A

LIFESTYLE PORTRAYAL

From

A TO Z

❧

Delectable savory soup
For the famished ravenous soul;
Generously and graciously served
In a sterling silver bowl.

❧

Reuben Matiko

© Copyright 2001 Reuben Matiko.
All rights reserved. No part of this publication may be reproduced, stored in a retrieval system, or transmitted, in any form or by any means, electronic, mechanical, photocopying, recording, or otherwise, without the written prior permission of the author.

Phone: (250) 592-6579
Fax: (250) 592-6579
E-mail: loonbay2@shaw.ca

Loon Bay Publishers
VICTORIA, B.C.

National Library of Canada Cataloguing in Publication Data

Matiko, Reuben, 1920-
  A lifestyle portrayal from A to Z

ISBN 1-55212-620-X

  1. Lifestyles--Quotations, maxims, etc. I. Title.
PN6084.L53M37 2001   C818'.5402   C2001-910135-X

Printed in Victoria, BC, Canada. Printed on paper with minimum 30% recycled fibre. Trafford's print shop runs on "green energy" from solar, wind and other environmentally-friendly power sources.

Offices in Canada, USA, Ireland and UK
This book was published *on-demand* in cooperation with Trafford Publishing. On-demand publishing is a unique process and service of making a book available for retail sale to the public taking advantage of on-demand manufacturing and Internet marketing. On-demand publishing includes promotions, retail sales, manufacturing, order fulfilment, accounting and collecting royalties on behalf of the author.

Book sales for North America and international:
Trafford Publishing, 6E–2333 Government St.,
Victoria, BC V8T 4P4 CANADA
phone 250 383 6864 (toll-free 1 888 232 4444)
fax 250 383 6804; email to orders@trafford.com
Book sales in Europe:
Trafford Publishing (UK) Limited, 9 Park End Street, 2nd Floor
Oxford, UK OX1 1HH UNITED KINGDOM
phone 44 (0)1865 722 113 (local rate 0845 230 9601)
facsimile 44 (0)1865 722 868; info.uk@trafford.com
Order online at:
trafford.com/01-0022

30 29 28 27 26 25 24 23 22 21

DEDICATION

To
Son James and his wife Becky Sue,
Jenifer and her brother Matthew,
Son Robbyn and his wife Pamela Sue,
Jonathan and Gregory, brothers two.

ACKNOWLEDGMENT

This book is a lovely bouquet
Of flowers that others have grown;
Nothing but a sterling silver bowl
That holds them together is my own.
I do not make rival claim
To transcendent misleading originality,
It's putting others' thoughts into verse
That gives them that unique profundity.

∼

Many words that you'll see you've no doubt seen before,
And perhaps you have read and heard o'er and o'er.
Please note that at this particular moment in time
Those same thought-initiators have been put into rhyme.

∼

There is this one thing we must never ignore,
Most things have been thought of or said years before.

PROLOGUE

Dr. Matiko is a man of many talents and, unlike his particular breed, he's a man capable of recognizing humor in many aspects of our lives. There are, of course, many people who possess that enviable ability to observe humor in our day to day lifestyle and activities that unfold on the local, national or international stage. We are all aware of the comedians who thrive in the political agendas of the day, no matter what the level. They make us laugh about the political gaffs, the injustice of the justice system, or the lack of care of our Canadian Medicare system. Then there are those certain few who, in addition to their ability to make the requisite observation, also possess the ability not only to convey it to the rest of us, but the talent to do it in verse form which serves to enhance the overall effect. Such a talent is Dr. Matiko.

I have known him for several years as a fellow director of a major financial institution. As with any corporation there are times when the company's fortunes are up or down or in between, but the "Doc" is always "up." He unfailingly regales us with humorous verse preceding each board meeting. Just say one simple word, or mention any topic that may be of interest that particular day, and Dr. Matiko has a verse that will lighten our load, dissipate our concerns, or out and out make us laugh convulsively.

But there is another side to Doctor Matiko,- the philosopher and linguist.

How many times in our lives have we heard expressions from the past that convey a certain meaning from something experienced by our predecessors – perhaps, one or two lines, perhaps from some pioneer, an original thinker or a Biblical verse. Note his succinct acknowledgment: "This book is a lovely bouquet of flowers that others have grown."

There are as well many words in our English language that may be used somewhat ambiguously to suit the orator's specific need at the time. It is easy for us to look up a definition of a word in a dictionary, but to make verse with that word gives it special meaning and an appropriate place in our lives. Dr. Matiko has taken many of these expressions and words and has put them in verse form, as well as attaching his own philosophy to some of the simplest words in our language. Indeed, he traverses the entire alphabet in his own unique style.

This book contains a collection of universal truths; however, many of these truths are presented with a sprinkling of humor and wit. For instance in the section that deals with aging:

> "At twenty we wonder what others think of us;
> We care less at forty - we don't make a fuss.
> At sixty we discover they us don't discuss."

And then there is this one:

> "You have money to burn when you're ready to retire,
> But you've hit a huge snag; you haven't any fire."

Then, on a more serious note, Dr. Matiko reminds us that when it comes to our daily living:

> "Be it something you do or something you say,
> To do a wrong thing there is no right way."

Further on, in two short lines he sums up the true purpose in life:

> "We're placed here to add, not to selfishly subtract.
> To truly achieve we must dauntlessly act."

His description of a bigot as "the idiot that slams his mind in your face." opens the door for a tongue-in-cheek poem about ego:

> "You must not accept your dog's admiration
> As conclusive evidence of another's veneration."

Dr. Matiko's book is a delightful collection of entertaining, thought-provoking ideas that serve to remind us who we are as human beings, but it also provides an insight of how we can attain greater heights, or at least make us think about it.

I know you will enjoy reading Dr. Matiko's book, "*A Lifestyle Portrayal from A to Z.*"

His Honor, Judge John M. Robbins,
Retired

INTRODUCTION
-About the Author

My love of poetry dates back many years, while still in my pre-teens, attending grade school in a single coal-heated room, in the absence of inside plumbing. It was situated on the correction line, four miles away from our farm home on the bald, open prairies of Saskatchewan, approximately fifty miles west of the city of Saskatoon. It wasn't Shakespeare or the classics that riveted my attention. It was the simple lines that I would glean from the "Winnipeg Free Press Prairie Farmer." I recall clipping some of the poems and pasting them into a six by nine loose leaf booklet which I have in my possession to this day. These were simple metered verses that spoke about life and its experiences on the prairies in the 'twenties' and 'thirties.' They were short creations, four, eight or twelve lines, some a bit longer, that in many cases didn't give recognition to the author. It was the Edgar Guest type of poetry. This form of verse was printed for the edification of us common farm folk. As an example, one of these compositions was "The Weatherman." Here it is:

When your forecast is snow, the street cleaner prays
That the bad spell will last just a couple of days.
The coal dealer orders six carloads at once,
He hopes freezing weather will hang on for months.
When the forecast is rain, the wheat farmer grins,
Says, "Now we can fill those north granary bins."
His daughter twelve fusses, "Rain go away,
The Sunday School picnic is at Locust today."
When your forecast is fair, the magistrate beams,
"The trial is postponed, there's trout in the streams."
The café owner grumbles, "My business is bad,
When weather is pleasant and customers gad."
What a job, Weather Man, keeping folk satisfied;
No wonder you are Dr. Jekyll and Mr. Hyde.
-Sadie Stuart Hager

Another one that was apropos for the bachelor farmer was: "Attention Ladies!"

Wanted - a wife! Come, who will apply?
Her's shall be everything a love can supply.
Of plain earthly things I have but a few,
A table, a cot, a comfy chair for two,
And a pot in which my coffee to brew.
She should be healthy, wealthy and witty,
Be able to dance well, keep house and stay pretty.
In society she should shine, bright as a star,

> For others to admire – but only from afar,
> Then nothing our happiness should chance to mar.
>
> She also needs to be joyous and lovable,
> Myself to regard as something adorable;
> Ever ready to help me - to be my mate,
> For a girl like this, I'm willing to wait,
> Be she a princess or a country milk maid.

Much water has gone under the bridge since those days. Being bent in my early years on becoming a physician, I attended a parochial boarding junior college in Alberta for three depression years, 1936-1939, completing high school and beginning my pre-med. One autumn my parents sold twelve head of cattle for the sum of one hundred and twenty five dollars, which was to go as a down payment for tuition, room and board for my school year. Labor in those days was very cheap. I worked at the College for seven and fifteen cents an hour to help defray the expenses for my schooling. I remained at home for one year to take three years of Latin by correspondence, a requirement, then went on to Walla Walla College in the fall of 1940 to complete my pre-med course for acceptance to medical school at Loma Linda University. Prior to hitch-hiking to Loma Linda, California, I remained in the Everett, Washington and Marysville area during the summer months, selling a medical book for the home from door to door.

During my freshman year in medicine, I remember very well the Japanese aerial attack on Pearl Harbor in December of 1941. Medical training was cut down to eight months with four weeks for vacation. During my vacation month I worked as a surgical orderly at the Hollywood Presbyterian Hospital in Los Angeles, earning the sum of one hundred dollars. After my second year I was deeply in debt.

For my vacation month after the second year I made the decision to go to Brawley, California, situated in Imperial valley, during the month of March to work as a door to door book salesman. That was an exciting story in itself for my clients were itinerant Mexican folk who spoke little or no English, and I knew no Spanish. A conundrum indeed. I was attempting to sell a medical book for the home that was in the Spanish language. Orders for the book were taken for two weeks, then I made deliveries in a 1926 business Dodge which an acquaintance kindly loaned me to use in the delivery of my sales.

During those four weeks I was exceedingly blessed, earning not one hundred dollars, but almost fourteen hundred dollars, - enough money to pay my tuition for the next two years. One of the professors remarked, "What in the world do you want to study Medicine for?" For our junior and senior years we medical students moved to the Los Angeles division to continue our training at the Los Angeles County and the White Memorial Hospitals. There was no vacation break between the junior and senior years.

In what little spare time I had I did janitorial work, worked in the admitting office and did some door to door selling in the surrounding area. For transportation, I didn't have any wheels, not even a bicycle. I felt the need of some mode of transport as I had obtained night work at the Queen of Angels Hospital 'specialing' surgical cases from 7:00 p.m. to 7:00 a.m., and so I purchased a 1934 Ford V-8. This auto had white-walled tires, and they were bald – totally void of rubber tread. In fact, a band of white cord, where the rubber used to meet the road, four to five inches wide, was clearly visible for the entire circumference of both front tires. These were the war years! Automobile tires were difficult to obtain, and so I was very careful in driving over streetcar tracks for fear of a blowout. Eventually I did obtain a voucher giving me permission to purchase a set of new tires as I was employed in an essential service. However, I did not buy new tires, for I was in my senior year and it was my plan to go back to Canada for my internship. The car and the voucher were sold to a happy customer.

At the Queen of Angels Hospital I worked a stretch of thirty nights, while still attending clinics and lectures during the day. My pay was twelve dollars for the twelve hour shift. During all the rigors of medical school I managed to find time to court a lovely young lady for four years who eventually became my wife on D-Day, June 6, 1944. We were married in Glendale, California, at the Wee Kirk o' the Heather in Forest Lawn Memorial Park. Nestled against a hillside amid green slopes purpled with heather, Forest Lawn's Wee Kirk o' the Heather is a faithful reconstruction of the church in Scotland where Annie Laurie worshipped more than 300 years ago.

Following graduation, in the fall of 1944, and I might say, I graduated debt-free, Frances and I traveled by train to Vancouver, B. C. where I interned at St. Paul's Hospital with two of my classmates, Drs Gustave Hoehn and Irwin J. Horsley. In July of 1945, we sailed on the Princess Adelaide to the northern part of Vancouver Island, to Port Alice, where I was to become the resident physician for the B. C. Pulp and Paper Company. My retainer was the sum of three hundred and fifty dollars. Along with the industrial practice, I took care of the population of the northern part of the Island, which included a total of eight communities. The main industries in the area were logging, lumbering, fishing and whaling, as well as the pulp mill that manufactured paper pulp that was used to manufacture newsprint.

In later years, our eldest son, who, after internship, spent four years in orthopedic residency training, two years fellowship in hand surgery and six months in arthroscopic surgery, on occasions expressed that my situation had been awesome, for I had no medical personnel to consult with, to give an anesthetic, nor to assist in surgery.

To abbreviate a long story, my wife and I moved to Victoria in 1951. During my years in Victoria I purposed to practice Preventive Medicine. In the early fifties, I frequently spoke to various groups on the dangers of smoking. This was deemed a "No" "No" by the medical establishment. It was definitely considered unprofessional and so I was called on the 'Red Carpet' by the executive committee of the Victoria Medical Society to give answer for my 'unethical behavior.' As a matter of fact, a colleague, who was on the executive, mentioned to me years later that they were considering recommending that my name be taken off the medical register. Upon my request I was given the opportunity to make my presentation to the executive committee on the harmful effects of smoking. My talk included a movie film entitled, "One in Twenty Thousand," featuring a surgical procedure on cancer of the lung.

A meeting was arranged for a Sunday evening in a lecture hall at the Royal Jubilee Hospital to show the film and to give my lecture. After a brief discussion the committee decided that it would be permissible for me to carry on with my speaking engagements, providing I first obtained permission by letter from the executive. That same evening I mentioned to them that I had been requested to address the members of the B. C. Legislative Assembly on Monday, the following evening. To this the president of the Victoria Medical Society remarked, "You can't do that!" "That's fine," I said, "I'll have to inform them that the Victoria Medical Society will not allow me to make my presentation." His response was, "You can't say that." After some discussion, it was finally agreed that I would be permitted to speak to the members of the Legislative Assembly providing the president of the Victoria Medical Society introduced me. At the conclusion of the meeting one of the more prominent internists of our medical community, who at a later date became the president of the Canadian Medical Society, came to me and said, "Reuben, carry on with what you are doing. I think there is merit in your crusade. I still smoke a pipe, but I'm a —— fool for doing that." The following day I was introduced by the president of the Victoria Medical Society to the members of the Legislative Assembly. In his introductory remarks the president mentioned that there wasn't enough evidence linking tobacco to lung cancer.

A few years later my wife and I were involved in establishing in Victoria a Health Education Centre. To head the program we had qualified health educators in charge. The centre was in existence for 20 years. Lectures were given in nutrition. Classes in vegetarian cookery were very popular, as well as lectures on the prevention and treatment of obesity. Lectures in Stress Control were in demand. A very successful Five Day program was featured to help folk stop smoking. Later on this program was called "Breathe Free." It was during this period that we were able to initiate a ten day 'Live-In' program that we called, "New Start." This program focused on fitness and prevention of heart disease, featuring a low cholesterol diet. The "Live-In," program was held at our church camp at Hope, B. C. It was during these programs at Hope that I seriously became involved in poetry. Every morning, prior to breakfast I recited poetry that was apropos to a positive lifestyle. One day I resolved to put into poetic verse a touching story that I had read about the painting entitled, "Praying Hands," by Albrecht Durer. I recall writing most of it during a visit to Loma Linda University to attend a biannual board meeting. This was my first effort at writing. You will find the poem in the section, entitled, "Hands."

Writing simple, metered poetic verse, much of it in the 'proverb' motif, became a hobby of mine. Several years ago I published a booklet, "Proverbs To Live By," and a leather-bound book entitled, "Living is Loving, and Loving is Giving.". The latter had three printings. It was used as a gift to donors to the university, by the Department of Development and Advancement at Loma Linda University, my alma mater. LLU is located about forty miles west of Palm Springs. It is where infant heart transplants are done. A number of infants from Victoria have been operated on there. Over three hundred infants under six months of age have had heart transplants there.

Over the past fifteen years I have continued to write for my own pleasure and enjoyment, putting into simple poetic verse, thousands of two to four liners, some, much longer. Many of my friends and acquaintances encouraged me to put my verse into book form. One day, in my musings I wondered as to what I should name the book. In mulling things over I realized that all that we do in life portrays our "LIFESTYLE." I decided that I should give it the title, "A Lifestyle Portrayal from A to Z". And so this is my concise life's story leading up to the compilation of: "A Lifestyle Portrayal from A to Z." There are well over five hundred titled topics. As a starter, turn to the largest, the broadest and most provocative section under the title, "Lifestyle, Per Se," beginning with page 228.

Read it,- live it,- enjoy it.

Dr. Matiko vaccinating Bushmen in the Kalihari Desert

LIFESTYLE

For a healthy lifestyle practice wise prudence.
To maintain body strength take wholesome sustenance.

Accidents are the result of thoughtless negligence.
You can't correct wrong with spiteful vengeance.

May your life exhibit a child's sweet innocence,
Pleasance, elegance, and sparkling radiance.

Forget not to express compassionate condolence.
May the words you convey have worthwhile substance.

If your toil is accompanied with brilliance and performance,
The result - you'll have a life full of pertinent relevance.

To the meek and the lowly, Christ-like forbearance;
Always maintaining a clear quickening conscience.

Hold not in your heart against a brother a grievance.
Allow not little things to cause any annoyance.

To have perfect peace, do practice awed silence.
The key to most everything is untiring patience.

Never openly display your contented opulence.
Hyphenate your affluence with serendipitous benevolence.

Your own intimate lifestyle is your life's profile;
It ultimately involves much practiced self-denial.

Take time for the needy, for their needs be solicitous;
Be charitable lest wealth make thee exceedingly covetous.

Read more than you write, you'll become erudite,
Darkness will be daylight and you'll have more insight.

Your 'LIFESTYLE is STEWARDSHIP - the life you live,
What to God and His creation you gratuitously give.

A LIFESTYLE PORTRAYAL From A TO Z

Proverbial sayings are drawn from experience.
The latter in itself is the mother of all sciences.
    -Miguel de Cervantes

Between these book covers you'll find many a noteworthy proverb.
I trust that your calm composure they won't emotionally disturb.
Instead, may they deeply inspire your carefree lifestyle to curb.

Proverbs are siblings of experience.
They attract a discriminating audience.

Proverbs bear age, they shall not pass.
Bear fully in mind, they're your looking glass.

The wisdom of the wise are experienced notations
Perceptibly preserved with poetic quotations.

Aphorisms are stimulating, they're thought-provoking blurbs.
A country can be judged by its notable proverbs.

Proverbs are made through public voice.
To live them positively should be our clear choice.

Proverbs are intended for giving knowledge and prudence to the young;
'Twill thoughtfully comfort your living, and give sound wisdom to the tongue.

Proverbs, aphorisms and maxims, carry a great deal of weight.
They're singular, luminous messages to which we should intimately relate.

Fundamental rules, we should intimately hold;
They're embodied in proverbs - our lifestyle they'll mold.

My sole lofty aim isn't to cause a sensation,
Just hope a line or two will reach its destination.

What I'm about to say, to some, empty chatter,
To others an opportunity to tickle their gray matter.

All poetry should be read with calm thought – at leisure,
For one to obtain greater insight and pleasure.

Verse without rhyme is a body without soul.
    -Jonathan Swift

A LIFESTYLE PORTRAYAL From A TO Z

Intellectual poetic thoughts, yes, occasionally a rare gem;
Some may even a questionable lifestyle condemn.

So many wise maxims o'er the years have been written.
It should now behoove us by them to be smitten.

Two classes of people o'er the years I have met.
Some read to remember and there are those who forget.

Not later, rather sooner - now and then, a bit of humor.
The brief words of humor originate from faint rumor.
Most are quite terse, all in metered poetic verse.

There is nothing one writes, though desiring it be good,
That will turn out as virtuous as one would hope it would.

This analysis of writing very few have heard.
Journalese is writing old words in any order.
Good prose is the selection of thoughtful word,
Poetry, superb words – of unique order a hoarder.

Poetry is quite simply a lovely method of addressing.
It's a visually impressive, effective mode of expressing.
It conveys deep significance and permanence with resonance,
Speaking with quiet elegance and exquisite timely eloquence.

Poetry is an art that selects and arranges
Symbols of thought that excite heart changes.

Paintings are poetry, silent thought they seek,
On the other hand, proverbs are paintings that speak.

My aim is to write verse, putting feeling into words,
Expressing thoughtful wisdom and occasional wit;
Proverbs and aphorisms - lifestyles to direct,
Simple truth put beautifully so folk will want to live it.

Proverbs and maxims, one surely can't deny,
Are 'wisdoms' that we should attempt to live by.

ABILITY

Each one of us can bring to fruition, innate God-given abilities.
-George H Bender

A LIFESTYLE PORTRAYAL From A TO Z

We all have a measure of ability; more importantly, it's having credibility.

One's ability will never catch up to the demand that there is for that cup.

You must sharply zero in on your unique abilities,
Rather than focusing on questionable probabilities.

Don't be proud of your ability, mistakes are lessons in humility.

It is most admirable to proceed and persist,
In fact, a singular duty we must not resist,
As if the confined limits of our abilities don't exist.

The greatest ability is to have ability, emotional stability, endless capability,
Tender sensibility, amiable compatibility, instant availability, diplomatic flexibility,
Moral accountability, sacred responsibility, unending reliability, implicit credibility,
And radiant spirituality.

You'll find that the difference between a luxury and an absolute necessity,
Is usually directly proportional to your ability to solve the perplexity.

Our proven ability is soundly rated by what we have completely finished,
Not by what's been feebly attempted and then reluctantly relinquished.

Ability and determination can overcome bad luck,
And effectively they can help to earn a needy buck.

Executive ability is the ability to decide
Who's to do the work while playing Club Countryside.

The ability to accept moral responsibility is a positive sign in the column of credibility.

Executive ability is deciding quickly.

Superior ability is initiating opportunity.

You say you can for you think you can, so, go ahead man, enact your plan.

Why would you fume, fuss, rave and rant? Knock the letter "t" off the "I can't."

To the person who pronounces, "It cannot be done!"
Obtrude not the imperative, "It can be won."

A LIFESTYLE PORTRAYAL From A TO Z

A BORE - BOREDOM

*A*gain I hear the creaking step, he's rapping at the door!
Too well I know the boding sound that rushes in a bore.
-John Godfrey Saxe

*W*hen a speaker begins drilling the spirit may be willing,
But when he begins boring a body starts snoring.

*W*e gracefully pardon those who habitually snore;
Can't say the same for those who regretfully bore.

*B*ores do not usually set out to offend you,
But then they don't care an iota if they do.

*I*f you talk about others you'll be labeled a gossip,
Particularly if you don't know the score.
If you talk about self and all of your wealth
You'll be considered a veritable bore.

*W*hen you're bored or boring you're not amiable or adoring.

*N*ever give the impression that people bore you;
Be so credibly outstanding that they can't ignore you.

*O*ne can never be inclined to be a bore, when he tacitly consents to soar.

*M*ost bores are verbally aggressive; unquestionably they're socially recessive.

*O*ccasionally permit yourself to be bored,
From all your activity determine to cease.
After some practice you'll experience release;
Boredom will be replaced with a feeling of peace.

ABSURDITIES

*A*n ostentatious man will rather relate a blunder
or an absurdity that he has committed,
than be debarred from talking of his own dear person.
-Joseph Addison

*S*ome impudent, ludicrous absurdities give folks an apoplectic fit,
Yet every nonsensical 'ridiculousity' has formidable champions to defend it.

Ludicrous absurdities have an irrational tone;
A belief that's totally inconsistent with one's own.

ACCEPTANCE

The art of acceptance is a high form of art,
Thanking the donor for what he graciously did impart.
Even though he may have done a very small favor,
It truly makes him feel, "Should have done something greater."

Graciously accept, gifts do not spurn, if you do not accept you'll have nothing to return.

ACCOMMODATION

A hotel has the nerve to call me their guest,
And then in the next breath, a large fee they request.

ACCOMPLISHMENT

The difficulties and struggles of today are but the price we must pay
for the accomplishments and victories of tomorrow.
-William J.H. Boetcker

No one can pick a peck of pickled peppers,
They have to be picked before they are pickled.

Remember one thing, if you're to amount, don't count the days, make the days count.

To accomplish great things you must not just dream,
You must act confidently, believe and scheme.

To accomplish something for someone, to devote a portion of one's leisure,
To lift, to comfort and to give, are the highest forms of pleasure.

You may never know when you're making a memory.
Whatever you do don't take a full century.

A lack of accomplishment is a frequent complaint by many a sister and a brother.
Societal success is virtually determined by the problems we solve for another.

Make your own route to the top - when you get there don't stop.

*A*ccomplishment and will to win cannot be reckoned as sin,
As long as in the just process you don't try to do someone in.

*B*e it something you do or something you say,
To do a wrong thing there is no right way.

*W*e've been created for mental accomplishment,
We're awesomely engineered for success.
The Scripture is our book of explicit instructions;
God's word we must daily address.

*I*n the field of attainment, here's an axiom so true,
"Success usually stops when one chooses to stop too."

*I*f you wish to accomplish, get rid of glum mope.
Worthwhile entities are realized with high hope.

*W*hat counts is not the number of precious hours
You toil to sow seeds or plant lovely flowers.
It's what you accomplish during working hours.

*I*n order to accomplish what we've done to last,
We have to improve on what we've done in the past.

*T*o live long and have wealth, for many a prime wish.
It's not length of one's life, it's what we accomplish.

*T*o truly accomplish you must actually count
The blessings to others your actions did amount.

*M*ost of us can do more than we think we can do,
But we usually do less than we claim we do.

*I*f what you've accomplished lives after you leave,
Recognized, true greatness you did achieve.

*S*ome folk duly dream of noteworthy accomplishment.
There are those who stay awake - the result, pure astonishment.

ACCOUNTABILITY

*T*he heaviest obligation rests upon him who has been made
a steward of the greatest abilities.
-E. G. White

We increase our stability, ability and credibility,
When we've truly exhibited a measure of accountability.

Be free from moral bias, from stiff inflexibility,
From bigotry and egotism, but full of accountability.

ACCURACY

Related to accuracy is twin-sister honesty.

ACHIEVEMENT

Faith that a thing can be done is essential
For any great achievement to become a potential.

There's very little limit to what you can achieve
If your motto is not to deliberately deceive.

In the quest for achievement, don't hold your breath;
Fear of acrid criticism is the kiss of death.

When I'm tempted to say, "Wow, look what I've done,
All that I've accomplished and achieved by myself."
I'm reminded seeing a turtle on top of a fence post,
I know that that turtle didn't get there by itself.

If it requires no initiative, nor sound judgment,
There won't be any glory in its lasting achievement.

Do your level best, let God do the rest.

Do not just try - achieving don't deny.

This pertinent axiom you must truly believe,
"Nothing stops the one who desires to achieve."

ACTION

Out of the strain of Doing, into the peace of Done.
-Julian Louise Woodruff

A LIFESTYLE PORTRAYAL From A TO Z

*D*o not indulge in fantasy, instead, create sound vision.
Action is totally inherent in every favorable decision.

*W*ords may show a man's impulsive leaning,
But actions exhibit his inexpressible meaning.

*I*nitiating a running start is half the battle; mere meditation could just be prattle.

*A*ctions speak louder, let us be unique,
Let our mouths give our hands full permission to speak.

*T*hey speak louder than words, a heart they can soften;
It's kind acts my friend, do make them often.

*E*very right action and every prudent thought
Come from a character that cannot be bought.

*P*rudent people plan resolute action; doing good we must fully sanction.

*W*hatever you're inclination, do it now, lest you sorrow.
Remember, you may never get a convenient tomorrow.

*P*lease, pay less attention to what others may say.
Instead, observe carefully what their actions convey.

*T*he actions of a bigot are quite easy to trace.
He's the idiot who slams his mind in your face.

*W*e're placed on this earth to add, not subtract.
To truly achieve we must dauntlessly act.

"*I* must do something, effort I mustn't shun,"
Accomplishes much more than, "Something must be done."

*G*reat fame one can gain by actions that are great;
Ones that are questionable can soil the whole slate.

*W*hat you think you can do or dream you can do,
Begin, attack it, your boldness will subdue.

*A*ction's in the mind, that's where it starts; it's up to me to use my 'smarts.'

"*B*etter," is the enemy of "Good." "Should," should follow "Could."
"I will," gets you over the hill.

Fashion noble action to your word, it doesn't always have to be heard.
ও
Be cautious of the one who prompts an action
In which he himself doesn't risk an impaction.
ও
Decide, act, and assail, as if it were impossible to fail.
ও
If you should delay immediate action, the final result could be putrefaction
ও

ADMIRATION

Fools admire but men of sense approve.
-Alexander Pope
ও
You must not accept your dog's admiration
As conclusive evidence of another's veneration.
ও
Admiration so frequently is a short-lived passion;
An attribute that so oft we tend to ration.
ও
Affectionate admiration is a lover's creation.
ও

ADMONITION

So you're having a date - you're so neatly primped;
Keep your easy buttons buttoned and you're zippy zippers zipped.
ও

ADOPTION

Once there were two women who never knew each other;
One you do not know, the other you call Mother.
Two totally different lives were shaped to make you one,
One became your star, the other became your sun.

The first one gave you life, the second taught to live it;
The first gave a need for love, the second was there to give it.
One gave you a nationality, the other gave you your name;
One gave the seed of talent, the other gave you an aim.

One gave you your emotions, the other calmed your fears;
One saw your first smile, the other dried your tears.

The first one gave you up, 'twas all that she could do,
The other prayed for a child and God led her to you.

With hesitation you might ask, through loving smiles and tears,
That simple age-old question that has come down through the years,
Is it hereditary or environment, which are you the product of?
Neither, my darling, just two different kinds of love.
-Author unknown

ADORATION

If you humbly adore Christ as your Savior,
You'll daily be mindful of your insulting behavior.

Many may be deserving of heartfelt admiration;
Christ, the sacrificial lamb, is worthy of adoration.

Smart women I adore, they talk less but say more.

ADVERSITY

The virtue of adversity is fortitude.
-Francis Bacon

Put up with adversity, in it faith can flourish.
You must have simple faith if your soul you're to nourish.

When adversity is ready to strike and maim us,
The Almighty is willing to lift and strengthen us.

Adversity is frequently the parent of opportunity.

Adversity and affliction are not for sighing,
For irksome trying times are times for trying.

Adversity introduces a man to himself, much more readily than the absence of pelf.

Adversity can strengthen intellectual courtesy.

An oppressive opportunity a friendship oft ends.
Adversity is the scale that weighs its friends.

A LIFESTYLE PORTRAYAL From A TO Z

The cause of many problems, just one may I mention,
Like trouble and weeds they thrive on inattention.

It's been said that prosperity is a great teacher;
Adversity, on the other hand, a judicious preacher.

Greatness, a product of adversity; fools, oft the result of prosperity.

Many an adversity conceals a possibility.

ADVERTISEMENTS

A newspaper advertisement can gratify your wish.
The same leading paper wraps tomorrow's fish.

Many folk focus on the 'coulds', 'shoulds' and 'woulds';
It doesn't pay to advertise unless you have the goods.

ADVICE

Many receive advice, only the wise profit by it.
-Publililus Syrus

We love to give advice by the proverbial bucket;
When others give it, we try to duck it.

Good advice goes in one ear and out the other;
Comparable to fashions, in one year and out the other.

We readily give advice which has no fault; we take it from others with a grain of salt.

Advice is least heeded, when it's most needed.

Don't always give advice, at times, a ready hand;
Give cordial encouragement, never publicly reprimand.

Some folk give others admirable advice; to accept it themselves, it's too big a price.

The best way to succeed and be a blessing to a brother
Is to act on the advice that you give to another.

I recall sound advice my Grandpa gave to Clem,
"If good knots you can't tie, tie plenty of them."

To you these brief words of good honest wisdom,
I must this moment most clearly reveal.
These few curt words of kindly advice,
Though they to you may not quite appeal.
On attaining this day your distinct promotion,
Allow it not your soaring spirit to be damp.
Please do remember, though you've been advanced,
It mustn't be beneath you to lick a tiny stamp.

In the giving of advice, consent to be concise, more importantly, be nice.

The offering of advice may be timely and grand, but it isn't the same as a helping hand.

There is a sharp difference between leek and kelp,
Likewise, a glaring gap between advice and help.

Some pertinent advice for peoples, in this world of nations and races,
Allow not narrow waist and broad mind, ever to decide to change places.

AFFECTION

To feel much for others and little for ourselves,
to restrain our selfishness and exercise our benevolent affection,
constitutes the perfection of human nature.
-Adam Smith

Affection for another can always be improved.
Love is a relationship where selfishness is removed.

In casting affection, do note the direction.

The words of Will Rogers we should mentally mike,
"I never met a man I did not like."

AGE

It is age that forms the man, not man that forms the age.
-Thomas B. Macaully

A LIFESTYLE PORTRAYAL From A TO Z

As we gradually grow older, we're definitely not stronger,
Our frail bodies are shorter and our anecdotes get longer.

∽

Draw from the wisdom of age to avoid the mistakes of youth.
This singular directive is paramount in avoiding the proverbial steel booth.

∽

It can be said that aging is the only endeavor
Where advancement is guaranteed without being clever.

∽

"Please, do tell me, how old are you dear?" "I'm approaching forty," said Fern.
"The only way that you could be nearing forty is by making a full U-turn."

∽

He seemed to be anxious for the years to rush by,
"Why so?" I asked my pal Sid.
He told me he wanted to stretch it to forty before his waistline did.

∽

We cannot avoid growing old, but we can avoid being cold.

∽

There's a thing about aging that's an equestrian truth,
One becomes older when he's long in the tooth.

∽

You're only young once, full of glee, free as a bee;
Being young at my age would probably kill me.

∽

The reason some people over fifty, don't feel or look too nifty,
With multitudinous aches and pains, it's because they're over sixty.

∽

I would say one's life has reached its peak,
When the spirit is willing but the flesh is weak.

∽

A distinctive notable feature in those who've lived long,
Their unflinching, furrowed faces tell more than their tongue.

∽

Pay attention to the elderly, respect their rich years;
Listen with your eyes as well as your ears.

∽

You must be attentive to life's countdown; don't let death tell you, "You must slow down."

∽

The secret to longevity many seek to know; the answer, quite simply, be born years ago.

∽

The older we get, lengthy waits we deplore;
The less things seem worth standing in lines for.

∽

Age is oft comparable to an odometer in a car;
You know it's been set back but you don't know how far.

∽

A LIFESTYLE PORTRAYAL From A TO Z

An inevitable midlife crisis is when you realize
That your children and clothes are about the same size.

If you pray for long life, why fear old age?
A thought-provoking question by an elderly sage.

As a humble octogenarian my soul trills a truth,
I've quadrupled the satisfaction of a twenty-year old youth.

Do not despair about aging, remember with each passing day,
There'll always be someone else to celebrate their birthday.

"*You* know you're getting old," says my dear friend, Sid,
"When you cannot go out because your sacroiliac did."

Old age is no substitute for youth, neither is sincerity for truth.

Age is the acknowledgement of a term of years.
Maturity, on the other hand, is the glory of tears.

Never put down an infant after feeding unless some burping does ensue.
When you get old, you'll be put down if prolonged belching you pursue.

The years passing by to many doesn't please.
Age is not important unless you're a cheese.

How old would be your life's brief pause if you didn't know how old you was?

"*Anything* for gray hair?" was the dowager's request.
"Madam, I have nothing but the greatest respect."

It's natural for the elderly pensive quietness to tout;
They have so much more to be quiet about.

To have prolonged youth is the rage - oh, to have youth in old age.
There's a fabled story on the go that I think is quite apropos.
Two Eskimos paddled their kayak to open sea.
They encountered a breeze that was somewhat chilly.
They elected to be build a fire – for real – not a prank,
And as the sane would expect, their trusty kayak sank.
There's a lesson to be learned as you sail life's blue,
You can't have your kayak and heat it too.

A LIFESTYLE PORTRAYAL From A TO Z

There's definitely a problem with middle age, it's extremely difficult to get hired,
And it takes much longer to rest than it does for one to get tired.

❧

It could be slowed down, this dreary aging process,
If it gradually had to work its way through Congress.

❧

A firm fact of old age, we obviously get tuckered,
And surely, eventually, we do get puckered.

❧

I share a succinct truth, years ago I was told,
"If you want to live long you've got to grow old."

❧

In youth or old age it's imperative to avoid rage.

❧

Be careful to pass judgment on those old and gray,
For even a stopped clock tells correct time twice a day.

❧

I find that when one gets old, one must not be quite so bold,
Nor must one be too old to learn, or too wise to ever be told.

❧

My retentive memory is good, I just have trouble retrieving.
I precisely know where I'm going, but my feet inextricably keep weaving.

❧

Don't lose sight of the rumor that the elderly need very little;
The elderly need a great deal, for aging becomes so brittle.

❧

Forty isn't old, it appears to me, as long as you are a sturdy oak tree.

❧

I visited a home for the elderly today,
So many mentally teetering on the brink.
Said a patient of mine, "I'm thankful for my blessings,
Though I can't walk I can still clearly think.

❧

The way some minds seem to gradually drift
Is a sign they are ripe for a well earned pause.
Years have a propensity for fluctuant change;
You've become what you is, you aren't what you was.

❧

When you've reached your fortieth, this axiom you must heed,
"When you're over the hill you'll be picking up speed."

❧

When you've passed your fortieth, you're over the hill;
Believe me, being under it wouldn't be a thrill.

❧

A LIFESTYLE PORTRAYAL From A TO Z

At twenty we wonder what others think of us.
We care less at forty, we don't make a fuss.
At sixty we discover, they us don't discuss.

❧

You're getting much older, when you begin to realize
That caution is the entity you must mindfully exercise.
You are considerably older, when inclines you can't make;
You're exceedingly old when candles out-price the cake.

❧

As I pensively reflect on my past, I'm aware of my waning strength.
The thing that I regret the most is its lamentable decreasing short length.

❧

It's no wonder that girls live longer than men;
They're longer being girls before becoming women.

❧

You know you're getting older, you have a sense of disgust.
You realize you're still kicking but not raising any dust.

❧

You have money to burn, when you're ready to retire,
But you've hit a huge snag, you haven't any fire.

❧

Of those over sixty, one-third have a fall.
There could be safety features that we should install.

❧

As one gets older, his vision gets bleary;
He definitely gets older when of him all are weary.

❧

Age doesn't always bring wisdom, sometimes it comes empty-handed.

❧

Age is merely a quality of mind, if you have left your years behind,
If love is cold;
If you no longer look ahead, if your ambition's fire is dead,
Then you are old.
But if from life you take the best, and if in life you keep the jest,
If love you hold;
No matter how the years go by, no matter how the birthdays fly,
You are not old!
-Anonymous

❧

We're called middle-aged, not because we are slowing,
It's because our middles just keep on growing.

❧

A LIFESTYLE PORTRAYAL From A TO Z

*T*he elderly are worth a fortune, be they in a robe or a sheath.
They have shiny silver in their hair, pure, bright gold in their teeth.
They've stones in their hard-worked kidneys, an abundance of heavy lead in their feet,
Gas aplenty in their gurgling stomachs; who with them can compete?

*B*y the time we realize how short life-span takes,
It's far too late to slam on the brakes.

*W*hy use the mirror overmuch and dwell upon your age?
Remember, in the book of life, youth is but one page.
Why use the mirror overmuch, looking for uncomely trace,
Betraying that the toll of years is showing on your face?
Why use the mirror overmuch, forgetting that the spring
With its fresh blown prettiness is but a transient thing?
So do not ever panic when silver lights your hair,
Nor fear the touch of summer sun on skin for which you care.
Why use the mirror overmuch, searching for those signs
That your fretfulness effectuates, those cruel, tell-tale lines?
Remember, when you gaze again into that candid glass,
The mellow years of dreary autumn, how slow they are to pass.
So, SMILE you must serenely, eyeing mirror on the wall,
Reflecting in your maturity the BEAUTY of the fall.
-Anonymous.

*A*s the long years gradually slip by, how does one his duration gauge?
In the words of perceptive Plato, an ancient philosopher and venerated sage,
"He who is of a calm and happy nature will hardly feel the pressure of age."

*L*est we inadvertently forget, we mustn't ever neglect
To handle with due respect the idiosyncrasies of the elderly.

*A*re CARING and SHARING old?
Are CREDENCE and ALLEGIANCE old?
Are ADHERENCE and PERSEVERANCE old?
Are KINDLINESS and HAPPINESS old?
Are COURAGE and ENCOURAGEMENT old?
Are TRUTH and KNOWLEDGE old?
Are COMELINESS AND MEEKNESS old?
Are AFFECTION and FRIENDLINESS old?
Are FAITH and PRAYER old?
Are PEACE and PATIENCE old?
Are HOPE and WISDOM old?
Are LOVE and COMPASSION old?
Though they take years to mold,
These qualities are definitely not old,

Nor are they considered icy cold.
On their beautiful attributes I'm sold,
They are more precious than gold.
May I be so audaciously bold,-
"BEING OLD" can be "BEAUTIFUL!"

Why must I get old, a question in my book,
Before someone tells me how young I look?

If I'm blessed to live to hallowed years one hundred,
Will I be exceptional ? – For what, I've wondered.

About your elderly years let no one be a mocker.
If they're viciously critical, squash their toes with your rocker.

For keeping fit, age shouldn't be a threat; one is never too old to gently sweat.

'Twas a biweekly routine, visiting a home for the elderly,
To see a nonagenarian, my senior by far.
"Do you know who I am?" – into her hear I half-shouted.
"Do go to the front desk, they'll tell you who you are."

Age does speak, it makes one meek.

Your midlife crisis, turn it to your betterment-
It's a time of evaluation of your body and mind.
Why would you stand by, hopeless and shiftless,
Watching you faculties slowly decline?

When one enjoys life in his own pursuance,
The years causing old age will not be a nuisance.

A distinguishing feature, in those who live long,
Their unflinching, furrowed faces tell more than their tongue.

Grow old with me! The best is yet to be.
-Robert Browning

AGONY - AGONIZE - AGONIZING

He who in life does not economize will have to 'ere long painfully agonize.

Do not spend agonizing about days long gone,
The waywardness you've traveled, the evil you did nurture.
Should the devil take issue with your shameful wicked past,
Gently jog his memory of his hopeless, hellish future.

Pain makes us think, thinking makes us wise,
Wisdom makes life bearable, we needn't agonize.

Never allow agony to turn into tragedy.

AGREE - AGREEABLE - AGREEMENT

My idea of an agreeable person is a person who agrees with me.
-Benjamin Disraeli

Though our agreements aren't always achievable,
Our differences don't have to be outrageously disagreeable.

Man is at his best when there's full accord,
And when he is stimulated by the hope of reward.

AGGRESSIVENESS

Lightning is great, it is impressive, so is thunder, it's so aggressive.

AIM

What leads to unhappiness is making pleasure the chief aim.
-William Shenstone

An aim is important, most essential I figure,
Nonetheless, it is worthless if you don't pull the trigger.

Make your veiled goal then press the mold.
Don't lose desire to aim and aspire.

There is no limit to the heights we can attain if being on the level we aim to sustain.

On unmerited luck don't ever rely, you must carefully aim at something high.

ALERTNESS

You can be a standout without a red shirt by working very hard and by being alert.

Hyphenate fitness with mental alertness.

AMBITION
There should be no age limit placed on ambition.
-George Matthew Adams

Unbounded ambition can become your ammunition.

Aggressive ambition can't be bought or sold; munificent fortune usually favors the bold.

You won't be thought hopeless if you exhibit ambition.
Achieve automatic drive and you won't be deemed shiftless.

Ambition, a good thing, on candid reflection,
Providing you're heading it in the right direction.

If you truly have ambition and volition, you can overcome hardship and opposition.

So many are deficient in ambition, they lack determination and resolve.
Scores are like instant hot chocolate, when they're in hot water they dissolve.

If ambition doesn't weary you ambition is not within you.

Though we must be ambitious if we're to survive,
We must watch our health if we wish to stay alive.

In the absence of hope, there's no noble desire.
Without innate ambition there is no inward fire.

Make your ambition a positive notion; calculable chance favors those in motion.

A man's matchless worth and intellectual premonition
Isn't any greater than his singular ambition.

Ambition is not going to work if unending aspiration you shirk.

Ambition is a commendable, a fundamental platitude;
'Tis best when it's coupled with versatile aptitude.

A LIFESTYLE PORTRAYAL From A TO Z

ANGER

*L*et anger's fire be slow to burn.
-George Herbert

*T*he size of a man is measured by many
By the size of that something that makes him angry.

*S*peak when you're angry, in your opinion be set
And you'll make the best speech that forever you'll regret.

*V*ile anger oft leads to treason - the physician for anger is reason.

*F*lying off the handle is not the solution; blowing your stack will add to pollution.

*S*o many get angry in due season; they get angry again on returning to reason.

*A*nger in a sense is but sheer madness; do control wrath, lest you reap sadness.

"*A*nger" is only one letter short of danger; never introduce it to a stranger.

*H*ot anger is an attribute that can grow into hate.
Patience is a virtue that carries great wait.

*T*oo much agreement kills many a chat; too much vengeful anger results in a spat.

*N*ever vile anger in any argument; sensible reason it will not augment.

*A*nger and resentment give one headaches and tenseness;
Lightness and laughter return with forgiveness.

*B*e he black or white, from Afghan or Iran, beware of the fury of a quiet, patient man.

*F*olks who inadvertently fly into a rage, don't perform pleasingly or speak like a sage.

*S*hrewd words spoken by a gentle old sage, "Don't pacify a man at the height of his rage."

*Y*our sudden anger will never score - you must creatively think before.

*P*roud anger is exceedingly difficult to budge; the heaviest item to carry is a grudge.

*A*n angry man is considered unwise, he opens his mouth and shuts his eyes.

A LIFESTYLE PORTRAYAL From A TO Z

You must watch what you say or unkindly convey, lest you regret it tomorrow.
If you are patient in a moment of anger, you'll escape many days of sorrow.

Lest anger spread throughout your big chest, "Guard your tongue," - the mind's request.

Never get angry, never make a threat, never do anything that will cause regret.

Anger makes your mouth spout words unkind.
It makes your tongue travel much faster than your mind.

Blunt, stern anger opens your mouth, simultaneously it closes your mind,
And undeniably you'll have to agree, most assuredly it's blatantly unkind.

Anger and jealousy are debasing tools, they usually reside in the bosom of fools.
Harsh words of ire stir up bitter wrath, but an answer that is soft is a perfumed bath.

The person who consistently angers you, is invariably the one who dominates you.

If habits are destructive, bitter anger seems to flow.
Evil tendencies will follow wherever you go.

Do your words anger convey? The remedy for anger is delay.

Avoid frustration – don't attempt to exfoliate your energy with negative emotions.
Flood your dear soul with love and serene joy - energy creators called endorphins.

Some try hiding anger and their fiery pride;
They're calm on the exterior, but they're jumping inside.

Bitter, vile anger, envy and strife – all three will shorten a man's idyllic life.

When have you spoken or acted in anger?
Why become a spectacle in front of a stranger?

Holding on to vile anger won't give you any hustle.
It only tends to give you more than one tense muscle.

Anger is momentary madness; invariably it brings on sadness.

Being slow to anger keeps a man out of danger.

For senseless anger be an abater; no worthy conquest is any greater.

Rule your anger to the letter; to prevent it is much better.

A LIFESTYLE PORTRAYAL From A TO Z

Anger can make one totally irrational; exhibit happiness - be sensational.

When there is anger on the floor, patent reason rushes out the door.

Some folks when angry can't control what they do.
React with loving kindness, bitter thoughts you'll subdue.

Words spoken in anger cannot be effaced,
Unless with forgiveness they're completely erased.

To pacify his anger, said I to brother Steven,
"You can never get ahead by trying to get even."

Anger is an emotion and so is meek love; it's pertinent to remember, they don't tail-dove.

Carrying a grudge is definitely a curse; like a run in a stocking it can only get worse.

On this earth war and peace so frequently rub shoulders,
While anger and vile passion continue to smolder.
Thank God, through faith of a new era I'm a beholder.

You're not angry for long with someone you adore.
It's difficult to stay angry at someone you pray for.

Sullen anger is a hindrance to wisdom; with it one cannot enter Christendom.

A hot-tempered anger makes one totally unruly,
And it usually manages most everything very poorly.

ANGUISH

Can you fully picture the anguish on Calvary's face?
Man can't truly fathom the breadth of God's grace.

ANNIVERSARIES

Anniversaries can be life's precious memories;
Allow them not to be your milepost's burglaries.

A LIFESTYLE PORTRAYAL From A TO Z

Grandpa's Birthday

It was grandpa's birthday, he was seventy-nine.
The years were telling, he was far past his prime.
He got up quite early, he showered and shaved,
He put on some new duds from money he had saved.
He tidied his room, neatness was his aim,
So things would look neat when his family came.
He skipped his daily walk to the town café,
Where he routinely had coffee with his cronies each day.
He arranged his porch chair so he could have a better view;
His children were coming, anytime they were due.
At noon, though tired, he would skip his nap,
But no one showed up,- did they have a mishap?
The afternoon was spent near his telephone,
In case some one called, maybe Tom. Dick or Joan.
He had nine children, oh, to see each face!
A daughter and son lived but ten miles from his place.
No one had visited him for a very long time,
But today was his birthday, expectations were prime.
A suppertime he left the birthday cake untouched,
For his children were coming; to anticipation he clutched.
After supper he sat pensively on the porch and waited,
For some reason their visit to him was belated.
On retiring he left a note, as he uttered, "Ho Hum,
Be sure you awaken me whenever you come."
It was Grandpa's birthday – he was seventy-nine.
-Thoughts of an anonymous writer, paraphrased into verse

APATHY

The apathy of the people is enough to make every statue
leap from its pedestal and hasten the resurrection of the dead.
-William Lloyd Garrison

Dull, stagnant apathy is the shoe into which evil puts its foot in.
Insensibility, coolness and lethargy, without question are its next of kin.

Despairing apathy can result in tragedy.

APOLOGY

Apologies only account for that which they do not alter.
-Benjamin Disraeli

∼

Tell me, has it ever to your feeble mind occurred
That the husband who apologizes always has the last word?

∼

When you're apologizing, tell the truth, don't lie.
When you say, "I'm sorry," look the person in the eye.

∼

She lets him have the last word, when he's sincerely apologizing.
Eventually she'll have her turn, when she's tearfully eulogizing.

∼

APPEARANCE

If a beard were all, goats could preach. –Danish Proverb

∼

Appearance is secondary, it's the plate on the door;
"No rich man is ugly," says Zsa Zsa Gabor

∼

Dress conservatively when you go to borrow money.
Do make it a point to wear a countenance that's sunny.

∼

What people are like so oft clearly shows
In there scuffed up shoes and their dirty tattered clothes.

∼

Mutton-chop sideburns and multicolored coats appear at all ages from kids to old goats.

∼

In preparing to go out, remember young man,
It's difficult to look spick if you have too much span.

∼

Always keep your body and your appearance in good taste -
Spare tire in the trunk - not around your waist.

∼

A ring in one's nose and a tattoo are inanity; the latter, the result of temporary insanity.

∼

Looks can be very deceptive – so many individuals are fabled.
Some should be done up in packages with their ingredients clearly labeled.

∼

The velocity of the wind is directly proportionate
To the extravagant cost of a hairdo inordinate.

∼

A LIFESTYLE PORTRAYAL From A TO Z

Men wake up, good looking at daylight; women, somehow, deteriorate during the night.

Be mindful of word, appearance and action, for certain, shun mental recession.
Remember, you never get a second chance to make that first impression.

It's strange how bright sun will lighten one's hair,
But the skin grows darker, it doesn't turn fair.

Why do so many corpulent women encase their bodies in tight-fitting pants,
When cloaking their persons in lovely modest dresses,
They would their beauty and appearance enhance.

APPLAUSE - APPRECIATION

From self alone expect applause.
-Marion L. Burton

Applause, virtually proves nothing, in it there may be absolute void;
Many barnyard hens loudly cackle – you'd think they laid an asteroid.

An applause at the beginning is a sign of hope,
When it comes at the end it's frequently soft soap.

One's whole-hearted, sincere, appreciation, magnifies a soul's rapturous radiation.

Nice people, so oft in compliments may wallow;
Remember, like perfume, inhale, don't swallow.

You must never be cheap on sincere appreciation,
If your ardent desire is to improve the relation.

Living for God's approval - working in His just cause,
Is exceedingly far better than living for man's applause.

ARGUMENT

Be calm in arguing; for fierceness makes error a fault
and truth discourtesy.
-Sir William Temple

For many live debate engenders keen enjoyment;
Then comes a vital fact - thereby ending the argument.

Most arguments don't generate audible approbation;
Astute minds are changed by simple observation.

Your arguments you will hurt if vital facts you pervert.

So many people argue, to win they are bound;
So oft their argument is sound, merely sound.

A delightful married couple will stubbornly argue,
Logomachy they'll vehemently and soundly belabor.
In time they'll learn that their deplorable debate
Is clearly heard by their next door neighbor.

Whether in an argument or when you're on the hop,
When you see bright red it's time to stop.

Most arguments are a poor form of conversation.
Frequently they result in sordid defamation.

An argument can produce a fair amount of heat,
And frequently bright light it chooses to delete.

His noisy argument can be likened to percussion.
It invariably interrupts my spirited discussion.

Argument, then quarrel, result in a cost; in quarreling some truth is always lost.

Don't point out faults to a man who is proud;
He'll arrogantly argue, oblivious to the crowd.

A young lad got into an argument with boys who were twice his size.
He boldly drew a line in the dirt, then challenged that they cross the divide.
The big boys accepted his challenge, they promptly crossed the line;
Whereupon the little guy smiled – "Now you are on my side."

Strive not with superiors, arguments are an oddity;
Always submit judgment to others with modesty.

Don't argue or confront, definitely do not fight;
It's just small stuff trying to be right.

Shun argument of any kind, friendship it doesn't bind.

It seems so immoral that two will quarrel.
One or two can start it - takes only one to stop it.

Always being right means defending your position;
Being right does signify you're in direct opposition.

The tiniest disagreement in your plans can frequently effectively tie your hands.

ARROGANCE

When men are most sure and arrogant, they are commonly most mistaken.
-David Hume

Never allow arrogance to hold you ransom, lest it rob you of rich precious wisdom.

If haughty arrogance you choose to employ,
Your lofty lingering pride is bound to destroy.

So frequently I find the haughty let off steam,
And the naughty and proud their impious esteem.

Arrogance puffs up like a balloon with hot air.
It can easily be punctured, of arrogance beware.

With some, why does the head continue to swell,
When one stops growing, my friend, pray tell?

Being haughty and overbearing is arrogance; too often it's the companion of excellence.

ASPIRATION

Hitch your wagon to a star.
-Ralph Waldo Emerson

Most lofty, awakened aspirations exceed the required perspiration.

Aspire to inspire before you retire.

If you diligently aspire to earn top wages,
Be cognizant of the fact, "Good Enough" seldom is.

It takes a certain level of meaningful aspiration
Before an opportunity becomes a unique creation.

Our highest aspiration should be, to accept in our lives Christ's victory.

ASSOCIATION

When a dove begins to associate with crows,
its feathers remain white but its heart grows black.
-German Proverb

❧

Associate yourself with men of profound quality, of merited repute and sterling fidelity.

❧

ASTUTENESS

In a large city hotel there was a man who checked hats
At the dining room door 'midst much laughter and chats.
A frequenting salesman became thoroughly intrigued,
How checks for their hats guests never received.
How the hat man managed of many hats to keep track –
Not once did he see a wrong hat being passed back.
The travelling salesman then questioned a man
In charge of the check room, 'bout the man they called Ben.
"He's been doing it for years, he never makes a mistake,
I can assure you, dear sir, the hat man's no fake."
As the salesman was leaving, Ben passed him his hat,
So promptly, with a flurry, not an eye did he bat.
"Now, how do you know that this hat is really mine,"
The puzzled salesman asked, as he stood in line.
"Oh, I don't know that," the hat man admitted;
A queried expression the salesman's face committed.
"Then, why give it to me, this I truly cannot see?"
"Well, when you walked in, you personally gave it to me."

❧

Habitual astuteness is void of rash rudeness.

❧

ATTEMPT

Trying is ambition's spying.

❧

Times can be trying for those who aren't trying.

❧

Attempt the impossible, let me give you a clue,
No one can do things that he thinks he can't do.

❧

Trying repeatedly one must never shirk; what isn't tried is bound not to work.

❧

Do attempt the allegedly impossible; end up making it totally accomplishable.

ATTENTION

One day at Nordstrom's exotic perfume counter, I heard a sweet lady say,
"Would you like something that will instantly turn a cold fish into the catch of the day?"

An axiom worthy of mention, 'Your lifestyle needs your attention.'

To get maximum attention, be it hard to take,
It is difficult to beat a great big mistake.

Surrender your need for attention, you'll find you won't be sorry.
Share in the earth-born joy of someone's bountiful glory.

ATTITUDE

Your attitude controls your endeavors, your willingness, your fervor and your might.
"Whether you think you are able, or think you can't, you're right."
-Henry Ford

Preserve a right mental attitude, an attitude of courage and good cheer.
Carry your chin in and head high; God answers every prayer that's sincere.

Problems encountered are not as important as is our mind-set toward them.
Our outlook determines our success or failure; attitude can vanquish each problem.

Have you ever noticed that the word "gratitude"
Is primarily composed of philanthropic attitude?

Grumbling, crabbing, complaining, seldom expressing any gratitude -
Can a person be deemed a smart cookie, entertaining a vile, crummy attitude?

Be cognizant of your attitude, restrain boundless latitude;
By showing your gratitude you'll increase your altitude.

A person has to be a contortionist these days.
His anatomy is positioned in so many variant ways.
Firstly, he must keep his back to the wall,
His ear to the ground, a position that prevents fall.
He's expected to keep his shoulder to the wheel,
By now I wonder how his torso would feel.
The nose to the grindstone must persistently abound,

While keeping a level head and both feet on the ground.
With his noggin in the clouds searching for the silver lining,
He must stand tall while lazily reclining.

❧

An entity that is most sublime – a positive attitude all the time.

❧

Never let your attitude be filled with helplessness,
And never let it be governed by debasing selfishness.

❧

A mind set of gracious loving attitude can sprout in one's life a beatitude.

❧

To be healthy is more than exercise and diet,
It's a positive attitude – never defy it.

❧

To change your altitude why not change your attitude.

❧

AUTHORITY

How a minority, reaching majority, seizing authority, hates a minority.
-Leonard H. Robbins

❧

Authority is insecure, it can lack credibility,
Unless it is based on outstanding ability.

❧

Authority is usually conferred; power by most is preferred.
Authority is frequently spurned; power is something that is earned.

❧

Most people will submit to authority, though they don't necessarily rejoice.
They invariably do it because they have no other wise choice.

❧

It's interesting how an aggressive minority will strive for leading authority.

❧

Some strive energetically for despotic authority,
Though they're not part of the vocal majority.
Forget not to be graciously and genuinely mindful
Of the nation's needful, significant minority.

❧

In accepting acknowledged authority,
Be cognizant of your sacred responsibility.

❧

AWARENESS

To know ourselves diseased is half our cure.
-Alexander Pope

❧

Increased awareness, you must address; keen, sharp insight is the key to success.

❧

BEATITUDES

May your prime response to the Beatitudes be assurance,
May happiness be engendered but quick.
Beatitudes are indeed to one's spiritual life, what the octave is to live music.

❧

For each and every beatitude we must express our gratitude.

❧

While on earth, Lord Jesus, precious blessings unfurled;
Beatitudes are His promises to a helpless, needy world.

❧

The Beatitudes, like the fruit of the Spirit, are all part and parcel of the whole.
The candidate for the Kingdom of God will possess all these graces in his soul.

❧

The object of the second Beatitude, mortal, mental anguish is its twin,
Is to teach us the value and importance of sincere godly sorrow for sin.

❧

BEAUTY

If beauty is made for seeing, then beauty is its own excuse for being.
-Ralph Waldo Emerson

❧

The best of beauty no photo can impress; it takes select words inner beauty to express.

❧

Rouge, mascara - all makeup are liars;
Contentment and cheerfulness are the greatest beautifiers.

❧

So oft a face is what it ain't; a beautiful face needs no paint.

❧

God is more interested in inner grace,
Considerably more than the geography of our face.

❧

Don't think of the misery that your mind retains,
Think of all the beauty that still remains.

❧

A LIFESTYLE PORTRAYAL From A TO Z

A woman's natural beauty isn't portrayed in a mole.
Her beauty is reflected in her harmonious unblemished soul.
It's the caring she lovingly gives, the passion she devoutly shows;
With years this beauty luxuriously grows.

❧

Take no credit for beauty at sixteen, at age sixty-five is when it's best seen.

❧

She thinks that beauty is part and parcel of class;
She neglects her heart, she studies the glass.

❧

A raving beauty, the one who'll protest -
She finished last in a beauty contest.

❧

BEHAVIOR

Behavior is a mirror in which everyone shows his image.
-Goethe

❧

Today, people live as they jolly well please; things known as sin now considered a disease.

❧

One's demonstrative behavior, a lifelong perilous pilgrimage,
Is a shiny reflective mirror in which one shows off his image.

❧

One's behavior is a reflective mirror that exhibits more than its showy exterior.

❧

To attain high principles of wholesome behavior,
Is to live with unbending integrity.
Make your faithful promises and solemn commitments
Prime examples of sterling sincerity.

❧

Good behavior is a singular factor – decidedly so in structuring right character.

❧

For a change in behavior, talk to the Savior.

❧

BELIEVE

You will never succeed if in self you don't believe.
-William J. H. Boetcker

❧

Man says, "Seeing is believing." God says, "Believing is seeing."

❧

If you can conceive and believe you'll achieve.

❧

A LIFESTYLE PORTRAYAL From A TO Z

*N*othing is so firmly believed, as that which isn't fully perceived.

*T*rust in yourself, though a beginner; assert yourself, believe as a winner.

*T*o believe with certainty begin with sincerity.

*B*elieve in yourself, though unclassified; who else than you is better qualified.

*Y*ou'll believe that your life has been worthwhile living,
If you believe that you should be involved in more giving.

*F*ew things special have ever been achieved, except by those who dared to believe.

*F*ully believe that life is worth living, and that of ourselves we should be more giving.

*B*elieve, you'll achieve, if you doubt, you're out.

*T*oo quickly believed is too readily deceived.

*M*any folk keep saying, "There is no God."
Explicitly and emphatically their words do prod.
Has anyone ever seen electricity or the wind?
And yet, no Deity, they are determined.

A med student dissected a cadaver completely.
He opened every organ, he did it so neatly.
The student was asked, "When you opened the brain,
Did you find an idea, or did you search in vain?

"When you cut open the heart, did you find sweet love,
And did you find peace in the form of a dove?
He said, "No," repeatedly, though questions did persist -
Though things aren't seen isn't proof they don't exist.

*W*hile you are sincerely believing, blessings you will be receiving.

"*A*t times, believe not all you hear;" words from the rich wisdom of an elderly seer.

*B*elieve that life is worth living; your believing will create thanksgiving.

*W*ith the practical effect of a firm belief, one can to others initiate relief.

"*B*elieve on the Lord, so shall you prosper;"
Words from Scripture - what a magnanimous offer.

Believe in the sun, even when it's cloudy,
Believe in warmth though you're chilled to the bone.
Believe in God, even when He's silent, believe in love, even when you're alone.

≈

The believing person who kneels to the Lord
Will stand up to anything – prayer is his sword.

≈

"God, said it, I believe it; that's all there is to it."

≈

BELITTLING

Try not to belittle, instead, be big.

≈

Rogues differ little, they all belittle.

≈

It's a great mistake to do nothing, because you can do so little.
Do what you can, my friend, but never attempt to belittle.

≈

Souls are not meant for you to shun, neither are they meant to be trampled upon.

≈

It's a mistake to unkindly belittle; be duly aware, life can be brittle.

≈

BELLIGERENCE

Contentious, incorrigible belligerence, frequently the result of blind ignorance.

≈

Belligerence and negligence, deep anxiety they bring;
Hot heads and cold hearts never solve a goodly thing.

≈

BENEVOLENCE - GENEROSITY - PHILANTROPHY

If there be any truer measure of a man than what he does,
it must be by what he gives.
-Robert South

≈

Some label benevolence as religiosity; sacrifice is the true measure of generosity.

≈

If a soul hasn't discovered something he could give,
He hasn't discovered how he should daily live.

≈

Generosity gives rice instead of advice.

≈

A LIFESTYLE PORTRAYAL From A TO Z

To right the world we must all labor; we must begin with helping our neighbor.

❧

As recorded in the Scripture, years ago, King Solomon,
A proverb on giving wisely uttered,
Generously cast your bread upon sky-hued waters,
It will come back to you buttered.

❧

The person who thinks the world owes him a living
Is rarely ever found in the mood of giving.

❧

To right the world, we must all labor; we must begin with helping our neighbor.

❧

A person would have to pay a great big fee for what a mother does so abundantly.

❧

One thing you can give and still always keep,
It's your honest word; true words aren't cheap,

❧

This morning I beg, more than one question for your celestial, your mental digestion.
In giving to the Lord, what's your attitude? Is it initiated by duty or gratitude?
Your clear objective, what is it in the main? Is it prompted by heavenly gain?
Is your giving a joy or a big pain? Do your thoughts have a tendency to complain?
What does your freewill offering say? Does it to God thankfulness convey?
God so freely, loved that He gave; Christ died on the cross for us to save.
And so, what is your reason to continue living, if it isn't to be joyfully giving?

❧

Beneficence is a virtue, many souls it has thrilled;
As the purse is emptied, needy hearts are filled.

❧

If a man hasn't discovered something he could die for,
In the tournament of life what would be his score?

❧

Serendipitous generous giving is a message from the heart;
The brain doesn't direct if it's not on its chart.

❧

Beneficence is duty, full of love and beauty.

❧

If a gift or great favor to someone is conveyed,
And reciprocation is expected, it's not a gift, it's a trade.

❧

A gift to God is a gift to the needy, it's blankets to those who shiver.
Nothing atones for the insult of a gift like the sincere love of a giver.

❧

Benevolence exalts, it satisfies, it truly elevates and magnifies,
It graciously honors and it glorifies.

❧

A LIFESTYLE PORTRAYAL From A TO Z

Giving is a year-round virtue; serendipitous benevolence won't hurt you.

All people should give from the heart, not economics.
When the need is recognized one should move off his coccyx.

Practice viable generosity - avoid contemptuous pomposity.

Benevolence and compassion are invariably clear-sighted;
Merit and good deeds are always united.

Generosity is a spiritual gift, ingrained in those who lift.

In spite of the enormous high cost of living,
Forget not to set aside a good portion for giving.

Permit your wealth to do good while living.
Accomplish that good simply by giving.
You will not experience that pleasure when you're dead;
All said and done, what more need be said.

Best not to display your contented opulence.
Hyphenate your affluence with kindly beneficence.

We design costly garments that make ladies swoon.
We spend many billions that send men to the moon.
It costs millions upon millions to build and launch rockets,
But money for God - it's still in our pockets.

I truly and most sincerely believe that it is God's divine intention -
Free-will offerings are worthy of being, part of His plan of redemption.

Give and you'll be rich, grasp and you'll be poor; hoard and you'll need, and that's for sure.

Do note all around us, there are needs to meet.
Try to be God's heart, His hands and His feet.

Don't let the devil golden thought impede;
"Giving," the only proof you've overcome greed.

Judicious generosity in design, of a great man, an encouraging sign.

Giving isn't what benevolence is all about; an amiable helping hand, better than a handout.

If with a meager income, your giving spells reluctance,
Will you become generous, when living with abundance?

A LIFESTYLE PORTRAYAL From A TO Z

Whenever you give, don't fret, and when receiving, don't forget.

Cultivate your capacity to give, others by years you'll outlive.

In the absence of beneficence there can be no true joy;
Compassion and liberality endeavor to employ.

You have helped by being generous; in helping you'll be prosperous.
-Proverbs 11:25

Philanthropy is a gracious, a radiant ministry,
A kindly, sacred calling, full of benevolent artistry.

Philanthropy is defined as love for mankind.

Most people will never understand, unless needs of others they perceive.
If they aren't willing to give they'll never be able to receive.

Give of your increase, love grows, so does peace.

Every man in this nation has a distinct obligation
To put back to this world the equal of his ration.

Some people think that they're generous by giving their free advice.
What they really should be giving is clothing and whole rice.

Giving to the needy is an exercise sublime;
Can't wear two pairs of shoes at the same time.

Water that is far is deemed unavailable
To swiftly extinguish a raging fire that's near.
Misery and poverty, likewise, are unassailable,
When funds for their abatement do not appear.

In deciding to give, seek not to impress, seek to inspire and to graciously bless.

The flowers of benevolence you cannot grow if seeds of caring you do not sow.

If you're able to give, give God what's right; do not limit it to a measly mite.

Benevolence can't be bartered, can't be bought or sold.
It's an amazing virtue - so beautiful to behold.

Cultivating a productive capacity to give, should be a basic requirement to live.

A LIFESTYLE PORTRAYAL From A TO Z

When it comes to giving, many stop at nothing.

Man receives from God by the bushel; so oft in return God gets but a nickel.

Benevolence, an attribute that can result in a lift.
A blessed miracle can be the effect of a gift.

Don't give them a stone, when they need bread.
Why would you build walls - build bridges instead.

BITTERNESS

If ire you should fire, do take a long pause,
For critical, bitter words are a sign of a weak cause.

Don't let bitter feelings cause heartache and despair.
They can be sweetened, mention them in prayer.

As long as vile vengeance within you seems sweet,
Deep, nasty bitterness in your heart won't retreat.

Bitterness kept secretly is anger, most agree it doesn't always show.
Nonetheless, it still is inner anger, though silent, it is on the go.

BLABBERMOUTH

The jawbone of an ass is as treacherous today as it was years ago in Samson's day.

If you're to save face, moving jaws oft erase.

Loquacity is a cousin to pomposity.

BLESSINGS

For blessings never wait, nor should you debate, they'll come if you rate.

BOOKS

God be thanked for books.
-William Ellert Channing.

A LIFESTYLE PORTRAYAL From A TO Z

The purpose of good books is to trap the ready mind,
To do its own thinking, leaving ignorance behind.

~

Incisive books are exceedingly special; they never interrupt with a dull commercial.

~

A man of rare intellect, a sound character breeds.
Of him we should inquire as to what books he reads.

~

Books are not bundles of inanimate paper,
They're treasures of intellect, giving life its caper.

~

Books like friends, should be carefully selected;
The Bible is paramount for a life to be perfected.

~

The Bible is an informative, thought-provoking book.
It gives us examples how our lives should look.

~

Good books are the greatest - they should be well used.
Never should they ever be neglected or abused.

~

Determine to read, make it a habit, even though initially it be scant.
The person who won't read has no advantage over the person who can't.

~

You must not read to contradict or confuse.
That isn't the way good books should be used.

~

A good book should be a magnifying mirror.
The primary function is to make things clearer.

~

A great many books inform, it takes but one Bible to transform.

~

Samuel Johnson, years ago is known to have said,
"I don't converse with a man whose written more than he's read."

~

The covers of some books are too far apart.
My advice in reading them, near the end you should start.

~

Read not to contradict, gainsay or refute, to learn, to envision and one's prejudices boot.

~

I was able to read him discernibly like a book,
But to shut him up, it much longer took.

~

Good books have wise things to say; they invariably have instant replay.

~

A LIFESTYLE PORTRAYAL From A TO Z

BRAGGING - BOASTING

The honor is overpaid, when he that did the act is commentator.
-James Shirley

When brash boasting ends, calm dignity begins.
When self-seeking ceases, love somehow wins.

A person is never so empty as when of himself he is plenty.

Some egotistical, blatant boasting, requires occasional roasting.

Bragging and boasting are worthless and vain.
It's not the steam whistle that pulls the train.

He who is an ass but thinks he's a stag will learn his error when attempting the crag.

Some people have pride, others have clout.
Most everyone has something to brag about.

The more a man knows the less he blows.

Don't blow your trumpet about years spent in college,
Lest you darken counsel by words without knowledge.

The man who is constantly boasting and crowing
Is usually not the one who is used to rowing.

The person who begins with, "May I say without boasting,"
You'll find invariably, he himself will be toasting.

A boorish boastful man has a crystal clear plan.
His verbosity flows, telling more than he knows.

Years ago, I knew a man - let's call him Joe.
One would think the sun rose just to hear him crow.

When someone attempts to sing his own praises,
Too high the pitch he invariably raises.

Jactation is something we can ill afford; "Let him who boasts, boast in the Lord."

Be careful, don't ever blow your own horn.
Likewise, don't play leapfrog with a unicorn.

Do bite your tongue, don't brag, don't try to increase your score.
Instead, just say, "That's wonderful!" or "Sir, please tell me more."

Bragging, boasting and crowing, your ego invariably they'll corrupt.
Good deeds speak for themselves, so why would you choose to interrupt.

Don't pat yourself," says Uncle Ben, "Even a blind sow finds acorns now and then."

A conceited, pompous ass loves to hear himself bray.
Do not allow bragging to be your mainstay.

BUSINESS

It is not the crook in modern business that we fear
but the honest man who does not know what he is doing.
-Owen D. Young

Some say, "Don't let business interfere with your pleasure,"
But it's business that gives many pleasures its measure.

CARELESSNESS

Many little leaks can sink a ship.
-Thomas Fuller

Carelessness can be so costly; caution is the parent of safety.

CELEBRATION

Christ's celestial, eternal resurrection is glorious cause for our joyful celebration.

CHAIRPERSON

What a good chair so frequently fears - 'When everyone talks, no one then hears.'

CHANCE

Chance is the providence of adventurers.
-Napoleon Bonaparte

A LIFESTYLE PORTRAYAL From A TO Z

Go for it, take a chance - don't give it another glance.
There's a time you must strut with that feeling in your gut.

✎

Give others a chance their image to enhance.

✎

Fat chance and slim chance have always the same chance.

✎

Some stumble into fortune seemingly by chance.
Remember, when you stumble you always advance.

✎

Trusting happenings to chance?- Lottery of one's life makes no sense.

✎

The chances are totally remote for our world to become greener and cleaner.
Moreover, the devil is an optimist if he thinks he can make man meaner.

✎

A flea and a fly were hiding in a teepee.
"Let us flee," said the fly,- "I can't fly," said the flea.
"Why don't you just hop, chances are we'll be free."

✎

Necessity is the mother of invention, 'tis also the parent of taking chances.

✎

Taking slim chances, bravery enhances; chance is oft lost by giving but a glance.

✎

No man has ever found happiness by chance; a yawn or a wish will never life enhance.

✎

It's too beautiful a world to appear just by chance;
Without the hand of God – this starry expanse?

✎

Life is unpredictable, it's unforeseen chance.
No one can write his autobiography in advance.

✎

Life guarantees a perceptible chance; never does it give just a cursory glance.

✎

Trusting all things to favorable chance, fashions lottery of one's life in advance.

✎

CHANGE

Life belongs to the living, and he who lives must be prepared for changes.
-Johann Wolfgang Von Goethe

✎

Open your stout arms to healthful change.
Your own rare values you might have to rearrange.

✎

Visible change is inevitable, repeatedly this I have seen.
Except, I might knowingly add, from a miserly vending machine.

Change like sunshine can be a friend or a foe, a blessing or a curse, a come or a go.

To change and to improve are two different things.
Ponder the change, what betterment will it bring?
While improving you grow a new pair of wings.

May the banner of change now and then be unfurled.
Be that subtle change you want to see in this world.

CHARACTER

Character contributes to beauty - it fortifies a woman as youth fades.
A mode of conduct, a standard of courage, discipline, fortitude and integrity
can do a great deal to make a woman beautiful.
-Jacqueline Bisset

To one's illustrious character, a virtuous life is a benefactor.

Upright moral character is a reserve force
That we with overt action should fully endorse.

A man's task is light if his heart is right.

One of the crying needs of our sensitive society
Is the acquiring of gentleness and habitual sobriety.

If you want to know what's in a man's heart, listen to his mouth, that's a good start.

Character isn't fully defined by a single self-confident act.
It's how in our daily living we habitually, intuitively react.

A person's true character is revealed by actions he has repeatedly concealed.

The backbone of character is the discipline of desire,
And how often for others it's pragmatically on fire.

A gem can't be polished without sufficient friction,
Nor character perfected without some restriction.

Character, seldom developed in peace and quiet -
So oft, in adversity, like suffering while on a diet.

A LIFESTYLE PORTRAYAL From A TO Z

*A*lways maintain the ethical code, you must avoid character regression.
A second chance you will never get to make that first impression.

*P*eople rarely disclose their character so sincerely
As when they describe someone else's so clearly.

A singular maxim that all should address, "Character is basic for all forms of success."

*A*ll obnoxious traits should be slated for removal.
A man can't be comfortable without his approval.

*P*eople will listen to character, not to what you habitually say.
Your courageous actions will tell, they make or break your day.

*A*n upright character is never uncomfortable,
And mindfully I might add, it's not transferable.

*N*ever measure a man by the size of his head.
Try putting the tape around his heart instead.

*G*racious character, a precious habit; others will invariably want to nab it.

*P*opularity, an accident, fame, but a vapor; riches take flight - what stays is character.

*T*he measure of character is what one would do
If he knew he would never leave a flawless clue.

*I*f your character is upright and incredibly pure,
You'll encourage others to imitate yours.

*T*ake care of your character much more than your wealth.
Hyphenated to the above, take care of your health.

*C*haracter is created by many a soul, through industry, thrift, and self-control.

*T*o instill in your children a character sublime,
Spend half as much money and twice as much of your time.

A man who is at ease is a gentleman that'll please.
The intolerable arrogant man has a coercive plan.

*T*he gold of gentleness and resilience is richer than intellectual brilliance.

*T*here's a thing that I've learned as o'er years I've traveled,
You can latch onto ropes without getting unraveled.

A LIFESTYLE PORTRAYAL From A TO Z

The character of your children tomorrow is what you teach them today.
You'll find that it largely depends on teaching them how to obey.

❧

A person reveals character by the jokes he presents,
Likewise, by jocularity he habitually resents.

❧

The measure of a man's true character, is being to fellow men a benefactor.

❧

Moral character is made by what you stand for;
Reputation, on the other hand, by what you fall for.

❧

I've learned that it's free, you don't have to pay a price.
It doesn't cost anything in trying to be nice.

❧

It can't be denied, spotless character is scriptural.
In today's business world it's priceless collateral.

❧

You can't dream into self, virtuous, pristine character.
You must hammer and forge to be its benefactor.

❧

Character is power, it's with us every hour.
It's power of the will, to be active or still.
It's power of restraint, being free of complaint.
It's power to live right, conscience free every night.
It's command over feeling, being honest, no stealing.
It's unassailable reputation, worthy of salutation.

❧

Some virtuous characters have a malady, they choose to find fault, not a remedy.

❧

CHARITY

Alas for the rarity of Christian charity.
-Thomas Hood

❧

Charity, the ardent, generous spirit that prompts us to give things away;
That item we haven't used in years – that something we labeled, "Throw Away."

❧

FAITH – HOPE – CHARITY;
If we had more of the first two, the latter would not be a rarity.

❧

So much of our charity is not outright giving,
For certain it smacks of seduction.
Philanthropy years ago was a distinct virtue,
And not a sought-after deduction.

❧

A LIFESTYLE PORTRAYAL From A TO Z

True charity is the desire to be useful to others,
With no thought of reward from any of our brothers.

❧

There are six essential qualities that are keys to one's success:
Courtesy, humility, wisdom – sincerity and personal integrity.
I have only mentioned five - the sixth stands out with clarity.
Last, but not the least, it's gracious, unsolicited charity.

❧

Charity it is said, begins at home, but it truly should much farther roam.

❧

These days some think, charity is a rarity.
Every token of liberality is a gift to charity.

❧

Remedial charity should not be a rarity,

❧

Charity is the epitome of morality.

❧

CHARM

The charm of a deed is its doing, the charm of a life is its living.
-Eugene Fitch Ware

❧

Having outward charm is a delightful thing;
Coupled with the above, something praiseworthy bring.

❧

Don't always depend on your exquisite charm;
Beware lest it do you untold harm.

❧

Charm can disarm, walking arm in arm,
Be it city or farm, with a sweet schoolmarm.

❧

Charm is the rarest, the least used of powers.
It captures with a glance like a bouquet of flowers.

Can be likened to love, it can move without force.
It grows like the daylight; abundant is its source.

It bears gifts galore, it responds so sweetly,
It isn't at all punitive, it captures completely.

It disarms itself fully by being disarmed;
It strikes without wounds – no one is harmed.

It wins without battle though it has its victim,
It is modest in dress, always neat and trim.

He who falls in battle let him fall to charm,
He'll never see defeat, he'll walk arm in arm

In the armory of man charm is enchanting;
It is light and subtle, it is most convincing.

But it can be deceptive like a sense of humor,
If you think you have it , it may just be rumor.
-Paraphrased from a description of charm by Laurie Lee

CHOICE - CHOOSING

To every man the choice is continually being offered,
and by the manner of his choosing, you may fairly measure him.
-Ben Ames Williams

When choosing your selection between two besetting evils,
Determine to choose neither, lest it cause an upheaval.

Choose your models with care, lest they become a snare.

Choosing not to respond about a criticism about you,
Shows strength of character that dwells within you.

Never allow the conduct of a fool to be your model, lest evil overrule.

Choose the path of love with indomitable persistence.
Renounce vile hatred and hardened indifference.

May that silent inner voice administer your clear choice.

Irresistible compulsion is the devil's domain.
Force, fear, vile cruelty and ferociousness are his reign.
On the other hand, God gives us the freedom of choice.
My friend, respond promptly to His beckoning voice.

I can choose to give up, recoil, defeated,
Or follow the One who has never retreated.

Now is the time to choose the Lord;
Later may never come - that you can't afford.

A LIFESTYLE PORTRAYAL From A TO Z

When you're faced with a choice it's important to choose.
If you're sitting on the fence you are bound to lose.

∽

In purchasing a house, its plans some belabor.
It is far more important to choose the right neighbor.

∽

Choose being kind over being right; choose to be giving over being tight.

∽

The giving of gifts is a dangerous art,
Unless you choose to give from the heart.

∽

Beware of the person who has nothing to lose.
You are bound to be at odds if that person you choose.

∽

Appeasement or conflict, sweet peace or grim wars,
Placid patience or shortness - choice absolute is yours.

∽

If you choose to carry a load with a frown,
'Ere long the load will wear you down.

∽

To respond to God's voice is entirely your choice.

∽

If you choose to dive into a sea of thought,
You could find pearls that cannot be bought.

∽

In a lap-hazard manner, a precarious way to eat;
My choice would rather be at a table to have a seat.

∽

As a youngster, my menu, one could scarcely believe it,
Consisted of two choices, "Take it," or "Leave it."

∽

Why would you the date of your demise advance?
Live healthfully by choice and not by chance.

∽

Our unlimited choices must be weighed, not ignored,
For they will determine our future reward.

∽

We have two ends from which to choose; I say this not just to lightly amuse.
With one we think, with the other sit and snooze.
Our success depends on which one we choose – heads, we win, tails, we lose.

∽

One's greatest wealth is the freedom to choose,
But you'll not retain it if your decision is booze.

∽

When you don't choose right, in essence you are choosing;
The devil is then winning and you are losing.

❧

You and you alone have control of your soul.
No one but you can choose your goal.

❧

A lean, hungry lion was roaming the Savannah,
Seeking for something he might choose to devour.
In a secluded spot he spotted two men,
One, reading a book, the other wrote by the hour.
Which one would he choose - the creative, prolific writer,
Or would it be the reader sitting under a gamp?
He chose the book-worm, a wise choice you'll agree
For readers digest, but writer's cramp.

❧

Determine to choose to look forward, likewise choose to look back;
Can't tell which way the train travels, merely by looking at the track.

❧

You're more likely to rejoice if you make the right choice.

❧

How odd of God to choose the Jews,
But odder still are those who choose
To choose the God who chose the Jews.
I'm not Jewish, but I wish I were;
With this some folk may not fully concur.
You see, dear friend, my best friend was a Jew,
He loved us so much, He died for us too.
He did it to save us - His name is Christ Jesus.

❧

In making your choices, avoid ignominy; your choices determine your future destiny.

❧

Those who choose to conform, don't always scrupulously perform.

❧

I'm unable to choose how today I might feel,
But precisely I can choose how with others I deal.

❧

We're the sum of our choices as well as our voices.

❧

CHRIST

Make Christ the head of your house, and He will transform religion into life.
-Ralph Stockman

❧

A LIFESTYLE PORTRAYAL From A TO Z

You may be worthy of singular admiration,
But Jesus alone is worthy of adoration.

It is truly amazing what one can endure,
When you know you're winning - Christ is the answer.

Of Christ we're the picture that some will ever see.
To portray that picture, it's up to you and me.

The more you love Christ, to have Him within,
The more you'll comply to fully hate sin.

A picture of Christ that's completely reliable;
Just one place to look, it's in the Holy Bible.

If we are like Jesus, some folk may not like us.

Christ, our Savior, the epitome of love; to die for us He came from above.

Christ's resurrection assures what Calvary's cross secures.

Christ came to this earth to work among the poor.
They required the greatest share of His attention.
Today, in the person of you and I, His children,
He visits the needy, I hasten to mention.
-E. G White
(paraphrased)

Not only did He die on the cross for us,
He ascended to heaven to prepare a home for us.
Even now, Christ appears in the Sanctuary for us;
He is our High Priest, He intercedes for us.
He's perpetually and deeply concerned for us.

Christ, the only way to the heavenly mansions, no need for gloom, there's room.
All other pathways, roadways and crossways are but weary detours to doom.

Believing Christ died, some say, "That's history."
That he died for me - ah, glorious, divine mystery.

He said, "It is finished," you will recall, Jesus' great sacrifice was once and for all.
He'll truly forgive, you must on him call.

The Rehabilitation Act of A. D. 33, extends to each of us boundless mercy.

Use Christ for reliance when looking for guidance.

When Christ is the center of your focus, the Spirit will have achieved His purpose.

No Jesus, no peace - know Jesus, know peace.

Invest in God's future - in Christ a child nurture.

Christ endured the darkness that we may enjoy Light.

Christ bridges the gap in eternity's span, between infinite God and immortal man.

God's word will endure, Christ's blood makes us pure.

Christ crossed out our sins at the cross.

Christ paid a debt He did not owe to satisfy an amount we couldn't pay escrow.

THE LORD IS MY SHEPHERD

The Lord is my shepherd – I shall never truly want.
He maketh me so peacefully to lie
In pastures green,
Calm waters are seen;
Sweet rest He so abundantly doth supply.

He restoreth completely my failing faltering health,
In Him my soul is revived.
He helps me to do
What's best in His view;
Paths of holiness are so graciously supplied.

While calmly walking through the dark valley of death,
I shan't for a moment be afraid,
For Thou art beside me,
I know thou will guide me;
My enemies by thee will be stayed.

Thy rod and Thy staff, they direct, they lead me,
They correct, guide and comfort all the way.
Should I slip and fall,
Thou dost instantly call;
Solicitude Thou truly dost display.

A LIFESTYLE PORTRAYAL From A TO Z

Thou providest me a spread in the presence of my adversary;
Am supplied with life's needs – they're the best.
My blessings overflow,
Thy love Thou dost show;
Am welcomed as your beloved honored guest.

Surely goodness and loving kindness – these blessings they do bind us,
These gifts freely given are adored.
My Shepherd I will follow,
My covenant is not hollow;
I shall dwell in the house of the Lord.
-Psalm XXIII, paraphrased

❧

*W*ith Jesus, my shepherd, my reliance, is the only lasting, reliable alliance.

❧

*F*or God so loved that to us He gave His only begotten Son that us He might save.

❧

A sincere, deep longing for Christ's second coming
Is constraining, compelling and totally overwhelming.

❧

"*L*ooking unto Jesus," the secret of life,
His words are destined to nullify strife.
"Looking unto Jesus," in the Bible we learn
What we should do, and what we should spurn.
"Looking unto Jesus," that the brightness of His face
May enlighten our darkness by His redeeming grace.
"Looking unto Jesus," our Lord crucified -
Our ransom, our pardon   for us Jesus died.
"Looking unto Jesus,"- He is risen again,
We find that his righteousness will justify and amend.
"Looking unto Jesus," He'll teach us to look
To the words of instruction - He's the author of the Book.
"Looking unto Jesus," the author of our faith,
He is also the finisher, so the Good Book saith.
"Looking unto Jesus," He is the Way,
If we follow Him faithfully we won't go astray.
"Looking unto Jesus," and not to our meekness;
We can't become stronger by lamenting our weakness.
"Looking unto Jesus," and not to our sins,
Meditating on His life is what eventually wins.
"Looking unto Jesus," and not to any other,
He is our salvation, He is our brother.
"Looking unto Jesus," and not to our brethren,
Not even to the dedicated and most beloved of men.

A LIFESTYLE PORTRAYAL From A TO Z

"Looking unto Jesus," not the depth of our sorrow
That we feel for our sin, today and tomorrow.
"Looking unto Jesus," not the things of mirth,
Nor to the anxieties of this temporal earth.
"Looking unto Jesus," and not to the law,
For the law condemns - I am an outlaw.
"Looking unto Jesus," for redeeming grace,
That is freely supplied to the whole human race.
"Looking unto Jesus,"- through the days allotted here;
The cares of unknown future we need not fear,
For His promised second coming will soon be here.
-An article from the Adventist Review paraphrased into verse.

༄

Jesus always listens, that's his strict rule; He's never too busy, His schedule, never full.

༄

The priest and the rabbis, Christ death desired;
Christ's sacrifice for man in God's plan was required.

༄

If man's intellect is on the eternal, his life with Jesus will be fraternal.

༄

I Refuse !

I totally refuse discouragement, to be somewhat sorrowful or cry.
I refuse to be downhearted, and here is my reason why.
I have a God who's Almighty, who's Sovereign and He's Supreme;
I have a God who loves me, He keeps me on His team.
He is all-wise and powerful, Christ Jesus is His name,
Though all is prone to be changeable, Jesus is always the same.

My God knows all life's happenings, from its beginning to the end,
His nearness is my comfort, He is my dearest friend.
If sickness should happen to come to bring my head bowed low,
I'll call on eternal God - into His arms I shall go.
If misfortune should threaten to rob me of my peace,
He will hold me to His breast, all my struggles will cease.

When my feverish heart melts and weakness takes control,
He takes me in His arms, He soothes both heart and soul.
The great "I AM," is with me, my life is in His hand;
My companion, the "Son of God," in His strength I'll stand.
I totally refuse discouragement, my eyes are on eternal God;
He promises to be constantly with me as through life's journey I trod.

A LIFESTYLE PORTRAYAL From A TO Z

I'm looking past all circumstances to God's eternal throne above;
My prayers have reached my Savior, I'm peacefully resting in His love.
I give God thanks in everything, my eyes are on His face;
The battle is His - my victory, He helps me win the race.
-Original thoughts by an unknown author.

❧

Christ is the epitome of unquestioned authenticity.

❧

Christ's cross provides eternal serenity - the only safe crossing into endless eternity.

❧

Christ to heaven departed that His Spirit could be imparted.

❧

Christ our Savior, the sole benefactor in the recreation of our sinful character.

❧

Christ died for us once, don't choose to die twice.

❧

Proclaim it to the world every tribe and nation;
Christ is the rock of eternal salvation.

❧

If you want your friends and neighbors, to know what Jesus can do,
Your life should show and tell what the Savior has done for you.

❧

You gave up your throne, gracious Lord, precious Jesus.
You became a miracle, you died for us.

❧

"Who is this Christ?" - see pages 483 and 484.

❧

CHRISTIANITY

Christianity is the good man's text; his life the illustration.
-Joseph P. Thompson

❧

Christianity is the path you walk, likewise, the vocabulary you talk.

❧

Hedonism is proclaimed as the doctrine that pleasure
Is the only proper goal of moral behavior.
A Christian, however, has more to treasure,
He has in his heart, Christ Jesus, his Savior.

❧

A saint that is godly makes virtue attractive
With an abundance of patience - seldom negatively reactive.

❧

We as living saints, please God when our walk
Qualitatively and quantitatively lives up to our talk.

❧

A LIFESTYLE PORTRAYAL From A TO Z

Christianity is the root of all democracy;
Based on love, not hard-hearted bureaucracy.

❧

There is no graded scale in Christianity's view,
So why should a white man a black man subdue.

❧

Molding some clay doesn't make a Dresden;
Attendance at church doesn't make a Christian.

❧

A smooth sharp tongue, not a sign of mental fitness;
A biting, scoffing tongue can dull a Christian's witness.

❧

Choose to be a person of faith than of fame.
This should always be a true Christian's aim.

❧

If Christians were Christians, why would they hate Jews?
Christ Jesus was a Jew, so why Jews eschew?

❧

To all professing Christians, I tenderly appeal,
Reveal to your neighbor that you know God is real.

❧

Double occupancy is taboo in the heart of a Christian.
You can't expect pardon serving God and Mammon.

❧

Too many Christians are sitting on the premises.
They should be faithfully standing on Christ's promises.

❧

God's promises are eternal, and they're never too late.
Furthermore, I might add, they're never out of date.

❧

Christ-likeness doesn't defile, nor does it go out of style.

❧

If you were arrested for being a Christian,
Would there be enough evidence for viable prosecution?

❧

In the Christian battle, to be a solid winner,
Refrain from vile sin, and encourage the sinner.

❧

A believer at war with a Christian brother cannot be at peace with his heavenly Father.

❧

A Christian is inspired God's grace to receive, but it isn't a license to live as you please.

❧

God speaks to us through His sacred word; to those who will listen, He will be heard.

❧

A LIFESTYLE PORTRAYAL From A TO Z

Christ's saintly soldiers seldom stand at ease.
Routinely they fight best when they're on their knees.

❧

The Christian who carries a cross with a song will carry it easier than dragging it along.

❧

Born once, you'll die twice, this undeniably is a fact;
Born twice, you'll die once. if you accept God's contract.

❧

If your Christian experience is to fully mature,
Close friendship with God you must daily nurture.

❧

If your Christian experience is a great big drag,
Rid the worldly weights that are in your bag.

❧

It's good to be a Christian and know it; better still to be one and show it.

❧

When there is enmity and vicious backbiting,
This ponderous thought I must briefly mention.
There is no place in the body of Christ for that jutting bone of critical contention.

❧

Christianity isn't prattle - it's an uphill battle.

❧

If you truly are Christians, you're His chosen saints.
This is the clear picture the good book paints.

❧

Christians are not sinless, but they should sin less.

❧

When the world is at its worst, Christians must be at their best.

❧

God's, endearing, unparalleled ways, deserve our joyous, our boundless praise.

❧

Note well this maxim, "What you sow you reap."
No one becomes a saint while he's in his sleep.

❧

A collapse in a Christian, with some, so to speak,
Is seldom a blowout, it's usually a slow leak.

❧

When Christians get closer to Christ their Brother, they then get closer to one another.

❧

A bright red ember that separates, isn't capable to clearly remember
That its brilliant red glow decreases, be it January, June or December.
Likewise, the church-attendee, as commitment begins to roam,
His spiritual radiance diminishes - he decides to stay at home.

❧

An empty tomb and a living Savior should guide and control our Christian behavior.

❧

A LIFESTYLE PORTRAYAL From A TO Z

"So live that no one can despise your Savior."
That means we must always watch our behavior.

☙

God is truth, He is man's hope; without His presence how would one cope?

☙

On deciding to go to worship Almighty God,
Did your dear spouse have to coax and prod?
Attendance at church is more than a fellowship,
It's an opportunity to develop with Christ a friendship.

☙

A strong healthy heart is not just to please us,
It's a heart that beats with a love for Jesus.

☙

If humans were truly sons of God, almost with angels on par,
Satan would try to persuade that they doubt who they really are.

☙

Holiness is not a matter of one's survival, it's to live in a state of perpetual revival.

☙

Holiness is not a virus to be caught, it's a way of life that must be sought.

☙

Some intellectuals betray their beleaguered vanity.
They dogmatically assume that Christianity is insanity.

☙

A clearer vision of end-time should give us
Compassion for those who are no longer with us.
Our solemn commitment should be to acquaint them
With the love of our Savior, our Lord, Christ Jesus.

☙

In our Christian journey we must daily keep pace.
We're rewarded not for running but for finishing the race.

☙

We repeatedly flunk tests in Christian sociology,
Our glacial demeanor plots to be unkind.
It's sad how our frailties are unable to overtake
The serpentine tongue and caustic cruel mind.

☙

As a devout Christian, remember, the devil can also inspire.
Theology one must never rewrite to accommodate an evil desire.

☙

The badge of Christianity is not an outward sign of wearing a crown or a cross,
It's that which reveals union of man with God – obedience is the sign – disobedience toss!

☙

CHRIST'S SECOND COMING

We know that Jesus is coming; do you know the Jesus that's coming?

Our Lord, who holds the stars in their place
Will surely be capable of carrying saints through space.

Much greater than man's fabulous trip to the moon
Is Christ's glorious coming to take place real soon.

The glories of heaven will totally eclipse
The glories of this earth - assures the Apocalypse.

Look not into the future with eyes of dread and fear;
Jesus' second coming is just about here.

Unless we are following Jesus, our calculated wisdom is folly.
Prepare for His inevitable coming; don't plan on taking the last trolley.

CHURCH

It is illogical to abolish churches, just because they haven't abolished sin.
-C. Donald Dallas

You need the church and the church needs you.
The world needs both its plight to subdue.

We should go to church to worship, not whisper,
To commune, not criticize with words so oft crisper.

We should invite people to the edifice with the steeple,
But it's only God's Spirit that convicts and saves people.

The church must preach or perish; saving precious souls it must cherish.

Just the other day, I sat and pondered, why people would choose to absent be,
And so I've penned a provocative message that should gently nudge both you and me.

Are you a zealous church attendee my friend,
Or do you have a question in deciding to attend?
Don't wait 'till the hearse hauls you off to the church,
Come now, join your family, don't leave them in a lurch.
If you wait, hesitate, vacillate, procrastinate -
You'll go, regardless of rain, wind or snow,

A LIFESTYLE PORTRAYAL From A TO Z

You'll go though you have no one with you to go.
You'll go, no matter how you're needed at work.
You'll go even though trips to church you did shirk.
You'll go no matter how you're needed at home.
You'll go, though luscious meadows you'd much rather roam.
You won't be concerned 'bout your makeup or attire,
Nor worry about a taxi that you frequently hire.
You'll go, regardless how your family may feel,
You'll go, whether or not, you hear church bells peal.
Prayers will be there, but they won't touch your heart,
You won't shed any tears when with friends you part.
The minister may relate lovely things about you,
But you won't hear a thing, though you're near the front pew.
Aren't you glad to be alive, hale and hearty, full of zest,
Happy to fellowship - to draw near in God's rest?

❧

*S*ome folk sow wild oats throughout the whole week,
On weekends go to church a crop failure to seek.

❧

A church sign caught my I eye, I thought it a blast,
"Heaven only knows when you were here last."

❧

*E*very church member must be actively caring,
Coupled with the above, the "Good News" sharing.

❧

*A*ttendance at church is a habit of mine, skipping is the beginning of spiritual decline.

❧

*G*oing to church on Saturday or Sunday, doesn't excuse one to live right on Monday.

❧

*C*hurch services are meant for our sobering reflection
On Christ's sacrificial death and His glorious resurrection.

❧

*T*he preacher may be preaching – as a church are we reaching?

❧

*F*or just a brief moment may your ear be bent
As I relate a short story about a tiny copper cent.
A two tone *'twonie' and a little copper cent
Rolled slowly along as together they went.
Rolling nonchalantly along the sidewalk,
The twonie remarked for dollars can talk.
"You poor copper cent, you tiny little mite,
I am much bigger and many times as bright.
I am worth far more, fully two hundred fold,
And engraved in me is a bear, quite bold."
"Yes, I know," said the cent, "I'm a wee little mite,
I'm not very big, nor especially bright,

A LIFESTYLE PORTRAYAL From A TO Z

But yet," said the cent with a meek little sigh,
"You don't go to church as often as I."
[*A Canadian two dollar coin]
There's a moral to this story, don't leave dollars in the lurch;
Invite and encourage them to come regularly to church.

≈

*D*on't knock the church, the house of prayer,
It may have improved since last you were there.

≈

*W*hat kind of church would my church be if all of its members were just like me?

≈

*T*he church it is said, is the army of God however, o'er the years I've sadly concluded,
These troops planted firm on this earthly sod
Is the army that so oft shoots its own wounded.

≈

*T*o all a sincere welcome to this sacred hour of prayer,
As we to the Lord our thanks and petitions bare.

≈

"*C*ome unto me and I will give you rest," is our Savior's promise, I trust you'll be blest.

≈

*W*e welcome each saint that is with us today.
May the blessings of heaven rest on you, I pray.

≈

*Y*our presence today will result in a gift – a gift from the Lord, a priceless faith lift.

≈

*A*bsence from church won't make you grow fonder,
Nor will it prepare you for the up-yonder.

≈

*F*uneral *S*ervices for a *D*ead *C*hurch

*T*he little old church had been closed for some years.
Clergy after clergy had left it in tears.
Minister after minister, how they've tried to revive it,

But there came no support to help revitalize it.
Then at last there came an energetic, able man,
With zeal and devotion he had a great plan.
But as much as he tried, he could not instill fervor,
Each parishioner played well the part of an observer.

A brother spoke bluntly, to the Padre, he said,
"Taint no use in trying, the church is stone dead."
"Then why don't we bury it," said the cleric, "If it's dead?"
The brother sized the pastor – questioned what he said.

A LIFESTYLE PORTRAYAL From A TO Z

"The church being dead, we must arrange for a burial;
An early date I will set for a fitting memorial."
The village weekly came out, early Saturday morn,
There was this terse announcement in concise, simple form.

"Dead,- the village church – funeral Sunday at two-thirty;"
Many people were perturbed, others felt a bit squirmy.
On that bright afternoon, the local kirk, so neglected,
But to come to that service, more came than expected.

In front of the pulpit were casket and floral bouquet
Of beautiful white flowers, how lovely they did lay.
The preacher gave the sermon then requested all to file
To look at the remains, "Please do come down the aisle."

They all were very eager, the short, stout and thin,
They were extremely anxious to look in the coffin.
To view the dead church, they viewed as they were told;
In a mirror they themselves they truly did behold.
     -Anonymous thoughts, put into verse

"Pillars of the Church," can have a negative notion.
Pillars stand still – have no motion or emotion,
On the other hand, most pillars show solid devotion.

For the saving, transforming power of Christ,
The church, you and me, is the best advert;
Helping the needy, be it but a fresh loaf,
Or for a child, a pair of shoes or a shirt.

We as a church can help people spiritually,
Only to the degree that we help them physically.

How the church outside its walls enthralls is just as important as inside its walls.

About leaving the church, a fitting maxim has been writ,
"Folk, like some autos, start missing then quit."

Why would you go to the church in the morning,
When your plan is to go to the devil in the evening?

The church is the place where of counsel there's no lack,
Where someone speaks to me and I don' talk back.

A LIFESTYLE PORTRAYAL From A TO Z

To all a sincere welcome to this sacred hour of prayer,
As we to the Lord our thanks and petitions bear.

∞

When you leave this place, your step will be brisker.
I trust you'll feel, you've been in touch with the Master.

∞

COMMENDATION

When an accolade to someone is publicly unfurled,
You portray sound leadership, unchallenged in the world.

∞

COMMITMENT

You shall be careful to perform what has passed your lips
for you have voluntarily vowed unto the Lord your God
what you have promised with your mouth.
-Deuteronomy 23:23

∞

There are a few things you can get for a dollar,-
Shiny nickels, silver dimes and a quarter,
But priceless is the entity of total commitment,
A steadfastness akin to brick and mortar.

∞

When making your positive commitments, bear in mind those negative 'omitments.'

∞

"Honor your commitments, for goodness sake," my father thus years ago spake.
"Make it a goal to make good on your promises, no matter how long it will take."

∞

He works six days and fourteen hours a day, some would say, this man is plucky.
I would venture to note that this eager beaver is invariably the man who gets lucky.

∞

Winning doesn't depend on strength, nor does it depend on habit.
It does not depend on size; could a cow ever catch a rabbit?

∞

Every morning in Africa, when a gazelle wakes up
It knows it must run lest it be gobbled up.
Likewise, the lion, when lazily he awakens,
He knows he must dash, lest starvation overtake him.
When you personally get up, don't plan all day sunning;
Though not a gazelle, you had better be running.

∞

A childhood commitment represents the potential, of a whole life lived for the Lord.
Why then would a child's request for baptism be rejected by the local church board?

*C*ommitment to Christ, the Scripture demand;
Commitment to His church go hand-in-hand.

*P*eople can achieve a fuller meaning in their lives
Only if they've made full commitments;
Commitments that extend far beyond the selfish self,
Commitments that embody 'omitments.'
Commitments to religion, to loved ones and fellow humans,
To excellence and concepts of moral order.
Commitments give a wholeness and completeness to lives,
And a steadfastness akin to brink and mortar.
-John William Gardner (paraphrased)

COMMON SENSE

*I*f a man can have only one kind of sense, let him have good common sense.
-Henry Ward Beecher

*D*o the right thing at the proper time; it's just common sense embodied in rhyme.

*C*ombine common sense with the precious Golden Rule;
For success you'll find this to be a useful tool.

*C*ommon sense an oddity - an uncommon commodity.

*S*uaveness can never be used as defense.
Sophistication can't be valued above common sense.

*F*or happiness in life one requires, appreciation for occasional nonsense.
Incidentally, I hasten to add, couple it with good common sense.

*C*ommon sense in medicine is no pretender; surreptitiously it can be a wholesome mender.

*Y*our own common sense can be your recompense.

*T*here's a thing that I've noticed about common sense,
It isn't always common, oft specious pretense.

*S*ome sense the ridiculous but haven't sense of humor.
Some skip the full truth - they love to propel rumor.

"In the race of life," so wise men say, "Good common sense has the right-of-way."

Nothing astonishes and is so appealing as good common sense and clean, honest dealing.

No need being tense, use good, common sense.

Common sense is seeing entities as they are,
Embodying a reminder of the things one must bar.

Happiness is not a matter of events, it depends a great deal on one's common sense.

COMMUNICATION

The fantastic advances in the field of electronic communication
constitute a greater danger to the privacy of an individual.
-Earl Warren

Communication is defined as imparting and transmitting
Information and ideas, and promises committing.

In effective communication, make expression your choice;
Be careful not to use a minacious tone of voice.

In fulfilling communication with insightful thirst,
Understanding others must always come first.

There are people we trust, their character we know,
Though they're not eloquent they're true.
What we really are communicates far more than what we say or do.

If you talked much less and calculated the score,
You would more than likely communicate a lot more.

So much thoughtless speech on this earth does abound;
The vessel that is empty makes the biggest sound.

Some talk incessantly their ego to feed; all talk and no listen is a form of greed.

When someone is speaking , my friend. are you listening,
Or are you yawning with your tonsils glistening?

Do consider what you're about to say.
Are your words true blue, do you argue and subdue?
Do you attack and condemn, do your words cause mayhem?

A LIFESTYLE PORTRAYAL From A TO Z

Do you cut people to size, constantly criticize?
Do you love to find fault, with words do you assault?
With words do you flatter, are they empty chatter?
Do your words express ire? Hatred is like fire.
Does your speech express ecstasy or does it show jealousy?
Does your talk uplift? Kind words are a gift.
Words expressing gratitude can change a person's attitude.
Thoughtful words giving praise, endorphins will raise.
All people have a choice to grumble or rejoice.
If others you're to reach you must watch your speech.

❧

The material value of sound communication isn't primarily remembering what was said.
It is in remembering what you candidly think, as a result of what was verbally fed.

❧

Do you have a problem in the field of communication? Do try using this simple key.
To help initiate a pleasant conversation, use these simple words, "Friend, please, tell me."

❧

Calm, meaningful communication - the fulcrum of human relation.

❧

Allow a time gap before your jaws snap.

❧

Uplifting communication depends on whether two committed people can pray together.

❧

The art of communication is not only to say
The right thing, the right time and right place.
It's to leave unsaid at the ill-starred moment
Things lacking compassion and grace.

❧

If you've courage to speak, say it well, let it glisten,
But it must be matched by the wisdom to listen.

❧

So much of our talk is but empty squawk.

❧

Tell me not what I love to hear, just tell me what I ought to fear.

❧

The concrete essence of meaningful communication
Is based on one another's astute observation.

❧

A propensity to growl creates words that bite,
Resulting in one feeling dog-tired at night.

❧

In a beauty parlor, women talk and share; some of the conversation could curl one's hair.

❧

Let us open the channels, let us gracefully communicate;
To permanently bond, congeniality hyphenate.

❧

With friendly communication we can live in the world,
But don't let worldliness in your life be unfurled.

The fulcrum of communication is to avoid retaliation,
To clear militant air, to be honest and fair.

The purpose of the Bible, a means of communication,
To dispense information for our eternal salvation.

Some statesmen believe that ongoing powwows
Will prevent their countries from going to the bow-wows.

There's a great deal one can say with an enchanting bouquet.

The fantastic advance in the field of communication
Constitutes a great danger – verbal fabrication.

The careful application of full approbation is also a form of meaningful communication.

COMPASSION

Wisdom, compassion and courage, these are the most
universally accepted qualities of man.
-Confucius

May compassion be the law of human coexistence.
May it be accompanied by indomitable persistence.

The thought-provoking parable of the Good Samaritan
Was singularly recorded for a purpose.
It truly behooves us, individually and collectively,
To seek out that incomparable litmus.

The Priest passed by courting a solemn, proud air,
"My appointment is sacred, my office beyond compare."
Cerebrated the Academician, "This sight I can't bear,
And at this particular moment precious time I can't spare."
The compassionate Samaritan, in reflection quite rare,
"What is mine is ours, with you I will share."

The Priest displayed arrogance, disregard for human life,
His egotism he could not hide;
"He's not my concern, it's beneath my dignity,"

A LIFESTYLE PORTRAYAL From A TO Z

Humility he exchanged for pride.
The self-centered Levite had an attitude problem,
"Oh, that's a hopeless situation.
I'm in too much of a hurry, I don't scrub toilets,
Academia is my occupation."
The compassionate Samaritan was ready to serve,
Time limits were not a distraction.
"This poor man needs help, I'll pay his expenses."
He was primitive Christianity in action.

✺

Your heart on your sleeve, not the practical test,
Wear it inside where it will function the best.

✺

True, tender compassion is love in action.

✺

Man may dismiss compassion from his heart, but God never will.
-William Cowper

✺

So many a dear heart has a mountain to climb;
Do give it a moment of your precious time.

✺

An abundance of compassion, a singular obligation,
Should be as natural as one's rhythmic respiration.

✺

If I lack sincere compassion, I'm unable to quicken respect,
Nor am I able to inspire to lead, my counsel they'll totally reject.

✺

In order to be a compassionate man
One must be dedicated and totally committed
To something much greater than the common self;
Befriending humanity must not be omitted.

✺

Compassion is the law of human coexistence.
It should be natural, it should be persistent.

✺

It isn't our words, it's our kind deeds
That help to supply one another's needs.

✺

Compassion is more than an emotional response,
Compassion is more than tenderness for another.
Compassion is pathos, hyphenated with action,
It's giving assistance unselfishly to a brother.

✺

Do good, leave behind a memorial of virtue
Over which storms of time can never prevail.

A LIFESTYLE PORTRAYAL From A TO Z

Etch your fair kindness in humility and compassion
On the hearts of those who attempt to assail.

A good way to console is with your ears;
Pity comes with listening, not with tears.

*M*any are in need - respond, don't resist;
One can't show compassion holding a clenched fist.

*C*ompassion is more than empathy in the main,
It's unreservedly forgiving those who cause pain.

*T*ears may be dry, but never a heart's eye.

*T*ender compassion we must always impart.
The bleakest prison is a sealed callous heart.

*C*ompassion has a hidden capacity - showing love in adversity.

*L*ord, teach me to care, others' burdens to bear,
My blessings to share, to say, "I'll be there,"-
My humble fervent prayer.

A few kind words take seconds to say, but their echo goes on for a year and a day.

*H*e who is ignorant of the art of compassion,
He who hasn't learned how to generously give;
He who's been unable to make new friends,
Hasn't learned the art how harmoniously to live.

*H*e who lacks compassion, can't inspire respect;
While attempting to lead, his counsel they'll reject.

*T*he epitome of compassion is superbly complete,
When walking in shoes of those who haven't feet.

*W*hen a person hasn't fire in his heart, when he hasn't love for his brothers,
When he's totally void of compassion, it's impossible for him to warm others.

*D*uring world War II a general was waiting
At an airport for a plane that he was to be taking.
To the wicket rushed a sailor to ask for a seat,
"I want to see mother before joining the fleet."

A LIFESTYLE PORTRAYAL From A TO Z

The clerk at the counter was not impressed,
"There's a war on, young man," she ignored his request.
General Roosevelt overheard the brief conversation,
He said to the agent, "Give him my reservation."

A friend said, "Teddy, aren't you in a hurry?"
The General showed no sign of concern or worry.
"It's a matter of rank, this is no pun,
I'm only a General, he is a son."

&

A stubbly prospector is trapped under stone,
Head skewed to one side, with gashes to bone.
A comrade is trying to help his buddy,
Toiling very hard to set his friend free.
A third sourdough of contrasting mold
Is minding his own, busily panning for gold.

There's the one who is crushed with anxieties of life,
Has difficulty coping, full of worry and strife.
Another's distinct lifestyle has a salutary mode,
He takes hold of opportunities to help ease the load.
The third is unconcerned, he has selfish intent,
On caching his wealth he's continually bent.

&

*Y*our gold and silver are corroded, their corrosion shall be a witness against your ways.
It will eat your flesh like fire; you have heaped up treasure in the last days.
-James 5:3

&

*L*et there be empathy on every page, let's make compassion the glory of our age.

&

*B*e kind to your children wherever they roam;
Eventually they'll choose your nursing home.

&

*T*he dew of compassion is a tear that we mustn't be ashamed of or fear.

&

*T*here is no future in just making a profession.
The future resides in the person with compassion.

&

*M*ake room for wisdom, may knowledge abide,
Compassion your motto - rid ugly pride.

&

*W*hy don't you dare to affectionately share and to show you care?

&

*I*f you would that your day be compassionate and kind,
Remember, you must always keep 'others' in mind,

&

A LIFESTYLE PORTRAYAL From A TO Z

COMPLAINING

Constant complaining is never witty,
And I might add, it never gets pity.

Never feed on the fuel of deep-seated irritations;
On triumphant success it sets limitations.

On a daily basis decide not to complain -
Your decision will prevent much untold gnawing pain.

So many are involved in negative encounter.
They spend most of life at the complaint counter.

If you stumble don't grumble, just try to be humble.

You repeatedly grumble, "I'm physically unfit."
Never constantly complain about lifestyle you permit.

If you must lament, do it with soul;
Accomplish it promptly toward your goal.

So many find it tough, much gripe is unfurled,
There is envy and malice, vile anger is hurled;
Their garbage disposal eats considerably better
Than a large percentage of the people in this world.

I complained about the bills that my wife kept bringing.
Her reply, "Birds have bills, but they keep on singing."

Breathes there a soul that drinks Brazilian coffee,
To satisfy his sweet tooth he consumes English toffee.
He devours French pastry, wears a Swiss tick-tick,
Drives home in a German car after seeing an Italian flick.
He complains about his business, he's all out of sorts,
He demands that the government stop the flood of imports.

Dwelling on the negative increases its power.
Negativity won't get you to the top of the tower.

Some gripe about the heat, the sun they don't relish,
They crab and complain, discomfiture they embellish.
If we didn't have sunshine, this thought I have weighed,
Trees wouldn't be able to give us cool shade.

Negate negativity, pursue objectivity.

When one is perpetually complaining, conjointly he's needlessly detaining.

COMPREHENSION - UNDERSTANDING

Understanding is more than simply comprehending.
It begs overt action, not idiotically pretending.

We're given a rich abundant life with an explicit deep understanding,
So its singular purpose would be, God's love more fully comprehending.

To know a little less, to understand much more,
Is what we all should be striving for.

Understanding is the greatest amongst all riches;
Burdens we don't need, let's get rid of excess inches.

COMPROMISE

Better to bend than to break.
    -Scottish Proverb

A workable compromise is contention's demise.

Of the trips that are made along life's pathway,
The most highly rated, meeting people half way.

A compromise though lean can be so precious,
Much more-so than a fat lawsuit contentious.

When compromise is suspended, human rights are abandoned.

CONCEIT

Every man thinks his own geese, swans.
    -Proverb

Conceit, said or writ sires more speech than wit.
It's a form of "I" strain in a character that is vain.

Beware of the folk puffed up with importance - gross egotism and conceit.
They're desire is to pay a generous compliment, expecting a tax-deductible receipt.

❧

Self-centeredness, a characteristic, that the world must endure.
It's an inherent malady that our doctors cannot cure.

❧

Self-serving conceit, smugness and rigidity;
Egotism, the anesthetic that dulls pain of stupidity.

❧

CONCENTRATION

When driving one stares grim death in the face;
Keen concentration continually embrace.

❧

Concentration is imperative for practical achievement,
Likewise it's essential for professional advancement.

❧

CONCERN

Dad's, be concerned about your offspring,
Much more so than your follow-through golf-swing.

❧

Don't be so concerned with your inalienable rights;
If you fly off the handle you'll start ugly fights.

❧

Never let your phantasmic illusions or delusions
Make you jump erroneously to erratic conclusions.

❧

If you have a concern, God's will you must learn.

❧

CONDEMNATION

Be you male or femme, choose not to condemn.

❧

I must not choose to condemn, instead, I must show I care.
Criticism is the devil's proxy for effectual intercessory prayer.

❧

Condemnation prior to total examination,
Intense investigation, and unreserved communication,
Is certainly a far cry from the fullest of information,
Determination, verification and fair adjudication.

❧

CONDOLENCE - SYMPATHY

Sympathy is a virtue rarely known in nature.
-Paul Eipper

Forget not to express compassionate condolence.
May the words you convey have worthwhile substance.

It takes a big man to sympathize, only a small mind to criticize.

CONFESSION

A fault confessed is half redressed.
-Proverb

Confession heals, confession justifies, it grants man pardon of sin.
All hope consists in honest confession; a calm peace enters within.

Don't let your pride, self-esteem or self-righteousness,
Keep you from confessing your sin.
No point in trying to keep secrets from God -
And neglect not confessions to brethren.

As the result of sincere confession, we can obtain unequivocal absolution.

Coming clean of evil we shouldn't be flagging;
Confession without repentance is simply bragging.

CONFIDENCE

For they can conquer who believe they can.
Ralph Waldo Emerson

Of confidence I must be a professor; confidence inspires its possessor.

Inspiring confidence in a student - a singular function of a professor.
Confidence imparts inspiration to the student and his assessor.

The self-confidence and assurance you lucidly address
Is bound to determine your future success.

Calm, supreme confidence is a sweet emulsion.
It can't be stimulated or produced by compulsion.

✑

Have confidence in God, come what may; listen and obey to what God has to say.

✑

Confidence will thrill while doubt stands still.

✑

Retain calm confidence, avoid moral laxity;
When you have confidence you have capacity.

✑

CONFIDENTIALITY

Things confidential, not meant to be seen, are oft retrieved from a copying machine.

✑

Maintaining strict confidentiality, the few that can do it is scant.
I can keep enrapturing secrets, it's those I tell that can't.

✑

If friends don't respond to words deemed influential,
Attract them with a packet marked, "Strictly Confidential."

✑

CONFLICT - DISCONTENT

There is no conflict between the Old and the New.
The conflict is between the False and the True.
-Henry Van Dyke

✑

The source of all conflict, the secret I have found,
It wasn't the apple, it was the pair on the ground.

✑

Appeasement or conflict, sweet peace or grim wars,
Patience or impatience, the choice is yours.

✑

Conflict prevention always needs our attention.

✑

We must play fair, we mustn't make a fuss,
Blaming others for something that's wrong with us.

✑

Expecting one's life to be fashioned to all-inclusive specifications -
It's temptingly, cordially inviting those enduring, fruitless frustrations.

✑

CONFRONTATION - BATTLE

Be kind, every one you meet is fighting a hard battle.
-Ian Maclaren

So little lowers more the level of conversation
Than raising the voice, it becomes confrontation.

Avoid confrontation, argument you must shun;
It's easier to start a fight than it is to stop one.

CONGENIALITY

One's congeniality has a penetrating insight.
Wholesome morality is doing what is right.

Much better than the savor of exotic spices and herbs,
Are added luscious sauce of amiable congeniality,
Than are the pretty dishes of signal, saucy pride,
And colorful cloisonne bowls of carnal sensuality.

CONGRATULATIONS

When you give a friend a voluble felicitation,
He'll try to live up to your exaggerated summation.

Congratulations, felicitations, humble thanks to all missionaries,
Who give and who gave of their talent, skill and time,
Who gave of their lives in God's concessionaires;
The work of their hands have been immeasurably sublime.

CONSCIENCE

The worm of conscience keeps the same hours as the owl.
-Schiller

One's conscience wants to talk with the proud and the meek,
But the line is oft busy when it desires to speak.

One's conscience, a voice of values deeply infused in one's blood;
On occasion a subtle reminder, employing a bright photoflood.

A LIFESTYLE PORTRAYAL From A TO Z

Conscience is the language of ideals; it has of compassion a preponderance.
Love is not only the source, it is the substance of conscience.

☙

Some folk do wonder where conscience resides;
It takes up more room than all of my insides.

☙

A good, clear conscience is a great companion,
Just like a little salt is to a green onion.

☙

Do what your conscience tells you to.

☙

Carry a clear conscience, sing a happy song;
Conscience is the voice that "no's" what is wrong.

☙

A guilty conscience in the soul, can be as heavy as lead;
Endeavor to clear it with God – obtain sweet peace instead.

☙

Conscience, comparable to a buzzing bee; it can make a fellow uneasy.

☙

Consider your conscience as your very best friend.
He's exceedingly tactful, he'll never offend.

☙

When you have a fight with conscience and get licked,
You win, not lose, when your moral sense is pricked.

☙

Conscience and the precious Holy Spirit, prosecutors of body and soul,
Unquestionably are the two great informers that help to make man whole.

☙

A trustworthy compass, one's conscience – heeding it is considered prudence.

☙

Dread guilt, a wide billow - a clear conscience, a sweet pillow.

☙

A mute, guilty conscience truly does matter.
It's a knowledgeable mirror that does not flatter.

☙

Conscience, for certain, gives direction, it helps to prevent future fears;
Though it is that still inner voice you've been trying to silence for years.

☙

Unsilenced conscience, a small voice of sorts, that makes exceedingly major reports.

☙

There are no walls that can hide our sin;
Stubborn, nosey conscience is always peeking in.

☙

One's conscience, the still voice, disobeyed makes us smaller.
On the other hand, when obeyed, 'twill make us feel taller.

☙

A conscience clear in any season is the heartbeat of potent reason.

For puritanical morality our conscience is a tutor.
If not sincerely heeded, it becomes a prosecutor.

A conscience mute, gives us a strict clue; it reminds us of things that we shouldn't do.

A keen conscience always strives for conviction, to make us happy through confession.

A conscience that dwells in your chest, is a witness that won't let you rest.

Quickening conscience, hideously hurts, when with repressed feelings one boldly flirts.

Conscience, that still, repetitive voice that makes one consider another choice.

There is no wisdom so trustworthy and astute
As clear quickening conscience, though it be mute.

Just like a pungent savory smell, tells us something is cooking,
So conscience is a silent inner voice that tells us someone is looking.

CONSOLATION

A wise way to console is with listening ears;
Compassion with action, not with unshed tears.

"Do keep a stiff upper lip," one says, to console.
It's really the lower we should try to control.

CONTENTION

They carp, crab and grumble, they perpetually beg,
Their point of contention the astute clearly tag.
When an obstinate husband portrays a stubborn mule,
His darling, loving wife becomes a nag.

CONTENTMENT

But godliness with contentment is great gain.
    -1 Timothy 6:6

What's total contentment?
It's calm peace in your heart - bright sunshine in your soul,
Abiding love in your home - nutritious food in your bowl.

❧

Understanding is the greatest amongst our acquisitions.
Contentment is the zenith amongst earthly possessions.

❧

To achieve contentment, set limits on resentment.

❧

The secret of contentment is to fully realize,
Life's not only a right, it's a priceless prize.

❧

A contented soul need not be demented;
Treasure your health that others take for granted.

❧

To live contentedly, gently and quietly,
Bravely and cheerfully, respectably and spiritually,
In absolute harmony, this is my task.

❧

Contentment is wanting what you have, not having everything you want.

❧

If we lived our lives, filled with abiding contentment,
We wouldn't hang onto our sordid resentment.

❧

To be completely content with little, though difficult, some say it's possible.
To be totally happy with a great deal, you'll admit it's virtually impossible.

❧

This Japanese proverb to mankind has been sent,
"He's miserably poor who doesn't feel content."

❧

Contentment isn't getting everything we want,
It's virtually being happy with what we've got.

❧

Covetousness displays a lack of contentment.
Turn your lack into a positive amendment.

❧

CONUNDRUMS

How do noses run, and how do feet smell,
And why would some people keep themselves in a shell?
And how do heated arguments cause atmospheres that are chilly?
These baffling conundrums are absolutely silly.

❧

Our natives who beat drums to drive off evil spirits,
To many of us they're objects of scorn.
And yet, as North Americans, to break up traffic jams,
We invariably resort to an impatient car horn.

CONVENTIONS

People go to conventions to improve skills and mind;
When they're attending, convention is left behind.

Political conventions are booked in haste;
Why not in winter months? Hot air they wouldn't waste.

A convention, a conference where people work shirk.
They take time off to talk about work.

CONVERSATION

"The art of discreet conversation, should be like well-planned Santa Fe.
It should have stops in many places to give others the right of way."

The commonest and cheapest of pleasures - conversation.
Don't make it a frustration, more appropriately an elevation.

A profitable conversation is being able to disagree,
To carry on with your speech and still collect a fee.

She told me that you told her what I told you not to tell her.
From this I must conclude, you're not a trusting fellow.
I also know you told her not to tell me - agree,
Now, don't you go and tell her that I told you she told me.

Many people are totally overcome, with disquietude and visible consternation,
When their friends habitually jaywalk over their every ongoing conversation.

What one really says, truly does matter, for good conversation is mind over chatter.

Regardless how brilliant or original you are,
In monopolizing conversation minds will wander afar.

The cheapest of all pleasures is common conversation;
To be kept in moderation, not carried to saturation.

The person who's in the habit of hogging conversation
Can be likened to a porker; he takes more than his ration.

❧

"Sedate conversation," someone once did say,
"Is like a defensive driver, he yields the right-of-way."

❧

If you think that the art of conversation is dead,
Try telling a child that he should go to bed.

❧

So many monopolize casual conversation,
Party-givers with them, are oft distraught.
Hostesses cannot help but sometimes wonder,
If they've retained any unexpressed thought.

❧

A good conversationalist remembers what was said,
And graciously conveys what he's retained in his head.

❧

Blessed is the woman or man, who has very little to say,
Refrains from giving evidence in an ignorant, wordy display.

❧

A bore talks arrogantly in the first person,
While patiently listening one's listening will worsen.
An idle, malicious gossip circulates rumor in the third,
He purposely says things that should not be heard.
A good conversationalist is the one to be reckoned -
His words are selected to talk in the second.

❧

CONVERSION

Man's conversion, takes only a moment – his forgiveness, takes Christ's atonement.

❧

CONVICTION

The men who succeed best in public life are those
who take the risk of standing by their own convictions.
-James A. Garfield

❧

A "No" that is said with firm conviction
Is better than a "Yes," without any restriction.

❧

The merit of conscientious conviction, be it but self-propelled,
Consists in the precise steadfastness in which it is passionately held.

❧

A LIFESTYLE PORTRAYAL From A TO Z

*B*e unimpeachably loyal to your deep conviction.
You alone over it have complete jurisdiction.

*S*trong convictions embody restrictions.

COOPERATION

*S*incere solicitude for our fellow man
We express not with words that are biting.
True brotherhood we'll never truly accomplish
While hatred we are boldly inciting.
In the very vast field of benevolent endeavor,
Remember, dear friend, there's a hitch,
We can't help the needy with whole heart and soul
By robbing the so-called filthy rich.
We certainly can't help the proverbial 'little guy'
By blatantly tearing down the 'big'.
Never forget, that to lighten the heavy load
These men exert effort and dig.
We surely can't oblige most people by doing
What literally they could do for themselves.
These precious same souls will treasure far more
What they've achieved for their own willing selves.
We cannot to this land bring fame and good fortune
By discouraging our forefathers shrewd thrift.
We cannot to this land bring the fullest abundance
By refusing our own gears to shift.
To be sure we can't lift the industrious wage earner
By downgrading providers of work;
We as workers must verily so fully accomplish,
For certain we our tasks mustn't shirk.
As individuals, as governments, and as a distinct people,
How can we keep out of trouble?
If we much expend, much more than we gain,
We are bound to burst the big bubble.
We cannot build confidence, peace, love and gain courage,
By stifling pure initiative, so oft clever.
We must duly inspire amongst us a distinct people
That'll create a cooperative endeavor.
-Anonymous thoughts paraphrased into verse

*I*f you've ever been involved in a mixed-farming operation
You'll appreciate this illustration of meaningful cooperation.

In shooing bull flies and hauling heavy freight, it's always much wiser to fully cooperate.
This is a singular truth all horses know – they've learned it so many long centuries ago.
When days are hot and flies are very thick - intimate cooperation does the deft trick.
One tail on duty at the blind rear can't reach the pesky fly behind the right ear,
But two long tails when arranged with craft, give full protection both fore and aft.

Do choose openness and timely cooperation,
Not fierce conflict and moral degradation.

There's a pertinent adage that I've learned on the farm,
'You may not see eye to eye but you can walk arm in arm.'

For when was honey made with one bee in the hive.
-Thomas Hood

CORRECTION

Correction does much but encouragement does more.
-Goethe

Take correction, it will never do you harm.
It provides an opportunity to be collective and calm.

If you should insist on absolute perfection, demand of yourself total correction.

When you're kindly and tactfully corrected
It doesn't mean you're being rejected.

COUNSEL

In great straits and when hope is small, the boldest counsels are the safest.
-Livy

In the giving of counsel, and in rendering a report,
Counsel with caution and do make it short.

Your father's counsel don't ever begrudge; time is the fairest and wisest judge.

Before making a decision consider all the facts;
Seek wise counsel, the Almighty contact.

COURAGE

*C*ourage is that virtue that champions the cause of right.
-Cicero

*Y*ou're your own doctor when you're in the hot seat,
As well as when it comes to curing cold feet.

*F*aint-heartedness mend, make courage your friend.

*C*ourage, can be said, is a unique type of fear;
A fear that encourages bravery to appear.

"*W*ithout courage all virtues lose their meaning."
A quote from Churchill that's worth repeating.

*C*ourage does not put on airs, it's fear that has said its prayers.

*L*ook grim fear squarely in the face; peerless courage choose to embrace.

*I*t's easy to stand with the crowd, a choice to which men are avowed.
There's a stance to which few are prone; it takes courage to stand alone.

*C*ourage cannot see around corners, and it isn't at all fearful of scorners.

*F*or emotional courage it takes physical fitness.
Couple it with spirituality to become a true witness.

*T*he one that's outstanding, of courage does not lack,
So do not be reticent to stand out from the pack.

A man with courage isn't prone to discourage.

*I*t is said, it takes courage to use the word "Yes."
The impact of that decision we must morally address.
On the other hand, there is that two letter word "No,"
If we use it prudently 'twill prevent tears to flow.
It takes singular courage which rightly to choose;
The vision of that decision never choose to lose.

*B*e bold and courageous but never outrageous.

*M*ore effectual than the will to win is the ardent courage to earnestly begin.

*L*ife shrinks or expands proportionately to one's courage.
Quite oft it can be likened to a floating mirage.

*C*ourage is important, you can't it abuse; it's like one's muscle – strengthened by use.

*I*n times of distress, how have you fared? There can be no courage unless you are scared.

COURTESY

*P*oliteness is the ritual of society, as prayers are of the church.
-Ralph Waldo Emerson

*C*ourtesy stands tall like a dazzling church steeple.
It is the shortest distance between two people.

*B*e known for your courtesy, couple it with diplomacy.

*C*ourteous patience, let's all face it - more should be known to embrace it.

*C*ourtesy is treating other folk as though they are as important as they think so.

*C*ourtesy we mustn't abort, life is far too short.

*C*ourtesy sells, disrespect smells.

*M*anliness and politeness are precious; no man is too big to be courteous.

*D*on't half-listen or rudely interrupt; courtesy at times means to promptly shut up.

*B*e courteous to all, never exhibit fury, for you'll never know who'll show up in the jury.

*D*ignified courtesy and praise, forget not to continually sing.
It can be bestowed on others without you losing a thing.

*O*ne never loses anything by being polite; experience does more than good eyesight.

*B*e courteous to all, but intimate with few,
Those few well tried; bid rudeness adieu.

CREATION - NATURE

I love to think of nature as an unlimited broadcasting station
through which God speaks to us every hour, if we only will tune in.
-George Washington Carver

*M*an is a wonderful creature, sitting, standing and running;
A created being with an assembly of ingenious portable plumbing.

*M*an was created a little lower than the angels,
This truth the Bible does clearly convince.
However, o'er the years, most will agree,
Man has progressively become a lot lower since.

*T*ake needful lessons from God's awed nature, wild storms eventually lose to the sun.
Do blend them with mild-mannered creatures, they are the ones we're to be among.

*M*ysterious nature is amazing, it has abundant know-how.
Just think, a built-in fly swatter at the end of a contented cow.

*H*uman nature is an entity that gives man a certain bent.
It's what makes kids treasure, writing on fresh cement.

*T*he sky, like a bolt of blue silk unfurled, adds so much beauty to this magnificent world.

*N*ature is in verity, a name for an effect, whose cause is God; this truth some reject.

*A*nyone can count the seeds in a pear; counting pears in a seed - no one would dare.

A rough coral reef doesn't innocently malign.
A host of colorful creatures cavort in its brine.
Their beauty could embarrass a colorful neon sign.

*A*t first I was a tadpole, slender and thin, then I was a froggie with my tail tucked in,
Then I was a monkey swinging from a tree, now I'm a physician with an M.D. degree.

*D*on't ever make a monkey out of yourself, evolution is not the supreme adjudicator.
You were fashioned, you were made perfect, by Almighty God, the Omnipotent Creator.

*O*ur beautiful world with things so natural
Bear the signature of a creator supernatural.

Bright sparkling snow, the peanut butter of nature,
Most kids love it as well as my spouse.
It's crunchy, it's cool, all love it at school,
As it tenaciously clings to the roof of the house.

CREATIVITY

It is wise to learn; it is God-like to create.
-John Saxe

Creativity is so delicate a flower; praise tends to make it tower.

By activating singular motility, a hunch can lead to creativity.

Michelangelo was once asked how he created superb statue,
Magnificence it surely did spell.
"If an angel I was to carve, I'd keep chiseling away
Everything that wasn't an angel."
From sculptor Michelangelo, a lesson we can learn
In this world of disappointment and strife.
Take courage my friend, keep chiseling away
All that shouldn't be in your life.

To foster creativity in yourself or others,
Be willing to tolerate the aberrant in your brothers.

Overcoming the unforeseen and discovering the unknown,
Kindles the spirit and energizes the backbone.

CREDIT

Of personal credit cards do not be a hoarder.
At times plastic surgery is definitely in order.

CRITICISM

It is much easier to be critical than correct.
-Benjamin Disraeli

Adverse criticisms will maliciously hurt if with sharp witticisms you choose to flirt.

A LIFESTYLE PORTRAYAL From A TO Z

If you choose to criticize and unjustly condemn,
Irrepressible. raw hatred you will never stem.

Why be critical? Choose to be analytical.

Give guarded attention to what critics say,
No statue is erected to honor their day.

Do not be quick to nick, pick or kick, for certain, do not rain on another's picnic.

Criticism mustn't ever encompass defamation;
'Tis best when it sounds like a meaningful explanation.

People asking for criticism, truly amaze, for all they want is unstinted praise.

If ire you should fire, do take a long pause,
For critical, bitter words are a sign of a weak cause.

Never let criticisms defile, complement a bald man on his smile.

The people who lift are the ones who encourage;
The ones who criticize do duly discourage.

Before embarking on becoming a critic,
You must take time to be a learnedly analytic.

It's safe if it's painful to criticize someone,
Doing it without being emotionally high-strung.
But if you take pleasure in castigating that one,
It's best that you hold your chastening tongue.

Constructive criticism, positives initiate.
Do avoid using it to horribly humiliate.

In bringing up children, don't criticize and condemn;
Your children will treat you the way you treat them.

If you're not big enough to take needful criticism,
You are far too small to exhibit magnetism.

Be slow to criticize - never make it demeaning.
Praise does wonders for the sense of hearing.

Never use a sharp witticism to initiate painful criticism.

A LIFESTYLE PORTRAYAL From A TO Z

*T*aking harsh criticism will never do us harm.
It provides an opportunity to be collective and calm.

*W*hen critics have a verbal race, is our world a much better place?

*A*ttempt agreeing with criticism, when it's directed toward you,
Then watch it slowly disappear; you then they'll differently view.

*R*esist the urge to criticize, 'twill increase your stature's size.

*W*e can all learn a lesson from foul, inclement weather,
Just censure and criticism it ignores altogether.

*T*urn your criticism into tolerance, 'twill prevent a friendship's severance.

*T*ake not costly time to harshly criticize, instead sympathize and duly harmonize.

*W*e need people and people need friends, let us in our speech make needful amends.
We can by avoiding sarcastic witticisms and equally omitting painful criticisms.

*I*f you think that a criticism of you is unfounded,
Ask a friend to reveal where it is grounded.

*C*riticism can be painful like a sting of a bee;
So frequently it's a form of intense jealousy.

*C*hoosing not to respond to a criticism about you
Shows strength of character that dwells within you.

*S*ome well-meaning critics this world try to alter;
Comparable to peashooters shooting at Gibraltar.

*I*t is much better to be criticized than disparaged and ostracized.

*I*f you haven't the will to improve or change it,
Why would you effort to criticize and attack it.

*W*hen you're criticizing, attacking and complaining,
Do not forget, the Almighty is listening.

*H*e can be so blatantly insufferable,
Unbearable, obscene, insulting and intolerable,
Scornful, defamatory, invective, denunciatory,
Disparaging, depreciatory, slanderous and derogatory,

A LIFESTYLE PORTRAYAL From A TO Z

Fulminatory, licentious, offensive and evasive;
To remove the rough spots will require an abrasive.

Men, before you criticize another, look closely at your sister's brother.

Take scathing criticism in your stride; may singular humility forever abide.

Do not unduly fault frank criticism, at times it could be a glistening gold nugget.
It may not hit the black bull's eye, but it could very well be right on target.

In the battle of one's life it's not the critic that counts,
Not the one who expounds how the other guy to trounce;
How the doer of a good deed could've done much better,
How more he could've accomplished had he lived to the letter.

Why no, full credit is with the man in the arena,
The stalwart who steps forth without a subpoena.
With face heavily stained with grime, sweat and blood,
He's the man whose not afraid of getting his feet in the mud.

He's the man who strives valiantly full of courage and devotion,
With ambition and set goal he puts his frame into motion.
He's the man though he errs and comes short now and then,
For certain he's the man who keeps trying again.

He gives freely of himself to many a worthy cause;
He works hard and long, seldom taking a pause.
His place shall never be with those faint-hearted souls
Who have never tasted victory - they've been afraid to set goals.

He best knows in the end the triumph of his achievements,
While his critics sit back and marvel in deep amazement.
-Theodore Roosevelt, 1858-1919, (paraphrased)

CYNICISM

A cynic is a man who when he smells flowers, looks around for a coffin.
H. L. Mencken

Don't be a cynic, bewail and bemoan, neither should you carry a heart of stone.

An optimist lets his son take his car on a date.
A pessimist would never to the same act relate.
A cynic once did - now bemoans his car's fate.

A LIFESTYLE PORTRAYAL From A TO Z

Cynicism is oft humor that bears ill-health.
It features jealousy when talking of wealth.

∽

Not only can cynicism be hurtful and uncouth, it is a thorny way of telling the truth.

∽

Cynicism will never a broken friendship heal.
At times, pinch yourself to know how others feel.

∽

DANGER

Dangers and perils cause tears; dangers are less numerous than fears.

∽

"Though constant exposure to dangers, will breed for them contempt,"
Philosopher Seneca alludes, "some dangers we should attempt."

∽

DEATH

Death levels all things.
   -Claudian

∽

"Death is nature's expert advice;" while living it teaches us to always be nice.

∽

Shrouds have no deep pockets; you won't be piloting rockets.

∽

The Scripture tells me that death is a sound sleep.
My concern should be, 'What resurrection will reap?'

∽

About Elvis being alive – a rumor wildly spread;
One wonders about humans – they think God is dead.

∽

For you as a human, what thoughts does death spawn?
For the Christian it's the last shadow before heaven's dawn.

∽

If you live for eternity you'll die with serenity.

∽

DEBATE

Honest differences of views and honest debate are not disunity.
They are the vital process of policy-making among free men.
   -Herbert Hoover

∽

In all your debates, may truth be your aim;
Endeavor to make gain, do not expose shame.

❧

There's a question that has started so many live debates,
"If the world is getting smaller, why the raise in postal rates?"

❧

In open debate or while having chit chat, never proudly say, "My child wouldn't do that."

❧

DEBT

A small debt produces a debtor, a large one, an enemy.
-Publilius Syrus

❧

Running into debt can be obviously bad; running into creditors can also be sad.

❧

Canada and America span the continent of the free.
They've one thing in common, they're far from debt-free.

❧

DECEPTION

Hateful to me as the gates of Hades is the man who hides
one thing in his heart and speaks another.
-Homer

❧

Deception can be likened to a soiled short sheet.
If I pull it o'er my face it exposes dirty feet.

❧

Fool me once, shame on you, fool me twice, I'll say, "Adieu.".

❧

DECISION - INDECISION - DELIBERATION

Deliberate with caution, but act with decision;
and yield with graciousness or oppose with firmness.
-Charles Hole

❧

In making a decision, some folks can't sense.
They'll risk getting slivers sitting on the fence.

❧

Make God's promised unalterable provision
The sound foundation for your moral decision.

❧

A LIFESTYLE PORTRAYAL From A TO Z

When faced with a decision make a decision to decide.
When faced with a choice make a decision to choose.
Sitting on the fence is just a pretense -
If you don't make a decision, you could win or lose.

❧

Is it "Yes", or "No?" I must wisely contemplate;
Decision, a sharp knife that cuts clean and straight.

❧

Decisions involve scrutiny, they determine one's destiny.

❧

When making a decision, think omission and precision.

❧

There are moments of indecision in this bureaucratic world,
Some bureaucratic questions that are frequently hurled.
Is there a rule touching what you're about to do,
Or a rule that you mustn't - just what does one do?

❧

A decision to commit less energy to worry and more to your goal,
Will give you a lot more incentive to be much gentler to your soul.

❧

Your decisions could take you out of God's will.
Your peace with Him may not always be still.
Your decision may give others sound reason to impeach.
Do not allow self to be out of God's reach.

❧

If I should ever question as to whether I ought to -
Must determine to know enough - when to know not to.

❧

One's decision-making is a very slow process, in minutiae and trivia many drown;
By the time they figure out where they firmly stand, they find it is time to lie down.

❧

Decision, a sharp knife that cuts clean and straight.
Indecision, a dull one – it tends to mutilate.

❧

In moments of indecision give your gray cells a ring.
Inspire them to accomplish nothing but the right thing.

❧

In making a decision accommodate precision.

❧

I must make a decision what to put into my mind if I'm to become the keen thinking kind.

❧

There is always hope when I fully decide to take time to sit down to hear the other side.

❧

In hours of deliberation choose not to assail; drop to your knees, God answers knee-mail.

❧

In choosing not to act, smacks of derision, in not deciding, you've made a decision.

If love is to be a supreme acquisition, you must make love your singular decision.

DELINQUENCY

A juvenile delinquent is a lad, that yourself you have frequently wrought.
There is a glaring inconformity, a delinquent is a lad who gets caught.

DEPENDABILITY

Without the help of thousands of others, any one of us would die naked and starved.
-Alfred E. Smith

Today, my schedule I'll try not to botch, instead, I'll try to be a vigilant watch;
Pure gold, open-faced, always present, on time,
Dependable, busy, of good works sublime.

DEPRESSION

He has fully turned his life around, the man distressingly obsessed.
He used to be depressed and miserable, now he is miserable and depressed.

Mental obsession can cause a depression.
We're greatly blessed, so why be depressed.

DERISION - RIDICULE

Ridicule is the language of the devil.
-Thomas Carlyle

Most mates would cease each other to deride
If they understood clearly they were on the same side.

Never make it a habit another's character to deride.
Don't let your conscience be another person's guide.

Merciless, ruthless ridicule, comes from the tongue of a fool.

Most expert advise, "Begin with a joke."
My advice to you, "Don't fun at others poke."

DESIGN

Our sweater manufacturers design to womanize.
Their goal is to pull the wool over women's eyes.

DESIRE - DESIRES - WANTS

All human effort is prompted by desire.
- Bertrand Russell

Regardless of how much we possess, we continually expand our desires.
We'll never be filled with happiness unless we put out those fires.

Seldom do we get what we're after from life's font,
Unless, far in advance we know what we want.

It's easier to suppress that first warm desire,
Than when it becomes a blazing raging fire.

Most everyone desires bus service to the door,
But no one wants buses on their street to roar.

Fulfilling desires can light many fires.

You'll become as small as your controlling desire,
Conversely, as great as you purposely aspire.

The four D's leading to the path of impunity,
Desire + Direction + Destination = Destiny.

DESPAIR

The name of the Slough was Despond.
-John Bunyan

Never tell a young man he is losing his hair.
Without question he knows it, you'll add to despair.

Say "Yes" to right, say "No" to wrong; avoid despair, give way to song.

It profits no one to nurse despair; a world in despair needs humans that care.

Despair and despondency are a shocking scene.
Hope, like an anchor is fixed to the unseen.

Whenever you see small print anywhere, remember to read it - 'twill prevent despair.

DETERMINATION

A determined soul will do more with a rusty monkey wrench
than a loafer will accomplish with all the tools in a machine shop.
-Ruper Hughes

Dedication and determination are a powerful combination.

DEVOTION

Of all devotions the best devotion is to utter the name of God,
-Arjan

Some churches share commotion and emotion.
It should be replaced with sincere devotion.

The surge of man's spirit is oft named as emotion.
Thought trained heavenward, is termed true devotion.

Sacred devotion is a spiritual notion.

Ignore pain involved – a most positive notion.
Consecrate yourself to the object of devotion.

There is no devotion without some virtue;
Commit yourself fully - it will never hurt you.

DICTATION

The advantage of dictating your letters is that you can use many a word
That you're unable to spell, and perhaps your steno hasn't heard.

A LIFESTYLE PORTRAYAL From A TO Z

DIET - DIETING

*W*hy do I diet? – It ain't no mystery,
I want to improve my medical history.
My doctor says, "You've got to lose weight,"
Strange, he agrees with my lovely wife Kate.
My muscles are flabby - have a big pot belly -
My derriere it shakes like a bowl full of jelly.
My saggy bodily frame just seems to hang loose;
My friends, they tell me I look like a caboose.
Losing avoirdupois will take loads off my heart,
'Twill also prevent pants seems coming apart.
I've got to eat less, got to watch what I eat,
This abominable state I've just got to beat,
And putting on weight I must not repeat.
I've got to lose pounds, and yes, several inches,
Then when climbing stairs there'll be no need for winches.

*D*iets are so strict nowadays, a consensus that still remains.
It appears that the most conscientious are allowed to have hunger pains.

*M*y wife oft reminds me, on dieting she is sold,
"The refrigerator keep closed, you're liable to catch a cold."

*T*o our daily diet we should be more attentive,
And to our lifestyle a lot more preventive.

*W*hat Sophia Loren says, applies to me,
"Everything you see I owe to spaghetti."
We are what we eat; this is nature's feat.

I know that I could lose much weight
If I only ate what was on my plate,
But my good intentions they have a way of fading,
I begin to munch what I should be evading.
No foil-wrapped crumb escapes my theft,
I eat what's right and then eat what's left.

*I*f excess calories you continue to coddle,
Eventually you won't walk, you'll wiggle and waddle.

*R*ash gluttony can perniciously trigger, your dieting it can truly botch.
If you pensively don't watch your figure, you'll have considerably more to watch.

A LIFESTYLE PORTRAYAL From A TO Z

The chances of a diet succeeding real soon
Depends on how you use knife, fork and spoon.

❧

Let your eating be guided by desire for good health;
Control your appetite for attaining great wealth.

❧

It's one appetite that makes eating a delight.

❧

Beware of the eye-catching, tall golden arches,
To all my dear friends, be cautious, I share.
If you choose to imbibe repeatedly in their fare
You'll be heading prematurely, only heaven knows where.

❧

Most folk lack strength on going on a diet,
They also lack will about it to keep quiet.

❧

People who are thick and tired of it
Should strictly diet and become physically fit.

❧

It isn't a woman's will that makes her diet –
Most assuredly it's her ego – she can't deny it.

❧

Initiating will power for many is rough,
They keep putting on while putting it off.

❧

"And how should I slice your pizza. shipmate?"
Said the seaman to the waiter, "Into six – can't eat eight."

❧

It is most interesting to know that many a statistic does show
That those who are continually eating their demise will sooner be meeting.

❧

Why not accept loss as a distinct gain; obviously losing weight is a worthy aim.

❧

Some link excess weight to the time spent at a table,
Relating so many quaint legends.
For excess avoirdupois, don't blame the minutes, the cause is the abominable seconds.

❧

Dieting involves persistence, watching calories at a distance.

❧

The cost of animal products, heart disease can stall,
By lowering the blood level of sticky cholesterol.

❧

Said a diner in a café, "This soup's not fit to eat,"
"Who told you," said the waitress, so pert, cute and sweet.
"If you really want to know," with voice, this time mellow,
Retorted the upset diner, "It was a little swallow."

DIFFICULTIES

Difficulties mastered are opportunities won.
-Sir Winston Churchill

Most inherent difficulties are guidelines; they're never meant to be stop signs.

When encountering difficulties don't give up and scoot;
Tumultuous storms make trees take deeper root.

Be thankful for problems, don't let difficulties rob;
Someone with less ability might take your job.

Most difficulties that are great can be quickly overcome.
It's only the imaginary that take time to succumb.

To overcome difficulties is to fully experience
The full excitement of one's existence.

Difficulties mastered are opportunities captured.

Difficulties encountered should be surmounted;
Good deeds are to be accomplished, never to be counted.

With relatives so oft it's hard to make amends.
Let's be thankful we can choose good, trusty friends.

DILIGENCE

Few things are impossible to diligence or skill.
-Samuel Johnson

If you diligently aspire to earn top wages,
Be cognizant of the fact, "Good enough," seldom is.

Diligence is as important as intelligence.

Do with due diligence what you have to do; thrift in itself results in revenue.

Be diligent, to giving up may you never succumb;
Prepare, some day your chance will come.

Be diligent each day, do work and pray, tomorrow you'll be proud of yesterday.

DIPLOMACY

A drop of honey catches more flies than a hogshead of vinegar.
-Proverb

He who has learned to disagree without being at all disagreeable
Has discovered the secret of a diplomat; his objectives will be achievable.

Diplomacy is making for troubled waters a dash
Without producing a huge, resounding splash.

Many diplomacy hate, they believe that it's lying in state.

It's been said that diplomacy is a lot of hot air that diplomats are fashioned to pump;
But that's what is in our automobile tires, you'll agree, it eases a bump.

A diplomat is a person who engages in ducking.
He's the one who thinks twice and then says nothing.

Diplomacy is using subtle tact while relating an unforeseen fact.

Diplomacy is an art that is here to stay.
It's a skill that lets someone have your own way.

DIRECTION

If you cry "Forward," you must without fail make plain
in what direction you are going.
-Anton Chekhov

Socrates was once asked, "How do I get there,
Mount Olympus is my selection?"
The philosopher replied, "Make certain every step
Takes you in that impulsive direction."

*Direction is much more important than speed;
An axiom that we all should strive to heed.*

❧

To avoid deception seek God's direction.

❧

*Direction is paramount, it's the set of the sail
That determines your success or whether you fail.*

❧

*Invariably men and women that meet my selection
Possess sound objectives and a sense of direction.*

❧

*It's what you stand for and what seeds you're sowing.
More importantly it is the direction you are going.*

❧

*To firmly stay on course, these words must be heard,
"Trust the sure compass of God's holy word."*

❧

Contemplating life's direction involves astute selection.

❧

*Note all the details on those rugged mountain trails,
Don't with them be carelessly toying.
Lest you will find you'll be somewhere else
If you don't watch where you are going.*

❧

DISAPPROVAL - OBJECTION

Men of age object too much, consult too long, adventure too little.
- Francis Bacon

❧

A blue-black eye, before one's removal is a definite mark of distinct disapproval.

❧

DISCERNMENT

Sound judgement with discernment is the best of seers.
-Euripides

❧

*Bernard Shaw was approached by his gardener one day,
"I request that you change your method of pay.
Instead of making payments in hard cash, I beseech
That you make out checks of ten shillings each.
There's reason for my request, it's not for a laugh,
You see, I could sell them, they'd bear your autograph."*

Shaw was very pleased with the gardener's request.
The checks would have potential of never being cashed.

You can readily discern the pulse of a nation
By intelligent listening and by keen observation.

Ordinary people are also important; put into practice shrewd discernment.

DISCIPLINE

Discipline is doing what you have to do,
Whether or not you want to, you have to.

He who has learned to obey, can readily show others the way.

Of discipline and diligent application,
Don't choose to be physically weary.
An ounce of seasoned practice
Is worth more than a pound of theory.

Strict discipline begins with small things done daily,
Like faithfully practicing your treasured ukulele.

What's singularly paramount? – It's virtuous discipline.
If it's absent in your life, you'll lose, not win.

Give to a pig every time it grunts, and to a child each time it cries.
Eventually you'll have a very fat pig, and a child that continually defies.

He who is disciplined to obey, the Almighty will never betray.

DISCLOSURE

We had our first test, we were awaiting results,
The professor's entrance caused a lull.
He solemnly announced, "The cow is a widow –
Most of you just shot the bull."

DISCORD - DISCONTENT

He who with a little cannot be content, endures an everlasting punishment.
-Robert Herrick

You cannot afford to sow bitter discord.

It's common for people to anticipate indigestion,
When meals are spiced with discord and question.

Smoldering discontent is the catalyst for change;
An abounding forbearance a better future will arrange.

Intelligent discontent, poverty can prevent.

DISCOURAGEMENT - DESPONDENCY

Blessed is he who expects nothing, for he shall never be disappointed.
Alexander Pope

If you're having trouble coping, why don't you in God try hoping?

In hours of discouragement, try God for encouragement.

Lack of self-reliance breeds discontent; a mental ailment where will is absent.

When everything seems to be going against you, and you feel you are not quite with it,
Remember that the airplane takes off into the wind, seldom does it take off with it.

Some folk get the feeling that they're intentionally slighted,
That life is a big party and they're not invited.

To help avoiding pain, discouragement and sorrow,
Plan wisely for today, but live for tomorrow.

Make the best of your world, do not be dismayed.
If the world gives you lemons, make fresh lemonade.

In times of discouragement a thought sublime –
"Sadness falls away on the wings of time."

Bitter disappointment should be regarded as a stimulant;
Never should it be viewed as profound discouragement.

It's permissible to sit on your 'pity-pot', now and then,
But don't forget to flush it when you're done.

DISCRETION

For good and evil our actions meet; wicked, not much worse than indiscreet.
-John Dunne

Oft conscience gets credit for one being discreet,
When usually the credit should belong to cold feet.

When reasoning with a child, discretion must be shown
To reach the child's reason without wrecking your own.

DISPARAGE

You won't wear a crown putting other people down.

DISPUTE - DISSENSION

A long dispute means both parties are wrong.
-Voltaire

Both parties end up with grave ill-repute, if they are involved in prolonged dispute.

For certain, dissension is best to avoid.
It's while you are quarreling that truth becomes void.

A beautiful truth my dear mother taught,
"One can't start a quarrel if the other will not."

DISREGARD - IGNORE

In talking to yourself there is nothing wrong, many parents do, been doing it for long.

DISTRESS

A man may survive distress not disgrace.
-Sir Philip Sidney

A great deal of distress has been caused in this world;
So-called intelligence but little wisdom unfurled.

If you have distress, why don't you confess.

DIVORCE

Munificent alimony is paid by many a man.
I'd say it's divorce on the installment plan.

Some think divorce a panacea for all ill; soon they learn it becomes a bitter pill.

Divorce is comparable to losing a limb.
Eventually you survive it but you have less vim.

Think long and hard before choosing divorce.
The direction you choose may be the wrong course.

It is said, "Love is Grand," divorce, a hundred grand.

DOUBT

Doubt is a pain too lonely to know, that pain is its twin brother.
-Khalil Gibran

"Feed your strong faith," the wise man saith,
"Then your faint doubts will starve to death."

Doubt sees the obstacles, faith sees the way,
Doubt sees the darkest night, faith sees the day.
Doubt dreads to take a step, faith soars on high.
Doubt questions, "Who believes?" Faith answers, "I."
-Anonymous

Cynical doubt is a traitor; vile anger acts as a 'berater.'

When you sulk and pout you ventilate doubt.

Those who doubt, usually pout, they have little clout.

If you must doubt, doubt your doubts; perhaps you should doubt your whereabouts.

Doubt is not a pleasant circumstance, nor will it ever certainty enhance.

Don't ever doubt the value of doubt; you must be certain what your doubt is about.

Doubt indulged becomes doubt realized.

Faith is important, doubt don't deride;
Not always antagonists, work them side by side.

Prodigious wonderment, the root of knowledge, rather than impending, grisly doubt,
And inevitably you'll have to agree, knowledge has considerably more clout.

DUTY

I slept and dreamed that life was Beauty; I woke, and found that life was Duty.
-Ellen Hooper

Our children from duty should not be 'shrinkers,'
For spoiled, wayward kids become little stinkers.

When in doubt about whose turn it is to take out the daily trash,
Don't argue or pout, go ahead, take it out, pretend you're having a bash.

It's the soul's duty to keep inward beauty.

Duty by itself can be drudgery, particularly if it is compulsory.
Duty alone is a right; duty with love is delight.

Our duty is to be useful, truthful and fruitful.

In fulfilling one's duty, discharge it with beauty.

Exacting duty a constraint, a solemn obligation, no doubt;
It's something we perniciously hate, but we love to brag about.

Though there are duties we've repeatedly neglected,
We still keep on doing what we've never expected.

There's hope for the man who duty doesn't shirk,
And for that someone who's not afraid of work.

This planet is not meant to be loaded with passengers,
We're part of the team including the managers.

When hyphenated with duty life can be beauty.

Duty without enthusiasm is laborious; duty with enthusiasm becomes glorious.

ECONOMY

Economy is a distributive virtue, it consists, not in saving, but selection.
-Burke

Economists do watch strong indicators to forecast our vulnerable economy.
For something to do while they're wrong, they turn to the stars, astrology.

Practice economy, it's a worthwhile venue; it can of itself be worthwhile revenue.

Practice economy in days of plenty; 'twill be far too late when coffers are empty.

To check on the economy, I inquired with pleasantness,
"Just a simple question, how is business?"
I questioned a sculptor, who worked with vigor,
"I would say it's great, I'm making six figures."
A photographer remarked, his words had a motive,
"Our negative results are always positive."
An optometrist replied in phrased vernacular,
"I cannot complain, it's simply spectacular."

Practicing economy and self-denial are positive virtues of a prudent lifestyle.

EDUCATION

The aim in education should be to convert the mind
into a living fountain, not a reservoir.
-John M. Mason

Education should survive all of our lives.

Learn and compare, seek out the facts; you'll be further ahead, exploiting with acts.

With ability to learn a person need not worsen.
It will help to produce an astute productive person.

A LIFESTYLE PORTRAYAL From A TO Z

The primary object of education, wisdom must be unfurled
To open wide the window through which we view the world.

The roots of education can be so bitter, but the fruit thereof make us so much fitter.

If excellence in education is to be fully achieved, intellectual integrity must be believed.

Many graduates aren't interested in the experience of learning
As much as they look forward to the encounter with earning.

Verily, most everyone should be educated enough
To know that education in itself is not enough.

Education can alleviate one's inner strife; with it be in contact throughout your life.

Education is what survives after what you've learned nosedives.

Education, not just learning, as so many are inclined,
It's exercise and development of the powers of the mind.

Education is a safeguard of liberty; only the educated are truly free.

Education is definitely a preference; it's a discovery of our primitive ignorance.

It is well to drink plenty from the font of education,
Gargling is not enough – it gives a poor foundation.

Next to the spirituality of our repentant souls,
The education of our children should be our set goals.

Education, experience and memories, regardless of what big governments may do,
Are the three operative entities that no one can take from you.

'Tis best that a fool you ignore or bypass; an ass in a tuxedo is still full of gas.

Education is not the pumping of a tire, it's gathering kindling, then lighting a fire.

Though the cost of education is high, on ignorance one can never rely.

Education, an ornament in prosperity, and a sheltered refuge in adversity.

An astute, studious scholar profound knowledge seeks.
He examines what is said and him who speaks.

Education is the discovery of our humble ignorance,
Our denseness, unawareness and our lack of experience.
⊷
A college education is no magic carpet;
If you don't move your butt your goal won't be met.
⊷
What education does, is open the mind; it's up to the brain to move your behind.
⊷
Experience, ups and downs, and verbal condemnation
Are all part and parcel of compulsory education.
⊷
Education develops one's distinct personality,
And the obvious significance of life's reality.
⊷
Quoting Aristotle, the philosopher and sage,
"Education is the timeliest provision for old age."
⊷
Education is a companion that nothing can destroy;
In solitude it's solace, in the workplace, 'employ.'
⊷
A man's education is never complete.
One must never cease to actively compete.
⊷
"One's vivid imagination, more important than knowledge;"
Words by Einstein, it's needful in college.
⊷

EFFORT

There is no development physically or intellectually without effort.
-Calvin Coolidge
⊷
Persistent effort, invariably does count; one's direction, decidedly paramount.
⊷
Effort is required to aim high, you can't on daydreaming rely.
⊷
To one's best efforts there's a two-edged sword,
The fear of punishment and the hope of reward.
⊷

EGO - EGOTISM

Conceit may puff a man up, but never prop him up.
-John Ruskin
⊷

An egotist is a person who praises himself; he gives me no time to talk about myself.

❧

Ego is part of you, but don't ever frame it; you can't destroy it, but do try to tame it.

❧

One's egotism, its been said, is obesity of the head.

❧

Undisguised egotism is defined as ruthless self-intoxication.
Intuitive braggadocio is spelled out as glorified self-exaltation.

❧

Stultifying egotism and gross conceit, we should actively attempt to eschew.
Complacent vanity, a selfish vice will never encourage one's high virtue.

❧

Egotism is an alphabet of one letter; one couldn't describe it any better.

❧

Some folk get into a deep rut, they're not inclined to move.
Their ego makes them ideate that they're in the proverbial groove.

❧

Parading your importance is a good way to lose it.
A person of distinction doesn't ever abuse it.

❧

He's the kind of a guy, he displays his own charms,
And would rather die in his own rapturous arms.

❧

"Take a good look at me, don't you think I'm special?
I know my spicy story is more exciting than yours."
Our assertive inflated ego is that proud part of us,
That desires to be seen, much respected, and heard.

❧

Those who shoot from their big fat lip will eventually find that ego trips trip.

❧

ELOQUENCE

True eloquence consists in saying all that is proper, and nothing more.
-Francois De La Rochefoucauld

❧

The finest eloquence under journeying sun
Is the working kind, it gets thing done.

❧

Lofty articulation shouldn't be used to mock;
Fiery eloquence shows the orator can talk.

❧

EMBARRASSMENT

A prudent intuitive tongue won't generate any harassment.
Likewise, a stitch in time can prevent painful embarrassment.

※

EMOTION

Passions, emotions, may be made popular, but reason
remains ever the property of the few.
-Goethe

※

Some folk are so emotional, they have leaky eye sockets.
Their glistening eyes drip like worn out water faucets.

※

Most everyone has a deep emotional need;
Appreciation of others we must always heed.

※

EMPATHY

Empathy is your pain that's present in my heart.
It's compassion transferred to another's aching heart.

※

ENCOURAGEMENT

Correction does much, but encouragement does more.
-Johann Wolfgang Von Goethe

※

A little encouragement can ease discouragement.

※

Be mindful of the lonely, encourage the despondent;
Discouraged, hanging heads need shoulders abundant.

※

Never be a carrier of discouragement, instead, be a bearer of encouragement.

※

Consistent encouragement can spark a thwarted ambition's worthy mark.

※

Words of fresh encouragement, fan the flames of achievement.
The slightest bit of reassurance can spark substantial accomplishment.

※

Encourage that person who's endeavoring voluntarily
To improve himself mentally, physically and spiritually.

※

*E*ven when you think you have little to give,
Give them encouragement - show them how to live.

*S*o many folk bear the yoke of discouragement;
Be compassionately involved in the ministry of encouragement.

*E*ncourage achievement by letting people know
That they can accomplish because you think so.

*P*ainstaking creativity is a most fragile flower,
Cordial encouragement tends to make it bloom.
Withering criticism, oft nips it in the bud;
Be a wise stimulator, not a bearer of gloom.

A word of encouragement can magically spawn
The difference between quitting and methodically going on.

*B*e cautious, use wisdom, sympathize with others' woes;
A sunbeam of encouragement drives away dark shadows.

*E*ncourage your children to diligently work,
And teach them that duty they mustn't ever shirk.

*E*ncouragement will bestow metal to one's successor.
Confidence gives inspiration to its potential possessor.

"*C*ome to the edge," but they delayed.
"Come to the edge," but they were afraid.
"Come to the edge," she urged anew;
She gave them a push and off they flew.

ENDEAVOR

*O*pportunity is the best captain of all endeavor.
    -Sophocles

*I*n the field of endeavor this one thing I've observed,
Pure chance only favors the mind that's prepared.

*T*he captain of endeavor need not be at all clever.
If he'll just look around, opportunity will be found.

*Y*ou don't have to be clever to enthusiastically endeavor.

It is by endeavor, overcoming and ascending, that we get a glimpse of fortitude.
It is by compassion and magnanimous liberality that others observe our magnitude.

Though you deem to be wise, notably brilliant and clever,
It's best you lay your life upon the altar of endeavor.

Don't just survive, endeavor to thrive.

ENDURANCE

Whatever necessity lays upon thee endure; whatever she commands, do.
Endurance is patience concentrated.
-Thomas Carlyle

Just as one's tears are part of bereavement,
So essential is endurance to lasting achievement.

Learn to endure the betrayal of false friends,
And be willing to make needful amends.

Nothing is so impressive as the capacity for endurance,
Sacrifice, true love, compassion and reassurance.

ENTERTAINMENT

Leisure may prove to be a curse rather than a blessing,
unless education teaches a flippant world
that leisure is not a synonym for entertainment.
-William J. Bogan

In preparing to entertain you must wisely ascertain.

ENTHUSIASM

Enthusiasm is the genus of sincerity, and truth accomplishes no victories without it.
-Bulwer-Lytton

The person who with enthusiasm is fired, is usually the person that gets hired.

Irrepressible enthusiasm creates ambitious plans.
It's comparable to having two strong right hands.

Enthusiasm and success, regardless of the weather,
To me seem destined to always go together.

❧

A salesman that's good must have spirit, he must have a passion for work.
A salesman lacking warm enthusiasm is emulating a plodding clerk.

❧

Manufacture enthusiasm as you go, you'll attain success as you grow.

❧

Your enthusiasm for work is a priceless ingredient,
In the discreet formula for living.
Hyphenated with the above, don't fail to include
The precious element of giving.

❧

We need more people who can bring to their jobs a rapt enthusiasm that's terrific;
The same enthusiasm for getting ahead, as frequently displayed in heavy traffic.

❧

To have enthusiasm, 'tis great, it's prolific.
It's definitely first-rate when it's highly specific.

❧

It is difficult for many a young employee to see
That those who aren't fired with enthusiasm soon will be.

❧

Rapt enthusiasm is caught, when it is energetically sought.
It can never be bought, nor can it ever be taught.

❧

Though he may forget to wear proper attire,
If he has enthusiasm, he's the one to hire.

❧

Time wrinkles one's features, stress has its toll,
But to lack enthusiasm wrinkles the soul.

❧

ENVY - JEALOUSY

Fools may our scorn, not envy raise, for mad envy is a kind of praise.
-John Gay

❧

Unjust, harsh criticism is a compliment in disguise,
For you've aroused envy in the jealous and unwise.

❧

Jealous envy berates - hot anger fights –
Saucy pride divides - deep humility unites.

❧

Criticism can be distressingly painful, like the sudden sting of a bee.
So frequently and invariably I find it's an analog of gnawing envy.

❧

A LIFESTYLE PORTRAYAL From A TO Z

If you're reared without envy you're prone to be less angry.

If you should take potshots of riddled envy at another,
You're bound to wound self, and ardor you'll smother.

*S*cripture tells us where there's envy there's strife;
Confusion and evil can manipulate one's life.

*I*ntense, petty jealousy, and a critical nature,
A poor self-image is bound to nurture.

"*O*n the other side of the fence," the grass may appear much greener,
But don't attempt to be envious, the rewards could be much leaner.

*K*nocking is a sign of dirty carbon or envy.
More often it's the latter, love is the remedy.

*D*on't envy your neighbor, his status, his abode,
The grass on his side still has to be mowed.

*A*s a rule, intense jealousy isn't all that bad.
So oft it's the fun that you surmise they had.

*M*an feels that it's nobler to be envied, than it is to be tenderly pitied.

*V*ile envy destroys another man's joy, and despises the assets that others employ.

*J*ealousy, the monster, can eventually burst your bubble.
When you're green with envy you could be ripe for trouble.

*B*itter envy, so oft will amaze - inadvertently it can mean high praise.

*S*ecret jealousy is a viable sin; God's approval it doesn't win.

*W*here envy and strife surround, confusion and evil abound.

*F*orever keep in mind this simple childish rhyme,
"You cannot be envious and happy the same time."

*V*ile envy is a hate, ardent passion a desire,
Rare talent is a flame, mature genius is a fire.

*R*egardless of one's position, stature or clan, vile envy has never enriched any man.

*E*nvy is an insult to one's personal character; to a prudent lifestyle it's not a benefactor.

Envy is libelous, so frequently it cheats; it's very thin, though it bites it never eats.

EQUALITY

Perfect equality it is said, is a relentless futile pursuit.
Equality of matchless opportunity depends on an individual's input.

EULOGY

"I want it whispered about me by those acquainted with my tread,
That I've toiled to remove a weed and to replace it with a flower instead."

EVOLUTION

The question is this: Is man an ape or an angel? I am on the side of the angel. I repudiate with indignation these new fangled theories.
-Benjamin Disraeli

Mystic, regressive evolution, the devil's deceitful intrusion.

EXAGGERATION

Some folk never exaggerate, they just remember big.
-Audrey Snead

It was once a simple truth, now it's bold exaggeration;
Some people like to call it, grossly added imagination.

Over-statement you must shun, gross exaggeration, do elude it;
The more you stretch the truth the easier to see through it.

A sparkling diamond is a gem that's derived from pure black coal.
Gross exaggeration is a truth that's gone completely out of control.

EXAMPLE

Example is contagious behavior.
-Charles Reade

A LIFESTYLE PORTRAYAL From A TO Z

The priceless gift we can give, the total of it must be ample,
Especially for our beloved children, it's the gift of good example.

If you're looking for a man that you wish to hire,
Observe him with a woman with child and flat tire.

Do unto others, deeds kind and true; do as you'd have them deal with you.

An outstanding magnificent example gathers more followers than reason.
It's something that on a regular basis is never found out of season.

Incline to be a perpetual sunbeam - two ways of spreading the light,
Be a candle or reflecting mirror; both are acceptable in God's sight.

Some children choose to close ears to advice;
To example, big eyes open, be it good or be it vice.

If a man of himself will repeatedly take stock,
People will then set their watches by his clock.

Don't ever drive as if you owned the road.
You must strive to drive according to code.

A shiny example has outstanding power, an impact that's impossible to resist;
That wisdom, that influence, that force, that direction; in your life may it ever persist.

Give to your child a good example, to your client the best of service,
To your opponent, kindly tolerance, to an enemy, total forgiveness.

To live an exemplary life, a true Christian you needn't prod.
He is in verity the keyhole through which other folk see God.

An exemplary life, to live is most vital.
Life's testimony is superior to having a title.

Endeavor to follow, to model, when observing that exemplary person.
When you see that someone unfitting, pull out all stops not to worsen.

To be exemplary do endeavor; a sage would reckon it's being clever.

EXCELLENCE

The man who has ceased to grow up intellectually has begun to go down.
-William Matthews

*S*trive for rare excellence; be a positive influence.

*T*he mystery of joy in accomplishment isn't bolstered by indolence.
To know how to accomplish commendably, the secret lies in excellence.

*S*triving for excellence motivates; aspiring for perfection enervates.

*T*here are no shortcuts to doing a job well.
Hold aloft excellence if your goal is to sell.

EXCUSES

*H*e that is good for making excuses is seldom good for fruitful uses.

*Y*ou're wondering who I am, - no, I'm not from Islam.
An introduction I shall try, my name is "Obuteye."
I don't like to take those fluctuating slim chances,
My name oft changes, it depends on circumstances.

Obuteye couldn't do it now - obuteye wouldn't know how.

Obuteye'm much too tired - obuteye'm already hired.

Obuteye'm extremely shy - couldn't do it if I did try.

Obuteye'm much too old - obuteye'm far from bold.

Obuteye'm just too busy - obuteye'd be in a tizzy.

Obuteye think she would do it - obuteye know he would do it.

Obuteye'm just not well enough - obuteye think the job's tough.

Obuteye couldn't do it steady - obuteye have a job already.

Obuteye'll be away, this next busy week.
Obuteye think someone else you should try to seek.

Obuteye'm too involved in living - obuteye'm a-a-a-already giving.

I note, you recognize me now, in the future don't use me, no how.
I say this with voice and pen – Goodbye, may we never meet again.

Your coy excuse will never win if you intentionally use the excuse to sin.

Excuses, excuses, repetitive excuses, never initiate bona fide uses.

Excuses and lies are seen through most eyes.

Excuses won't get you to the top of the tower.
They show lack of faith in your ability and power.

Prudent people will know when you aren't an excuse.
They'll know you're truly serious, when you begin to produce.

The evil sins we so frequently excuse will return someday to publicly accuse.

He who is in the habit of making specious excuses,
Has the potential of being involved in abuses.

An excuse can't commendably effectuate a truce,
Nor can sin be conquered with a specious excuse.

Be it vile anger or petty envy, or abominable pernicious abuse;
Dark, deadly sin cannot be conquered with a voluble, plausible excuse.

Do not substitute excuses for service; think of the blessings you're about to miss.

Innocent ignorance of the law is not a plausible excuse,
And so the dutiful state trooper you mustn't ever abuse.

He who is good at making excuses is seldom good for worthy uses.

About your invention, don't give me excuses, all I hear is "Perhaps" and "Maybe."
I don't want to hear about your labor pains, all I want to see is a live baby.

EXERCISE

There is no exercise better for the heart than reaching down and lifting people up.
-Johne Andrew Holmes

"Atrophy," an award, some do surmise, that is given to those who don't exercise.

They call it a 'fun-run,' but why aren't they smiling?
They seem to be in pain - grimacing, almost crying.

A LIFESTYLE PORTRAYAL From A TO Z

For an hour of work-out my son pays much more
Than I got for a week's wages in nineteen-thirty-four.

Nowadays, the only student who will walk a mile -
You'll have to admit it cramps his lifestyle.
He's the one who can't find a parking spot for his car,
Otherwise, he wouldn't be walking quite so far.

There are so many venues for aerobic exercise, exercise surely is in style.
The exercise that drastically changes one's life is walking the center isle.

Regular body action, not striving for position,
Is better for one's health than many a physician.

Not to exercise I cannot afford; I must daily walk with the Lord.

EXPEDIENCY

Expedients are the hour but principles are for the ages.
 -Beecher

What has expediency o'er the years justly solved?
Be deaf to expediency where principle is involved.

EXPERIENCE

It is costly wisdom that is bought by experience.
 -Roger Ascham.

Don't rely on your intellectual brilliance
To the total exclusion of personal experience.

Experience is a teacher, some say the best,
But she's far from being the cutest or cheapest.

Experience is that entity that allows us some days
To be totally stupid in many ignorant ways.

Experience is acquired - most folk aren't enthralled.
It's a comb nature gives when we gradually grow bald.

A LIFESTYLE PORTRAYAL From A TO Z

Experience won't allow any cowardly copouts,
  Nor does it sanction deliberate dropouts.

❧

Experience is not really what happens to you,
  It's what you do with what happens to you.

❧

What have you done that'll lessen tomorrow's strife?
Experience is of no value unless translated into life.

❧

Experience, a great teacher, not governed by a board;
  She gives the test first, the lesson afterward.

❧

When a man with money meets a man with experience,
  The man with experience ends up with the money.
It's then that the former ends up with experience;
  Believe me, my friend, I'm not being funny.

❧

Experience is something we cannot borrow.
It's a name that we give to our screw-ups and sorrow.

❧

By the time that you have the experience to be smart,
  Your memory is shorter and there's no hair to part.

❧

Experience tells you what to do; confidence inclines you to pursue.

❧

"Experience is schooling," he said with a sigh,
"I'd enjoy it much more if the fees weren't so high."

❧

Don't be a lone prisoner of your own experience.
Share your enlightenment with utmost expedience.

❧

Experience is invariably what you get, when you fail to get what you bet.

❧

Experience can cause sorrow, at times it causes laughter.
Experience is what you get and not what you were after.

❧

Good judgement we get from prolonged experience.
Experience is what we get from repeated poor judgment.

❧

Experience, a great teacher, she very seldom thrills.
Of one thing you can be certain – she sends huge bills.

❧

EYE CONTACT - EYESIGHT

Sight is a faculty, seeing is an art.
What does your vision to others impart?

❧

Have you ever noticed how little eye contact
Most of us have with strangers?
Are we afraid? Let us open our hearts;
Smiles to affability are arrangers.

❧

Treat strangers not only with a smile and eye contact.
You must treat them with kindness and due respect.

❧

You must always hold your head high,
And look at everyone straight in the eye.
Forget not to do it as they're passing by.

❧

FAILURE - BANKRUPTCIES

A man of intellect without energy added to it is a failure.
-Sebastion R. N. Chamfort

❧

Henry Ford, years ago, said by word and pen,
"Failure is the opportunity to begin again."

❧

The keys to success are too many to recall,
But the key to failure is trying to please all.

❧

Choose failure with honor than success by fraud.
Would you rather please the devil or have favor with God?

❧

Failure an entity we should avoid denying.
There is no failure except in not trying,
Nor is there defeat unless will is dying.

❧

Fear of grim failure by many timid souls
Keeps many folk from setting great goals.

❧

You may be discouraged if you should fail, but you are doomed if you do not assail.

❧

When you think you're failing, your effort do not lessen.
When you don't succeed, do remember the lesson.

❧

*F*ailure for certain is not a welcome word;
Success invariably is much more preferred.

*Y*ou can become a failure but don't blame yourself.
You're not a total fizzle till you fault someone else.

*M*ost of past failures we should fully address.
They are our guideposts for future success.

*F*ailure as a rule has little resistance.
It's the narrow path of least persistence.

*G*rim failure won't stand in the way of success,
Providing the "Why?" you painstakingly address.

*I*f you don't fear failure, success you will meet.
Failure is a detour, not a dead-end street.

*F*ailure, a state of mind you must duly address.
It's a learning experience along the road to success.

*B*ankruptcies and failures are not good news.
The greatest of assets are the feet in one's shoes.

*I*f you don't succeed, stop crying, instead, why don't you repeat trying.

*W*hen heading for failure use your derailleur.
If you don't learn now, how to change your gears,
You'll get a reminder in your later years.

*P*eople who are prosperous dismal failure address.
Wisdom comes from failure and not from success.

*T*he story of failure - at first you are hired,
Then you get mired and then you are fired.

*A*bject failure, does oft impress us.
We learn more from failure than our successes.

FAITH

*F*aith is a higher faculty than reason.
-Philip James Bailey

A LIFESTYLE PORTRAYAL From A TO Z

Our faith grows stronger as we climb higher,
And when our love for Christ is on fire.

❧

Simple faith is knowing my character is perfected.
It's having the assurance I'm not being rejected.

❧

Abiding faith is to know, rich blessings He will bestow.
Then why would you worry and be glum? The best is yet to come.

❧

Faith is counting on God, without the slightest reservation;
What is beyond one's belief, beyond a worldling's expectation.

❧

Faith is the Holy Spirit's power that vanquishes many a barrier;
Overcoming many an obstacle; of God's love it's a constant carrier.

❧

Faith a divine gift void of self and pretense.
To live God's way without doubt makes sense.

❧

Faith is acknowledging life seemingly is unfair,
But eventually the Judge, "Well done," will declare.

❧

Have no faith in the devil's wraith.

❧

A haunting wraith, the devil's apparition;
Unwavering faith, a Christian's rendition.

❧

Faith is believing in the truthfulness of Scripture.
It is a prime virtue I must daily nurture.

❧

Faith is the acceptance of God's divine favor
Extended to man through Jesus our Savior.

❧

Faith is a dimension that supplies prayer with wings
That soar to heaven– divine peace it brings.

❧

Faith is a little light that shines in the night,
When it's in sight it scares away fright.

❧

Faith isn't a leap in the dark, nor is it a walk in the night;
With eyes focused on Calvary, we're stepping into His light.

❧

Fear sees the obstacle, faith sees opportunity.

❧

Lacking divine faith in God is comparable to driving in a fog.

❧

A LIFESTYLE PORTRAYAL From A TO Z

Faith in essence is a willingness on my part
To be a partaker of the events on God's chart.

My faith, I would say is virtually misplaced
If with Jesus it isn't totally interfaced.

Faith, an entity, oft read and heard; it simply means taking God at His word.

Faith is leaving the ever-present future
To the Almighty God who controls the future.

Faith is taking my eyes off me so that my Savior I may fully see.

Faith is believing and trusting Christ's grace.
At His soon coming I'll see Him face to face.

Our faith in God grows greater, on recognizing the greatness of God.

Have faith to come to Jesus - He chose to come to us.

Faith in God is the essential element for spiritual change in any climate.

Faith is believing the precious word of God.
It's unequivocally rejecting what the devil tries to prod.

Faith is giving up the thought of rejection.
It's knowing through Christ I can gain perfection.

Faith is knowing God always comes through
With His promises if I'm faithful and true.

Faith has its work to do; frequently it is far overdue.

It is better to walk with God by faith
Than to go it alone, so the good book saith.

Faith with works is a force – without genuine works it's a farce.

Faith is the humble, trusting hand, reaching out to shoreless eternity;
Climaxing in Jesus' soon return, ushering in God's glorious infinity.

True faith, in no sense is an ally of presumption.
The latter, a transgression, a specious assumption.

Sorrow looks back, fear looks around, but faith looks up - peace you'll have found.

A LIFESTYLE PORTRAYAL From A TO Z

*P*rofound faith is believing that God can heal.
The entries in the Bible aren't fables, they're real.

*F*aith always tells me, "You've committed sin."
It allows the Holy Spirit to enter in
To tell me that Jesus has pardoned my sin.

*C*hildlike faith, that precious Spirit's spark
That gives us the ability to see God in the dark.

*F*aith is knowing, God is trustworthy - that through His Son we become worthy.

*F*aith is a precious heavenly grace acquired, by the experience of years;
A virtue that helps us to overcome a multitude of fears and tears.

*T*rue faith is believing in God's approbation without the slightest mental reservation.

*J*oyful faith is trusting that I'll be more loving,
Compassionate, more patient, polite not shoving.
Not pushing through crowds, not first to be grabbing,
And certainly not with cutting words jabbing.

*F*aith and freedom from doubt, acceptable success will enhance.
An ounce of profound believability is worth a pound of perchance.

*F*aith is fully accepting the Divine Agent of change.
The precious, pleading Holy Spirit transformation will arrange.

*T*he business of faith is to believe with your might
The things you can't reach, the things out of sight.

*U*nfailing faith is a soul's heartbeat; it gives me courage, it discourages retreat.

*G*enuine faith is securing, enduring and assuring.

*F*aith is a bridge from this world to the next,
Providing it is genuine - never a pretext.

*T*he Greek word "pistis," has thoughts that in it dwell.
It means not only faith but belief and trust as well.

*F*aith in God mustn't be a pretense; trusting in him fully is your sure defense.

*R*emember, as you travel this sphere, faith is the only cure for fear.

A LIFESTYLE PORTRAYAL From A TO Z

Faith is believing God is working in me, that his Spirit is striving to set me free.

Through faith in Christ we step out of sin's slavery,
And then we step into salvation's liberty.

Humble faith is the ultimate for the faithful insider.
It's also the answer for a repentant backslider.

The essence of faith, 'tis very clear to me,
Is willingness to serve without expecting a fee.

In the bosom of mankind faith is oft rare.
I must develop faith in a God that is there.

Faith in Christ makes extraordinary heroes
Out of ordinary people - it avoids making Neros.

Our faith is being tested through frustrating disillusionment,
Through conflict and failure, through hardship and disappointment.

Genuine faith is a fabric that endures, it cannot unravel with strain;
A fabric that trials cannot rend and insidious temptations cannot stain.

Without faith a prayer has no heart, without faith a prayer is not warm,
Without faith a prayer has no spark, without faith a prayer is not norm.

Without faith it's impossible to love God and serve Him.
Christianity without faith is but an idle whim.

Faith makes my expectations precious, it makes my outlook bright.
It creates a footing that calms, faith makes my future a delight.

About keeping the faith, advice that is sound,
Instead of hoarding it, let's spread it around.

Faith is making a Spirit-filled decision, it's claiming the promise of 20/20 vision.

Remind me, O God, that your servant James, years ago, these wise words said,
"But wilt thou know, oh you vain man, that faith without works is dead?"

Faith is a fact with unruffled equanimity, that I am accepted in my total unacceptability.

Faith that the thing can be done is essential
For any great achievement to be a potential.

A LIFESTYLE PORTRAYAL From A TO Z

Faith, like an anchor is fixed to the unseen; the Spirit invites us on Him to lean.

≈

"For by grace we are saved through faith, not of works if anyone should boast.
Faith without works is dead," without it we could become toast.

≈

The world crowns triumphant success; God crowns long-term faithfulness.

≈

An abiding faith means increase in vigor,
A conquering power which the Spirit doth trigger.

≈

True faith obeys without doubt or delay, obeys like old Abraham, that's the sure way.

≈

Faith is not turbulent emotion, to Omnipotent God it's humble devotion.

≈

Faith is a virtue we must not shun; hope is a risk that we must run.

≈

Faith is the faculty with which God endows us
So we can live joyfully and He can trust us.

≈

True faith in Jesus is the power by which we can triumph over evil;
Revealing His character at all times, while waging the final upheaval.

≈

Faith is clinging to Christ for His grace, it's believing my sins He'll completely erase.

≈

When fear knocks at the door, that's what trusting faith is for.

≈

There's an intimate relationship between faith and healing.
For an abundance of both be prayerfully appealing.

≈

Hear ye, hear ye, peoples of all nations,
"Expect from God what's beyond all expectations."

≈

The rule of conduct for faith is patience.
Hyphenate with patience the presence of prudence.

≈

Faith can sustain all effort; it will satisfy and comfort.

≈

If your faith is worth having, it should be worth sharing.

≈

Faith and hope we must daily nurture; it will direct us to the eternal future.

≈

For faith, history tells us many men have fought.
Though faith is oft sought it can never be bought.
Only by the power of God is it wrought.

≈

Faith, like love, loyalty and hope
Is an important dimension with which to cope.
It's secluded in the brain where reason cannot reach,
And our sharpest intellect can't explain or teach.

Faith is knowing that God does care; if I'm faithful to Him, my life He'll spare.

Faith is looking forward to eternal salvation.
It's expecting from God what's beyond expectation.

Faith is knowing my poor record is corrected;
No longer is my life to eternal death subjected.

Faith is anticipation beyond expectation,
Redemption, liberation and promised salvation.

Faith is doing to others good, as every faithful Christian should.

Faith is divine, God sees it as a sign, if I accept it as mine and keep it in line,
Love and truth I combine, eternity is mine.

Faith is seeing a rainbow in each tear; it can wash away that inward fear.

Faith is knowing, I am God's treasure.
His blessings are bountiful, they're far beyond measure.

Faith is remembering that I grow by adjusting, and more importantly, by fully trusting.

Faith is a cure for worry and fear; it quickly suppresses many a tear.

FALSEHOOD

The united voice of millions cannot lend the smallest foundation to falsehood.
-Oliver Goldsmith

Those who concoct little fibs, frequently get into a bind.
Relating white lies will eventually make one quite color-blind.

A lie will go the circumference of the world,
While simple truth is being gradually unfurled.

The biggest liar most any day, more than likely is, "They say."

A LIFESTYLE PORTRAYAL From A TO Z

*F*alsehood Is that "something" that's said in a hurry,
That invariably results in anxiety and worry.

*G*lib white lies are a dark abomination; they make dark stains on one's reputation.

*T*he war up in heaven was started in the choir.
The leader of the group was a notorious liar.

*M*any, their character deceptively disguise.
One cannot help but read between the lies.

*I*f we swindle habitually, prevaricate and cheat,
Our children the same are bound to repeat.

A liar should always have a retentive memory.
He would be much safer with a well-kept diary.

*I*t is difficult to let a half-truth pass by; it's twice as hard as a deliberate lie.

*T*he price of prim pride can be very high.
You can never uphold it with a deliberate lie.

*S*in has many tools as I vividly recall; a lie is a handle that fits them all.

*T*o utter falsehood we have the ability; we must fully realize it's a sinful liability.

*D*ishonesty is never an accident; truth must always be precedent.

*T*here are two entities that never lie or fail,
It's the smile of a baby and the wag of Rover's tail.

*H*e begins to die when he starts to lie.

*L*ying gives rest to your head only when it's done in bed.

A middle-aged visage doesn't ever lie - the featured, lined face, truth doesn't defy.

"*I*t didn't work, but I really tried,"- is much better than, "I lied."

*T*he way to avoid falsehood about something that's revealed,
Is to absolutely do nothing that needs to be concealed.

*I*n stretching the truth or launching a wisecrack,
One must be careful lest it snap back.

A LIFESTYLE PORTRAYAL From A TO Z

Do not believe all that you hear; from a lying tongue do stay clear.

A plausible lie may take care of the present.
However, for the future it wouldn't be pleasant.

Liars, so oft figure how to make figures lie.
They're the ones who can't look you straight in the eye.

"It's not at all worth it," says the dishonest buyer.
After he has purchased he's thrilled he did acquire.

Beware of half-truths from employers or staff,
Lest you latch on to the despicable wrong half.

Many folk do not say exactly what they think.
Instead of telling truth, so oft they just wink.

It is better to suffer for the sacred truth
Than rewarded for a lie, penned in a steel booth.

A prevaricator is the one who from truth subtracts.
One might say that he dwells on the wrong side of the facts.

White lies, misrepresentations, now and then an inflection,
Introduce hostile characters of a darker complexion.

Dishonesty in the workplace makes supervisors tense.
There's nothing so damaging to integrity as pretense.

A deliberate sly lie has it's day of disclosure.
Yes, innocent white lies get tanned from exposure.

A half-truth and a half-lie, the two one can't tie;
You will have to admit they're both a whole lie.

There are three entities that a man cannot hide,
When in love, when he's drunk and when he has lied.

A lie can never condone or nurture;
May take care of the present but never the future.

History informs us that men become wise, when they've exhausted all of their lies.

False testimony in court is deemed rank perjury;
Prescriptions are preferable to radical surgery.

If you haven't lied you have nothing to hide.

FAMILY - HOME

Take the word "Family," strike out the letter 'm' for mother
and the "y" for youth -and all you'll have left is "Fail."
-Omar Burleson

FAMILY = (F)ather (A)nd (M)other (I) (L)ove (Y)ou.

One daily gets tired with confusion and clatter.
It's refreshing to come home to feet that pitter patter.

Never let your child be a lazy slob - don't pick up after him, that's his job.

Children are inclined to brighten up a home, especially during the hours of the night.
O'er the years I've learned it's invariably because they never turn off the light.

A child is less errant having a godly parent.

Many children would love to be physicians, they contemplate having heaps of dough,
Till they learn that doctors who operate have to wash hands and arms above elbow.

When you have to wash the soap before you can use it,
That family usually has a five year old in it.

Said a father to his daughter, "Heavy traffic, do beware,"
And some added precaution, "Drive with fender-loving care."

A little boy and his mother went to a food store.
This joy they had shared many times before.
On getting needed items, such as eggs and fresh trout,
They then both proceeded to the grocery checkout.
Just ahead of them was a man - one would say he was huge.
O'er the years, scores of calories in his hulk took refuge.
The man's pager went off - the little tyke clipped, "Yup!
Let's get out of here, he's going to back up."

A quiet drooling baby is too young to be errant.
It's certainly a spitting image of its parent

A little boy went to a mall with Grandma,
He was totally enthralled with the things he saw.
On checking the purchases - pantyhose was a surprise,

A LIFESTYLE PORTRAYAL From A TO Z

He slowly sounded out the words, "Queen Size."
He turned to his Grandma and excitedly said,
"You wear the same size as our waterbed."

✦

All good mothers say before daughter's debut,
"Everybody may be doing it - but you're not going to!"

✦

Said a mother to her daughter who was bent on 'elopin,'
"When my eyes become closed yours will become open."

✦

Much more importantly is the family to come,
Than the proud family that you once came from.

✦

As mothers go, so goes propriety - as mothers go, so goes society.

✦

A child leaving home learns for the very first time -
It gives up fridge benefits, some deem this a crime.

✦

Show your sweet love and hug them at home,
They then won't have a marked tendency to roam.

✦

A home is the locale where you wear your old breeches.
It's also the place where you scratch when it itches.

✦

When a woman has forgiven her man, it's past.
She shouldn't reheat his sins for breakfast.

✦

Home, sweet home - you can act like a clown,
You can put your feet up and let your hair down.

✦

Not only do they need sweet coddles, children need exemplary models.

✦

Brothers and sisters, legally I have none, but this man's father is my father's son.

✦

A home is loving understanding, a haven when things go wrong,
Where cares are lightened with kindness, where joys are livened with a song.
Contentment, a light in the window, an open door, welcoming with a smile,
Happiness to carry where we go, 'cause love is the dweller's lifestyle.
-Anonymous

✦

A family altar direction can alter.

✦

FANATIC

The worst vice of a fanatic, sincerity.
-Oscar Wilde

A fanatic is a person whose tongue he doesn't budget.
He won't change his mind nor will he the subject.

I commiserate with utmost clarity, a fanatics worst vice is sincerity.

FAST-TALKER

Beware of the fast-talker, listen carefully to his yup.
Why don't we place cheese in his big mouth-trap?

Avoid the fast-talker, be careful whom you trust.
You can always judge men by the size of their exhaust.

FAULT-FINDING

We can often do more for other men by correcting
our own faults than by trying to correct theirs.
-Francois Fenelon

Avoid finding fault, deem it pollution;
Be practical, be effective in finding a solution.

Do think of your faults while awake, the first part of the night as a rule;
Of the faults of others while asleep, it's then that you can't ridicule.

Finding fault in others many search and hope.
It's best they use a mirror than a peering microscope.

His multitudinous idiosyncrasies give us abundant clues.
We learn considerably more from his faults than virtues.

Fault-finding, incomprehensible - sharp wit, indispensable.

There are defects in some, imperfections in others;
Faults are the easiest to find in our brothers.

A LIFESTYLE PORTRAYAL From A TO Z

*H*e who emphasizes the faults of his brothers,
Underestimates his own, compared to all others.

*L*ook for the good, not faults - never make verbal assaults.

*D*on't lay blame, regardless of the tragedy.
Never find fault, discover a remedy.

*W*hen something goes wrong, don't others frame;
Talk about fixing it than who to blame.

*S*ome folk have faults, they try to defend them.
The real faults are to have them and not try to mend them.

*T*he faults observed by all good doers is usually proportional to the number of viewers.

*I*f you are looking for faults to correct,
Try looking in a mirror, you may be the subject.

*F*aults are thick when love is thin, confess your faults then love will win.

A earthly fault confessed is honest character addressed.

*P*eople keep counting and they keep on debating
The faults of those who keep them waiting.

FAUX PAS

A breach of etiquette is courtesy's neglect.

*T*he *R*ed-*F*aced *C*olonel

*T*he colonel was conducting a routine inspection.
In the scores of shiny boots he could see his reflection.
He bellowed at a soldier that he deemed lacked luster.
This unfortunate young man didn't pass his muster.
"Button up that pocket," the shrill voice hammered.
Rattled the young soldier, visibly trembled and stammered.
"Should I do it right now?" he hesitatingly questioned.
"Why of course, right now." the colonel demanded.
The hands of the young soldier shot up like a rocket
To button the flap on the colonel's shirt pocket.

FEAR

*T*hings done well and with care, exempt themselves from fear.
-Shakespeare

*F*ear will make one hesitate, 'twill also make one procrastinate.

*Y*ou'll live with fear if evil thou wilt; fear is the tax conscience pays to guilt.

*F*ear in our souls keeps us from setting set goals.

*B*eing fearful or frantic is a non-essential;
You immobilize yourself from your greatest potential.

*W*hy would one sorrow and fear tomorrow?
Do not despair, God, punctually is there.

*I*f yourself you accept and bid fears adieu,
You'll find that more people will be attracted to you.

*W*e need not fear the perils around us
If we invoke God's power to completely surround us.

*F*ear frequently makes one go into tizzy;
It's nature's warning sign for one to get busy.

*H*orrible imaginings depress, present fears aren't any less.

*F*ear is the darkroom where negatives are developed.
Hatred is when bitterness in the heart is enveloped.

A fear that is definitely common to most, especially with those who are meek,
Is that we will be over the hill before we have reached its peak.

*F*ear not that life shall come to an end,
That it has been worthwhile is what we must vend.

*W*hen you're out on a limb or straddled on the ropes,
Let not fear hold you back from pursuing your hopes.

*F*ear has a tendency to discourage; it takes a man far from courage.

*F*ear is invariably of our own creation.
It's never as bad as is our imagination.

Thinking, by itself, will not cure fear.
I must include action in ideation's sphere.

&

If fear is nurtured, it will become stronger.
If faith is cultivated, fear is no longer.

&

There are endless obstacles, so many it appears.
The root of them all, stark, palpating fears.

&

"Fear is an instructor of great sagacity."
This definition by Emerson has proven veracity.

&

When a man harbors fear, it permeates his thinking.
It damages personality, and his courage will be shrinking. .

&

"We have absolutely nothing to fear for the future,
Except as we neglect our spirituality to nurture.
We mustn't forget how we've been led by His Majesty,
Nor reject His teaching in our past history."
-E. G. White (paraphrased)

&

FEELINGS

The young man who hasn't wept is a savage,
and the old man who hasn't laughed is a fool.
-George Sanatyana

&

The seat of feelings for discouragement is derision.
The soul of dispatch is prompt decision.

&

To change the way you feel, change the way you deal,
Alter the way you think – strict honesty doesn't wink.

&

There are feelings physical and mental; do consider being graciously gentle.

&

Whenever you feel blue, don't count to ten -
It's much more important to start breathing again.

&

FELLOWSHIP

We need the fellowship of the godly to safeguard our fellowship with the ungodly.
-Ralph W, Sockman

&

A LIFESTYLE PORTRAYAL From A TO Z

Fellowship needs action, love must have feeling, both are called for in our daily dealing.

To attain sainthood, firstly have brotherhood.

FINANCE

The essence of any plan for financing old age is saving.
-Bernard M. Baruch

One of fettered life's most trying disappointments,
Accompanied so frequently with solid moans and groans,
Is discovering that the person who writes ads for the banks
Is surprisingly not the one who approves the loans.

Finance is an art of exchanging money, it appears,
From one hand to another till it totally disappears.

Never let banks keep you years in their clutch.
It's pertinent to remember, some money costs too much.

Be ruthlessly realistic with your financial statistics.

Into a bank in a city in Oklahoma, one day a native Indian came,
To secure a loan of two hundred dollars was Chief Lott's distinct aim.
"And what security do you have, my friend, if this money to you I were to lend?"
"I am the owner of two hundred horses that are pastured out at Big Bend."
A short time later the Big Chief returned with two thousand dollars in cash.
He saw the banker, he paid his loan, the rest he was stashing in his cache.
"Why don't you let us keep it for you?" the banker asked, Chief Lott;
Looking the banker straight in the eye, "And how many horses have you got?"

When you lend people money, I caution, don't be liberal.
Make certain their character exceeds their collateral.

If you mind your own business you won't be annoyed.
Succinctly, I might add, you won't be unemployed.

Noah was the greatest, the wisest financier,
He worked at it diligently for many a long year.
He eventually floated stock with full approbation,
While the rest of the world was in total liquidation.

Remarked a Jewish mother about her Paulette,
"So what if she's short, she can stand on her wallet.

It's not bears and bulls that put investors in arrears,
More oft you'll discover it's the proverbial bum steers.

If prime rate is what chartered banks charge their friends,
Let us not be enemies - banks, let's make amends.

Think of tomorrow, divide your pay, take what you need, the rest lay away.

Excessive borrowing can result in sorrowing.

In paying his light bills he was late and defiant,
And so the power company wrote to their client.
If you would pay when due, we would be delighted,
If you choose to delay – you'll be de-lighted.

How do you do? Some folk pay when due, some pay when overdue,
Some, never do - how about you? Please do - won't you? Thank you.

FLATTERY

A flattering mouth worketh ruin.
-Old Testament: Proverbs 36:28

You can buy servile flattery, though by many it is spurned,
But do always remember that envy must be earned.

Don't fall for flattery, it could be a lie.
Remember, the best mirror is a friend's eye.

Never allow flattery to be part of camaraderie.

When a salesman you encounter, beware of the 'praiser;'
Like a barber he lathers before using the razor.

He who knows how to chatter knows also how to flatter.

When flatterers meet, when a liar is a winner,
When jealousy prevails, the devil goes to dinner.

When someone toots your audacious horn,
The music is sweet, you feel airborne.

Blazoned flattery is from the teeth out;
In my big book it doesn't have any clout.

Talk gently, go slow - don't let it overflow.

*Flattery, like chewing gum, chew it, don't wallow in it.
You can enjoy it briefly but don't ever swallow it.*

*Choose your companions with care;
Of smoothness and flattery beware.*

*Flattery in itself is verily soft soap.
In it you mustn't ever put your vague hope.*

*God does not use flattery or beguiling deceit.
For love and recognition He does compete.*

FLEXIBILITY

*The cornerstone of flexibility is availability, sensibility,
Practicability, manageability, pliability and adaptability.*

*Flexibility is the cornerstone of moral progress,
Progress is impossible without change.
If you are unable to shift your thinking,
Progress will be difficult to arrange.*

Be patient with stupidity and flexible with rigidity.

FOCUS

*Unless Jesus is the center of interest, our lives will be totally out of focus.
Unless to Him we fully surrender, how can we expect the Lord to save us?*

Focus on the positive, don't idly dream, recognize the building blocks of high esteem.

To focus a bright light, don't ever tire; some day you may set the world on fire.

FOOD GROUPS

*Said a Wall Street broker to his family physician,
Specializing in Nutrition, "Well I'll be daft.
I thought that the four major food groups were,
General Foods, Nabisco, General Mills and Kraft."*

Eating strong onion and beans en masse, results in the production of subtle teargas.

❧

FOOL - FOOLISHNESS

"The man is a fool," the psalmist doth prod, "Who says to himself, there is no God."
-Psalm 14:1

❧

FORBEARANCE

The two powers constituting a wise man are bearing and forbearing.
-Epictetus

❧

Learn to acquire forbearance, to it you must add observance;
But the highest tuition ever paid is for the school of experience.

❧

FORGIVENESS

Those who forgive most, shall be most forgiven.
-Philip James Bailey

❧

Force may subdue, it may even reign,
But love and forgiveness will spiritually sustain.

❧

"I can forgive, but I cannot forget," is a way of saying, "Forgiveness I'll regret."

❧

There's nothing more admirable or enchantingly desirable
As when a loving couple agree to make amends;
Seeing eye to eye, as husband and wife,
Confounding their adversaries, but delighting their friends.

❧

To forgive and forget is truly sublime.
Some folk think it's easy, but not at the same time.

❧

To forgive does not mean to give up or give in,
It means to let go, in the end both will win.

❧

To forgive is to set a prisoner free, and to discover that it does include me.

❧

Forgiveness should not only be guided by love,
It's an act that's advocated by our God above.

❧

A LIFESTYLE PORTRAYAL From A TO Z

*F*orgiveness should not be an occasional act,
It should be a habit we repeatedly enact.

❧

*S*ome folk can't seem to forget, grievances they hide in deep thought.
They may say, "I've buried the hatchet," simultaneously they mark the hidden spot.

❧

*T*o gracefully forgive is considered moral; he who forgives will forget the quarrel.

❧

*F*orgiveness is the key that opens the entrance to freedom of resentment;
Resulting in one's peace of mind with gratification and glorious contentment.

❧

*T*o have forgiveness one must be forgiving.

❧

*T*he only people that God will forgive
Are those that confess; Jesus is supportive.

❧

*B*e kind, be courteous, forgive, never tattle;
Everyone you meet fights an uphill battle.

❧

*F*orgiveness is an attribute of the resolutely strong.
Forbearance in the weak seems seldom to belong.

❧

*F*orgiveness for your sins, when to church you roam?
Hold it, my friend, firstly, pray at home.

❧

*W*ouldn't it be wonderful if we could extend
Gracious, loving-kindness to everyone we meet.
Compassion we'd exhibit if we could forgive,
Like forgiving teenagers' behavior that's offbeat.

❧

*F*or implored forgiveness confess - it's not at all worth it to obsess.

❧

*F*or gracious living we must be forgiving.

❧

*T*o err is mine, to forgive is divine.

❧

*F*orgive and forget, you'll never regret.

❧

*S*ome folk can be likened to an assertive dog
That's determined not to give up its bone.
Their minds continue to vigorously chew -
To forgiveness their thoughts aren't prone.

❧

*M*ealy-mouthed forgiveness can be easily diagnosed,
So don't bury the hatchet with the handle exposed.

❧

To forgive some choose not, be they next of kin.
If that be your choice, choose not to sin.

To forgive those who hurt you we must never cease.
'Tis a singular pathway to inner peace.

Forgiveness is the path to action and freedom,
And it's a signpost to God's eternal kingdom.

When God forgives, it's not just soft soap;
God's loving forgiveness is our only hope.

To suppress explosiveness, ask for forgiveness.

FRAGRANCE

Sweet, lovely fragrance always flows from the loving hand that gives a rose.

FREEDOM

The cause of freedom is the cause of God.
-William Lisle Bowles

Some talk about keeping the flame of freedom lit;
When asked to pay the gas bill, they almost have a fit.

Freedom and education - of happiness the summation.

My priceless freedom does not come free; self-determination is up to me.

Everyone has the freedom to accept heaven or hell.
Forgiveness, an entity only love can compel.

A belligerent man is not a free man.

We should try to reserve the goals of freedom
In our beloved country, our enduring kingdom -
Freedom from want and freedom from taunt,
Freedom from oppression and freedom from suppression,
Freedom from starvation, and freedom from deprivation,
Freedom from fear and freedom from the spear.

*O*ur greatest freedom is freedom from sin.
To effect that freedom, keep Christ within.

*I*t is said that liberty is exceedingly high priced.
Precious freedom is free in surrendering to Christ.

*F*reedom is the right to be wrong, it's not the right to do wrong.

*T*he soul of freedom we must cherish; we mustn't ever allow it to perish;

*F*reedom is in doing what you know is right,
Without any fear; it maintains clear insight.

*A*ll of the citizens of our family tree,
Though not always wise, we were all born free.

*T*he love of freedom is to love others;
Beneficence and caring for others it mothers.

*F*reedom rings where opinions clash.
-Adlai Stevenson

FRIENDSHIP - COMPANIONSHIP

*F*riendship without self interest is one of the rare
and beautiful things of life.
-James Francis Byrnes

*F*riendship is always a sweet responsibility.
Never forsake this enviable opportunity.

*F*riendliness, loneliness, not difficult to conceive;
That's why Creator God gave Adam comely Eve.

*T*rue, devout friendship in this world is rare;
Jealousy and mistrust so oft is the fare.

*B*eware of the person who has nothing to lose;
Not the type of friend that you should choose.

A friend of man you cannot make if you haven't confidence in him.
Converting a man you won't succeed if you have silenced him.

A LIFESTYLE PORTRAYAL From A TO Z

The vitamin for making good friends, my son, unquestionably, conclusively is B 1.

❧

A true friend is someone who still is a friend,
Though your bank loan by him isn't backed.
A true friend says that you're a good egg,
Even though he knows that you're slightly cracked.

❧

True friendship is loyal camaraderie; in life it's a genus of luxury.

❧

A valued friend can call at 3:a.m, be he or a she, a male or a femme.

❧

In choosing your friends, let me give you a clue,
A person stealing an egg steals chickens too.

❧

A true friend is someone who reaches for your hand
And touches your heart, he seems to understand.

❧

A friend is a gift that's much greater than pelf.
It's an intrinsic endowment that you give to yourself.

❧

Friends they truly are, of needs comprehending;
A precious abiding love with a deep understanding.

❧

Most everyone hears what you say.
Good friends listen to what you say.
True friends listen to what you don't say.

❧

True friends I note, over the elderly fuss.
They are God's way of taking care of us.

❧

True friends are the ones you meet in prosperity.
They firmly remain in bitter adversity.

❧

Friendship is being quite close in heart,
Even though we may be many miles apart.

❧

If you don't have nice things about your friends to say,
You should get some new ones without further delay.

❧

Permit me to ask you, friendship how do you rate?
Is it average or great, does it include your mate?
What's on its slate, does it foolishly prate,
Abusively berate, and harbor vile hate?
Is it always straight and does it carry weight?
What verbiage does it spate. does it patiently wait?

A LIFESTYLE PORTRAYAL From A TO Z

And let me ask you, what is its present state?
Fashion it, improve it, lest it be too late.
Most certainly don't leave it to uncompromising fate.

୶

*I*f you aim to keep a congenial friend, uphold, do honor and do not offend.

୶

*C*ultivate friendship in feeling and thought.
Lasting companionship can never be bought.

୶

*F*riendship with evil will cause an upheaval.

୶

*N*ever expect a friend to be ideal; are you perfect? - let's be real!

୶

*I*f you should own a precious painting, would you hang it out of sight?
Treat your friends as priceless canvas, place them in the best of light.

୶

*F*riends are ministering angels on whom we can trustfully rely.
They gently raise us to our feet, when our wings can no longer fly.

୶

*W*hile travelling life's seas, choose the right ship;
Your journey will be smoother sailing a sturdy friendship.

୶

A lifelong, loyal, unquenchable friendship
Can perpetually trigger a sigh of relief.
Not only does it multiply inward joy,
It has great potential to divide one's grief.

୶

*F*riendships aren't purchased with penurious pelf.
A friend is a gift that you give to yourself.

୶

A pathway to friendship we should try to employ.
It's sharing and experiencing another person's joy.

୶

A true friend is ready to make amends.
Misfortune reveals those who aren't true friends.

୶

*W*ords spoken years ago are not at all errant,
"In tight places true friends are always apparent."

୶

*M*ake him your friend but don't envy him,
The man with material prosperity.
Much greater the man who goes to a friend
Who's afflicted with deep adversity.

୶

It topples governments, it wrecks many marriages,
It reprehensibly increases the count of baby carriages.
It causes cruel heartaches, nightmares and indigestion,
Ruins careers, a many, and sullies reputation.
Makes headlines and headaches, it causes much grief,
And of precious time it becomes a subtle thief.
It spawns shrewd suspicions, it makes people cry,
And on its veracity one cannot rely.
The name is GOSSIP, at party or shop,
It's not at all necessary, so why not shut up.
Ask yourself, friend, before repeating a story,
"Is it kind, is it true, will it give another glory?"

Not everyone repeats gossip, some prefer to start it.

To perpetuate gossip we are all so capable.
To spread the Good News, let's gossip the gospel.

GRACE

The grace of Christ alone can change a heart of stone.
-E. G. White

No one can fathom the depth of His grace, nor picture the anguish on Calvary's face.

God's grace accepted is God's peace perfected.

God's free offer of his loving, saving grace, is available to all for a limited time space.

God gives amazing grace for whatever we face.

God's grace is immeasurable, His love inestimable,
His mercy inexhaustible, His peace inexpressible.

He who eternally holds the stars in space, has for all a sufficient amount of His grace.

We're saved by grace through Christ's atonement.
Determine not to make indefinite postponement.

The will of God is not inclined to take you to where His grace will not protect you.

I must ask for grace before I think, and before I dip my shy pen in ink.

GRATITUDE - INGRATITUDE

How sharper than a serpent's tooth it is to have a thankless child.
-Shakespeare

When you've thanked the Lord for every blessing sent,
You'll have little time to murmur or lament.

Blessings that are hemmed with gratitude and praise
Aren't prone to unravel, their duration will amaze.

From your lips may gratitude flow; contentment enables you to grow.

"Thank You," should be a prudent policy; sincere gratitude is a form of courtesy.

Gratitude is the rarest of virtue; you always expect it, don't you?

Write injuries in the dust, don't over them moan.
Be thankful for small mercies, carve them in stone.

Gratitude, a heart's fuzzy feeling, for it many people do yearn,
For that expression in words and for one's giving in return.

Gratitude, when articulated with the least of emotion,
Should be the prime part of our daily devotion.

Gratitude is the least of virtues, ingratitude the worst of vices.

Gratitude is the soul in which joy thrives.
Try it my friend, you'll find it saves lives.

True gratitude is not a sugared platitude,
It is in verity a God-honored attitude.

Always make gratitude a continuous attitude.

Gratitude to God should not be a feat,
On the contrary, it should be a treat.
It's something that we should always repeat.
It should be as regular as our trusty heartbeat.

Gratitude fosters good cheer - express it to God, child and peer -
Proclaim it throughout the whole year.

If you wake up in the morning with gratitude on your mind,
Your day will be sprinkled with deeds that are kind.

Gratitude, indeed, is a small price to pay
For affection and goodwill that comes our way.

Virtuous, gracious gratitude is the heart void of blindness.
It's tearfully remembering a past loving kindness.

"What – giving again," I asked in dismay,
And must I keep giving and giving away?"
"Oh, no!" said the angel, looking me through and through,
"Just give till the Master stops giving to you."
-Anonymous

It's another's frailty if he isn't grateful,
But I am the culprit if in giving I'm not faithful.

A solemn sacred duty resides in a life
That of this world's goods is so treasured and plenteous.
A trust, an obligation it must truly fulfill,
For poverty verily robs the right to be generous.

Ingratitude is not a beatitude.

GREATNESS - FAME

What makes greatness is starting something that lives after you.
-Ralph W. Sockman

He is a great man who listens to a little man.

Don't lust for fame – it's an overrated game.

A person that is great doesn't ever get irate,
His temper he will bate, he will always keep a date,
He doesn't make you wait, always courteous to his mate,
He doesn't show hate, he doesn't ever prate,
His dealings are straight, he has a wise pate,
With his friends he'll highly rate and he makes you feel great.

You can be great and you don't have to wait,
There's no payment of a fee, no waiting for a degree.
You can be great now, let me tell you how,

A LIFESTYLE PORTRAYAL From A TO Z

Just determine to serve, it doesn't take nerve.
For a great new start put love in your heart.
Love in one's soul can make man whole.

❧

You needn't ever be afraid of greatness,
As long as you live a life of 'straightness.'

❧

Deeds, not granite, are the deeds of the great.
In expressing our gratitude we're oft so late.

❧

True greatness is indeed a spiritual condition
That stimulates interest, love and admiration.

❧

Great fame is when you dominate conversation,
But you aren't present to make the presentation.

❧

It's noble to give birth, much greater to give life;
Exhilarating to have mirth than perpetual strife.

❧

Greatness is to do a common gracious thing
That joy and high esteem to others 'twill bring.

❧

It is never too late to do something great.

❧

If you determine to be a great soul in the future,
You must with greatness your soul daily nurture.

❧

A great man, though powerful, he does not abuse it.
For certain, he's the one who knows best how to use it.

❧

True greatness lies not in being very strong,
It's the right use of strength where it belongs.

❧

The price of greatness - responsibility - it's generously coupled with fidelity.

❧

Greatness is not trying to be somebody,
It's conscientiously endeavoring to help somebody.

❧

A retentive, canny memory, without question, it's priceless,
But the ability to forget is the true sign of greatness.

❧

Great men are honest where small men lie.
Likewise, they envision where small men sigh.

❧

It is not what we have that will make us great,
It is what we bestow without a debate.

GREED

Avarice corrupts man's humanity.
-E. G. White

We're all born naive, distrustful and greedy,
Overflowing with self, forgetting the needy.

Greed makes Neros, difficulties make heroes.

There is no greater tragedy than greed; one's lavish desires calamities feed.

Cleanse your heart from greed; it is man's obligation to feed.

At times it's quite difficult to accept religious creed
From people when observing their outrageous, filthy greed.

One's miserly greed will eventually impede.

The miser wants more of the wealth that has grown,
And a plenteous amount of what he doesn't own.

Maturely assess your daily need; make certain it isn't miserly greed.

There's an apparent difficulty in distinguishing one's need
From the despicable, miserly, entrenched, filthy greed.

Resist the miserly song of greed, lest your salvation it does impede.

A deliberate, deceptive mind of greed should not think of wants, only of need.

A tenet of culture - don't be a vulture.

The earth has enough for every man's need, but not enough for his miserly greed.

GRIEF

One's mental worry and mental anxiety are a troubled soul's shrewd, subtle thief.
Sincere, open-hearted praise to God can lift a heavy burden of silent grief.

*D*o you believe that your excessive grieving the hosts of heaven will please?
One's silent grief weakens the defenses that fight despicable disease.

*G*rief is a shrewd, subtle thief - replace it with faith and belief;
Wholesome laughter can relieve one's grief.

*T*enderly, may time heal your sadness, compassionately, may friends ease your pain,
Tranquilly, may peace replace anguish, warm memories may they ever remain.

*D*on't allow your grief to impair your belief.

*C*ompare your grief with other men; you'll find that you'll be more thankful then.

GROOMING - DRESS

*N*eatness is the asepsis of clothes.
-Sir William Osler

*D*olly Parton was asked, "Who does your hair?"
"Wouldn't know," was the reply, "I'm never there."

*S*aid a man to his wife, "That dress don't take off,
It's 50% cotton, and 50% off."

*T*hose perfumed ads make me run to the sink.
I wish that some people would take time to think.
There's nothing in our constitution about freedom to stink.

*S*o often a man of his manner will be careful,
His dress, his appearance, avoiding sullen scowl,
But a boy's priority is to keep face clean,
To confirm it he uses a clean white towel.

*G*ood grooming will get you through the door; good manners, usually, past the foyer.

GRUMBLING

*I*t is a general error to suppose the loudest complainers
for the public to be the most anxious for their welfare.
-Burke

*E*veryone has a choice to grumble or rejoice.

A LIFESTYLE PORTRAYAL From A TO Z

A man will sit patiently in a swamp all day
To shoot a wild duck that might come his way,
And yet he'll gripe when dinner is late;
They then become miserable, both he and wife Kate.

❧

Working to reach high keeps a man on his toes;
Grumbling and complaining magnifies his woes.

❧

Grumbling, crabbing, and complaining is pathetic.
Joy in a woman's life is the best cosmetic.

❧

GUILT

Guilt is present in its very hesitation, even though the deed be not committed.
-Cicero

❧

Everyone is guilty of the good he didn't do, this most likely includes both me and you.

❧

He who refuses to come to trial, confesses himself guilty with his denial.

❧

God never intended His children to bear guilt as a burden - the remedy is prayer.

❧

HABIT

Habit becomes a kind of second nature, which acts as a motive for many of our actions.
-Cicero

❧

It's only when good habits exist that principles of right influence persist.

❧

A despicable habit is easy to desire, and it can be so easy to readily acquire.

❧

Habits involve actions we are prone to repeat.
Choose to have wings not weights to your feet.

❧

Make your happiness a matter of habit.
Others will notice it –they'll be inclined to ape it.

❧

Habit, a strong rope that we twine every day; if it isn't broken, it is here to stay.

❧

If you should acquire a pernicious habit, you'll have to agree that "I" is the culprit

❧

If with a bad habit there's continual persistence,
  Chances are remote to combat resistance.

Habit and routine, watch how you employ;
  It's an unbelievable power to waste and destroy.

Abandon bad habits, lest you sorrow; it's easier done today than tomorrow.

HANDS BENEFICENT

There are hands of violence and hands of omission –
It's loving, giving hands that I rapturously envision.
The skilled dexterous hands of a calm, brilliant surgeon
  That determine to relieve dread disease;
The adept, intent hands of a proficient, comely seamstress
  That sew neatly and stitch deftly to please;
The nimble, rhythmic hands of an accomplished musician
  Whose artistry occasions such joy,
Do tell me, what creates more love and affection
  Than the grubby, chubby hands of a little boy.
The delicate, tiny hands of sweet, newborn baby
  That are loved by all ages, young and old;
The experienced, kind hands of a dear, loving grandpa
  That are loved by a grandchild, so I'm told.
The hard-working weathered hands of a seasoned prairie farmer
  That toil hard from early morn to late at night;
The ever-generous loving hands of a patient, caring father
  That share time with his young son and his kite.
The callused, iron hands of a resolute stone mason
  That snugly fit stone in the sea wall;
The intuitive, learned hands of a much lettered professor
  That train a young person to stand tall.
The creative, visionary hands of a persevering, astute sculptor
  That chisel and sculpt flawless form;
The anchored, steady hands of an undaunted ship's master
  That guide the frail barque through the storm.
The adroit, masterly hands of a self-assured artist
  That stroke and brush smoothly a masterpiece;
The heavily veined hands of an assertive house builder
  That erect with brawny muscular ease.
The esteemed, beloved hands of a faithful, caring mother,
  That console and gently dry painful tears;
Greatly treasured are the hands of a magnanimous philanthropist
  That generously impart through the years.

A hand stretched out in giving is in a position to receive.
It will enrich your living, happiness you will perceive.

*W*e have in our hands the power to lift,
To generously give and to annul rift

HANDS – HANDS – HANDS

*O*ur loving, heavenly Father gave us two hands –
They weren't created to humiliate;
Hands made with which to devotedly love,
Hands not with which to hate.

Hands, that we might freely that needed
Kind help to others give;
Hands, that are very own brothers and sisters,
So much the better might live.

Hands, with which our loved ones and friends
And ourselves we may defend;
Hands, on which our misfortunate neighbors,
So freely could depend.

Our God generously gave us our precious two hands
But we willingly use them to destroy;
Yes, those self-same, unworthy, evil hands
For wickedness we so oft employ.

Hands that were made to love and to cherish,
We use to deride and berate;
Hands, that were made to gently soothe,
We now use to castigate.

Hands, that should be used to conciliate,
We use them to be jabbing;
Hands, that humanity they should alleviate,
We use to be selfishly grabbing.

God, in his mercy stretched forth his hands
To a world itself destroying;
He sorrowfully embraced his rebellious creation,
With loving, caring hands imploring.

We nailed those gentle hands to a cruel, wicked cross, -
"God, - stay there," we did announce;
Yes, with our sinful, our own barbaric hands
His lowly, sweet spirit we did pounce.

Today he is walking our streets and our roadways,
With nail-scarred hands wide open;
Entreating, longing and anxiously waiting
While our hands in sin are groping.

We're intentionally stone-deaf to his beckoning call,
We are blind to see his face;
Our hands reject his long-standing invitation,
Our hands receive not his grace.

My friend, you must not delay any longer,
Respond to his pleading today;
Allow his kind hands to lovingly enfold you –
He'll graciously show you the way.

PRAYING HANDS

"*I* must show the whole world my love and appreciation
By painting his hands in divine supplication."
'Twas this thought that inspired artist Albrecht Durer;
So devoted a friend, one could find no one truer.

So longingly from childhood Albrecht wanted to paint,
Great ambition he had,- he labored like a saint.
Very clear was life's pathway, not at all was it muddy;
Eventually he left home with a renowned artist to study.

He acquainted with a fellow whose predilection was the same,
Similar goals they melded, their hearts were aflame.
Their means were very meager,- paying hours were needed;
Their mastery of skilled art was so grossly impeded.

Albrecht was to apprentice, 'twas on his comrades insistence,
While the latter was to labor to provide life's subsistence.
After relentless persuasion he reluctantly agreed,
While his companion toiled hard to provide daily need.

Albrecht studied faithfully and was crowned with success;
In time sold wood carvings, they were some of his best.

Now 'twas his friend's turn to tote palette and paint,
But hard work had stiffened his hands and his gait.

No longer was he able to use brush with sharp skill;
His life's aspiration he could no longer fulfill.
When Albrecht had learned what had befallen his friend,
He was filled with much sorrow - couldn't quite understand.

One day on returning to their humble abode -
As into their modest dwelling he unexpectedly strode,
He quietly climbed to the top of the stair,
There to find the gnarled hands reverently held in prayer.

Durer's deep gratitude became quite overwhelming,
And so captured that scene in this now famous painting.
Today we're so blessed with both beauty and thought
That this wondrous story of friendship has taught.

HANDSHAKE

A good firm handshake need not subtract.
It should be as binding as a wordy contract.

HAPPINESS - CHEERFULNESS - JOY

Happiness is not perfected until it is shared.
 - Jane Porter

Happiness you yourself must woo, it's rarely inclined to choose you.

Money and fame don't automatically win,
But happiness does, coming from within.

It's not always easy, it's not for the weak,
It's not for the timid, the wishy-washy, the sneak.
Happiness requires courage, great stamina, insistence,
Valor, vigor and bravery, much spunk and persistence.
It requires backbone, grit, guts and sheer pluck,
Yet, sometimes you get it with just plain luck.
It comes with tolerance, with reasoning and concentration,
With nerve and resilience, with power and implementation.
Much happiness can be achieved through kindness and love,
And with divine blessings that come from above.

A LIFESTYLE PORTRAYAL From A TO Z

A word about happiness, the salient fact is,
It is something that we should genuinely practice.

*L*earn to find pleasure in the simple things.
Invariably you'll find much happiness it brings.

*L*earn to be cheerful - if you aren't, fake it,
Believe it, work at it, eventually you'll make it.

*I*t's not so much our position as it is our innate disposition.

*T*here's an old Scottish proverb that's been so well said,
"Be happy while you're living for you're a long time dead."

*H*appiness, a unique discipline - enchantment is its twin.

*T*he epitome of happiness is to have joy and peace,
Integrated with a quickening, clear conscience.
Anger is a hindrance, avoid vile vengeance,
While practicing self-restrained patience.

*E*ntertain happiness, it's the way to wisdom.
Be joyful continuously, it's the road to Christendom.

*I*f you are happy cause you're saved by grace,
Why not make an effort to notify your face.

*H*appiness truly helps to make man whole;
A blessed inward virtue of the human soul.

*Y*ears ago, Lincoln spoke a thought meant for me,
"Most people become as happy as they determine to be."

*N*o one ever found true happiness by chance.
It's entirely up to me pure delight to advance.

*H*appiness can be likened to a beautiful butterfly,
It invariably eludes you as catching it you try.
But on turning your attention to some other thing,
It comes and sits softly on your outspread wing.

*D*o I want to be happy instead of being right?
To accomplish number one, my tongue I must bite.
Do you want to be happy or should you choose right?
They're mutually inclusive - keep happiness in sight.

A LIFESTYLE PORTRAYAL From A TO Z

*A*lways do strive to be happy, dire misfortunes are rare;
Those which just never happen are invariably the hardest to bear.

*J*oyous happiness, not a station you arrive at,
It accompanies travelling, it's the time you're at bat.

A prime, prudent proverb I give prominence in rhyme,
'The pursuit of happiness is a chase of a lifetime.'

*O*n this earth's sojourn let deep joy be a part.
He never grows old who has love in his heart.

*W*hen you choose to rejoice you make a wise choice.

*H*appiness is possible when one is very busy,
Not to be confused when one is in a tizzy.
A weary body must toil, the keen mind occupied,
The stomach must be full and the heart satisfied.

*T*rue happiness in your life shouldn't depend on your "boughts."
More importantly it should hinge on the characteristics of your thoughts.

*H*appiness comes from what you lovingly adore.
More importantly it's having so much to live for.

*W*hat joy and happiness the festive season brings.
Remember, the best gifts are tied with heartstrings.

*E*ffervescent exuberance is beauty; boundless happiness is high duty.

*H*appiness, an attribute that is always in;
Should be faithfully practiced like a violin.

*Y*ou'll gain great strength and joy if happiness you continually employ.

*W*hen we're in a good mood we tend to do good.

*H*appiness is not what we hoard or wear,
It's a byproduct of what we generously share.

*B*e cheerful, be happy, express charm and grace.
When you feel terrific you'll notify your face.

*A*dore simple pleasures, they are valued treasures.

A LIFESTYLE PORTRAYAL From A TO Z

Fun is natural pleasure - joy is spiritual treasure.

The secret of happiness is intellectual curiosity.
It's totally avoiding bloated pomposity.

True happiness isn't measured in terms
Of the specialness that you may impart,
But in terms of the peace of Christ
That reigns within your heart.

Happiness doesn't always come from our possessions,
Frequently it comes from honest confessions.

To be of a good spirit, being cheerful is contagious.
To promote happiness is not being outrageous.

You can show happiness by providing it; multiply happiness by dividing it.

The essentials of happiness, something to do, something to chew,
Knowing the score, something to hope for - Christ to adore.

Although up to its neck in hot water, the kettle continues to sing.
Take a lesson from the tea kettle, happiness to others you'll bring.

The perfect way to have a happiness bash
Is to count your blessings and not your cash.

Happiness, a state of mind we should highly rate,
So why don't we move to that joyful state.

Buoyant happiness, one cannot rob - radiant joy is an inside job.

If with humble happiness your life you saturate,
Eventually damp gloom is bound to evaporate.

Greater joy life brings, loving people, not things.

To be of good cheer, a straight course steer,
From courage never veer - have faith, not fear.

Multiply happiness, don't ever quit; this you'll accomplish by dividing it.

Happy is he who can readily arrange to bear the things he cannot change.

Happiness walks on busy feet; don't let happiness ever retreat.

To retain happiness be gainfully employed.
Dire misfortunes try to perpetually avoid.

Though happiness is free it must be sought.
Pleasures, on the other hand are frequently bought.

You appear intensely unhappy - consider how much more you could be.

If it isn't in your heart to make happiness and please,
My friend, you have a symptom of heart disease.

Practice being excited - you will be delighted.

HATRED

Like gluttony or drunkenness, hatred seems to be
an agreeable vice when you practice it yourself,
but disgusting when observed in others.
-William H. Irwin

Our God makes it abundantly clear - hatred and revenge we must fear.

Hatred is like a vicious barracuda; passion that is fiery never feed.
Envy can be likened to a baited trap; there's nothing comparable to miserly greed.

Hatred is a pastime one can ill afford,
An indulgence not sanctioned by our Loving Lord.

Hatred in your lifestyle is not an enhancer.
Rid it my friend, it's a genus of cancer.

Passionately avoiding and hating - the result of a petty spat,
Can be likened to burning your closet because of a filthy rat.

Hate damages the vessel in which it is stored,
As well as the object on which it is poured.

Avoid the occasions to indignantly berate.
One can never rid hatred with hideous hate.

With enemies, make amends, make them your friends.

Hatred of vile sin can make you a winner,
But this should not keep you from loving the sinner.

Hatred, revenge and lack of pardon
Are poisonous weeds in the devils garden.

HEALTH

Our prayers should be for a sound mind in a healthy body.
-Juvenal

Health is not merely the absence of illness,
It's the presence of joy and deep inside stillness.

Nothing tends more to promote health of soul
Than does a spirit of gratitude and praise.
In your daily living make room for giving,
It will for certain your endorphins raise.

Good, healthy health habits must be kept at a premium;
On their full benefits one can trustfully rely.
It's definitely the slowest possible highroad
On which an individual can peacefully die.

Health isn't valued till sickness comes; take care of yourself, thumbs up, my chum.

A picture of health is a countenance that is kind.
To attain this I must be in a good frame of mind.

The greatest health risk, night, morn or noon,
Is the uncontrollable knife, fork and spoon.

Men and women who relentlessly give in the restoration of one's personal health,
By virtue of their inordinate skill give more than they do of their personal wealth.

Be a health witness, focus on fitness.

God's health-care plan is designed with your and my needs in mind.

He who would be radiantly healthy, let him be pleasantly cheerful.

HEAVEN

What can be more foolish to think that all this rare fabric
of heaven and earth could come by chance,
when all the skill of art is not able to make an oyster.
-Jeremy Taylor

Heaven is a prepared place for a saintly prepared race.

Heaven's eternal delights will exceedingly far outweigh
The misery found on earth that evil angels convey.

Heaven, no pain, no fears - no night, no death, no tears.

Heaven isn't a place of misleading pretext.
With faith build a bridge from this world to the next.

If you wish to dwell in the place of many mansions,
You must make your reservation - don't take any chances.

HELP - HELPING

When a person is down in the world, an ounce of help
is worth more than a pound of preaching.
-Bulwer Lytton

Some people are willing to give a helping hand
To those who are a notch above their own clan;
But to help the unfortunate who are much below them,
They frequently think they're too far above them.

This earthly human race would perish from the earth
If we ceased to help from conception to birth.
So let us not ever, not a moment in time
Resign in our effort to assist mankind.

If I cannot help, someone far away, I have an alternative, I can always pray.

When a piano is being moved, be it at home or the school,
Do you reach for the sheet music or the lowly piano stool?

HEREAFTER

Heaven's gates are not so highly arched as princes palaces,
that they that enter there must go upon their knees.
-John Webster

Our minister came by, one lovely, bright day.
He was kindly invited for a few moments to stay.
He firmly suggested, "Think on the hereafter,
I have grave concern, this mustn't cause laughter."
I clearly explained, that I did it all the time.
I said this not just to structure a neat rhyme.
For on going up stairs, to storage near the rafters,
I've asked myself frequently, "What am I here after?"

HISTORY

The men who make history have not time to write it.

History most certainly is a capricious lady,
So in your assignments avoid things shady.

Yesterday is ancient history, tomorrow, an unsolved mystery.
Today is a precious gift, use it to give others a lift.

Early morning news, oft a strange mystery,
Becomes the first draft of social history.

HOLY SPIRIT

The abiding Holy Spirit, in a repentant soul
Is the prime catalyst to make man whole.
We should earnestly ask for the Spirit's control
Over every longing thought that sinks into the soul.

Obey the Holy Spirit - must He us prod?
Conscience can be our compass, our chart the word of God.

God generously will supply our dire daily needs;
Be careful to stay clear of vile attitudes and deeds.
Unreservedly do yield to the Spirit's control.
Choose to obey Him with whole heart and soul.

A Christian who neglects the abiding Holy Spirit
Can be likened to a lamp not plugged into an outlet.

If the Spirit should urge you to repent and be ready,
That wouldn't be the time for a feasibility study.

The Spirit enables the people of God
To understand and obey the will of God.

The Precious Holy Spirit's sharp paring knife
Enhances the Christian's fruit-bearing life.

The power that guides, sustains and compels us,
Comes from the Spirit that dwells within us.

Begin overcoming your obsession
By the power of the Spirit's intercession.

HONESTY - VERACITY

An honest man is the noblest work of God.
-Aslexander Pope

There is no legacy as rich as honesty.

An honest name has unqualified fame; to attain success, honesty acclaim.

Basic honesty is paramount, disappointment, oft absurd;
Frequently the latter lies in the oppressive broken word.

Unimpeachable honesty one cannot shout.
Likewise, it's an entity you cannot doubt.

Strict honesty in your dealings is an absolute must.
Truth will not injure maiden ventures that are just.

Rigid honesty first, then courage, then brains,
All are indispensable in life to make gains.

A scale of full measure, injures no man.
This maxim should be part of everyone's plan.

Honesty must prevail, avoid being crooked;
Life is tough – it's tougher if you're stupid.

A LIFESTYLE PORTRAYAL From A TO Z

I've known many pharmacists o'er scores of years,
Men of high honor, full of honesty and sobriety.
I gladly hasten to unequivocally state,
They truly have been the "Pillers" of society.

※

If basic honesty is blind, it's virtue of the wrong kind.

※

Unless you are sick, it's an immoral trick
To take honest sick days just to sun and laze.

※

Be honest in your dealings as you rake in the dough.
A crooked stick always casts a crooked shadow.

※

True honesty in a woman isn't love of her male,
It's the accuracy of the setting on her bathroom scale.

※

You mustn't deliberately cheat; with crystal honesty be replete.

※

Honesty and truth have the most clout.
If you tell the truth you'll be found out.

※

No one will know of your honesty, unless you exhibit true modesty.

※

There's an honest man that for long I've well-known.
With him I could play checkers over the telephone.

※

There's a succinct thought that we've so oft heard,
"One thing you can give and still keep is your word."

※

Stick to honesty, it is the best policy.

※

There are no grades of honesty, nor are there degrees of modesty.

※

Dishonesty in business does not belong,
It's either black or white, or it's right or wrong.

※

How can you ever get cornered, if you're on the straight and narrow?
Your business will meet with success if your dealings are straight as an arrow.

※

Honesty is the rarest of wealth that a person can ever possess.
This type of honesty I must strive in my life to fully confess.

※

A lad cycled leisurely down an idle street.
He chose to stop in front of a stranger's sandalled feet.

A LIFESTYLE PORTRAYAL From A TO Z

"Did you chance to lose a new five-dollar bill?"
The boy asked the man as the latter stood still.
"Yes, yes," said the man, while searching his pocket.
The youngster then readied to pedal his sprocket.
"Just wanted to know how many were lost today,
Yours is twenty-five," I heard the lad say.

*Honesty is an essence that in character stands out,
And it is an entity that one can't wear out.*

HONOR

*Mine honor is my life; both grow in one;
Take honor from me and my life is done.*
-Shakespeare

*In business it is better to have a clean face.
'Tis best to die in honor than live in disgrace.*

HOPE

*When things look hopeless, don't fret and mope.
Instead, look to God, the giver of hope.*

*Hopelessness is an entity that the devil tries to prod.
No one is hopeless whose hope is in God.*

*"Hope sees the invisible, feels the intangible,
And achieves the impossible."*

You say, "I'm unable to cope." There is no medicine like hope.

*In the face of uncertainty, how does one cope?
Bear fully in mind – nothing wrong with hope.*

A dull, misty morning doesn't mean 'twill be cloudy.

Hope is a thirst - prepare for the worst.

HOSPITAL

A patient while in hospital, in postoperative reflection,
Was approached by his nurse with a hypo for injection.
He was jabbed with a needle, passing out in agony;
"Just a little pain killer," as she rubbed his anatomy.

A hospital is the place where all good friends meet
To talk about their surgeries and leftovers to eat.

*S*o you have a health problem – doc says you're a heart case.
If you're in the heart ward, your heart's in the right place.

HOSPITALITY

*T*here is an emanation from the heart in genuine hospitality
which puts the stranger at once at ease.
-Washington Irving

*T*o her lovely home she frees the latch –
Her ready hospitality very few can match.

*C*ordial hospitality doesn't imply, size of house or food supply.
If you have love and a big heart, you will to others gladly impart.

*R*outinely practice genuine hospitality –
Angels become guests – make this your specialty.

*M*ake hospitality in your home a reality.

HUGGING

*I*f you don't want your kids to get hooked on drugs,
Start early in life to give lots of hugs.

*P*eople are oft greeted with a huge bear hug.
Then there are those who have their backs slapped.
Some are greeted with a great big smile;
They've recently had their eyeteeth gold-capped.

*I*t's so wondrous what a hug can do, a hug can cheer you when you're blue.
A hug can say, "I love you so," a hug it's warmth it does bestow.
A hug is, 'Welcome back again! It's great to see you, where've you been?'

A hug can soothe a small child's pain and bring a bright rainbow after the rain.
A hug, there's just no doubt about it, we scarcely could survive without it.
A hug delights, it warms, it charms, it must be why God gave us arms.
Hugs are great for fathers and mothers, sweet for sisters, swell for brothers.
And chances are some favorite aunt, loves them more than potted plants.
Kittens crave them, puppies love them, heads of state are not above them.
A hug can break the language barrier and make a dull day seem so much merrier.
Never fret about your store of them, the more you give, the more there's of them.
So stretch your arms without delay and give that someone a snug hug today.
-Author Unknown

Been thinking of you, this hug is overdue.

Your affectionate hug gives my heartstrings a big tug.

HUMILITY

True humility, the highest virtue, mother of them all.
-Tennyson

Humility has might, it sheds divine light.

There's something great about honest humility
That gently softens narrow-minded rigidity.

Arrogance we must shun, ugly pride eschew;
Humility, the foundation of honorable virtue.

It may not be thought very dashing, or deemed as somewhat smashing;
You wouldn't call it very stunning, but it is exceedingly becoming -
That virtuous cloak of humility.

Humility must never be equated with senility.

Meekness, a trait to be fully desired,
It's an attribute more precious than gold.
Lord, give me humility, I earnestly pray,
My character with this feature do mold.

The most honorary title since time first began -
"The inviolable character of a humble honest man."

False humility is definitely pride; this type of humility one cannot hide.

A LIFESTYLE PORTRAYAL From A TO Z

To maintain in your life tranquility, keep a profile of humility.

❧

Knowing God will make us humble; our intolerable arrogance is bound to tumble.

❧

Humility grows from one's strength, it justly increases with meekness.
Beware of ongoing prim pride, it gradually comes out of weakness.

❧

Humility and peace go hand in hand; an attribute that harmony does graciously demand.

❧

Do try to be humble, avoid shameful scorn.
Always blow your own nose, but don't toot your horn.

❧

To learn to walk humbly can be done with ease,
Repeatedly start out on 'bended' knees.

❧

Practice humility and self-denial; you have been placed on this earth on trial.

❧

Genuine humility may make you feel smaller,
But in the eyes of men, you'll stand much taller.

❧

Beware of the personage who is highly opinionated;
He who's truly humble cannot be humiliated.

❧

A humble, honest man is greatly admired.
He's the individual that invariably gets hired.

❧

Humility, without question is modesty of the soul.
It is part and parcel in making man whole.

❧

No cloak more becoming than the garb of humility,
When one approaches the age of senility.

❧

Be slow to be forward, at times draw inward;
The latter a prerequisite for reaching outward.

❧

You can ask the Lord for humility, but never attempt to thank him for it.
If you elected to do so, my friend - you'd be deemed as a pharisaical hypocrite.

❧

Some folk stand still, they're afraid they might stumble.
Some purse their thick lips, they're afraid they might mumble.
No one can fault you, when you try to be humble.

❧

Humility can be sought, but can never be bought.

❧

Not a day passes, but folk of humble note
Accomplish great things, they keep rowing the boat.

Consider the humble sheep – have you someone shorn?
Enemies are made, very seldom are they born.

Those who exercise arrogance and clout, don't seem to fathom what humility is all about.

HUMOR

A man isn't poor if he can still laugh.
-Raymond Hitchcock

All good humor should be painless and shameless,
And I must add, should be totally profaneless.

Our inborn five senses are far from complete.
It's the sixth, sense of humor, inadvertently we delete.

Good humor, the best shield against darts others wield.

Good humor, I must confess is a great article of dress.

A wholesome entity, to all this is known, is to have up one's sleeve a mirthful funny bone.

It's not restricted to this country, it's the same in Afghanistan.
Horse sense is what a horse has that prevents him from betting on man.

Laugh oft at yourself, season it with wit; pleasurable humor, one can't live without it.

Good humor is considered proper dress for fashionable, fastidious society;
Sarcasm and shady witticism, a shockingly despicable impropriety.

My recent cataract surgery, with my wife doesn't score,
For I see linear dimples I've never seen before.

Humor is a significant activity of the brain;
It should never cause one inner pain.

Most of us love to shoot the breeze - delightful, subtle humor we all adore.
Even the lofty, bright gilded eagle, needs a gentle breeze to gracefully soar.

Buoyant humor is usually spontaneous, it can be full of pleasant surprises.
So very frequently it is totally unplanned, and at times it has clever disguises.

A LIFESTYLE PORTRAYAL From A TO Z

The essence of good humor is its subtle surprise,
Not to mention how it brings happy tears to one's eyes.

❧

"What do the best paid free-lance writers write?"
A student of journalism queried one night.
"It's not those long sermons by a long-winded preacher,
It's doctor's prescriptions," so answered the teacher.

❧

You cannot completely replace the newspaper with a TV you love to eye.
Tell me, have you ever seen a sane person with a TV try to swat a fly?

❧

I've been recently singularly promoted, it certainly beats being demoted.
I now have some six hundred under me, I'm the caretaker of Rosebud Cemetery.

❧

The cleaner pays when he loses your suit, it's classed as an obvious misdemeanor.
Your gray-haired lawyer can lose your suit, and still he can take you to the cleaners.

❧

A landlord and tenant to the same goal are bent.
They both are trying to raise the rent.

❧

Allergy is a problem that is difficult to combat,
And the cost of treatment is nothing to sneeze at.

❧

If you drive carefully you'll avoid the mourning after,
And I might add, you'll postpone the hereafter.

❧

A salesman showed her half of his stock, but selections and funds didn't agree.
"Please, do you mind if I rest a while - Lady, your feet are killing me."

❧

Said a pitiful inebriate, as his head swam, "I'm not as think as you stoned I am."

❧

On seeing my dinner plate, done beautifully, I have a fit,
For I know that someone's fingers have been in it.

❧

By a roadside stand in letters quite bright,
"Our berries have slept in their beds last night."

❧

"Fate," says Clem, "is usually to blame for all the accidents under the sun,"
But he makes himself totally responsible whenever he makes a hole-in-one.

❧

An employer questioned a man - the latter a job was seeking.
"And what is your marital status?" His candid reply, "We're not speaking."

❧

One thing I can't figure when I'm counting sheep,
Is how a wee mosquito gets along without sleep.

❧

A LIFESTYLE PORTRAYAL From A TO Z

Why do some people lack private endeavor?
Yet to run our country they think they're so clever.

❧

A committee meeting, an event at great cost,
Where minutes are kept and the hours are lost.

❧

It's great to have a good sense of humor; never confuse it with sardonic rumor.

❧

In this world some do wish that a plenteous amount of vintage cheese did abound,
Then there wouldn't be that victimizing rat race if there were enough to go around.

❧

It's great to have a good sense of humor; never to be confused it with sardonic rumor.

❧

A politician says, "Consumer outlook better."
He wants you to believe it completely to the letter.
"Better lookout consumer," you should rather read.
Those are the words you must fully heed.

❧

So oft comes the question to the neuron of a moron,
What happens to the holes when the cheese is all gone?

❧

A playful, middle-aged graying wolf, sidled up to a cute brunette -
"Where've you been all my life?" - "Wasn't born for the first half of it."

❧

I remarked one late night as my wife was baking,
"I've come into the kitchen for the smell of it."
She curtly replied, as o'er the coals she raked me,
"Get out of the kitchen for the health of it."

❧

Humor is delightful - mustn't be lost; must be permanently preserved at all cost.

❧

A political convention is called to decide,
As to who's going to run and who's going to hide,
And it is to pick that singular 'smartie' who is going to be the life of the party.

❧

They say that man spends a third of his time soundly asleep under some feathers.
Pray tell me, my friend, where does he abide, when he says he is under the weather?

❧

A fox should not be a member of a jury
When a goose is on trial - that would be perjury.

❧

Pat, with puzzlement, questioned one day his partner semi recumbent Moriarty,
"Where would our suspenders business be if we didn't have the law of gravity?"

❧

A LIFESTYLE PORTRAYAL From A TO Z

I have those brief moments that are free from worry,
Those respites of panic, full of hurry and scurry.

❧

*H*umor, one of God's most wonderful gifts,
With smiles and laughter conversation it lifts.
Humor reveals roses, it hides prickly thorns,
Not meant to have spears or sharp, pointy horns.
It obscures the rough spots, makes one's burdens light,
It deflates the pompous, puts the arrogant out of sight.
-Anonymous

❧

*W*hen the chips are down, to my mind there's no doubt,
That it's definitely the time to get the dip out.

❧

A simple memo to you my dear, I trust you do not mind,
Lips need not be so strikingly colorful, as a baboon's broad behind.

❧

*A*nyone without a good sense of humor is a late bloomer, so goes the rumor.

❧

*B*en came to his doctor with two scorched ears.
The doctor remarked, "Bad burns it appears -
And how did this happen," the doctor inquired,
"It seems it's been caused by something that's been fired."
"I was pressing my slacks - had the phone on the board,
Suddenly the phone, - to my ear the iron soared."
"What about the other ear, what happened, Ben?"
"Believe it or not, the same fellow called again."

❧

A doctor remarked, to his old patient Joe, "The check you sent me was a placebo."

❧

*T*wo burly breezy truckers came into a café,
Thought they'd have fun with the waitress that day.
The bright young maiden clearly beat them to the punch
As the two huge hombres seated down to brunch.
"And how can I help you prevent minimum shrinkage?"
The portliest replied, "Give us hubcaps and linkage."
The waitress was puzzled as to what the order meant,
So her ear to the chef she quizzically bent.
The cook made it clear, "It is unique verbiage,
What they've really ordered is fried eggs and sausage."
The waitress was prompt, but with two bowls of beans.
The men piped up, "You're in error it seems."
"Oh no," she replied - "These are for starts -
Why not gas up, while you're waiting for parts?"

❧

A LIFESTYLE PORTRAYAL From A TO Z

*I*f you eat excessively beans and onions en masse,
You'll produce an abundance of pungent teargas.

*G*ood humor is a tonic for mind and body;
Sarcasm and cynicism express thoughts that are shady.

*W*hoever in their wisdom concocted 'mammogram?'
Putting a breast in an envelope then sending it to someone.

A tall truck driver was having his lunch
At a roadside café with the usual bunch,
When three shaggy hoodlums, sporting black jackets,
Garnished with skull and crossbones, drove in causing a racket.
They parked their motorcycles, then swaggered inside,
They spotted a tall trucker, then proceeded to deride.
They took away his plate, they insulted his age,
Pushed him off his seat, but his smarts they didn't gauge.
The man said not a word, he got up off the floor,
He paid for his lunch then walked out the door.
A biker was unhappy, he hadn't provoked a fight.
He said to a waitress, "He wasn't much for his height."
The waitress quite agreed, while glancing at the cycles,
"Nor is he a good driver, he's backed over three motorcycles."

*I*n American politics, the donkey and the elephant, play important roles to woo.
It's interesting to note, that at the same time, the bull plays an important role too.

*R*ecently, a well-known politician, while visiting a constituent said,
"Been reading many nice things about you, and saw you on TV, Ned.
Like many you'll end up in an urn, or buried beneath the heather;
Remember the size of your funeral will solely depend on the weather."

*O*n a bakery was a sign, "We're open at daylight,"
On a café, "We will wait, all night for you."
Foo Ling, a laundry proprietor, studied the signs,
Next morning his proud effort, "For service, me wake too."

*B*lessed is the day when you laughed at yourself,
Treasure it friend, much more than pelf.

*I*n the garden of Eden lived the first pair,
Fruits, nuts and grains were Adam's and Eve's fare.
No cooking for Eve - she called it paradise.
Most women today would be delighted, likewise.

A LIFESTYLE PORTRAYAL From A TO Z

*A*s a young lad I was clearly informed that the world revolved on its axis.
I've since learned, I've been totally misled –
It revolves on it's exorbitant taxes.

❧

*W*hen you go on a diet, so goes the rumor,
The first thing you lose is your sense of humor.

❧

A sense of ill humor provides room for rumor.

❧

*A*n elderly gent, to me well-known,
Elected to leave his comfort zone.
He drove his convertible - his few strands blown,
Bombing around town, he was minding his own,
Happily munching on a freshly baked scone.
He became a bit concerned about the motor's tone,
So he chose to drive in to an auto service zone.
He appealed to an attendant who was eating a cone,
"Please fill her up with testosterone."

❧

*T*he American and Dutch flags similar colors display;
The red, white and blue in a colorful array.
A Dutch visitor on occasion came to the U. S.,
Said he to a friend, "My flag doesn't impress.
The colors," he continued, "are symbols of my taxes.
Frankly, my composure it never relaxes.
Red is what I see while thinking about them;
White – seeing the demands, blue - after I've paid them."
The American agreed, "Peace of mind it mars.
It's the same with my flag - but I also see stars."

❧

A dinner for two is ME – N – U.

❧

*C*omposers had a meeting, a reporter wrote,
It's primary function was to compare their notes.

❧

"*M*iss Muffet was spoiled," I heard someone say,
It's because she always gets her own whey.

❧

*S*aid a wife, "I saw a mirror of exceptional value."
Said Hubby, "It's something that we should look into."

❧

A curt answer to the "Whys," not a lengthy clause,
It's simply a single word, the word is "Because."

❧

A LIFESTYLE PORTRAYAL From A TO Z

A maimed branch on a dogwood of unknown how -
A tree surgeon remarked, "It's simply a bough-wow."

To test Christmas tree bulbs needs little concentration.
It's easily accomplished by the process of illumination.

A crabby inspector is a cross examiner.

To operate a bakery a unique name is a must.
I think I would name it, "The Thin Upper Crust."

A well known drunk, so goes the rumor, is known to retain a rye sense of humor.

Beer drinking rabbits have their downs and ups.
The reason is simple, they're just full of hops.

Archery is not a perfect sport, it definitely has its drawbacks of sorts.

Why he didn't sign up for aerobics was no riddle.
The violinist insisted he was fit as a fiddle.

The surgeon refused to have his gown untied.
It was clearly evident, he was fit to be tied.

Conscience does no harm, it's a faults alarm.

The grapevine in every nation, a fruitful source of information.

A lad in rubber boots in a puddle was wandering.
One could frankly say that he was pondering.

Matches, need I mention, are a sure fire invention.

Babysitters don't impede, they have a crying need.

A pointless endeavor, no, it's not a stencil, it's trying to write with a broken pencil.

A meeting without chairs, one wouldn't call it a tea.
I'd decidedly say, "It's a standing committee."

I heard a patient say, "Can't stand sitting up."
The English vernacular doesn't seem to add up.

A mosquito, a conniver, a pesky skin diver.

A LIFESTYLE PORTRAYAL From A TO Z

An epitaph so oft spews forth with distinction.
Methinks, it's a mark of one's life's extinction.

Orthopedists are reputed to have what it takes.
To add to their fortune they get all the breaks.

An astute brain surgeon is compassionate and kind.
He routinely strives to have an open mind.

To attend an auction my wife kept on prodding.
We ended up getting many things for nodding.

What a garbage man did - he just flipped his lid.

A backseat driver annoys with carp – he's a person that's likened to a broken autoharp.

The church bell and clergy are not for hire.
What they have in common - they both inspire.

There are secrets in shoe stores - they never chew the rag.
Some have long tongues but they just never wag.

Said a frustrated ram who was quite in a stew,
"The whole long day I dream of ewe."

A determined snowplow will push, never sift.
One finds that eventually it gets the drift.

An inebriated golfer was weaving and conniving.
He eventually was charged for drinking while driving.

"Furniture disease," the doctor implores,
Is when a man's chest slips into his drawers.

Today's obstetrician with his manner and skill
Has in common with the stork, a very large bill.

A sense of ill humor provides room for rumor.

I heard this conversation between a dentist and his patient,-
"Had high temp, last week,- I just couldn't sleep,
I shivered and shook, I tried to count sheep."
"Did your teeth chatter when you were under the weather?"
"Well, I really don't know – we don't sleep together."

A LIFESTYLE PORTRAYAL From A TO Z

Two Elderly Campers

Mr. Holmes and Doctor Watson go on a camping trip.
They've seen scores of years but still think themselves hip.
They choose to climb a mountain that was somewhat steep.
They deftly set up tent then promptly fall asleep.
Hours later, Holmes awakens his illustrious friend,
"Watson, look at the sky, what thought does it blend?"
Watson sleepily replies, "I see millions of stars."
"Now, what does that tell you, aside from seeing Mars?"
"Astronomically speaking there are galaxies galore,
Time wise it appears to be a quarter past four.
Theologically it is evident that God is all powerful,
Meteorologically I've concluded, the morning will be beautiful.
And what do you see?" Holmes is silent for a moment;
"Watson, you idiot! - Our tent has been stolen!"

∼

A sense of gentle humor with its verbal contortions
Reduces people and problems to sensible proportions.

∼

As we walk the tightrope of life – to elude mental worry and strife,
A sense of humor is the long pole that gives floating balance to the soul.

∼

Said a diner in a café, "This soup's not fit to eat."
"Who told you," asked the waitress, so pert, cute and sweet.
"If you truly want to know," in a voice, somewhat mellow,
Retorted the upset diner, "It was a little swallow."

∼

An officer once stopped me while on patrol.
He asked for my license – 'must wear glasses,' he saw.
"But, officer," I stuttered, "I have my contacts."
"I don't care who you know – you're breaking the law."

∼

Go easy with your jokes – avoid deleterious pokes.

∼

A boy with no drink said to a boy with a drink,
"If I had a drink I would give it to you."
The boy with the drink said, "Why do you pout?
Can't you see I have one, what's the fussing about."

∼

At times you'll discover, some folk's sense of humor
Doesn't make any sense, it just vague rumor.

∼

*I*n paying his light bills he was late and defiant,
And so the power company wrote to their client.
"If you paid bills when due – we'd be delighted.
If you choose to delay - you'll be de-lighted."

*T*o Mike he announced that he lost his job.
"And how did that happen," Mike asked his friend Bob.
Bob briefly replied, "You know how foremen are,
They watch their men work then dash off to the bar."
Mike quickly interjected, "Why were you let go,
That certainly to me would be a big blow."
"I must truly confess, I'm not an artisan,
All the men thought that I was the foreman."

*Y*ou wonder why I'd rather relate funnies at the shore;
It's 'cause telling there the big breakers roar.

The Intolerable Big Shot

A bigoted big shot was admitted for a few days
To a local general hospital for some tests, not to laze.
He was extremely obnoxious – was a great big pain;
The nurses in attendance had good reason to complain.

One like him they hadn't seen this side of creation;
The head nurse decided to alter the situation.
One morning she walked in to have his temp taken.
She nudged him a few times, he was hard to awaken.

He held his lips tightly – he feigned to be mute,
"I'm sorry," said the nurse, "I'll be using the southern route."
To have his temp taken he was not too inclined,
But he finally turned over to bare his behind.

After the insertion, emphatically the nurse said,
"You must lie quietly and don't get out of bed!"
The nurse left the door open on her way out;
Irrationally he fretted, he did sputter and spout.

While passing through the hallway folk snickered while gawking;
They laughed hysterically as they kept on walking.
After waiting a long hour his doctor walked in.
He had on his face a wry, sheepish grin.

"Well, how are things going with my Lord Barrymore?"

"Haven't you ever seen a temp taken before?"

The doctor while laughing, "Yes, I have Bill." "Never have I seen it taken with a daffodil."

❧

A man leaving a café left a note without pay.
The proprietor said, "Joe, what does the note say?"
The simple note said, "I O U O 4 I 8 O."
"What does that mean, any idea Joe?"
The answer was simple – cash it didn't bring –
'I owe you nothing for I ate nothing.'

❧

*H*umor can be likened to one's needle and thread;
When used it can patch what's been inadvertently said.

❧

HYPOCRISY

*W*ho dares one thing, and another tell,
My heart detests him as the gates of hell.
-Alexander Pope

❧

*H*ypocrisy in the church, critics say is immense.
There is nothing so damaging as specious pretense.

❧

*H*ypocrisy will eventually hurt you; it's homage that vice pays to virtue.

❧

A pompous hypocrite never intends to turn into what he groundlessly pretends.

❧

*E*ven the hypocrite, righteousness admits; obviously that is why he tries to imitate it.

❧

*T*he hypocrite is unable Christian love impart,
While seeking to retain the world in his heart.

❧

IDEAS

*I*deas must work through the brains and the arms
of good and brave men, or they are not better than dreams.
-Emerson

❧

*D*on't signal good ideas a quick 'Bye, Bye,' instead, determine a significant try.

❧

Let's give our gray cells a determined buz-z.
The gleaming crown jewels are bright ideas.

To be successful let me give you a clue.
If ideas are to work you must work too.

Of relevant new ideas there's no shortage of innovators.
The pitiful shortage lies in accomplished creators.

Takes a singular idea, timely hurled, and a single action to move the world.

Instinct can configure, ideas pull the trigger.

You don't have to travel to Kampuchea;
Even a meek child can give you an idea.

IDLENESS - LEISURE - SLOTHFULNES

Idleness, the refuge of weak minds and the holiday of fools.
-Lord Chesterfield

Slothfulness and laziness can spell grim disaster;
Get down to brass tacks, you will rise much faster.

Idleness, so frequently and invariably reneges.
It's a nest into which mischief lays its eggs.

If idleness makes you feel you cannot make it,
You'll find that poverty will soon overtake it.

On idleness and slothfulness the Lord does frown;
One can't go to heaven on a bed of fluffy down.

A loafer is oft seen on many a busy street;
He's endeavoring to make both weekends meet.

Idleness, in verity is the enemy of the soul.
The foul nurse of sin can't make man whole.
Vile vagrancy abhor, honest labor do not shirk;
If the devil finds you idle he'll put you to work.

Idleness is an agency that can seriously endanger.
It will never conceive a viable money-changer.

At the end of each arm there's more than one finger.
To play life's tune, do not idly linger.

Idleness that's inert do not nurse; a purse that is empty is a curse.

Some folk can be likened to wheelbarrows, this dilemma I sadly regret.
So many of us have to be pushed, while others are easily upset.

The slothful man with time to burn doesn't give the world any light to discern.

Leisure to some is a lovely garment; for constant wear it is scanty raiment.

Idleness warps the mind, it puts you behind,
It's always inclined to put you in a bind,
And you will find it doesn't help mankind.

IGNORANCE

Ignorance is the night of the mind, but a night without moon or star.
-Confucius

It's a common thing for ignorance to demand,
And firmly denounce what it doesn't understand.

Indifference, intolerance, defiance and belligerence
Are frequently the result of deplorable ignorance.

Today's college fees are incredibly lacerant;
Costs are as great to be knowledgeable as ignorant.

In the presence of fools, temper your utterance;
Effectuate silence,- the best reply to ignorance.

Ignorance is oft credited as an attribute of youth.
It should be an incentive for the seeking of truth.

If you don't read but can you're an ignorant man.

Ignorance is a source of misery and vice, and so as a result so many pay a price.

So many choose to be ignorant, with needful learning they're bored.
Vital facts just cease to exist merely because they're ignored.

Ignorance is always a curable disease; treat it with knowledge, your life thereby ease.

☙

Knowledge is light, ignorance is blight, knowledge is treasure, ignorance lacks measure.

☙

ILLUMINATION

Nothing is great that doesn't illuminate.

☙

IMAGINATION

The human race is governed by its imagination.
-Napoleon Bonaparte

☙

Imagination equips us to illuminate, to see a reality we have yet to create.

☙

Imagination is one's sheltered reservoir; it's part and parcel of one's riches.
So very frequently I gladly discover, my intellect it charmingly bewitches.

☙

Imagination, an entity that a brain makes; it can stretch far but it never breaks.

☙

IMMORTALITY

After the resurrection of the body shall have taken place,
being set free from the condition of time, we shall enjoy eternal life,
with love ineffable and steadfastness without corruption.
-St. Augustine

☙

Immortality need not be a solar myth; Christ is what we need to reach it with.

☙

IMPATIENCE

The impatience we show is unnecessary and unwise.
It's a negative attribute that we can't minimize.
The symptoms of impetuosity we can never disguise.
I wish it were possible against it to immunize.
It's a nullifying characteristic that so many despise,
Nor can it be used to gently tranquilize.
We must not show anger when we try to socialize.
We must prudently watch the words we utilize.
It is a distinct quality that we can't compromise,

And it's a mortal feature that no one would prize.
It's a trait that no one would ever idolize,
Or for that matter, would they ever eulogize.

IMPRESSION

Those first impressions are lasting impressions,
Particularly when made in cemented depressions.

IMPROVEMENT

Where we cannot invent, we can at least improve.
-Colton

Be it for your children, yourself, or your spouse,
The room for improvement is the largest in your house.

To improve this old world some strive to create pelf.
Make certain you're involved in improving your own self.

INCOMPETENCE

Incompetence knows no obstacle; ability is an intimate miracle.

INDIFFERENCE

Indifference opens more doors to the enemy than does tyranny.
-Edwin McNeill Poteat

Indifference toward evil can result in an upheaval.

Indifference opens gates to the devil, our enemy.
For a decisive decision, prayer is the remedy.

INDOLENCE - LAZINESS

It is the common fate of the indolent, to see their rights become a prey to the active.
-John P. Curran

A LIFESTYLE PORTRAYAL From A TO Z

Said a teacher about indolent Clem, "He has great gifts - too lazy to unwrap them."

No idleness, no laziness, no procrastination, can produce an amazing exclamation.

Said a teacher to an indolent student, the latter, his studies he routinely neglected,
"The afternoon invariably, intuitively knows, what the listless morning never expected."

Some folk are unbelievably lazy, most certainly they do drive one crazy.
They continually try to impress, while waiting for the escalator to success.

He had great desire for physical repose and mental serenity, so laziness he chose.

She buys him loafers, as well as leisure slacks,
Then says he's lazy, his indolence she attacks.

It is said that leisure is prone to corrupt, so why should humans honest labor interrupt?

The successful usually do what has to be done.
The lazy, the dawdlers, to excuses succumb.

Shiftless people, it does appear, seldom get into notorious high gear.

INDUSTRY

Hard workers are usually honest; industry lifts them above temptation.
-Christian Bovee

Industry spotlights the character of people, be it winter, summer or fall;
Some roll up their sleeves, some turn up their noses, and some don't answer the roll-call.

From industry and duty I must never think scooting.
Big shots are the result of little shots that keep shooting.

About man's achievements and his brilliant success,
Much has been printed and scribed with pen.
The only creature that succeeded by sitting, is the lowly fowl, the matronly hen.

To be actively industrious is inordinately sublime;
Backbone beats wishbone - overtakes it every time.

"Go to the ant thou sluggard, consider her ways and be wise."
Man wasn't created for slumber; industry is where success lies.

"Earning a living," a miserable phrase; "Earning and living," a more intimate phase.

A LIFESTYLE PORTRAYAL From A TO Z

Ants have a reputation for being industrious.
They're always at picnics, the concept is preposterous.

INEQUITY

Some will always be above others.
Destroy the inequality today and it will appear again tomorrow.
-Emerson

There are so many gross inequities - a salient one may I candidly reveal,
When the jockey gets the venerated silver, how does the aggressive stallion feel?

INFLATION

Inflation is the enemy of the aged and those who expect to grow old.
-Bernard Baruch

One reason why inflation has successfully come to roost,
All segments of our society keep giving it a big boost.

During critical, inflationary times, spending habits we must try to heed.
It's a period when a sizeable nest-egg is prone to turn into chicken feed.

INFLUENCE

Character is formed, not by laws, commands and decrees,
but by quiet influence and personal guidance.
-Marion L. Burton

In influencing, example is not the main thing, philosophers tell us, it's the only thing.

Influence is not measured by the distance it covers,
But by the amount of malevolence it smothers.

Influence can be likened to a savings bank account;
The more you use it, the less the amount.

Influences are oscillations, quivering in space.
What vibes do you send to this our human race?

INITIATIVE - SELF-ASSURANCE

Initiative consists of doing the right thing without being told.
-Irving Mack

❧

Initiative is your own self-starter button.
It's something you create, not from someone gotten.

❧

There is an old adage, a mental bent you must form,
"If you light your own fire you'll be twice as much warm."

❧

If you're to leave footprints in the sand of time,
Don't drag your feet, you must aim to climb.

❧

People who have initiative never have to be told.
You'll find invariably they're worth their weight in gold.

❧

This verily is the sole, solemn truth, for certain it is not a mere silly prank.
If we were all automatic self-starters, our boss wouldn't have to be a veritable crank.

❧

Those with initiative are of a singular mold; initiative is doing without being told.

❧

Self-assurance and unfettered initiative, one must never shirk.
All elated exhilaration comes from courage and work.

❧

INSOMNIA

If you can't sleep, don't count sheep - talk to the Shepherd, you will be heard.

❧

INSPIRATION

So long as man still has inspiration and the will to go on,
he still exemplifies youth.
-Maurice J. Lui

❧

Embody this bit of fresh inspiration, it won't produce profuse perspiration.
You must boldly tell yourself, "There are tens of thousands
No more intelligent than thee.
They've triumphed o'er problems that are considerably more difficult
Than are those now confronting me."

❧

When you have on your hands a bonfire of frustration,
Forget not to take from it a spark of inspiration.

INSTINCT

Subtle instinct is not totally blind, it's the perceptive eye of the mind.

Instinct is intelligence, it frowns on belligerence.

You'll lead a rich life if your instinct is rife.

INSULT

If insult you catapult, you won't exult – could result in tumult.

"I hear you've been taunting the dean again;
For immediate expulsion the dye has been cast!"
"To call him a fish was not my wish - I casually said, 'That's our Dean,' real fast."

Unadulterated comedy is oft difficult; never allow it to be stinging insult.

INTEGRITY

To give real service you must add integrity.
-Donald A. Adams

Though it may be at times unpleasant, unpopular, perhaps full of plight,
Unimpeachable integrity demands that we consistently do what is right.

Unbending integrity, a marvelous virtue, it leaves its indelible mark.
Exceptional character is evidence clear, what that person is in the dark.

A person of integrity has nothing to hide.
He has nothing to retract 'cause he hasn't lied.

Integrity without knowledge is weak; knowledge with integrity we must seek.

There is no greater legacy than unassailable integrity.

I would give no thought what others thought of me,
If I could pass on to posterity integrity.

*I*ntegrity can be likened to fine textured cloth.
When a thread has been pulled, it's integrity is lost.

*I*ntegrity has no need of rules, nor does it require special tools.

*Y*our innate integrity is at stake if you don't keep promises you make.

*I*ndisputable integrity inevitably pays; at times there seem to be long delays.

*V*eritable integrity, a true mark of a celebrity.

INTELLIGENCE

*A*ll men see the same objects, but all men do not equally understand them.
Intelligence is the tongue that discerns and tastes them.
-Thomas Traherne

*T*here is no limit to intelligence, likewise, to primitive ignorance.

*T*o all my dear friends, be you young or old, rid your neck bands I sincerely beck.
How intelligent can you be, wearing a snug noose around your neck?

*Y*ou must read widely, intelligence you will bind.
You can't think clearly on a shallow, vacant mind.

*A*lways keep intellect in season; never use rudeness for reason.

INTENTIONS

*W*hen any great design thou dost intend, think on the means, the manner and the end.
-Sir John Denham

*G*ood intentions are totally mortal, unquestionably they're perishable things.
If they're not brought to full fruition, you'll find they're just spent innings.

*T*he smallest act of prevention is greater than the grandest intention.

*Y*our prospects are bright if your intentions are right.

INTERRUPTIONS

Control your interruptions with a solid point question.
A non-threatening query shouldn't cause an objection.
How can I help you? What brings you around?
For you what can I do? Such questions are sound.
Point questions transfer the ownership of conversation
To the obtrusive interrupter to justify his transgression.

✌

The insidious tendency to arbitrarily interrupt
A friendly conversation is bound to corrupt.
As a startling result an argument may erupt,
Especially when one inclines to be rudely abrupt.

✌

Do you interrupt or finish their sentences?
For certain, not before a sentence commences.

✌

INTERVENTION

Those who in quarrels interpose, must often wipe a bloody nose.
-John Gay

✌

God intervenes in the affairs of men by kindly invitation, by Spirit and Pen.

✌

INTOLERANCE

The actions of a bigot are easy to trace; he's the man who slams his mind in your face.

✌

Intolerance causes a great deal sorrow; we continue to have it today and the morrow.

✌

Unchecked intolerance is a bitter curse; do tell me my friend, what could be worse?

✌

Intolerance has been an irritable curse throughout the ages of our universe.

✌

INTUITION - INSIGHT

Intuition is a gift that enables a person
To quickly arrive at a decision,
That's incredible, impeccable, infallible, irreversible;
It oft comes without aid of reason.

✌

Intuition is a strange power of insight that enables a woman to guess right.

A woman's intuition is the greatest by far; it can be defined as feminine radar.

More often then not the man with insight is usually inclined to do things right.

INVITATION

All of us love to be asked to go,
Even though our intention is to refuse with a "No."

INTRODUCTION

Our next guest speaker is in the preaching biz;
He needs no introduction, he knows who he is.

IRREVERENCE

Particularly do avoid articulating broad ignorance,
Arrogance, malevolence, and blasphemous irreverence.

JEST

The jest loses its point when he who makes it is the first to laugh.
-Johann Von Schiller

A good wife laughs at her husband's jokes and tricks,
Not because they're clever, but because she is.

At times wise words are spoken in subtle jest.
On the other hand, foolish ones are spoken in earnest.

JOY

Weeping may endure for the night, but joy comes in the morning.
-Old Testament: Psalms, 30:5

Spirit-piercing joy doesn't have to be sung.
It dwells in the heart, more so than the tongue.

In this world the joys that are prone to last, "Are the tender shadows our sorrows cast."

Tranquil pleasures are oft the strongest - they are the ones that last the longest.

Joy is a byproduct of obedience; our actions give us sound credence.

JUDGMENT

Call it astuteness or shrewdness - perception, insight, discernment.
People complain of their memory, few of their unmerciful judgment.

The way to judge most celebrated people is to observe how they usually treat,
Those who do them absolutely no good, and those with whom they routinely compete.

Our senses don't deceive us, it's our judgment that grieves us.

Never be too hasty to judge others' factions.
You may not know what's behind their actions.

Don't ever prejudge nor keep a grudge.

You can't judge a horse by the beauty of its harness,
Likewise, a man, though he may join Kiwanis.

The prudent judge by what they see, the foolish by what they hear at tea.
God judges us not by what others say, but by what we do, what our lives convey.

Consider judging the ordinary man by his thought-provoking questions,
Rather than by his shabby appearance, and his vague, speculative intentions.

For judicious selection use intuitive introspection.

JUSTICE - INJUSTICE

Justice is truth in action.
-Benjamin Disraeli

Because passions of men don't always conform
To dictates of reason, justice becomes norm.

In today's plutocratic society our criminal justice is totally upended.
In the old days, 'twas the guilty criminal, not the sentence that was suspended.

Inordinate justice has a savory flavor; it is what we get when it's in our favor.

The justice system so many will fail; good common sense should always prevail.

To do an injustice is more disgraceful than it is to suffer, though it be painful.

Justice is better when it prevents, rather than punishes – makes sound sense.

Whatever is powerful must be just; whatever is just must be powerful.

KINDNESS

A kindness loses its grace by being noised abroad.
Who desires it to be remembered should forget it.
-Pierre Corneille

How great and beautiful a day can be, when your angelic kindness touches me.

Sometimes the best witness is thoughtful loving kindness.

Kindness wins battles that force and wisdom lose,
So temper interaction with compassion – ne'er abuse.

The cloak of human kindness I must never eschew.
He's obviously ill clothed who is bare of this virtue.

At times may your kindness embody some blindness.

He was graciously kind, he would take the pain
Of holding an umbrella over a duckling in the rain.

Kindness does not hurt the tongue; with compassion no one gets stung.

Kindness is envisioned in so many, many ways.
It's poetry of the soul, a melody in trying days.
It's a bright, golden chain binding society together,
It's a fountain of gladness in sun or stormy weather.
We all know the pleasure of receiving a pleasant look,
A greeting, a helping hand, or the gift of a good book.
Kind hearts are a coronet, their orchids in a bowl,
They produce lovely images in the mirror of a soul.
A kind gesture can be made at so little expense,
Gratitude in return is one's recompense.
Anonymous

A LIFESTYLE PORTRAYAL From A TO Z

Feelings of love leave you a debtor; acts of kindness are inevitably better.

Bear this in mind, you can always be kind.

Hindrances to kind deeds, a cold heart and cold feet;
Oh, yes, there's another, a comfortable soft seat.

Kindness induces morality; the latter, practical liberality.

Assuredly it can be said of Boaz, he obviously was filled with kindness.
Before he contemplated marriage, it's recorded that he was Ruthless.

The devil doesn't care what kindness we convey
As long as he knows it won't be today.

As children of God, we must be of one accord.
To be absent from the Spirit we can ill afford.
Kindly traits of character are imparted to all
Who accept Christ Jesus, Savior and Lord.

KNOWLEDGE

It is the providence of knowledge to speak, and it is the privilege of wisdom to listen.
  -Oliver Wendell Holmes

Knowledge is pleased that it knows the score.
Wisdom is content that it knows a lot more.

My friend, how do you your extensive knowledge handle?
"A candle loses nothing by lighting another candle."

One may go to college and obtain much knowledge,
But he'll lack satisfaction if there is no action.

As knowledge increases, one's ignorance decreases.

The person who knows what he's told must know
That so many of the things he is told aren't so.

To acquire superb knowledge one must diligently study.
To obtain sound wisdom observation must be a buddy.

Knowledge is oft free - some ask for a retainer.
Regardless of the choice, you supply the container.

A LIFESTYLE PORTRAYAL From A TO Z

Do not worry about a crowded college, it won't in any way drain all knowledge.

Share your knowledge, espouse true morality,
Be involved in giving of means and congeniality.
It's a way to gain on this earth immortality.

The person who knows "how," will always have a job.
The person who knows "why," the boss's job will rob.

It's not the "I. Q.", it's the singular "I will"
That counts the most for knowledge to instill.

Vociferous people say what they think, their tongue with brain they oft do not link.

Put not profound knowledge on indefinite probation.
You must keep the "U" in your formal education.

Wonderment is so oft the root of knowledge; do read plenty, in or out of college.

Knowledge is light - ignorance is blight.

A brain becomes a mind on attending a college,
Providing it's fortified with abundant profound knowledge.

Knowledge burns up error, releasing light of truth;
A truth that is paramount for adults and youth.

The more you know, the more you owe.

Exfoliate your unproven obsolete ideas as the hardy eucalyptus sheds its old bark.
Make unique knowledge and practical wisdom your singular, symbolic, insured trademark.

Knowledge is a treasure, practice is its measure.

Be cognizant of this fact in obtaining profound knowledge,
'You must know a lot more than what you learned in college.'

This one thing I know for sure, sure does not always endure.

LANGUAGE

While struggling with the English language, with words like, tough, though and bough,
I couldn't see much rhyme or reason, to pronounce them I didn't know how.

A LIFESTYLE PORTRAYAL From A TO Z

And then, to add to my frustration, this conundrum lexicographers should address,
I saw in a newspaper headline, "BAZAAR IS PRONOUNCED SUCCESS."

Why is "Psychic" spelled with a "P?" The English language is a dilly!
Many a teacher will have to agree that it pcertainly pseems pso psilly.

Discrepancies in English so abundantly abound;
"Phonetics" should be spelled the way it sounds.

"*He* was much bent on seeing her" –
"Merely the sight of him doubled her up."
How can we learn what's truly meant?
I think our language is totally corrupt.

Who put the butter in butterfly? What was the reason, tell me, why?

Every man's language is an index of his mind.
One must always keep it compassionate and kind.

Our language like linen looks best when it's clean.
Never use language outrageously obscene.
If it's truly gracious we'll know it's not mean.

Our language, I would say, is with odd words piquing.
Frequently, you'll agree, they are figuratively speaking.
Young sprouts, our teens, feel their oats, full of beans.
Some men are just tops, others, full of hops.
The peppery smart cookies aren't always rookies.
Our salty, crusty oldsters aren't softies like custard,
Using beans and noodles to cut the sharp mustard.
The salt-of-the-earth eggs, so often take the cake;
They know their onions, they aren't half-baked.
Their lives, bowls of cherries, they are apples of our eye,
They are toast of our town, not pie in the sky.
-Anonymous

We're using sign language, undoubtedly, more and more,
We sign for about everything that we buy in the store.

Though dressed in top hat, white tie and tails,
Rhetorical, colorful language so frequently assails.

With command of language, spoken or written,
Many a humble heart has been mercilessly smitten.

A LIFESTYLE PORTRAYAL From A TO Z

"Johnny, write a sentence with the word 'fascinate.'
"My coat has nine buttons, but I can only fasten eight."

Do You Remember?

Remember, when HIPPY meant large hips,
And a TRIP meant travel in cars, planes and ships,
And BE-IN meant simply existing somewhere,
And FIX was a verb that meant mend or repair?

When BIRDS were winged creatures like robins and swallows,
And GROOVY meant furrowed with ridges and hollows?
When CHICKEN meant poultry and a BAG was a sack,
And JUNK was trash, castaways and bric-a-brac?

When COOL meant temperature de terra firma,
And HEAVY had reference to one's avoirdupois?
When FUZZ was a substance, so fluffy like lint,
And BREAD came from bakeries and not from the mint?

When GRASS was a ground cover, normally green,
And NEAT meant well organzed, tidy and clean?
When HANG-UP was something you did with the phone,
And a ROLL was a bun, and ROCK was a stone?

When HOOKED was what grandmother's rug might have been,
And POT was a vessel for cooking things in?
When RIPPED frequently meant the state of one's togs,
And SPACED had marked reference to a gear, and its cogs?

When a SWINGER was someone who would swing on a swing,
And a PAD was a sort of a soft, cushy thing?
When TOUGH described meat so unyielding to chew,
And MAKING A SCENE was a rude thing to do?

When PEACHY was fruit flavor, usually eaten with cream,
And PIG was a farm animal, by some deemed unclean?
When TURKEY was the big bird on the old homestead,
And CRASH was an accident and not going to bed?

When SCRATCH meant you itched and SPLIT was to share,
And BLEW-IT would fill your balloon up with air?
When a RAT was a rodent and SAP came from trees,
And FRUIT was grapefruit, and oranges, if you please?

A LIFESTYLE PORTRAYAL From A TO Z

When FAROUT meant distances akin to the North Pole,
And OUT OF THIS WORLD, mystic regions untold?
When HANG-OUT was Mom's method of drying the clothes,
And WEED was what would ruin a garden's prized rose?

When HIP was the big bone in the elderly so oft broken,
And DIG meant hard work, not lazin' and smokin'?
When HEAT was the result of the sun's rays beating down,
And GET-UP wasn't clothes that made you look like a clown?

When a SUCKER was candy that would last all day,
And a PANSY, a pert flower that bloomed brightly in May?
When GAS, a contrivance used in a past war,
And THREADS were for mending those swank trousers you tore?

When a DRIP was a sign that a new washer was due,
And a HUNK was a big chunk that you broke off to chew?
When TURN-ON meant switching the off switch to on,
And TIGHT described clothing with no room to yawn?

When STACKED was a method for piling things high,
And a TART, dainty pastry, a tasty mini pie?
When GROSS meant twelve dozen, not something very crude,
And STREAKING, variable striping, not dashing in the nude?

Remember when words, were once sensible and serious
Were not making FREAK SCENES like PSYCHODELERIOUS?
It's GROOVY, MAN, GROOVY, but English it's not,
Methinks that our language has gone straight to POT.
-Several lines, including the last stanza by an anonymous writer
were the inspiration for a much larger, "Do You Remember?"

❧

LAUGHTER

*L*aughter is the sun that drives winter from the human face.
-Victor Hugo

❧

*M*ay your laughter always be in season, with an absence of ulterior reason.

❧

*L*aughter, a tranquilizer with no side effect;
A wholesome entity we should never reject.

❧

*I*t stimulates endorphins, hearty laughter is fulfilling.
Another side benefit, it's moments we're not killing.

❧

A LIFESTYLE PORTRAYAL From A TO Z

A hearty, merry laugh is like sunshine in your house.
The brightest of sunbeams is a good, happy spouse.

*M*ake certain that your laughter leads not to sin.
If it's spiked with kindness it's surely bound to win.

*B*etter vigor and health can be real if you work and laugh a great deal.

*H*earty laughter does good like a medicine; to readily employ her don't be reticent.

*W*holesome laughter can relieve one's grief,
Generous giving gives the needy relief, libelous lying, scornful disbelief.

*I*n stone this thought duly cast, "The person who laughs heartily will last."

*D*elightful laughter is decidedly communication;
A merited side benefit, endorphin elevation.

*I*n this world there should be for laughter a great thirst.
We all should laugh at our own selves first.

*U*se laughter when you can, it's cheap medicine for man.

*M*an's singular qualities can't be kept under hat.
His character is revealed by what he laughs at.

*G*od is the Creator of wholesome laughter; I trust we will have it in the hereafter.

*T*here's a thing about laughter that I think is sublime,
One cannot worry and laugh the same time.

*I*t's totally amazing what a good laugh can do;
Tears and fears its inclined to subdue.

*L*augh at yourself now and then, season your day with wit;
Pleasurable, effervescent humor, one can't live without it.

*J*ust imagine in heaven, no disease outrageous;
Laughter, the only thing that will be contagious.

LAWS – LAWLESSNESS

*L*aw is a pledge that a citizen of a state will do justice to one another.
-Aristotle

A LIFESTYLE PORTRAYAL From A TO Z

God's law pinpoints our problem; His grace provides the solution.

God gave us His Ten Commandments; He didn't accommodate with amendments.

Serving God under law is duty; under love it's delight and beauty.

God's high standards for behavior are eternal, we must disregard the devil's derision.
This includes His Ten Commandments, they are not open for man's revision.
We as his children must acknowledge and obey; we must not delay that supreme decision.

"We're saved by grace, obedience isn't important,
The law has been done away with," many say.
In the Scripture there are three hundred and fifty texts
That admonish and command we obey.

Many sincere Christians choose to serve God, they obey his statutes explicitly,
But then there are those who clearly disobey, they serve in an advisory capacity.

It's not what I think, and it's not what you think,
It's what God thinks and says.

The Ten Commandment tablets were given to man.
They were meant to be kept by every human clan.
By following these directions we could save a lot,
And there wouldn't be need for 'med' tablets to be bought.

The Ten Commandments are God's supreme voice.
They were never meant to be multiple choice.

Laws like clothes should be made to fit the people they serve and those meant to hit.

Paul's law we've all heard before, "You cannot fall off the floor."

There's a rule that we all should hang on to but fast.
It's Dan Rather's rule – "The first thing is to last."

The noblest of rules that we should mold, is the golden rule, not the rule of gold.

In confirming God's law within your heart, remembering it is a preliminary start.

Law makers should not be law breakers.

A smoking section in our restaurants is frequently the local rule;
Never forget there's a voiding section in the local swimming pool?

Ignorance of the law, most reluctantly agree,
Does not prevent lawyers from collecting a fee.

Some people would believe in supreme law and order,
If they were involved in giving the order.

These words by Cicero, to our lives they're a key,
"We're in bondage to the law in order to be free."

As a matter of moral sense in our human race,
The law of the majority doesn't have any place.

Obey the law, never abuse it, it doesn't take talent, anyone can do it.

"An eye for an eye," makes both parties blind.
It's an old law that isn't very kind; to put it quite bluntly, it blows my mind.

The transgression of the law comes from within;
The eye and the heart are the agents of sin.

An officer once stopped me while on his patrol.
He asked for my license, 'must wear glasses' he saw.
"But officer," I stuttered, "I have my contacts."
"I don't care who you know – you're breaking the law."

Rash lawlessness prevails - some may class me a bigot.
It's because there's rarely an arrest for the wicked.

A good rule to follow, a tenet I long chose – "Never open a box that you didn't close."

LEADERSHIP - SUPERVISION

Reason and calm judgment, the qualities specially belonging to a leader.
-Tacitus

Top leaders never force individuals to conform.
They invite them on a journey, they continually inform.

How are you doing? Does your leadership inspire?
You're only as good as the people you hire.

The essence of leadership is to have focused vision.
It must also be void of wavering indecision.

A LIFESTYLE PORTRAYAL From A TO Z

If your desire is to rightly lead, you must be willing to daily read.

❧

Wise leaders are optimists, they have a strong hope.
They audit their gut feelings with an effective telescope.

❧

If stationary you remain, you won't reach the mark.
You can't lead to light if you stay in the dark.

❧

A sign of an excellent supervisor, he's one who can step on your toes,
Not making a mess of your shoeshine, and not dislocating your nose.

❧

Do lead or follow or get out of the way.
You'll find that it's more expedient that way.

❧

A leader has conviction that dreams can be achieved;
Knowledge and energy to accomplish is perceived.

❧

Great leadership does not adopt opinion polls.
It molds persuasion, solutions are its goals.

❧

Sound leadership is a combination of logistics and character.
Of the two, the latter is the greater benefactor.

❧

With keen intuition and keeping in touch,
A smart supervisor can prevent a huge botch.

❧

The burdens of leadership are great, some day you may be an emissary.
There is this one thing to remember, be unpopular when it is necessary.

❧

Leadership, assuredly, isn't about being wrong,
It's about being right - it's about being strong.

❧

When we're determined to lead, pertinent sage advice we should heed.

❧

Leaders are able – they think they're capable.

❧

Leaders are readers, they're not impeders.

❧

Good supervision is like a shot in the arm, without the sharp needle causing alarm.

❧

LEARNING

Much learning shows how little mortals know.
-Edward Young

❧

A LIFESTYLE PORTRAYAL From A TO Z

We all learn gradually by simple daily living;
Our learning, 'taint complete if we haven't learned giving.

Wide-eyed attention cultivates retention.

To keep on learning should be one's yearning.

Learning is an indispensable investment required.
In a knowledgeable age it should be desired.

First learn the meaning of what you would say,
Lest inadvertently your integrity you betray.

Do learn to use a handsaw and hammer, and take speech lessons to overcome stammer.

You must make an effort to listen intently,
For often opportunity will knock very softly.

You can't possibly pick a peck of pickled peppers,
Peppers must be picked prior to being pickled.
Likewise, you won't learn if learning you spurn;
For knowledge to be trickled, the mind must be tickled.

If you're always ready to learn, the more you'll eventually earn.

One must learn and fully realize, that bigger may not be better,
And to travel considerably faster, isn't necessarily the latter.

Only the stubbornly resolute, overcome the obstacles of learning.
Invariably the curious will learn, they'll be involved in earning.

The things worth learning, be it summer, spring or fall,
Are the things we haven't learned after we knew it all.

Enrique Solari, uttered words so sublime, "Oh, that one could learn, to learn in time."

You cannot learn from what you haven't read.
You cannot injure with what you haven't said.

"From this calm day, what freely did I learn?"
Must ask, "What have I given in return?"

There are men who learn by prudent observation,
An enlightened minority go to library book shelves,

Then there are those who choose to micturate
Discreetly on the electric fence themselves.

≈

*L*earn to see in another's calamity, the ills to avoid in one's incipient insanity.

≈

LEGACY

A man cannot leave a better legacy to the world than a well-educated family.
-Thomas Scott

≈

*A*fter years of hard work and rolled up sleeve,
What kind of a legacy will your life leave?

Will it improve lives or will it deceive - what benefit for others will it achieve?

Will it bring sunshine or will it much grieve - will it dishearten or joyously relieve?

Will it to someone grant a reprieve - what will your loved ones in it perceive?

As the years go by, what will it retrieve - will it to others noble thoughts conceive?

Will it disquiet and violently upheave, or will it calm and eradicate peeve?

Will it cause someone to underachieve, or will it explicitly direction weave?

Will it inspire to pilfer and thieve, or will it compel one to be on the qui vive?

Will it distress or give cause to believe – will it cause brothers and sisters to cleave?

Will it cause a life to be but a sleave,
[Sleave- tangled thread.}
Or will it protect, be a shield and a greave?
{Greave – piece of armour.}

Will it distress or give cause to believe –
Will it encourage brothers and sisters to cleave?

When the Good Lord returns, will it bring in a sheave,
Or will it, said and done, be a sad recitative?

≈

LIBERALITY

Frugality is good if liberality is joined with it.
 -William Penn

To be in the position of practicing liberality,
Consistently begin with exercising frugality.

We're never so generous, never quite so nice,
As when we're liberally giving others sound advice.

LIBERTY

He that would make his own liberty secure
must guard even his enemy from oppression.
 -Thomas Paine

It's easy to take your liberty for granted,
When you have never for it lamented.

A rocket scientist you don't have to be
To appreciate the blessings of precious liberty.

Liberty can be lost with cynical complacence;
To maintain your freedom, honor utmost vigilance.

You really can't have true freedom, my brother,
Unless you are willing to give it to another.

A LIFESTYLE POTPOURRI OF 'WISDOMS' PER SE

Your lifestyle is the standard of your life's profile.

What a great way to start a new day! Being able to wake up, to God humbly pray,
To get out of bed, to take a hot spray, to trimly dress up, with breakfast tank up,
To happily and energetically travel life's way.

A lovely sincere smile in your idyllic lifestyle is always worthwhile.

If you truly observe the benign rules of life,
Be compassionate to all, avoiding vile strife;

A LIFESTYLE PORTRAYAL From A TO Z

If you're temperate in action, your victuals and drink,
No gluttonous delight, you'll always be in the pink.

May your lifestyle speak, never let it shriek,
And continually may it be exclusively unique.

You are a distinct package with a special label on it.
On your unique parcel, what ribbons are there on it?

If you don't place a value on your God-given life,
Don't expect someone to raise the bidding price.

If you sit around the house, you certainly won't arrive.
The bee that makes honey doesn't hang around the hive.

In golf as in life, I love the inference,
It's the follow-through that makes the big difference.

Instead of living for human acclaim, resolve to do all in Jesus name.

The human spirit need not be paralyzed; if you are breathing dreams can be realized.

Whether you are near or be it far, where you arrive at there you are.

Some folk aren't able to forget, grievances they hide in deep thought.
They say, "I've buried the hatchet," simultaneously, they mark the hidden spot.

The fleeting past is but a guidepost - can't be reckoned as a hitching post -
Your immortal future is uppermost.

A life that's idyllic is never, yawned into being with a wish,
Nor are the hungry ever fed with an exotic empty dish.

Nothing but sunshine makes a desert – nothing but study makes an introvert.

We talk of independence, oh what vain folly!
We're dependent on each other, life's meant to be jolly.

Hindsight is wisdom forever; you must admit that it's clever.

Your porch attracts papers while you're away - just like a new tie, the soup of the day.

Unfortunately I came from a 'well-to-do' family,
May sound like a paradox, well, not necessarily.

A LIFESTYLE PORTRAYAL From A TO Z

In making a request, Mom would say to her Sonny,
"Well, to do that we haven't the money."

❧

*F*our things don't return, the word that is spoken,
Time past, an only chance, and the promise that is broken.

❧

*G*reat men continue to live though they die, but on death, for fame one mustn't rely.

❧

A wife can keep springtime in her loving husband's eye,
Wearing a lovely flower in her hair.
By supplying that flower, he'll keep springtime in her heart,
And she'll always be his maiden fair.

❧

*L*ongfellow, did disclose, "Joy and repose, slam the door on the doctor's nose."

❧

A large hollow building echoes all sounds; a mind that is vacant goes out of bounds.

❧

*D*o make changes in your lifestyle; more compassion should be unfurled.
Be the mutation you want to see in this hero-worshipping world.

❧

*T*o avoid old age be a tiger in a cage,
Outrageously overeating, be always in a meeting,
Be grossly overweight, always eating very late,
Be like a Trojan working, vacations always shirking,
And forever worrying, smoking and drinking.

❧

*H*igh speed can spell despicable disaster.
Why then would you choose to drive much faster?

❧

*L*ife is love, it's celestially sacred, and so it should be spiritually-mated.

❧

*S*leeping all night, having a good rest; the moment I wake up I find is the best.

❧

*W*hatever your boat - strive to stay afloat.

❧

*L*ive your LIFE, make it substantial; success is living up to a lasting potential;
A habitual ritual - to be highly effectual, 'tis best that it be incredibly intellectual.

❧

*T*he way spinning planets revolve around the sun,
Our lives should revolve around the Infinite One.

❧

*N*ot only communion and loving embraces, nor is it just having plenty of cash.
It's having three meals and place to lay head, and it's remembering to take out the trash.

❧

A LIFESTYLE PORTRAYAL From A TO Z

It takes more than shoeshine to give a man polish.
It takes more than charity for poverty to abolish.

❧

Efficiency in situ makes some folk hate you.

❧

The horn of plenty, how true, comes from the auto behind you.

❧

From animals have you wondered what difference a man makes?
It's the amount of medications that today's man takes.

❧

Before prescribing 'meds' I take this position,
Nature, time and patience can be one's best physician.

❧

The hardest thing to give is "give-in;" it's bound to prevent getting kicked in the shin.

❧

I have this feeling in this land of plenty, one should die content without owing a penny.
The trick is how to dismantle all riches, and how to appease all relatives' wishes.

❧

Do pay your bills, anxiety it stills.

❧

Take time to joyously marvel at the wonder of an infant's arrival.

❧

Spend not your brief life on vain pleasure and a casket;
Expend it on something that will far outlast it.

❧

A full sixty percent of death is eat, this flabby avoirdupois I've just got to beat.
Putting on extra pounds I must not repeat, on blubbered tummy and my big fat seat.

❧

'Eat,' a big portion of certain grim death; frequently it's the path to one's last breath.

❧

Tarnished is the man who builds his name on the unfortunate events of another's fame.

❧

Two it takes to start a quarrel, one can stop it, this is moral.

❧

Men's faces get characterized, women's faces get wrinkles;
Most men get mesmerized with the twinkles above the wrinkles.

❧

An eager person would gladly take his turn
Of caring for a fire where there's money to burn.

❧

Before hearing his lecture on his philosophy of life,
I would like to hear how he treats his children and wife.

❧

While cooking, many chefs constantly nibble in haste.
They're oblivious to the fact, frequent taste makes waist.

❧

A LIFESTYLE PORTRAYAL From A TO Z

A mule can't kick when a load he is pulling, neither can you and I, to pull let's be willing.

Always do your best at work or at bat; no goal is achieved that is better than that.

To ultimately become you have to overcome.

Nothing is more useful to the growth of one's worth
Than the contribution one makes to good mother earth.

Be your own self, be qualified; take hold of yourself, be dignified.

Don't put a question mark where God has put a period.

A lifestyle high-five makes one much longer survive;
But, no one, truly no one gets out of life alive.

It truly matters not how long you live, what matters is what to mankind you give.

Assertively never fail to read incoming mail.

You can't spell "brothers" without including "others."

By the time that you think you can make ends meet,
Someone move the ends, they disappear or retreat.

Be like a postage stamp, this maxim I share,
'Firmly stick to one thing until you arrive there.'

Determine to feed a stranger's parking meter;
Do good serendipitously, of beneficence be a repeater.

There's one thing in life you must fully understand,
If you can't face the music you won't lead the band.

You won't reach first base if you don't join the race.

Never let drive, ambition and expediency get in your way of compassion and decency.

When you sit on the beach - God isn't out of reach.

You'll never succeed relaxing making wishes.
Get to work and make a net if your desire is to catch fishes.

If it's not your desire that your merit be known,
Acknowledge what others o'er the years have sown.

A LIFESTYLE PORTRAYAL From A TO Z

There is no need for a pilgrimage, for one to display the right image.

≈

If with your close friends you want to have pull,
Return borrowed car with the gas tank full.

≈

If we don't have within us that which is above us,
It's likely we'll yield to the pressures around us.

≈

When meeting someone of humble, lowly fame,
Extend your right hand and give them your name.

≈

What am I doing, for Heaven's sake? For Heaven's sake, what are you doing?

≈

In the journey of life, to you I appeal, ask God to handle the steering wheel;
And I might add, one thing you must heed, there's more to life than increasing its speed.

≈

More and more, we as a people perfect, should ask ourselves repeatedly the question,
"If we are part of the challenging problem, why can't we be part of the elusive solution?"

≈

Life is so precious, savor each sip; express your gratitude while enjoying the trip.

≈

For many the high cost of living is due to the cost of high living.

≈

Expect to have blisters, when all is said and done,
If your desire is to retain an honorable place in the sun.

≈

Life has its ups and its trying downs too.
Some days you're the pigeon, on others the statue.

≈

If you are perpetually undisciplined and messy,
Love alone won't make you a person that's classy.

≈

The foundation for civilization is character - reach for it, 'twill be your benefactor.

≈

Rather than react, choose to interact.

≈

You don't have to be a graduate of Harvard to hold yourself to a higher standard.

≈

If success in your life is to be unfurled, you must gradually rise above this world.

≈

Suspicion is a clouded mental picture that's seen through an imaginary stricture.

≈

Drink, eat plenty and be merry, be silly, overweight and get drunk;
Be unkempt, be filthy and lazy, 'ere long you'll smell like a skunk.

≈

A LIFESTYLE PORTRAYAL From A TO Z

*Y*ou can usually tell how one fitly fares, taking two at a time, bitter pills or stairs.

*F*ortify yourself with personable elegance,
And hyphenate it with unequivocal effervescence.

*D*esserts can affect one's innards - be aware, it's "STRESSED" spelled backwards.

*I*f you strive in your life to put Christ first, you'll bring satisfaction to spiritual thirst.

*W*hy burden yourself with fears and tears?
Tame your fast tongue, words can be spears.
Let your life be an example to your peers.
The decided difference is between your ears.

A light that's amber spells caution - do take that extra precaution.

*S*ome people that we know, 'tis hard to figure out,
What really makes them tick and what they're all about.

*E*ach day I must live as if it were my last day,
In total conformity to God's heavenward way.

*L*ife frequently breaks us, but it also makes us.

*W*e've been put on this earth not to see through each other.
It's to see each other through; think it through, my brother.

*G*od's hope, let us be to someone today; a kindly reminder, He's but a prayer away.

*T*oday, people live as they jolly well please;
Behavior known as sin, now considered a disease.

*Y*ou can be too big for God to use, but you can't be too small for Him to choose.

*K*nowing myself should make me grumble; if I truly know God, He'll keep me humble.

*M*any folk spend hours, watching their health
Without taking time to do good with their wealth.

*Y*ou don't always need to express what you think;
With insidious negatives your mind do not link.

I asked my dear wife, "About dinner tonight?"
By the looks of her kitchen I timed it just right.
"Will it be, go out, take out or thaw out?"

A LIFESTYLE PORTRAYAL From A TO Z

Her quick wit reply, with a twinkle in her eye,
"There's no doubt, you're stout, how about going without?"

In your journey through life, may this be your goal,
Keep your eye on the doughnut and not on the hole.

Resolve to be tender and compassionate with the aged,
Sympathetic with the striving, positive with the strong;
To be tolerant and understanding and supportive of the young,
To be gentle and forgiving to the weak and the wronged.

Don't think of the dull misery that your mind retains,
Think of the sheer beauty that still remains.

There are two ways of spreading needful light,
Be a candle or mirror that reflect day and night.

Challenge incompetence, don't let it succeed,
Let calm, high efficiency be a definitive creed.
Fuller knowledge you'll feed the more if you read,
Learn well this sage precept I sincerely plead.
To be a brilliant leader, self don't impede,
On the contrary, determine how to lead.
Watch for the way marks, sure signs don't misread,
Sound wisdom heed, avoid miserly greed.
Choose well your words, bitter discord never breed,
Be kind and compassionate, help those in dire need.
Aim well, you'll hit the mark, you'll definitely succeed
If you continually keep your sharp eye on the bead.

Our ship would come in so very much sooner
If we would swim out to the approaching schooner.

Booze befuddled brains, means brawls, bumps and bruises.
I feel sorry for the individual who that lifestyle chooses.

The man who lifts the cup that cheers should not be used to shift the gears.

Loose brakes and tight drivers bring about non-arrivers.

If you drink before driving, what could be worse?
You are definitely putting the quart before hearse.

"One for the road," in his bright red racer;
Most likely he'll have a state trooper as a chaser.

A LIFESTYLE PORTRAYAL From A TO Z

"Meeting your daily bills," say Clem, "isn't as bad as dodging them."

❧

Hats off not so much to him who dares, but invariably to the one who nobly bears.
Acclaim to the heart that's compassionate and cares,
And to the benefactor who gratuitously shares.

❧

Definitely I shall try to be an enabler, a resource person, a guide, a stimulator.

❧

From thinking and doubting one must never shrink.
Think of doubting as an invitation to think.

❧

I find that the modest have a right to boast,
But they aren't the ones that need it the most.

❧

A true hypochondriac is verily the guy on whom a recital you can always rely.
If that organ recital you're not prepared to hear, ask him how he feels only once a year.

❧

Many a mute citizen misses the boat by failing to exercise his right to vote.

❧

On being introduced, oh, so oft I wish
That the hand wouldn't feel like a wobbly, dead fish.

❧

Our strength is shown in the things that we stand for.
Our weakness is shown in the things that we fall for.

❧

The most blessed thing you can do as a father,
For all of your children is to dearly love their mother.

❧

A paradox it would seem, it's hard to figure out,
How the man who fits in is the man who stands out.

❧

Never be afraid to say, "I'm sorry," as well as to say, "I do not know."
Love you'll release, you'll create inner peace,
And you will find your stature will grow.

❧

In travelling the rough road of life, there's a thought that's apparent to me,
We all can't play the same fiddle, but we should be in a harmonic key.

❧

No matter how soft or warm your bed, you still must get up to get ahead.

❧

A great pleasure it is to do good by stealth;
Endorphins are released, joy becomes wealth.

❧

Do watch your posture, be erect when you park;
Be an exclamation point, never a question mark.

❧

A LIFESTYLE PORTRAYAL From A TO Z

Don't casually accept "Good Enough" - "Good enough" is usually not enough.

You may have intelligence and heaps of information,
If you lack sound wisdom you won't reach your destination.

Anticipating the world to treat me fairly because I'm a venerable octogenarian,
Is expecting a ferocious bull not to charge or impale me because I'm a strict vegetarian.

Some facts, magnificent, although interesting are irrelevant.

You must to your body good care daily give.
If you don't, where else are you going to live?

Don't plan your life around regrets; give quality time to your begats.

To live like a light bulb we should daily strive.
We're meant to burn brightly the full length of our lives.

Now don't just lie there stretched flat on your back,
Get up, bypass the fridge, and dash out onto track.
My friend, pray tell me, where in health are you going?
I can see that your feet with the pantry have been toying.
Don't make it a fixed habit every few moments to indulge,
I'm telling you, if you do so, for certain you will bulge.
If with fiber in your diet you're not fully turned on,
Chances are before long you'll have a semi-colon.
If to your dear heart you're not true blue,
Someday, you'll find it may choose to attack you.
Against sweets and fats take a definitive stand,
Lest you have to buy the big waist brand.
If to your lovely teeth you're not at all true,
You'll find before long they'll be false to you.
There is a unique formula portraying the overweight,
This abominable state, spells U/8.
Be punctual, eat slowly, always use a small bowl;
Follow faithfully the prudent method of safe-girth control.

Regardless of the country, race, tribe or nation,
Heart attacks aren't sudden, they come with preparation.

The food we eat is the food we wear, not only on our tie, but also our derriere.

If you have what it takes, monitor what you grab,
Lest someone take you for what you don't have.

A LIFESTYLE PORTRAYAL From A TO Z

*P*rotect the birds – their destruction cease;
The stork brings exemptions, the dove brings peace.

*A*nalyze adequately what you are told, for what you may hear, water it won't hold.

*W*e cannot hold a torch on another man's path
Without brightening our own and obliterating wrath.

*T*wo women chanced talking about their dear mates.
Said one, "My husband is such a great sport,
He golfs and he swims, he works out in the gym,
And in his spare time he's out on the court."
Not to be outdone, the other did counter,
"My hubby spends hours on the balcony sunning.
Said I, 'For the health of it, get up and get going;'
Last week he was out all seven nights running."

*F*rom the king on the throne to the village cobbler,
We stuff and we dress the barnyard gobbler.
Then we dress and we primp and surround the table
To gobble and stuff till to move we're not able.

*S*tart the day out with a nod and a smile.
If you exercise daily, walk more than a mile,
Eventually you will be pleasingly gracile.
Exhibit a quick step, be flexible, be agile,
Holding head high will improve your profile.
Cleanliness is paramount, keep in mind the nail file.
Every day try doing something worthwhile.
In your business dealings, don't ever beguile.
A reminder to secretaries, don't ever misfile.
Control your temper, it mustn't be labile.
Be friendly to all, no, never hostile.

*Y*ou must adequately analyze what you are told,
For what you may hear, water it won't hold.

*O*ur lives lack meaning when full of empty chatter,
And the moment that we're silent about things that do matter.

A warning to teenagers, don't chew it for a thrill,
Remember, poisonous hemlock has potential to kill.

*Y*ou can't become a dynamic person, simply by blowing your top.
Neither can you reap a plentiful harvest if you haven't planted the crop.

A LIFESTYLE PORTRAYAL From A TO Z

If you do not care how soon you are dead,
Just keep on driving through lights that are red.

～

Be to others kind and true blue as you would have others be to you.

～

Do you manage your life based on principles of greed,
Materialism, and power? Beware, they'll impede.

～

To live such a life, you should be trying, as you'd wish to live when you are dying.

～

It's not what you know, nor is it what you do,
It is how you are known by those who know you.

～

Anyone, anywhere, anytime, may some day speak evil of you.
Your life should always so be, that no one would believe it to be true.

～

Work like you don't need the money, love like you've never been hurt,
Dance like no one is watching, constantly be on the alert.

～

Be it with the tiniest spark, one can make a hole in the dark.

～

Life's not obliged to grant what we desire and expect.
When the good comes, accept, when the bad comes, reject.

～

So oft says my spouse, "Let go of the mouse and get out of the house."

～

Wonderful memories don't come by chance, they must be planned for far in advance.

～

Regardless what may be your chosen territory, do strive to make it a beautiful memory.

～

To shorten our lives we're always on the hop, then we pay the doctor to tell us to stop.

～

If you want people to think you're fascinating,
Talk about things that are illustriously illuminating.

～

You don't have to look like an ape to be thought as being in good shape.

～

Take time to nurture adaptability; there's always room for flexibility.

～

Man's the only animal, the silly, stupid dunce,
He invariably allows himself to be skinned more than once.

～

There never has been a truly great man who in his daily living virtue didn't plan.

～

A LIFESTYLE PORTRAYAL From A TO Z

*C*onsciousness, an annoyance between my long naps;
I find that my strength it continually saps.

*I*t's totally amazing what a good laugh can do - tears and fears it's inclined to subdue.

*T*here's this one thing, you must learn, my son,
Even though you have pain, you mustn't be one.

I must be frank, with humanity I must level;
I can't walk with God while running with the devil.

*I*t takes more than shoeshine to give a man polish;
Depend not on moonshine for misery to abolish.

*W*hen a heart truly loves it does great things -
It's only then that intellect takes wings.

*E*veryone has opportunity to be moral or horrible.
If you can be virtuous, why be deplorable?

*I*f my dear people who are called by my name
Will humble themselves and earnestly pray,
And will seek my face and forsake their wicked ways,
Then will I listen and forgive them their sins;
I will hold their hand and heal their land.
2 Chronicles: 7:14
(paraphrased)

*S*ome live sincerely believing, many by gladly receiving,
Others by deliberately deceiving.

*D*etermine to keep your face to the sunshine;
Of dark shadows there'll be no visible incline.

*A*t times, stand aside with clear open eye,
Take a look at yourself as you jauntily pass by.

*W*hen you're over the hill and you don't feel fit,
Be calm, it's better than being six feet under it.

*I*n the battle of life, to decrease your sorrow,
Use the brains you have and all you can borrow.

*G*overning your lifestyle is always worthwhile.

A LIFESTYLE PORTRAYAL From A TO Z

Those who resolve to excel, unwillingness to work must expel.

President Abraham Lincoln made a solemn vow,
"I'll do my very best, the best I know how."
May that be our goal, let's begin doing it now.

Always attempt to do your humble job, the best that you possibly can,
And then just leave the rest, my friend, with the God who was once a man.

Do not let your I.Q stand still, more importantly, use the "I will."

Why be malicious when you can be gracious.

You'll never regret being circumspect.

Feed your strong points, on nourishment they rely;
Let your mortal weaknesses shrivel up and die.

Attempt to live slightly beneath your means,
Though oft it may mean baked beans and greens.

Give your casual clients your enthusiastic best,
You'll find that at night you'll much better rest.

Be a person of principle and intellectual purity,
Of righteous obedience and sterling integrity.

Do you chisel or do you carve? Do you feed or do you starve?

Get rid of your vices, replace them with virtues.

The greatest triumph is not stashing pelf.
The noblest victory is to conquer one's self.

The degree of pride is the measure of pomposity;
Sincere sacrifice is the measure of generosity.

It's not so much what a person possesses,
Much more significant, it's what he professes.

One's praiseworthy labor exhibits true behavior.

There are two distinct types of people in this world,
Their entrance is a contrast as the door comes ajar.

A LIFESTYLE PORTRAYAL From A TO Z

The one says pompously, "Here I am!"
The other unpretentiously, "Ah! - there you are."

❧

Never look down on a man unless you are picking him up.

❧

Let your life portray what you cannot say.

❧

It requires sincere interest in life to appreciate occasional nonsense.
I hasten to add, however, couple it with good common sense.

❧

The demanding person will meet resistance.
The defeated, carefree, runs into indifference.
The enterprising man has patient persistence.

❧

"Wild oats" and 'Old Rye" can make you feel high,
And then make you sigh and eventually cry.

❧

The person who makes most people at ease
Is inevitably the one who will decidedly please.
A salient characteristic about him can be said,
He is that person who's unquestionably well-bred.

❧

Speaking of employees who onto street at four pour,
Most likely their names won't be on the front door.

❧

Labor and ardent persistence is the soul of one's existence.

❧

Arise, move, go, proceed – depart, travel, heal, and feed.

❧

Prove, testify, teach - proclaim, persuade, preach.

❧

For fitness sake, get up at daybreak,
Take less intake, rich foods never bake,
Avoid that steak, honesty never fake,
Bribes never take, never a hissing snake,
Nor, ever be a flake. don't ever muckrake,
Never be a heartache, take a stretch-break,
Bones will less ache, you'll be more awake,
Be ready with a handshake, more friends you'll make,
Happiness you will stake.

❧

"Dost thou love life, then do not squander time."
Wise words of yesteryear placed in simple rhyme.

❧

A LIFESTYLE PORTRAYAL From A TO Z

If it weren't for the fact that the TV and the fridge were distanced so far apart,
Many folk wouldn't have ill-annexed opportunity
To exercise their weak, flabby heart.

∽

He who isn't busy about living is slowly but gradually dying.

∽

When actions and words do not agree, could that irresponsible individual be me?

∽

Living in the past has one thing in its favor,
It has considerably a much cheaper flavor.

∽

To preserve your credit, keep low your debit.

∽

Your signage requests that I wipe my feet;
Take off shoes and socks? - I shall promptly retreat.

∽

Take care of your soul, avoid getting drunk;
Be cognizant of the fact, there's no spare in your trunk.

∽

Humans can alter their lives, simply by being gentle and kind;
Filled, full of love and compassion and altering their attitude of mind.

∽

With many their ambition is the conquest of pelf.
No conquest is as great as victory over self.

∽

Learn the sweet luxury of doing some good.
To be involved in this luxury, everyone should.

∽

It's my plan at my age to stay home Saturday nights,
Waiting for the hour of slumber.
And if the telephone should chance to ring,
I would hope it would be the wrong number.

∽

Try using your self-control while handling the remote control.

∽

Good, healthy habits must be kept at a premium,
On their great benefits one can fully rely.
It is the safest, homeward highroad
On which an individual can peacefully die.

∽

If you mind your own business you won't be annoyed,
And I should add, you won't be unemployed.

∽

Giving of oneself creates joy of living; nothing can equal the passion of giving.

∽

A LIFESTYLE PORTRAYAL From A TO Z

*O*ur countenance can elicit a smile or a frown.
Our words have the power to build up or tear down.

*T*he years clearly show what the days never know.

"*W*here do you come from?" a quest oft annoying,
A query oft presented by the one who does employing.
More importantly he should ask, "Where are you going?"

*T*o handle yourself, use a sound head; to handle others, use heart instead.

*Y*ou don't have to brush all of your teeth,
Just brush the ones that you wish to keep.

"*S*hould-have," solves nothing, it has no clout;
It's the next thing to happen that needs thinking about.

*M*ay the following not be in your life a precedent,
Learning safety rules, simply by accident.

*D*on't be too concerned who your grandfather was,
Instead, be mindful of his grandson's cause.

*T*o make you feel inferior, some have a certain bent.
They can't make you inferior without your consent.

*I*f you stumble into fortune, seemingly by chance,
Bear in mind, when you stumble you gradually advance.

*L*ife is a series of encounters with the future.
It's the sum of what we are and what we nurture.

*T*wo questions could be asked of one's life, the latter may inadvertently belittle,
How could you have accomplished so much, and why have you done so little?

*I*f you duly obey and the Almighty revere,
You will have nothing in this world to fear.

*C*hrist came to this earth to serve among the poor.
They unquestionably received the greatest attention.
Today, in the person of you and I His children,
He visits the needy, I hasten to mention.
-E. G. White
(paraphrased)

A LIFESTYLE PORTRAYAL From A TO Z

In writing a book, what will I teach?
A query that I graciously and humbly beseech.

Regardless of the number written thought may reach,
Literature, good or evil, is immortality of one's speech.

Flagrant misconduct avoid - always logically deduct -
Never stupidly obstruct - choose someone to instruct.

The task ahead of us is never as great as when we allow God to fully participate.

It is not my nature my colleagues to deride -
Never go to a doctor whose plants have died.

Keep looking up, there's fortune in your soul;
Dream big dreams, they come before the goal.

Life is a vessel to be filled and maintained.
It's not a full cup to be perpetually drained.

We can do nothing, of ourselves we are nil.
We're saved by grace, Jesus paid the bill.

Lord, I am willing to be made willing; I'll do my utmost, may your Spirit do the rest.

Tough times don't last but tough people do;
Get going and accomplish what you've long planned to do.

Most folk won't know what we really are, till they see with their eyes what we bar.

Do more than average with nary a frown; not doing so will keep the average down.

The devil may be old, but he's not infirm.
Stay out of his reach, he can make you squirm.
This truth, Holy Scripture repeatedly confirm.

If your going gets easy with little input or will,
It's possible you may find you're going downhill.

If you don't watch your manners, be it now and then,
Someone will be noticing your lack of them.

Man is what he believes, retrieves, receives,
Perceives, conceives, and laboriously achieves.

A LIFESTYLE PORTRAYAL From A TO Z

Remember, there may not be another precious now,
So with this brief moment doing your best allow.

☙

To do all the talking we must impede; not stopping to listen is a form of greed.

☙

To gratefully live, on you is the onus; life is so short, every tomorrow is a bonus.

☙

How tall I am, how much I see, how far I go, depends on me.

☙

In your daily driving don't be conniving how two seconds earlier you could be arriving.

☙

Be conscious of keeping your life in balance;
You may have to utilize all of your talents.

☙

A life that is blameless engenders one's security;
Crooked sinful ways will inhale impurity.

☙

Be intent on well-doing, do decrease your slumber;
Keep company with the good, you'll increase their number.

☙

What you fail to eliminate in your life, is bound to give you incessant strife.

☙

Tidbits, finger food oft labeled as "fun food",
'Tis invariably the kind, so I note in my book,
If you eat too much of it, I can truthfully say,
People will be derisive of the way you look.

☙

To be 'fit as a fiddle' I must watch my middle.

☙

A seafood restaurant, where lobsters come to slaughter,
Where a strict 'vegan' feels like a fish out of water.

☙

So many think of changing humanity; few are thinking of deleting their inanity.

☙

You must not go where God is naught; so many years ago my mother taught.

☙

The devil goes seldom where he isn't welcome.

☙

After the verb "to love" is unfurled,
"I'll help," are the most beautiful words in the world.

☙

Avoid being a laggard, a coward or a drunkard;
Hold yourself responsible to a higher standard.

☙

A LIFESTYLE PORTRAYAL From A TO Z

If your deep-down desire is to live forever -
Your bonds with the devil you must daily sever.

To accomplish something for someone, to devote a portion of one's leisure,
To lift, to comfort, to enhance, are the highest forms of pleasure.

A maxim we should always keep in mind, "Every moment is the time to be kind."

Don't floss your teeth or use a toothpick, and never raw garlic when out in public.

Keep your own desk and work area neat; with comeliness and orderliness do be replete.

The key to mental wellness, most assuredly is education.
It has high priority, not pill pushing medication.

The words "I am," can be snooty and strong,
So don't ever use them where they don't belong.

It's what you do when you have nothing to do
That tattles on you; bid leisure adieu.

The company you continually keep will determine how you will sleep.

Be occupied with a purpose, not aimlessly busy -
You'll find it will be the best for your health.
For the exceedingly rich I have this admonition,
There's more to life than hoarding your wealth.

Don't let yellow gold become your mold.

Drinking doesn't happiness borrow, nor does it ever drown out sorrow.

Don't be thick-skinned when appraisal you face.
Take criticism calmly, worthy praise with grace.

Listen to these voices - "Control" and "Choices."

Never tell a person who's experiencing deep sorrow,
"I know how you feel" - you'll forget on the morrow.

Stand up to be seen, speak up to be heard, know when to sit down, always honest in word.

For happy heart and home, Jesus has propositioned
That we keep them both thoroughly prayer-conditioned.

A LIFESTYLE PORTRAYAL From A TO Z

Aim to be upright in everyone's sight.

The fridge door we open over twenty times a day.
We don't seem to know how to keep appetites away.

This Swedish proverb in verity does score,
'Fear less, hope more, eat less. chew more, talk less, say more, hate less, love more.'

It's wise with anything you do, to begin at the bottom when beginning.
A prudent, strict to rule to follow - one exception, it's when you learn swimming.

Life transpires at the level of an event; don't put it off, make it part of the present.

How I live and impart, can touch another's heart.

The essentials of life: something to adore, something to do, something to hope for.

"Begin to weave," someone has said, "and God will give you plenty of thread."

Be it peace or strife, one learns from daily life.

May your footprints in the sand of time, be the ones that initiate climb.

Learn to relax, don't get into a tizzy; the best time to relax is when you are busy.

To the world you may be but one person, but to one person you may be the world.

A maxim for the ambitious, I reckon apropos:
'Life is more meaningful when you're aspiring to grow.'

On life's pages, what have you writ? Every man's work of self is a portrait.

If you prayerfully choose to have Christ by your side,
You'll have an experience that will constantly abide.

I cannot expect God to intervene if I'm not willing with Him to be seen.

Life is a blend of laughter and tears; a subtle combination of joy and fears.

Let not a fool caress or kiss you, likewise, don't ever let a kiss fool you.

Men, to grow bald, don't be in a rush, a hair in your head is worth two in the brush.

One's daily persistent bodily exercise prevents a lazy muscle's demise.

A LIFESTYLE PORTRAYAL From A TO Z

*D*oes your life shed light or cast dark shadows?
Does it portray gloom or brilliant, bright rainbows?

❧

"*D*rink to your health and incalculable wealth."
A contradiction in term that I cannot affirm.

❧

*R*egardless how your past you daily did nurture,
Fully bear in mind, you have an ever-better future.

❧

*H*ave something to say, no sarcastic mocking; make it profound and then stop talking.

❧

*S*ome folks are a picture of health, they will even tell you it's so.
However, there is an inherent problem, so oft it's a retouched photo.

❧

*A*ctivity is better than gross inertia; choose to move muscles before it hurts you.

❧

*W*hat do we live for and what do we live off?
Do we effort to feed or do we seek for the trough?

❧

*P*erdition has three doors, lust, hate and greed.
The devil is the doorman, he'll gladly lead.

❧

*I*t could be fresh from the oven, and smell so utterly delicious,
Look so scrumptious and appetizing; if left untouched it's useless.

❧

*A*voiding exercise daily one cannot afford.
Why not make it a habit to walk with the Lord?

❧

*H*e who constantly fiddles, seldom solves life's riddles.

❧

*G*ood, better or best, rarely accomplished with rest.
Never rest till the good becomes better than the best.

❧

*I*t lies completely in your power, not to look offensively sour.

❧

*M*ost people emotionally and mentally healthy,
Know when to say, "No," and when to say "Whoopee."

❧

*N*ever abandon natural aptitude, live your vocation in quietude.
You will be blessed with gilded servitude.

❧

*T*he vocation of everyone should be, to serve mankind graciously.

❧

*W*e can't become what we need to be if we don't make an effort to battle gravity.

❧

A LIFESTYLE PORTRAYAL From A TO Z

Love your enemies, avoid verbal assaults; bear in mind, they'll tell you your faults.

Always have an answer to the question, "What would I do in a recession?"

We must seek to live a life so sublime, that it can be counted worthy of the time.

There is an old adage, a mental bent you must form,
"If you light your own fire you'll be twice as much warm."

If anyone should speak unkindness about you,
Live so that no one will believe it to be true.

Life's mental vexations and annoyances will swirl;
When irritations arise, make a lovely pink pearl.

Life is how we make it, coupled with how we take it.

Wear out your shoe soles, not the tires in your car;
You will live much longer and feel better by far.

To people who tail-gate, be polite, say "Shoo!" "Please, not so close, I hardly know you."

Watch your step carefully, Stu - others consistently do.

Learn to write your hurts in sand, and to carve your benefits in stone.

I wasn't born on enticing Vancouver Island, longingly to get there I wished I would,
And so I elected to do what I should, I elbowed and got here as fast as I could.

When people say, "You look fit as a fiddle,"
It's undoubtedly because you've been watching your middle.

With this weight-loss formula you're bound to score.
It's comprised of four words, "EAT LESS, MOVE MORE."

He lives who dies winning a lasting name, so in your daily living do not expose shame.
You must strive to play a tight fair game; determine not ever to ridicule or defame.
For certain, no never, should you attempt to maim.

An ounce of learning, one can't deny it, takes pounds of sense to skillfully apply it.

To build a huge estate this one thing you must learn,
You must expend less, much less than you earn.

A LIFESTYLE PORTRAYAL From A TO Z

Think of tomorrow, divide prudently your pay,
Take what you need, the rest lay away.

❧

A beautiful, wise proverb that has meant much to me,
"If you follow the river you will find open sea."

❧

"Yes, But"-ers, excuses hurl, "Not Now"-ers, deferrals unfurl,
"Why Not"-ers, move the world.

❧

If your wish is to positively achieve, you must learn to be on the run.
Plan to prepare to put up with blisters if you wish to have a place in the sun.

❧

An impatient patron, said to a waitress, "Will pots I have to scour?
I've been on nothing but bread and water for more than a whole half hour."

❧

"You can't have everything." says my sister Bridget,
"After all, my brother, where would you put it?"

❧

Never spit into a well, 'tis not a catch-all sink,
Lest from that deep font some day you'll want to drink.

❧

One virtuous wish changes nothing; a wise decision changes everything.

❧

Do not deem it danger to be courteous to a stranger.

❧

Give people much more than they ever expect,
Spontaneously and cheerfully, you'll never regret.

❧

Deliberate, conciliate, radiate, ideate, create, illuminate.

❧

Be exceedingly gentle with our sacred earth; for its respect there's a deplorable dearth.

❧

Allow no person to degrade your soul by making you hate him; may this be your goal.

❧

Disagreements are less likely to last if you don't keep bringing up the past.

❧

A man is no different than an infant, in hemispheres, north and south;
He smiles, he screams and cries, and he puts his foot in his mouth.

❧

To know how and when you should tacitly refuse
Is just as important as knowing how to choose.

❧

Dead men tell no secrets, but their biographies do,
So live that your issue may be proud of you.

❧

A LIFESTYLE PORTRAYAL From A TO Z

Take care to seek out the good in people,
And habitually bring self to the village steeple.

❧

Giving up completely is a tragedy for which there is very little remedy.

❧

The journey is within you – GO! But don't just go with the flow.

❧

Over scores of years this lesson I've learned, the forces that shape the pot
Are akin to the forces that shape our lives, this analogy do mentally jot.
Unless the frail vessel is truly centered, the clay flies off the wheel;
Unless one's life is favorably disciplined, it has no worthy appeal.

❧

A minister ordained a maxim worthwhile,
A precept to guide one's prudent lifestyle,
"If troubles are never big enough to pray about,
For certain they're not large enough to fret about."

❧

If aches and pains make you grimace and frown,
It is nature's way to communicate, "Slow down!"

❧

Never deprive others of hope, and never attempt to take dope.

❧

Do more than is expected of you, and never attempt to sniff glue.

❧

The lure of the distant and the difficult is deceptive;
Seize local opportunity, it is much more receptive.

❧

If jack you lack, get off your back, and out of the sack - a job attack.

❧

Is your mission on earth complete? If you're still alive - compete!

❧

Life can be fun, let it shine like the sun.

❧

Let us so live that when it's time to die, even the undertaker will be sad and cry.

❧

When people diminish esteeming, they usually cease to obey.
When people terminate believing, they invariably cease to pray.

❧

Accusing God, could resurrect His ire; could you be calling the Almighty a liar?

❧

When eating remember that the table's fare
Eventually becomes what's in the rocking chair.

❧

Living on earth is a challenge, but I do find the exercise fun.
Think of it, it yearly includes a trip around the warm sun.

❧

A LIFESTYLE PORTRAYAL From A TO Z

*Y*our good deeds restrict not to scheduled sense of duty.
Do practice impulsive kindness with serendipitous acts of beauty.

*K*eep your affairs in strict order, always keep track of the score;
Apply the same sound principle to your laundered underwear drawer.

*L*ooking down on people is a trait we must ban.
Only God is in a position to look down on man.

*L*ife isn't a duet, more oft it's a solo that should be sung with heart.
Others may supply the needed harmony, but no one can sing your part.

*E*arly to bed and early to rise, until you make enough to do otherwise.

*S*ome days you'll be happy on other days sad.
Be prepared to accept the good with the bad.

*I*t's in loving, not being loved that the heart finds its quest.
It's in giving not in getting that our lives are best blessed.

*G*ood is not good if it isn't perfected, and it isn't the best when better is expected.

*P*eople will never forget what we did, they won't forget how we made them feel.
People will never forget what we said, especially when we made them feel like a heel.

I am responsible for my own well-being, my happiness, my choices, my ways.
The decisions I make regarding my life do influence the quality of my days.
-Kathleen Andrew -(paraphrased)

*E*very time I do something that doesn't feel right,
On my life it ends up being an irreversible blight.

*W*hen invited to a banquet, express your delight;
'Tis prudent to rise, still with an appetite.

*A*s the sand in the hourglass continues to escape,
The clearer we see how our bodies we should shape.

*S*o many folk have a photographic memory;
The reloading of film with some is secondary.

*D*espite the high cost of living, I'm being good-naturedly jocular,
Have you noticed how it continues to be, so incredibly and amazingly popular.

A LIFESTYLE PORTRAYAL From A TO Z

In attaining lasting friendships, do note Fuller's verdict,
"You should never have friends if you expect them to be perfect."

≈

*W*ith the one hand you can throw multiple ringers,
On the other hand, you have five different fingers.

≈

In the rise of burial costs, how can we be forgiving,
When invariably they blame it on the high cost of living?

≈

*S*ome folk aren't dead, nor are they unbalanced,
They're just electroencephalographically challenged.

≈

*W*hen I don't have the strength to help in some way
That precious someone, I can always pray.

≈

*M*any times I have seen what a laugh can do; so oft unbearable tears it does subdue.

≈

*M*any have a gregarious propensity of having a conspicuous inclination
To pray for implored forgiveness, rather than to fight temptation.

≈

*K*now the difference between aerobics and fast walk;
Better still, the disparity between free speech and cheap talk.

≈

*R*eason without impulse is not the right stuff,
Neither is one's impulse without reason enough.

≈

A man in his life span, opportunities does seize.
With his unique lifestyle he duly tries to please.
It does have an encumbrance, it's incurable disease.

≈

*Y*ou're the best person to begin from scratch;
Compete with yourself, you won't find a better match.

≈

*D*o much for yourself is good sound advice;
He who gathers firewood, warms himself twice.

≈

*T*o avoid stumbling it doesn't take will, all you have to do is simply stand still.

≈

*T*o become wealthy, two things you must do,
You must work very hard and make your wants few.

≈

A brave arm that's strong makes a short sword long.

≈

A hero is a man who does all that he can.

≈

A LIFESTYLE PORTRAYAL From A TO Z

The pusher, the grabber, the offensive boaster, many folk would love to subdue.
Those that should have an inferiority complex, you'll note, invariably seldom do.

To be successful, to know how to live, follow the advice that to others you give.

Convenience is not man's sole spark for intention.
Necessity inevitably is the catalyst for invention.

God seldom calls the qualified, He invariably qualifies the called.

He who angers you, inevitably controls you.

A pathway with debts do not ever pave; a man with debts is a monastic slave.

It isn't paramount that all wishes be filled;
Through sickness one learns with good health one is thrilled.
Through evil one values the benefits of good;
Through hunger one recognizes the benefit of food.
Through hard work one enjoys the perks of rest;
Difficulties and trials of one's metal are a test.

Measure your shadow, it's never contradictory.
You'll find it's no greater than before your victory.

There's something we can do with no extra cost,
It's producing more horsepower with minimal exhaust.

Each day, each week, our living should be a creation of discipline, a conscious big key.

While strolling on the beach, saw a friend picking starfish,
Nonchalantly one by one he'd cast them to the sea.
"And what are you doing?" a man queried Bill,
"Surely you're not doing it for a paltry fee."
"I'm throwing these starfish into the ocean.
If I don't they'll die, for lack of needed oxygen."
"There are thousands, you can't possibly get to all of them.
There are far too many to make a big difference."
The friend just smiled, threw another toward the sun.
"You'll agree, 'twill make a big difference to that one."
This allegory tells a story, a justifiable inference,
'It is in one's power to make a big difference.'

It's best that I be cognizant of my future, forgetting my anxieties and strife,
For the future is where I'll be going to be thrilled eternally with life.

A LIFESTYLE PORTRAYAL From A TO Z

*W*isdom enables us to be commendably thrifty, inordinately wasteful would not be nifty,
Generous without being wantonly wasteful, pompously boastful is perpetually distasteful.

*I*n preparing to live, be prepared to give.

*I*f you should feel bored, penned in, unstimulated,
It's your responsibility to become highly motivated.

*R*egard your character, don't act like a clown; it's a long way up but a short way down.

*B*e cheerful, be happy, shed your cocoon, lest morale sag like a leaky balloon.

*I*n helping someone up a long steep hill, don't expect payment in pelf.
There's beautiful solace in helping a person - you get closer to the top yourself.

*T*he dividing slash between success and decline
Is expressed succinctly, "I dined on wine."

*O*verlook people's faults, admire their virtues.
It's the way to happiness, it's the road to choose.

*I*n your verbal interaction do not subdue, and fail not to see another's point of view.

*T*here are no shortcuts to a place worth going.
Remember this maxim when with aspiration you're toying.

*N*ow don't just stop at designing ambitious schemes.
Why not make realities out of your vivid dreams?

*W*e should never rile, much better a smile.

*I*t's not that people lack strength and skill, it's primarily the lack of one's basic will.

*S*tick-to-itiveness, an ingredient success demands.
A genius hasn't glue on his feet, just his hands.

*N*o one more confusing than he who gives advice,
While setting an example with a life filled with vice.

*O*ur lives would be extraordinarily versed if our second thoughts always came first.

*I*n a world that couldn't care less, resolve to care and bless.

*I*t's not wealth or splendor. it's tranquility and occupation,
Which give true happiness its appointed destination.

A LIFESTYLE PORTRAYAL From A TO Z

Though in great pain, Job wasn't inane, nor was he a pain.

∼

Fear thou not that life comes to an end; be anxious that it not have a despicable trend.

∼

Never give the devil a ride – he will energetically connive.
He'll want to take the steering wheel, he'll definitely want to drive.

∼

Why don't you do a good turn today, now don't you say, "I'm far too busy."
It's bound to raise lively endorphins; I promise it'll never make you dizzy.

∼

To maintain healthy teeth there are three basic rules,
The last has with it brisk frankness;
Brush after meals, see your dentist twice a year,
And always mind your own business.

∼

You won't excite nor will you delight,
If you don't do what's right with all your might.
Be thankful for sight, never start a fight
With words that smite, and don't ever backbite.
Watch what you write, use not words of spite,
Exhibit keen insight, avoid being tight.
Always give more than a tiny mite.
To be lint-white you must be upright.
You can avoid limelight without being a 'stylite.'
You don't have to be bright to shed some light.
If you study at night you'll become erudite.

∼

Avoid being unfaithful, neglectful, wasteful,
Distrustful, forgetful, regretful and fretful;
Wrongful, and slothful, resentful, distasteful,
Deceitful, disgraceful, lustful and remorseful;
Doubtful, dreadful, boastful, doleful,
Guileful, vengeful, hurtful and harmful;
Sinful, scornful, stressful, spiteful,
Unmindful, ungrateful, harmful and hateful;
Tearful and fearful, forceful, disdainful,
Doleful, a handful, wrathful and shameful.

∼

Instead, try to be peaceful and graceful, heedful, grateful, thoughtful and thankful,
Helpful, hopeful, cheerful, soulful, useful, fruitful, trustful and truthful;
Beautiful, dutiful, manful, purposeful, mirthful, meaningful, playful but mindful;
Skilful, and gainful, resourceful, successful, rightful, respectful, wonderful and merciful;
Watchful, tactful, joyful, and faithful, most of all, try to be healthful and prayerful.

∼

This axiom by Shakespeare we must not defy, "Our remedies oft in ourselves do lie."

∼

A LIFESTYLE PORTRAYAL From A TO Z

A maxim that shouldn't offer defiance, "Speak when you words are better than silence."

If you can't forgive and forget, my Son, you can at least forgive and move on.

Plan your funeral, your finances blending, but do not spend time planning on attending.

Always be forthright, entertain foresight,
Treasure your birthright, never forget hindsight.

Try not to insist that you aren't stubborn, others of you will not be fonder.
When you give in you won't be weaker, in fact 'twill make you considerably stronger.

If you live only for the praise of men, you'll lose the approval of most of them.

A home filled with kindness, a home full of mirth,
So oft is the healthiest place on this earth.

The quality of life soon greatly increases,
When you pick friends prudently, but not to pieces.

Do not get hung up on pride, instead, let humility abide;
May compassion lodge inside, may conscience be your guide.

Our value lies not in what we own, it's encompassed in what o'er the years we've sown.

Be it bitter disappointment or unrelenting rancor,
The fierce storms of life test the firmness of our anchor.

Acquiesce to the inevitable and the presumptuously improbable,
Accept the impossible, evade the unpredictable,
Do without the indispensable, endure the intolerable.

The die has been cast, don't live in the past.
Why would you dare, you've already been there.

Take time to rest, don't always be on the hop;
A field that has rested oft gives the best crop.

Strive not to be chief and don't always beef; life is too brief, give others relief.

You have only one life, few chances to do
The things that you're heart is inclined to pursue.

The people who are happy, do not necessarily
Have in their possession the best of everything.

A LIFESTYLE PORTRAYAL From A TO Z

He did not know that it couldn't be done, but he went ahead and with doing he won.

ಌ

Kindling intensifies one's subdued desire; takes overt action to light a fire.

ಌ

God is more interested in inner beauty and grace,
Exceedingly more than the geography of our face.

ಌ

Your interest should be in your future, that interest continually nurture.
The rest of life you'll spend there, so why not take time in prayer.

ಌ

Avoid vile ridicule and cutting sarcasm, show tender affection, never cruel clout.
Jealous, greasy envy is briskly rubbing it in, compassionate, abiding love is rubbing it out.

ಌ

Three things in life are important, the first is to be inordinately kind,
The second is to have a clear mind, the third, be spiritually inclined.

ಌ

There's an axiom that expresses one's life to the letter,
'No human ever lives long enough to know better.'

ಌ

An ancient historian would have written, many volumes about despot Nero,
And probably would not have even mentioned the blessed name of Paul, God's hero.
Today, we name our dogs Nero, to our sons we give the name of Paul.
I guess, how we live and what we live for is pretty important after all.
-Anonymous

ಌ

All people are significant, they deserve your attention;
Do learn their name, 'twill help to relieve tension.

ಌ

Our business in life shouldn't be, monetarily ahead of all others.
It's to pace ourselves and to be, beneficent to our needy brothers.

ಌ

In this world, a distinct want is the want of decent men,
Men who at no time can be bribed, bought or sold;
Men who are verily in their very inner core,
Dependable, true and honest, sincerely humble - so I'm told.
Men who do not fear to call sin by its name,
Men who are trustworthy in their very inner soul,
Men who aren't seekers of fleeting, worldly fame,
Men, true to duty ,as the needle to the pole.
-E. G. White (paraphrased)

ಌ

Action gives life its strength, moderation increase its length.

ಌ

There is no point in having a good memory,
Be it January, June or December,

A LIFESTYLE PORTRAYAL From A TO Z

Unless you can dip into memory's local bank
For something worthwhile for you to remember.

≈

In one's skirmish of daily life, never quibble about its odd quirks.
Just make certain you haven't become one of its lazy, incompetent jerks.

≈

Prudently avoid shops with Christmas sale banners.
They're certainly not the place one would learn good manners.

≈

Did I make anyone happier today, in a heart did I leave a sweet song?
Did I leave a sign of my kindness, today, did I right an old wrong?
Have I learned something new about life, have I lifted a soul by giving?
At the end of each day I must ask, "Has there been any loving in my living?"
-Author unknown.

≈

An unblemished name is better than fame.

≈

If you value your privileges above your principles,
'Ere long you'll lose both, your character it cripples.

≈

Better to be poor with fame than inordinately rich with shame.

≈

If there is pleasure in the work that you do,
You'll find that perfection will usually ensue.

≈

It's important to remember that we cannot become
What we need to be if to evil we succumb.

≈

Learn to use precious time intelligently; apply self to worthy causes diligently.

≈

Where there's a will there's a won't; where there's consent there's a don't.

≈

Whatever your location, avoid castigation,
Condemnation, confrontation, damnation, deprivation,
Fornication, inebriation, isolation, mutilation,
Manipulation, prevarication, retaliation, stagnation,
Temptation and vacillation, instead, seek motivation.
For competent concentration, seek intensive education,
Consultation, conciliation, inspiration and meditation.
Most importantly, above all, you must seek salvation.

≈

Capitalize on singular mentality to engender in your life morality.

≈

Health is the foremost amongst earthly treasures,
Talent is prime target amongst natural acquisitions.

A LIFESTYLE PORTRAYAL From A TO Z

Understanding is the greatest amongst all our riches,
Contentment is the zenith amongst our possessions.

❧

You may think you can stand between God and the devil,
Irrevocably uncommitted to goodness or evil;
When a fence you're straddling, you're not on the level.

❧

Life's tragedy is not that it ends so soon, it's we take too long with the baby spoon.

❧

Negative words that are spoken about you, allow not your ear to be bent.
No one can make you feel inferior without your personal consent.

❧

Life is too short to be wasted on mere living.
Be occupied with a purpose, doing good, generously giving.

❧

We are far too conscious of fatal disease,
Supplement generously with daily thanksgiving.
Let us get on with the business of life,
Let us hyphenate it with beneficent living.

❧

Why would you the date of your demise advance?
Live healthfully by choice and not by chance.

❧

In travelling life's journey, my advice, travel light;
Take off all your envies, your selfishness and spite.

❧

If you don't stand for something you'll fall for anything.

❧

A superior human is the one who's free from evil and its improprieties;
Free from selfishness and bitter envy, released from fear and anxieties.

❧

Some risks and challenges we must determine to meet,
Not hasty rationalization and then retreat.

❧

Rule your anger to the letter - prevention is much better.

❧

Consistently reject what the devil tries to prod;
Live justly, love mercy, walk humbly with God.

❧

Mr. Axel Munthie, a succinct thought does reveal,
"If a man can stand himself he can stand a great deal."

❧

Every living person is a silent propaganda, be he on the move or merely a bystander.
Strive to be a center of rapturous radiation, a luminous body, guiding your generation.

❧

A LIFESTYLE PORTRAYAL From A TO Z

Go placidly amid the noise and haste, feast on God's nature, enjoy its taste.

❧

He serves God best who gives self a rest.

❧

Some folk head for hell, they do so with speed.
They use three main roads, lust, rage and greed.

❧

If it be your desire to gain heavenly inheritance,
You must on this planet cultivate forbearance.

❧

He who knows and knows that he knows, is surely a wise man, follow his "knows."

❧

An intellectual wise man or a discerning seer,
Sees the wild storm before clouds appear.

❧

Be short on criticism, a good critic should know,
That others know something that he doesn't know.

❧

When minding a kind thought, there is no sanction –
Resurrect it to life, put it into action.

❧

Never be content to think a nice thought –
Express it to the world, happiness will be wrought.

❧

Things nasty about the farmer, never try to mutter
For farming is everyone's milk, bread and butter.

❧

Honor the old, consult the wise, instruct the young, evil despise.

❧

The select are those who readily will; the questionable non-elect, choose to stand still.

❧

What we learn from the past, so oft it doesn't last.

❧

My trusty heart beats 100,000 times a day; Lord, help me make it count, I pray.

❧

He who knows others is obviously clever; to know one's self one must endeavor.

❧

If knowingly you would take healthy habits to heart,
And to many others those same habits impart;
If traits of prudent lifestyle o'er the years you amass,
In years to come you won't need a bypass.

❧

A healthy lifestyle is heaven-sent, for a good healthy heart be always bent.
Likewise, a broken heart do try to prevent.

❧

A LIFESTYLE PORTRAYAL From A TO Z

*N*ever lose interest in life and the world; set a sound schedule as the day is unfurled.
Allow not yourself to be at all annoyed; may at all times your spirit be buoyed.
Get much bright sunlight and plenty of sleep; your physical frame many benefits will reap.

*I*t's an absolute fact, for my mind it's not a poser,
A wide road doesn't make one's destination any closer.

*O*ur greatest enemy is not disease, it's despicable despair and a life of ease.

*K*eep your mind active and your body in motion.
May this be a habit and not just a notion.

*H*ow fit must a man be to be fit to be tied, and why would he ever cool his heels,
And why a rag would he choose to chew - could there be a nutrient missing in his meals?

*H*ow can a highly paid chef today put great technology into his head,
And not put that knowledge into his mouth?
Can't help but wonder seeing the food being fed.

*P*eople will forget what you said, they won't forget what you did.

*T*here's a truth about animals, it isn't any guff,
They don't grab for more when they've had enough.

*L*oose brakes and tight drivers are catastrophic to survivors.

*W*hat you are is God's gift to you, some nod.
What you make of yourself is your gift to God.

A traffic warning sign about tempting booze: "Heads you win – cocktails, you lose."

*W*hy not make an effort to gradually begin to be the one you might have been.

I've come to an intelligible conclusion, man's perfection is an innocent illusion.

*A*ll the great things are relatively simple, they can be expressed in but a single word;
Words like freedom. justice and mercy, hope, honor and duty - words we've all heard.

A child of the king will never exhort, he will always display the manners of the court.

*T*o have a good name you don't pay a fee, and you'll have to agree it's totally tax free.

*N*o mortal disease is more deadly than sin;
Confess, ask forgiveness, with Christ you can win.

A LIFESTYLE PORTRAYAL From A TO Z

It makes little sense advancing rumor, instead, facilitate a good sense of humor.

Try to be much wiser today than you were but yesterday.

Do be generous with genuine respect, family and friends do not forget.

A differing opinion should never offend, never a motive for separation from a friend.

The older I get the more I realize that God's holy word I must idealize.

Each day is a new life, embrace it, live it; whatever you do, determine not to quit it.

Tenaciousness, an ingredient that success demands;
A genius has traction on his feet and his hands.

Harboring bitterness, one should never dare; happiness is bound to dock elsewhere.

Don't feel entitled, nor should you long for
Anything you didn't literally sweat or struggle for.

Behind every cloud there's a silver lining; remember, my friend. the sun is shining.

In spite of the tremendous high cost of living, we are continually needful air receiving.
Forget not to be thankful - be in the mode of giving.

A man's true wealth is unfurled in the good he does in this world.

You're truly living when you're contributing.

Life is partly what we make it, and by what's made by the friends we've created.

Don't do or say things to friend or host that you wouldn't want to see in the Daily Post.

Do you take disappointment in its sober stride,
Or do you discouragement attempt to hide?
Why not find solutions so it won't happen again,
Never to find someone to pin the blame on.

Concern propels some folk to distraction; it should be a goad to drive us into action.

Most of us carry our own stumbling block;
Frequently it's camouflaged with an old woolen sock.

To stay out of the heat, one must keep a cool head;
It's not easy to do, much harder than said.

A LIFESTYLE PORTRAYAL From A TO Z

Duties, distinct tasks, we anticipate with distaste,
Perform oft with dislike, think the whole time a waste.

A studious scholar profound knowledge seeks.
He examines what is said, and him who speaks.

He's the kind of guy that'll portray a mirage,
He'll pat you on the back then charge for a massage.

There is no doubt our people practice stealth;
Our country is abundant with unreported wealth.

There's nothing that governments can't give to us
Unless initially they extract it from us.

Frequently the person who usually laughs late, has a wobbly, insecure upper plate.

There's so much unrest, likewise of ill; many try to obtain long-lost peace from a pill.

Today give a stranger one of your lovely smiles;
You'll never know, he may be suffering from denials.

A feature that likens some men to animals,
Is the frequency with which some resemble cannibals.

The size of your torso you can surmount, the size of your brain has potential to count.
It's the size of your heart that inflates the amount.

Stubbornness is not that easy to take; it's better to bend than it is to break.

Retirees move south for warmth and fun,
And then do all they can to stay out of scorching sun.

It's said things desired come to those who wait,
But by then realize that they're totally out of date.

Green hospital gowns and health insurance, I'm certain that most of you have discovered,
Bear a remarkable, a surprising similarity, when you realize you're not fully covered.

What we 'off the cuff' say, tells; what we frequently laugh at smells.

Awareness you must fully address; insight is a key to success.

Articles for commerce: Brains and learning, muscles and skill.
Not for sale: Virtue and integrity, character and will.

A LIFESTYLE PORTRAYAL From A TO Z

There are two types of stores in our city, in some, no clerks, you wait, what a pity.
In others, the clerks are hired to ignore,
You just help yourself as you come through the door.

❧

The way we act behind the steering wheel,
Our nefarious character it does clearly reveal.

❧

Some people get drunk, just to unravel, and then end up standing before the gavel.

❧

Make the best of your world, do not be dismayed,
When the world gives you lemons, make fresh lemonade.

❧

The human spirit can bear reality, not artificiality or despicable sensuality.

❧

Do you chisel or do you carve - do you feed or do you starve?

❧

Sometimes, a person, needs a strong, steady hand
To help, to hold, and a heart to understand.

❧

Death and taxes, to many is a curse, but death, somehow, doesn't seem to get worse.

❧

A school has four walls - studious students, a surprise;
It's where our hope in a not-too-distant future lies.

❧

It is not in the probable nor in the likely possible;
What we need is people specializing in the impossible.

❧

Lives will be chock-full of living if our hearts are lovingly giving.

❧

If your life lives a lie, the second time you will die.

❧

You don't get to choose the method of your demise,
You choose how to live to prepare for the skies.

❧

Only what I choose to live by, is noticed by another's sharp eye.

❧

Life is like a pencil, be it slender or stout,
You can't make your mark without getting the lead out.

❧

The measure of a man is not how he's postured
In days of comfort and modern convenience.
It is where he stands in relationship to God,
And how he complies implicitly to obedience.

❧

A LIFESTYLE PORTRAYAL From A TO Z

There may be greatness in one's self-respect,
But a concern above another is a character defect.

❧

The past you'll note continues to last, but don't live in it, there's no future in it.

❧

You're not as young as you used to be, and you're not as old as you're going to be.

❧

When you give of yourself, you receive more than pelf.

❧

If your life is to rhyme, be the pilot of your time.

❧

My dog thinks I'm great – stable – never worsen;
My prayer, to always be that type of person.

❧

Through gradual growth, reform and change
We're prone our heavenly security to arrange.

❧

Some go to a physician due to physical obsession;
The malady, a result of gastronomical indiscretion.

❧

To be artfully astute doesn't come from a book,
It's so frequently knowing what things to overlook.

❧

If you keep on saying, "Things are going to be bad,"
Not later but sooner you'll be feeling very sad.

❧

Not only its length, live its depth and its breadth.
May your living follow the path the Scripture saith.

❧

This test of one's courage record on life's chart,
"Bear your reversals without losing heart."

❧

In our lives we must strive for a life of action,
Not of indolence or antagonistic reaction.

❧

Why would you rally to the stream in the valley,
When you can experience a fountain in the mountain?

❧

"Accomplished," is a word of achievement, "I won't" are words of retreat,
"Perhaps," a word foreboding, "I can't," are words of defeat.
"I should," are words of stern duty, "Must try," are words of each hour,
"I will," are words of sheer beauty, "I'm able," are words of power.
-Anonymous

❧

A LIFESTYLE PORTRAYAL From A TO Z

*G*od hates the human heart that devises wicked schemes,
The heart that's intent on destroying one's dreams.
He hates feet that are quick to rush into evil,
Stirring up dissension – causing an upheaval.
He hates a false witness, the one who spews lies,
The one who sheds blood and the one with haughty eyes.
Another prime evil, he hates adultery, and to the above he adds jealousy.
God deems these detestable; man's folly is regrettable.

*W*ho has troubles, who has pain? He who drinks wine will always complain.
He will have bruises and bloodshot eyes; he who imbibes is far from wise.

*W*here God guides, He graciously provides.

*L*ife's cosmetic is something to do; an active mind finds something new.

*P*ermit happy thoughts to run through your mind.
Your face will exhibit a countenance that is kind.

*T*oo many people miss the silver lining; for glittering gold they're usually pining

"*E*veryone is important," said my father, I recollect;
Must treat others with courtesy, dignity and respect.

*I*f you will observe the benign rules of life,
Compassionate to all, avoiding vile strife;
If you are temperate with your food and drink,
No gluttonous delight, you'll always be in the pink.

*I*f you would that your day lack not of energy,
Be watchful of NUTRITION, know well its quality.
If you would that your day be lively and viable,
A portion for EXCERCISE must be identifiable.
If you would that your day be happy and bright,
Drink plenty of WATER and enjoy the SUNLIGHT.
If you would that your day of cobwebs be clear,
It is very important to breathe FRESH AIR.
If you would that your day with REST be complete,
Your life must be TEMPERATE, with MODERATION be replete.
If you would that your day be free of distress,
TRUST fully in the Lord, He'll truly bless.

*T*hings just don't turn up in this big wide world,
Unless that "turn up" is by someone unfurled.

A LIFESTYLE PORTRAYAL From A TO Z

*B*etween most people there is very little difference,
But that little difference can make a big difference.

❧

*G*od makes time, but man makes haste; God makes beauty, but man makes waste.

❧

*L*uscious green grass can eventually turn into milk.
Likewise, from the mulberry we can get silk.

❧

A man to be successful has capacity for thinking,
And from positive action he mustn't be shrinking.

❧

*W*e didn't all migrate in the same ship,
But we're in the same boat, hoping it won't tip.

❧

*S*ome food preparations should be left unsung,
Like mother-in-law sandwiches, cold shoulder and tongue.

❧

*T*axes can be likened to playing the game of golf,
You put yourself into it, both body and soul.
You drive your heart out, trying to reach the green;
A paradoxical result, you end up in the hole.

❧

*W*hen you have been wronged, more than once,
An imperfect memory is the best response.

❧

*Y*ou may think you're on the right road because it's a well-beaten path;
Be extremely cautious my friend, lest it lead to misery and death.

❧

*W*e're forever getting ready to live, without giving thought when to give.

❧

*A*n old proverb tells us that social equality
Is present only in the neighboring cemetery.

❧

*I*nspiration and perspiration – not only do they rhyme,
They're always in step and they keep perfect time.

❧

*Y*ou'll honor the Lord on all that you do if you always live with eternity in view.

❧

*W*hen aiming for perfection, head it in the right direction.

❧

A step forward in obedience is a mountain top experience.

❧

A sinful heart, comparable to a crooked fence;
Paint won't straighten it, regardless of the expense.

❧

A LIFESTYLE PORTRAYAL From A TO Z

One cannot use force to make one achieve; I cannot be saved by a dogma I disbelieve.

If your heart is to be in it, you must put your mind to it.

God's law is the basis of civil society; it unequivocally points out man's impropriety.

Honor a man's virtue, avoid envy, be kind; as to his faults, strive to be blind.

If virtue in another you do not eschew, you're taking the first step toward virtue.

Virtue's triad: revering the inferior, respecting your peers, and honoring those superior.

For virtue to grow, keep a profile that's low.

Intelligence is the palate that detects and tastes, and auspicious time it never wastes.

Condescending moral equality is the hallowed law of humanity.

Although one's giving knows specific reason, true giving doesn't pin-point the season.

Wisdom is the essence of wealth, cheerfulness, the flower of health.

If you honestly believe and dream you are right,
You mustn't only dream, you must work and fight
With wisdom and might, keeping vision in sight.

Keep forging forward with full vigor and steam;
Only fish that are dead appear swimming downstream.

"The test of good manners," said I to my sons,
"Requires determination to be patient with bad ones."

Be not the first by whom the new is tried, nor be you the last to lay the old aside.
-Alexander Pope

Your wisdom will gradually recede if you don't feed your need to read.

Be exceedingly cautious of gleam and glitter,
Lest it lead you to the path called 'Bitter.'

Unlike space, time has direction; allow time's arrow to lead to perfection.

People who do more than of them is required
Are usually the ones who invariably get hired.

A LIFESTYLE PORTRAYAL From A TO Z

The fire you kindle for your enemy could seriously affect your destiny.

Temper your ambition, I humbly appeal, lest it become Achilles' heel.
[Ah-kill-ees-heel - A weak spot, vulnerable.]

With generous enthusiasm, carpe diem.
[car-pay-dee-um – Seize the day.]

To the hallowed triptych of our western society,
Money, beauty and youth, add prudent sobriety.
[trip-tick – A painting in three parts.]

We should live de jure, this is God's way.
[day-jur-ay - According to law.]

To be an astute apprentice you must be compos mentis.
[comp-os-meant-us – Mentally alert.]

Elan vital is available to all.
[eh-lan-vee-tall – Vital force.]

To live pari passu we should all strive to do.
[par-ee-pass-oo – Equal pace,- fairly.]

An adventurous esprit de corps is the mood we all should strive for.
[es-pree-duh-core – The mood of a group, togetherness, solidarity.]

Radio Moscow, once purported to be the U. S. S. R's vox populi,
Has virtually been proven to be not true democracy.
[vocks-pop-u-li – Voice of the people, popular opinion.]

Watch closely your actions, avoid contretemps,
Lest into an embarrassing situation you romp.
[con-tra-tomp - Misadventure.]

In selecting an agent provocateur, be certain that he is intellectually mature.
[ah-jawn-pro-vock-a-teur – Secret agent.]

Why exhibit hauteure when you can be demure.
[oh-tur – Haughtiness, arrogance.]

Spilled milk is fait accompli; crying over it would be silly.
[fete-a-com-plee – A done deal.- an action that is already completed.]

A LIFESTYLE PORTRAYAL From A TO Z

To wash hands frequently is de rigueur; this counsel, apropos for Mr. Restaurateur.
[du-ree-grr – Obligatory,- required by current custom.]

❧

A bore, if you virtually never want to become,
Never elevate your pet peeves ad nauseam.
[add-naw-zee-am – To an excessive, sickening degree.]

❧

Being graciously and compatibly simpatico, adds to one's life's mystical glow.
[If you get along with others and you relate well with them you are simpatico]

❧

The informed Fourth Estate to my thinking does rate.
[Journalists, the press, the media – The first three estates are clergy, baron and knights and the Commons.]

❧

Discouragement defy, hold your head high;
Your amour propre will carry you through.
[ah-moor-pro-pruh – Self-respect.]

❧

Support your alma mater, as one who is fully mature.
[ahl-muh-ma-tur –The college or university you attended.]

❧

We should all be looking toward ad infinitum.
God's eternity - a blessed event to come.
[Add-in-fin-eye-tum - To infinity,- without end or limit]

❧

Never lose interest in life and the world,
Set a sound schedule as the day is unfurled.
Allow not yourself to be at all annoyed,
At all times may your spirit be gently buoyed.
Get plenty of sunlight and adequate sleep,
Your physical frame many benefits will reap.
Eat regularly at set hours, plenty of water to drink,
If you follow these rules you always be in the pink.
Your doctor always see, consult him quite often;
Take plenty of exercise, with prayer your life hyphen.

❧

The measure of life is not its duration, but what to mankind has been its donation.

❧

Spend not your brief life on vain pleasure and a casket;
Expend it on something that will far outlast it.

❧

Put not off the joy of deeds that are needful;
The recipients of your acts will always be grateful.

❧

"As you would that men should do unto you, always do you also unto them."
This is long known as the golden rule; a profound Biblical injunction for man.

❧

You cannot help but have a perfect day, when you help someone who can't repay.

The measure of your calling, your profession - 'tis sharing;
Creating opportunities and others' burdens bearing.

Don't lose your head to gain a minute, you need your head your brains are in it.

Cautious rider to her reckless dear, let's have less bull and a lots more steer.

Speed was high, weather was not, tires were thin – X marks the spot.

Both hands on the wheel, your eyes on the road, that's the skilful driver's code.

Drove too long, driver snoozing, what happened next is not amusing.
Around the curve, lickety-split, it's a beautiful car, wasn't it?

No matter the price, no matter how new, the best safety device in the car is you.
-Burma Shave

High Tailing It

'I wasn't repairing binders, changing rods and engine pistons,
It was the 'blue bottle' that was the bane of my existence.

Eat at Joe's – millions of flies – could they be wrong?
Nonetheless, I shuddered when with food they played ping-pong.

I tell this brief story not for 'plause and vain glory;
They were the good ole days, so for me don't feel sorry.

Way back on the old farm, the pesky horsefly was so bad,
It made the herds restless, and yes, so very mad.

With tails up perpendicular, the cows would swiftly flow;
They'd dash for nearest poplars where the little beasties would let go.

You see that's where the utterance, 'High-Tailing-It,' came from.
Many think it strange – for cattle it wasn't dumb.

"Bill, you've forgotten my birthday again," their marriage was becoming somewhat colder.
"How can you expect me to remember your birthday when you never look a day older.

If you expect to have friends be friendly, to follow this maxim never fail.
Money can buy a pedigreed dog, but it can't buy a wag in his tail

A LIFESTYLE PORTRAYAL From A TO Z

If you'd like to have the last word, there are two words I guarantee
That are bound to settle any argument, they are simply, "I agree."

ᗩ

Do not be hasty in word, be not impulsive in thought.
We know through the voice of a fool, much transgression is wrought.

ᗩ

Someone has prudently said, seemingly with a sense of duty,
"Try practicing random kindness and senseless acts of beauty."
With an act of random kindness, someone's life you'll have brightened.
Furthermore, you'll get the feeling, your own troubles have been lightened.

ᗩ

To be duly prepared always look ahead; don't let yourself die until you are dead.

ᗩ

Blessed are the meek, they've increased their worth.
They are the people that will inherit the earth.

ᗩ

The crucial, selective tests of a truly virtuous man
Are based on high principles since life first began.
He's mild-mannered and amiable, exemplary and gracious,
Charming and caring, conscientious, not ostentatious.
He's alert, extremely able, committed and ambitious,
Contemplative, incorruptible, honest and vivacious.
He's kind and compassionate, not at all short on giving,
For beneficence is truly a great part of his living.

ᗩ

The thoughts in the two poems below, to one's lifestyle are quite apropos.

ᗩ

How Do You Live With Your Dash

I read of a man who stood up to speak at a funeral of a very close friend,
He pointed to the dates on his granite tombstone from their beginning to the end.

He noted that first came the date of his birth, and spoke of the last date with tears,
But he said what mattered the most of all – was the dash between those years.

For the dash represented all of the time that he spent alive on this earth . . .
And now only those who truly loved him know what that line is worth.

It really matters not how much we own, the cars – the house – the cash –
What matters the most, how we live and love, and what we do with our dash.

About this, my friend, think long and hard - are there things you would like to change?
For one never knows how much time is left, that can still be beautifully rearranged.

A LIFESTYLE PORTRAYAL From A TO Z

If we could take time to slow down enough, to consider what's meaningful and real,
And earnestly try to fully understand the way other people might feel.

And be less hasty to anger and debate, but to show appreciation much more,
And to love the people that touched our lives, liked we've never loved before.

If we would treat others with due respect, and more frequently wear a broad smile,
Always remembering that the short, special dash might last but a very short while.

So when your eulogy nostalgically is read, with your life's noble actions to rehash . . .
Would you be proud of the things they've said, about how you spent your dash?
-Anonymous

Take Time To Hear The Music Before The Song Is Over

Have you watched kids on a Merry-Go-Round,
Or listened to rain drops slapping the ground?

Ever followed a butterfly's spasmodic, erratic flight,
Or eyeballed setting sun into the fading night?

Do you run through each day, always on the fly?
When you ask, "How are you?" - do you hear the reply?

When dreary day is done, do you lie in your bed
With the next hundred chores running through you head?

To your child have you said, "We will do it tomorrow?
And in heedless haste you didn't see its sorrow.

Unmindfully losing touch – letting a good friendship die?
You didn't even call - just to say a brief, "Hi."

Too busy to accept a sister's invite to dinner. . . .
She dies in an accident – you're a loser not a winner.

"I'm going to," "I plan to when things are settled down."
Friend, seize the moment, why live a frown.

When you worry and hurry throughout the whole day,
It's comparable to a gift carelessly thrown away.
Have joy in your schedule, to self don't be mean;
Now and then depart from your rigid routine.

Life's not a race, friend, do take it slower;
Do listen to the music before the song is over.
-Anonymous - (paraphrased and enlarged)

An axiom that expresses one's life to the letter,
"No man ever lives long enough to know better."

Periodically pause to pray, you'll find 'twill make your day.

Climb high, climb far, your goal the sky, your aim the star.

LISTEN - LISTENING

While the right to talk may be the beginning of freedom,
the necessity of listening is what makes the right important.
-Will C. Crawford

To you what others say, don't attempt to evade,
You must listen carefully if you're to persuade.

To say the right thing at the right time we must carefully listen all the time.

Listen to wise voices, they're the sum of your choices.

When I should be listening, my motor keeps running;
My spouse's irate reaction is oft quite stunning.

If you're determined to give a listening ear, or a loving touch you are bound,
You have a remarkable, a lasting potential of turning a life around.

Too much a man of letters himself will eye;
So oft he's one letter, that letter is "I."

If you listen to another's point of view, he'll be more inclined to listen to you.

Said an acquaintance of mine who rarely spoke a brief line,
"I certainly can't learn when my tongue goes like a piston,
And so I talk little, I sit quietly and listen."

The mute word "listen" has the same letters as "silent."
I'll be more attentive, I'll be doubly compliant.

When others speak, be intently attentive;
May listening absorbingly be a renewed incentive.

A LIFESTYLE PORTRAYAL From A TO Z

When speaking if you sense that the listening is lessening,
Here's some sound advice, add to it shortening.

❧

I observe some people, I ideate to be such,
I listen to the people who don't talk too much.

❧

More time to listen, less time to scorn;
Why not grow an antenna instead of a sharp horn?

❧

The art of conversation is enhanced by auscultation.

❧

Amazingly a good listener is popular elsewhere.
He usually learns something that he can share.

❧

An attentive, sympathetic listener is reckoned a silent flatterer.

❧

A good listener is popular most everywhere he goes.
In time he adds much to what he already knows.

❧

It's amazing what one learns simply by eavesdropping;
Listening, very oft, more productive than talking.

❧

I know you believe you understand, what you think to you I have read,
But I'm not so sure that you realize, what you've heard is not what I've said.

❧

How can one listen to what someone is conveying,
When you rush to supply words that another attempts saying?

❧

A lesson for mankind, especially my peers,
You can win more friends not with words but with ears.

❧

Listening is not always what it seems to appear.
Intent, sincere listening is wanting to hear.

❧

Listening can result in more sales than talking.
Too much of the latter sends customers walking.

❧

The more and more you listen, the more and more you'll hear.
So frequently while you're listening understanding will appear.

❧

If others you're to persuade, listening you mustn't evade.

❧

You may think that he's listening, don't flatter yourself.
A listener is frequently thinking of something else.

❧

A LIFESTYLE PORTRAYAL From A TO Z

*L*isten to others, this you must do; do as you would have them listen to you.

*T*hose who love to chatter, their mouths go like a piston.
You'll find that they are the people who hate to listen.

*U*sing your ears can prevent many tears.

*E*ffective listening is being content
To listen to the entire spoken thought,
Rather than interrupting or impatiently waiting
To respond in your own time slot.

*L*isten attentively, don't deem it a chore.
You might hear something you've never heard before.

*L*istening is a very important thing to do.
It is wise to have the other's point of view.

*S*o very few people would listen to squawk
If they knew that they didn't have their own turn to talk.

*O*ne way to be popular is to listen attentively
To those things in the past that you've learned objectively.

*A*n intelligent, attentive listener becomes not only highly rated,
He becomes profoundly esteemed and illustriously celebrated.

*W*ith articulate sound speech the whole world one can reach.

*B*e a good listener, this thought carve in stone.
If you listen you'll get ideas that differ from your own.

*T*he most important thing you can do today
Is to silently listen to what God has to say.

LITIGATION

*P*otential litigants will settle their disputes the first day they come together if you put the idea of arbitration into their heads.
-Moses H. Grossman

*S*ome startling negatives for sowing wild oats,
It's vigorous rapid growth is hard to abort,

And the huge crop eventually reaped
Must be thoroughly threshed out in district court.

ℯ

Going to court, oft a hurtful spat.
It's losing a cow for the sake of a cat.

ℯ

LOGISTICS

Cause and effect are two sides of one fact.
-Ralph Waldo Emerson

ℯ

When logic is discovered underscoring your belief,
It gives you a good feeling, gives anxiety relief.

ℯ

LONELINESS - SOLITUDE

For solitude sometimes is best society.
-John Milton

ℯ

Loneliness is when you have something to share,
Your love, your thoughts, but no one is there.

ℯ

If you're lonely while alone, you're in bad company;
Do something about it, find a viable remedy.

ℯ

One's loneliness is not an absence of affection,
Very frequently it is the lack of direction.

ℯ

LORD'S SUPPER

For as often as you eat this bread and drink this cup,
you do show the Lord's death till he come.
-1 Corinthians 11:26

ℯ

Celebrating the Lord's Supper, endorphins will raise
To move our hearts, to mend our ways.
Neglect not to take part, the Good Book says.

ℯ

LOVE

*P*eace comes to us through love.
-Annette Victorin

❧

*S*ouls that don't love go empty in this world;
Let love, adoration and compassion be unfurled.

❧

*H*appy is the couple who lives and sings the life of love, honor it brings.

❧

*L*ove will endure if you keep it pure.

❧

*T*rue love is abiding, attentive, all-absorbing,
Deep-seeing, non-calculating, duteous, all-discerning;
Consoling, confiding, approving, condescending,
Endearing, enduring, forgiving, comprehending;
Spontaneous, so genuine, redeeming, assisting,
Stimulating, steadfast, passionately persisting;
Stupendous, responsive, unselfish, sacrificial,
Intimate, intense, remorseful and thoughtful;
Zealous, vivacious, virtuous, becoming,
Wondrous, unrelenting, undying and yearning;
Longsuffering, lifelong, matchless, and thankful,
Mutual, profound, so pure and faithful.

❧

*D*on't hug yourself, unwind your charms; love is initiated with open hands and arms.

❧

*L*ove is free of random provocation, and it's given without thought of reciprocation.

❧

*T*rue, genuine love if not fully unfurled is bound to go empty in this old wicked world.

❧

*T*he smile from heaven cannot be expected,
When the rules of God's love are summarily rejected.

❧

*L*ove is a welcome refreshing rain; lust is a promiscuous, tempestuous hurricane.

❧

*L*ove, one can't disguise, it starts in the eyes.

❧

*L*ove is a wholesome, a priceless commodity, on giving it away so many weep.
It's the only viable abstract entity that we can give and still have to keep.

❧

*W*hen love is full and mutually equal, a loving marriage is a beautiful sequel.

❧

*F*or some, self-love is a lifelong romance; to love mankind they don't take a chance.

❧

A LIFESTYLE PORTRAYAL From A TO Z

Love is a big hug that gives heartstrings a snug tug.

※

To truly love, one need not be passionate.
To be sincerely loved is to be highly fortunate.

※

People with a disability have profound credibility.
They have capability for surprising compatibility,
And a most precious ability to instinctively love.

※

You cannot get love from a heart that's been wrenched,
No more than get giving from a fist that is clenched.

※

Love does not say, "For me do more," nor does it attempt to keep any score.

※

Man loves glitter and he loves pelf; with so much to love why choose oneself?

※

Love is not prone to seek honor and vain glory,
And not at all reticent to say, "I'm sorry."

※

To lack fervent love is to lack sound wisdom.
We should all relate to this stimulating aphorism.

※

Vile confrontation - hatred seems to beckon;
In the presence of love, blessed mysteries happen.

※

Love is the expression of two people in such fashion
That each includes the other; it enriches without ration.

※

For love at first sight there's a remedy in my book.
It can usually be cured with a shrewd second look.

※

Responsible love cares, it doesn't put on airs,
It doesn't have affairs and it says its prayers.

※

Love that's sincere, void of pride and conceit, can build a stage on which all can meet.

※

With those who love, strive to be among; hearts that truly love will always stay young.

※

To love and be loved confides, it feels the sun on both sides.

※

Love does not offend nor a heart does it rend.
It's inclined to bend to mend and defend.

※

Love is the answer to the age-old riddle
Why two loving-hearts always sit in the middle.

A LIFESTYLE PORTRAYAL From A TO Z

Though the ends of the bench have much more room,
Togetherness in the center they lovingly assume.

❧

Love isn't a chore, nor is it a bore, we should ask for it less and be giving it more.

❧

We do things oft because of duty, but love persuades to do with beauty.

❧

To be most meaningful, let love be a verb, not only to be seen, it must also be heard.

❧

Food, a gift of God, so readily made edible;
A manifestation of His love that's totally incredible.

❧

It's not infatuation, nor is it mute lust; the true basic quality of love is trust.

❧

If love is blind, then how would you relate
To people dressing up every time they have a date?

❧

Love is a modifier, of compassion, an amplifier,
Of friendship, a magnifier, of right living, a qualifier,
Of character, a purifier, of goodness, an intensifier,
Of vile discord, a rectifier, of dissension, a pacifier.

❧

Live a life of love for life's survival; he who loves himself will have no rival.

❧

The basic need of our cold society is the revival of gentleness and love;
A gracious charity in equitably judging, initiated by God's abundant love.

❧

The object of love is to serve not win; lust, on the contrary leads on to sin.

❧

Love, compassion, and happiness within you; dignity and humility are part of virtue.

❧

Love is not love when you casually blow it, love is not love unless you show it.

❧

Can there be an atonement for that precious moment,
When my love was necessary, but I acted contrarily?

❧

To love, in truth, is rightly comprehending.
In verity, it's forgiving and graciously condescending.

❧

Living is loving, loving is giving, giving is sharing, loving is caring.

❧

Love can achieve unexpected majesty
On the mountainous peak of misfortune and tragedy.

❧

The love you take is the love you make.

❧

A LIFESTYLE PORTRAYAL From A TO Z

If you are lonely, friends you aren't making,
Remember, love is there, always there for the taking.

Take love from your life, you'll have incessant strife.

Use your given gifts to show love to people; never use talent for using people.

Love your enemies, bear their assaults,
Listen to their grievances, they point out your faults.

True love rejoices at the success of others; envy and resentment it always smothers.

How does love come? – comes unsought, unsent.
How does love go? – it wasn't love that went.

True love cares, it doesn't put on airs, it doesn't have affairs, it lovingly shares,
And it always says its prayers.

To truly love is to fully comprehend; before the sun sets, it's quarrels to mend.

Love purifies, it strengthens one's character;
For attaining stellar virtue it's a potent benefactor.

What does the Lord require - what does sacred conscience prod?
It's to love mercy and justice, it is to walk humbly with God.

One's love letters duly impart campaign promises of the anxious heart.

The love that we give is the love that we keep.
Give allegiance to this dictum if happiness we're to reap.

Love doesn't boast, love isn't loud, it does not envy, and it isn't proud;
Love is patient, pure love is true, and it remembers its neighbor too.

The magnanimous power of love is greater than the love of power.
Your compassion and acts of kindness above other acts will tower.

Some know not love, their peers haven't bothered,
And so their loveliness has not been discovered.

A love tap can be consequential, it's known to have great potential.

Love is a power, it's a spiritual force that elevates our thoughts, a love to endorse.

A LIFESTYLE PORTRAYAL From A TO Z

Let us have love, a great deal of love, a love that vanquishes our foes.
A love that succinctly calms opposition, a love that in a heart glows.

❧

The bit of love is the only bit that bridles the tongue, so Solomon writ.

❧

Let the radiant beauty of what you love be blessed by our gracious God above.

❧

In love and in politics - a truth therein - a well-known fact, you don't always win.

❧

Love can be likened to quicksilver in the hand, a gifted message it does relay.
Leave your hand open, you will note it stays, clutch it and you'll find it darts away.

❧

All children need love, much more than a bit,
Especially when we think they do not deserve it.

❧

Love involves acts of endless forgiveness,
Hyphenated with patience that suppresses explosiveness.

❧

Do love your neighbor, this duly pledge,
But don't love so much that you pull down your hedge.

❧

Love dares to abolish in our lives vile hassles.
Love lives in cottages, not only in castles.

❧

The language of love needs no interpreter; love of itself is a powerful transmitter.

❧

Divine love is the author of our amiable existence;
To show in my life I'll exercise persistence.

❧

A wee baby is born with a need to be loved, it never outgrows it, never aside shoved.

❧

For love to bind, it must be colorblind.

❧

Love is the doorway through which the human soul
Passes from selfishness to service as her goal.
It passes from solitude to unity of mind,
It's emotion put to motion, it's kinship with mankind.

❧

Beginning with a smile, if it's sincere, love grows with a kiss and ends with a tear.

❧

True love, most agree has a positive charge, that is if the battery isn't dead.
You won't experience full kick and great power if your love-battery is lead.

❧

Man wasn't given a loving, caring heart, for grabbing, for snatching, for stealing;
His heart was lit that he might know how love must be in his dealing.

❧

A LIFESTYLE PORTRAYAL From A TO Z

The quality of one's love isn't strained when it's shared;
It's not weakened or exhausted, it's strengthened, not impaired.

~

A mother's love is so dear, to me it's perfectly clear,
It always has a ready ear when to me it is near.
It's always bound to hear, it can nullify one's fear,
Can deliver joyous cheer, never a sardonic jeer,
Or a veiled subtle sneer; buoyant happiness she'll steer;
A fastidious love to revere!

~

People we like the least need our love the most.

~

Love is a fruit that's available every season;
Not to share it, there's never a plausible reason.

~

Occasionally give your spouse a gift for no reason,
Other than love, it's always in season.

~

All love is sweet, it does not weary - it's excitingly meaningful, it's not just theory.

~

The principle of God's love we should fully endorse.
It is so much stronger than the principle of force.

~

Love is not gazing at each other's reflection,
It's looking forward in the same direction.

~

When a heart truly loves it does great things,
Unquestionably it's then that intellect takes wings.

~

To the needy, some say, "Give them a fish."
This concept my friend is an ancient myth.
It's giving them a rod to catch fish with.

~

Love reduces friction to a fraction.

~

In helping others we mustn't be loath; love is a commitment to spiritual growth.

~

Love, you are bound to fully agree, is an irrepressible dancing desire
For an unquenchable burning flame, in another, love to set on fire.

~

Indifference fades away when love comes to stay.

~

Vile confrontation, aversion seems to beckon;
In the presence of love blessed miracles happen.

~

A LIFESTYLE PORTRAYAL From A TO Z

Meditating on God's love and His tender mercy
Will fill you with compassion - you'll rid controversy.

Love, a rule of conduct, a virtue of all virtues,
A power of all powers, a goodness we should choose.

Our love for humanity must widely be unfurled.
Souls that don't love go empty in this world.

Love that demands is usually spurned; a love that lasts must always be earned.

Giving, a way of sharing, love, a sign of caring.

When love and compassion work together for peace,
Expect nothing else but a beautiful masterpiece.

Can one truly fathom or fully count the cost, when love is missing, when love is lost?

To place a woman's heart on cupid's throne, a man must charmingly place his own.

A heart wherein love there is none is like a garden where there is no sun.

"*In* all our abundance, of love there is lack;" words by Hippocrates, many centuries back.

Love brings light and healing to the world, when with it generosity is graciously unfurled.

Love lights more fires than hate extinguishes;
Compassion and gratitude it never relinquishes.

Love is the beginning and the end of the law; passiveness and coolness it truly does thaw.

Though an abstract entity, love is profound; it must be earned, seldom is it found.

True love is not but a fleeting notion; it's complex emotion with profound, deep devotion.

Abiding love, forbearance does sire; in essence it can be deemed as a spiritual fire.

"*A* new commandment I give unto you, that you love one another," a divine thing to do.
-John 13:34

Love does not boast, love is not loud, it doesn't envy, and it isn't proud.
Love is patient, love is true, it always remembers its neighbor too.
-1 Corinthians 13 — see page 495

Love is a gift we can all afford - a gift of oneself without thought of reward.

A LIFESTYLE PORTRAYAL From A TO Z

This thought is sequential, its origin is mental,
"It's love that makes our hard hearts gentle."

&

When love and joy exist, apprehension and fear exit.

&

To love oneself, a lifelong romance, so many egocentrics dig.
I sincerely caution, I implore and beg - don't let your self-image get big.

&

Be a good lover, your love do cuddle;
'Tis better to be a geyser than a stagnant mud puddle.

&

"The love of humanity is the whole of morality."
-J. William Lloyd

&

LOYALTY

The strength of a country or a creed lies in the true
sense of loyalty it can arouse in the hearts of the people.
-Louis C. Gerstein

&

The best things in life need not be rationed;
Coupons aren't required when loyalty is fashioned.

&

Be loyal to your spouse and the children in your house.

&

MALIGNITY

A man's own venom is sure to poison him; usually a lot more than his innocent victim.

&

MARRIAGE - SINGLENES

Hail wedded love, mysterious law; true source of mysterious offspring.
-John Milton

&

Preceding a marriage an engagement is an urge
Of singular courage on the verge to merge.

&

Marriage, a relationship that has no equal;
The objectives are reciprocal and its love is mutual.

&

A LIFESTYLE PORTRAYAL From A TO Z

Never choose a mate if your freedom he curtails,
And when he delights taking the wind out of your sails.

~

Marriage, a moral status, for a couple it's scriptural,
But man must not ever act as a stubborn, intrepid general.

~

Would a great cellist need more than one cello to play the same piece of music?
Then why can't a man love just one woman? Just to one why can't he stick?

~

A good, happy marriage has its own peculiar charm,
It was never intended to do couples harm;
Freedom of communication between two lovely people,
Another basic rule, "Keep in touch with the steeple."

~

You can never guarantee a happy marriage with a ring,
No more than you can teach a fat sow to sing.

~

My friend, thank her now, lest you should sorrow;
You may not have opportunity to thank her tomorrow.

~

Marrying the one you can live with don't tout;
You should marry the one you can't live without.

~

Benjamin Franklin used his wise head,
When many years ago he so profoundly said,
"You cannot pluck roses without fear of thorns,
Nor enjoy a fine wife without danger of horns."

~

To demand of your love that there be no jealousy
Is to demand of marriage that there be no privacy.

~

Never try to overdo what's already been done;
Marriage is an exception, keep winning what's been won.

~

The more you invest in marriage, loving chums,
You'll find more magnetic your marriage becomes.

~

The more you invest in your marriage, the less there will be of disparage.

~

Defend, protect, champion your wife; be her best friend all of your life.

~

Oft marriage is the triumph of emotional imagination
Over sluggish intelligence, good counsel and frustration.

~

A LIFESTYLE PORTRAYAL From A TO Z

*M*arriage has reached a deep crisis, people do not marry as they should.
They marry for better or worse, but seldom do they marry for good.

A lasting, happy marriage designs, falling in love many times;
Invariably with the same person; a prudent thought, yes, sublime.

*F*or certain shaky marriages wouldn't have to skid
If couples who said, "I do," said, "We did."

*N*ever marry for money, you can borrow it cheaper.
If you marry for money you'll be a poor sleeper.

*T*o your dear wife your ear always bend, remember, she is your very best friend.

*M*arriage is a process for determining, so I've heard,
Just what sort of a mate your spouse would've preferred.

A lifetime of unquenchable marriage can trigger a sigh of relief.
Not only does it multiply joy, it's bound to divide one's grief.

*T*he moon, a heavenly body, many a couple it does woo.
It swings ocean tides and the untied too.

*T*o be happy without marriage is hard to conceive;
Even Adam wouldn't have been happy in Paradise without Eve.

*I*t is said that marriage is a two-way street;
For continued maintenance, marriage counselors compete.

*T*here's nothing more admirable or enchantingly desirable,
As when a loving couple agree to make amends;
Seeing eye to eye as husband and wife,
Confounding their adversaries and delighting their friends.

"*M*arriages are created in heaven," a message underscored every spring;
Someone has facetiously added, "and so are thunder and lightning,"

*W*hen love is full and avowedly equal, a lovely marriage is the sequel.

*T*hat her dear husband do the dishes, so very frequently a darling wife wishes.
Have you ever heard a man being shot for gladly volunteering to do the dishes?

*B*y all means marry if you choose a good wife,
But do be prepared for a little bit of strife.
Now if you should get one that's unquestionably bad,

A LIFESTYLE PORTRAYAL From A TO Z

In a way, that in itself isn't all that sad,
For you could become a pragmatic philosopher;
That vocation in itself lofty thoughts could spur.

❧

Marriage teaches loyalty, forbearance and restraint,
And attributes you wouldn't need if you didn't have a mate.

❧

Marriage is indeed a great institution,
So many bodies with whom you must mingle.
You can have happenings during those distressing times
That you wouldn't experience if you remained single.

❧

So your marriage gives out; has there been too much pout?
Have you put enough in to prevent it wearing thin?

❧

"Looks can be deceiving," said a man to his spouse,
"A man with vacant look could have a full house."

❧

Combine common sense with the golden rule;
For success in marriage, a most valuable tool.

❧

The hard-gained goal in a marriage, regardless of its inclement weather,
Is not necessarily to think alike, it's to think independently together.

❧

Success in marriage is more than a ritual, it's more than being that right individual.
In verity it's being contractually visual, conceptual, perceptual and devoutly spiritual.

❧

If you think that marriage is a 50-50 proposition,
You're deleting half of it, recoup the omission.

❧

"Were you or your wife ever married before?" An executive asked a young Scot.
The man glared indignantly, he was obviously annoyed, "Sir, please tell me, before what?"

❧

Choose your sweet love, duly live and rejoice.
To accomplish the latter, dearly love your sweet choice.

❧

Some think it is great to be rich and strong;
Much greater to know to your love you belong.

❧

"The reason for my tears of joy," at a beautiful wedding, said a mother,
"It's because my lovely young daughter married a man just like her father."

❧

My wife's elucidation of her vow is quite terse,
She succinctly puts it in concise poetic verse,
"I could've done better, you could've done worse."

❧

A LIFESTYLE PORTRAYAL From A TO Z

Said a bride to her husband, "When we get to the motel,
Let's pretend we've been married for years."
"That's great," said the husband, "You'll carry the bags."
"Oh no," she erupted in tears.

❧

A wife was vigorously powdering her nose before going out on the town.
"And why do you go to so much trouble, my dear?" said impatient hubby with a frown.
The wife's curt reply, "It's modesty my love, an attribute that's strictly all mine.
It's this way, my dear, no offense, but I haven't desire in public to shine."

❧

To be present at a conception, they're inexplicably delighted,
But to be present at a delivery, so many men are frightened.

❧

When a hubby brings flowers for his wife for no reason,
And if it happens to be totally out of season,
And matrimonial treason is not the reason,
There's bound to be some mysterious reason.

❧

In many good marriages you will find, that the husband is a solid provider.
Conversely you will also discover that the wife is invariably the decider.

❧

A woman dynamo static does bring, she is the woman that charges every thing.

❧

Now, why didn't you report the robbery right away?
Didn't you suspect something wrong the same day?
With tell-tale signs, gross disorder all about,
With all the drawers open, contents scattered about?"
"Yes,- I should've, officer, I wasn't fully alert,
I thought it was my husband frantically looking for a shirt."

❧

Be loyal to your spouse and the children in your house.

❧

A woman who insists on wearing the pants, a fur coat for another she's likely to enhance.

❧

A grammatically correct marriage is always tranquil;
The wife says, "You shall," and the husband, "I will."

❧

"Now, don't think you're going to play golf today!
Leaving me with the work,- well, what do you say?"
"It's the farthest from my mind," to his wife he did mutter
While eating his breakfast, "Honey, please pass the putter."

❧

A bride-to-be has a shower before walking that luring path,
But the groom, he never has one, instead, he's about to have a bath.

❧

A LIFESTYLE PORTRAYAL From A TO Z

A bride, these days, has so many showers in various seasons and climes.
A concern to her friends, many folk get soaked, some of them several times.

*T*o get more out of marriage, for love to win, you must work hard to put a lot more in.

*H*ere's to the first woman and to legend that's true,
Though very beautiful, she was but a side issue.

A maiden may be choosy about the man she would wed,
She may think he's unsightly and perhaps ill-bred.
She may see him as clumsy, though he may be quite deft,
She may think she is right, chances are she'll be left.

"*S*o you don't like my boyfriend!" said a daughter to her father.
"You'll notice that he comes in a swanky sports car."
"That's nothing," said the father, "When I courted your mother,
I took her in a trolley, worth much more by far."

A gallant, bona fide bachelor, many maidens have tried to win;
He has taken so many of them out, but to date has not been taken in.

*M*any bachelors prefer the circuitous route.
They firmly believe in "Happiness of Pursuit."

"*D*on't you get miserable being a lonely bachelor, why don't you marry someone?"
There's an entity far worse than being a bachelor - it's being a bachelor's son."

A bachelor, it would appear, has unique complacency.
He's a singular hombre with no wife expectancy.

A committed bachelor is permitted to flirt, though the buttons are missing on his shirt.
Even though he may have lost his shirt, a married man must stick to one skirt.

*W*edding expenses prolific, oft completely out of sight;
They're very frequently labeled as the nuptial bill of rights.

"*Y*ou must get rid of the 'ifs' in your life;" prudent admonition by a young, wise wife,

*M*arriage years ago was a binding contract; today it's an option with power to extract.

*C*ourtship is a period of doting and dating;
Marriage, a tedious time of waiting and debating.

A LIFESTYLE PORTRAYAL From A TO Z

It is said before marriage a man spoons around,
However, for marriage he is gallantly bound.
As time marches on he's no longer in clover,
He finds that he constantly has to fork over.

❧

Once upon a time, two brooms fell in love -
Said the male broom to the femme broom, "Let's get married my dove."
Just before the ceremony the bride informed the groom
That she was expecting a little whisk broom.
The broom groom was aghast, "Blow me over with a feather -
How could this have happened? We've never swept together."

❧

Do resolve making your marriage an edifice; conversely avoid it becoming a precipice.

❧

MATURITY

The mark of a mature man is that he wants to live humbly for a cause.
-William Stekel

❧

A good sign of maturity, a clever find, not a theft,
Is that the volume knob can also turn to the left.

❧

A token of maturity is having the ability
To be comfortable with people who are short on stability.

❧

Maturity is to have faith in the Almighty's surety.

❧

MEEKNESS

The meekness of Christ, manifested in the home will make the inmates happy.
-E. G. White

❧

If someone is to seek out the gentle meek, be the man that they wish to seek.
You can remove that vicious mean streak, just by trying to be meek for a week.

❧

To experience God's strength, recognize your weakness.
Rid ugly pride to experience true meekness.

❧

MESSAGE

God gave us a precious message to share; to keep it to ourselves, how would we dare.

❧

*Listen to the message, study the message, know the message, accept the message,
Claim the message, be part of the message, live the message, share the message.*

MIND - BRAIN - INTELLECT

The mind's the standard of the man.
        -Isaac Watts

Much reading swells the mind; one's exercise shrinks the behind.

The mind is not a deep-freeze storage; it should be a pilot for a lifetime voyage.

*Thousands seek work for a muscle to strain,
While the world is searching for a person with a brain.*

The more you use your brain, considerably more you'll retain.

*Cerebration creates wisdom, from brainwork never shrink;
Effective, lofty thoughts belong to those who think.*

Your mind is a sacred enclosure, it alone has control of its exposure.

*I must be cognizant of what goes into my mind
If I'm to become the prudent thinking kind.*

*It was Kettering who said, "Put bird cages in your mind."
To put something in them you'll eventually find.*

*Minds have been stretched so thinly o'er the years
That little of moral cells have been left between the ears.*

A chain is no stronger than its weakest link; likewise, the brain with its weakest think.

The human mind has many imitations; likewise, it has self-imposed limitations.

*Many dear people with their clear open minds
Are involved with pampering and coddling.
I truly believe that these same dear folk
Should have them closed for remodeling.*

*Fools and the dead don't change their mind.
Fools usually won't and the dead aren't inclined.*

Memory is so brief in a debtor, much better a memory in the creditor.

A LIFESTYLE PORTRAYAL From A TO Z

There's a question I can't get my thinker to win,
It's why heads grow bald but seldom the chin.

≈

A person who is endowed with a devotedly generous mind
Is benevolent, compassionate, unselfish and kind.

≈

Keep your mind busy and your body in motion.
May this be a habit, not just a notion.

≈

The brain can become an astute, keen mind,
When knowledge and wisdom are firmly combined.

≈

It's the mind that decides for good or for evil.
It's the mind that says, "I won't" or "I will."

≈

Great discoveries and improvements of all kinds,
Involve the cooperation of many astute minds.

≈

Your mind can be likened to a paper blotter; don't be with such a complement enamored.
You mustn't forget, 'tis prudent to remember, that blotters invariably get it all backward.

≈

Every time you give others a piece of your mind,
Their opinion of you falls far behind.

≈

My mind works like lightning, using computer or pen.
At times it exasperates - a flash - it's gone again.

≈

A body must be driven to survive by a mind that is very much alive.

≈

We must diligently search the good things of mind;
The pitifully insignificant are best left behind.

≈

When your brain is used more, the more you'll retain; determine your brain to tax.
Jumping to conclusions is not half as great an exercise as digging for facts.

≈

A great mind has purpose, a small mind has wishes.
A great mind is tenacious, a small mind relinquishes.

≈

The way that a man's mind is inclined to flow is the way that eventually he's likely to go.

≈

Convincing your mind that a bare, bad idea
Is a grand, great idea, could be a poor idea.

≈

If your heart and your brain seem to be far apart,
Listen to your head, there's no brain in your heart.

≈

A LIFESTYLE PORTRAYAL From A TO Z

Don't blow your top, be patient, use your mind.
Hot steam propels when it's totally confined.

≈

Your mind needs a break from its hectic routine.
Rest it now and then to help keep it keen.

≈

The woodpecker's success, so oft it's been said, is due to the fact that it uses its head.

≈

To those with open minds, be careful; rubbish could be thrown in, be prayerful.

≈

Some minds, like concrete oft get, all mixed up and permanently set.

≈

The brain could become an astute, trained mind,
When it chooses to attend a venerable college.
For then it's the time that its convoluted mass
Has the chance to be fortified with wisdom and knowledge.

≈

If your mind is on pelf it dwells upon self.

≈

In the words of President Woodrow Wilson, to prevent many problems and sorrow,
"Not only use the brains you've been endowed with, but also all the ones you can borrow."

≈

If the mind were very simple we could try to understand it,
But then we'd be too stupid to fully comprehend it.

≈

Doubtless the most moving moments of our lives,
Find us without words, the mind nosedives.

≈

Some people's minds are downright hazy,
Conceptualizing the difference between tired and lazy.

≈

What the mind can perceive, conceive and believe,
Most likely, eventually, 'twill successfully achieve.

≈

My brain is so active - it's always in a rush -
At times I can't remember what button to push.

≈

It's tragedy enough to be avertebral, but a total disaster to be acerebral.

≈

Take charge of your mind, leave worry behind;
Reading swells the mind, work shrinks the behind.

≈

No one can pick a peck of pickled peppers,
They have to be picked before they are pickled.

Very few can learn if education they spurn.
For knowledge to be down-trickled, the mind must be tickled.

❧

A devil-guided mind leads to sensuality.
Holy Spirit-guided intellect contributes to spirituality.

❧

Properly ventilate and illuminate your mind.
Leave needless fear and misfortune behind.

❧

A person grows as much as his brain vows, only as much as his horizon allows.

❧

Business, religion and pleasure of the right kind
Should be the ingredients of a prudent, thinking mind.

❧

Insects do have brains - how else could they figure out
Where you're having your picnic or where you'll be camping out.

❧

MISSIONARIES

Congratulations, felicitations, humble thanks to all missionaries,
Who give and who gave of their talent skill and time.
Who give and who gave of their lives in God's concessionaries;
The work of their hands has been immeasurably sublime.

❧

MISTAKES - WRONGDOING - ERROR

Who errs and mends, to God himself commends.
-Cervantes

❧

When you have realized you've made a mistake,
To correct it, my friend, right steps you must take.

❧

When something goes wrong, don't others frame,
Talk about fixing it rather than who to blame.

❧

To blatant wrongdoing some profess no claim.
They use a transmission that will shift the blame.

❧

Those who don't learn from mistakes, will invariably multiply heartaches.

❧

To make a mistake some deem it as terror;
Experience is the name that we give to error.

❧

A LIFESTYLE PORTRAYAL From A TO Z

Precisely you must know when to tune out,
Good sound judgment you must try to make.
If you should listen to too much advice,
You could end up making another's mistake.

❧

At other's mistakes do not ever revel.
Always keep your eyes on a friendly level.

❧

Most error is wrought through lack of sound thought.

❧

You're definitely skating on thin ice, when you make the same mistake twice.

❧

Never hesitate to ask dumb questions, they are not all that hard to take.
You'll find they're easier to regulate than is a frightfully stupid mistake.

❧

If immediate publicity you anxiously wish to make,
Become fully involved in a stupid mistake.

❧

"Admit your mistakes," says Uncle Clem, "before someone else exaggerates them."

❧

If a friend should make a mistake, don't of it an issue make.

❧

To avoid the mistakes of youth, draw from the wisdom of truth.

❧

Be able to admit you are wrong; an attribute that makes character strong.

❧

It could be misreckoning or idiotic misunderstanding
If you should make an administrative mistake.
But it is a lack of intellectual judgment
If prompt correction you don't undertake.

❧

Of errors in the past, so oft I've been the cause.
However, the past looks much better then it was.

❧

A mistake is evidence of the mark you were wide,
But it is corroboration that you sincerely tried.

❧

MODERATION

Fortify yourself with moderation, for this is an impregnable fortress.
-Epictetus

❧

True, practiced moderation avoids the odd binge.
Self-control in verity is a spiritual challenge.

❧

To practiced moderation your heart do incline.
Self-control is a pathway to the spiritually divine.

Moderation in all things is an ultimate worthy goal;
A time-honored attribute that lifts one's soul.

Fortify yourself with practiced moderation.
Make this your pillar of upright motivation.

Moderation in temper is always a virtue,
But moderation in principle is bound to hurt you.

The victuals that cause marked widening of the waist,
Cause narrowing of the arteries, to moderation make haste.

Powers that are exercised with violence cause ruination.
When practiced with moderation, the result, acclamation.

MODESTY

Modesty is the only sure bait when you angle for praise.
-Lord Chesterfield

Modesty is the art of being humble, a virtue that doesn't ever shout.
Surprisingly, however, it draws attention to whatever one is humble about.

The humble, lackluster citizen that's clad in a righteous cause,
Will prove to be mentally strong; he's bound to earn worthy applause.

There are no stages of honesty, nor are there degrees of modesty.

Meekness is not frailty, weakness and ineptness,
It's modesty, gentleness, forbearance and tenderness.

Modesty is the art of drawing one's attention
To whatever it is you're being humble about;
Freedom from sheer vanity, and excessive prim pride,
Void of derision or exhibition of clout.

True modesty and prim pride are difficult to hide.

MONEY

Put not your trust in money, but put your money in trust.
   -Oliver Wendell Holmes

❧

Money communicates - problems it duplicates.

❧

Matters not how much you accrue, money will not get you virtue.
However, when lofty virtue is attained, money is much more easily gained.

❧

It's quite well known that well-meant money talks, it usually has its own way.
Pinching poverty talks too, but very few stop to hear what it has to say.

❧

Make not making money your creed, lest your priority be greed.

❧

Money, a worthy servant but an injudicious master.
At times it's menacing, oft spelling disaster.

❧

"Money isn't everything," say those who have it;
Yet, with opportunity they enthusiastically grab it.

❧

"When money talks the truth is silent;"
An old Russian proverb with profound assessment.

❧

What language does it speak? They say money talks.
I know it's hard of hearing, when I call it balks.

❧

Money, a success symbol in our highfalutin culture.
To attain more of it, man swoops on it like a vulture.-

❧

Money is what one makes it - try to be keenly observant;
Never a tyrannical master, instead an honest servant.

❧

I have an old friend who keeps money in his fridge, he doesn't do it for a bash.
He stores it neatly in the freezer compartment – it's to have on hand cold cash.

❧

"For Sale, a carved desk - stands solid on fours,
For the discriminating lady, with thick legs and large drawers."

❧

When considering the food prices at our village grocery store,
You'll agree, spilled milk is worth crying for.

❧

To all you budding entrepreneurs - here's something I think you should know.
The ingenious creator of pretzels makes money out of crooked dough.

❧

A LIFESTYLE PORTRAYAL From A TO Z

Most money is flat – like it best when it's fat.

❧

Saving ample cash, has its recompense;
Dollars go further accompanied by sense.

❧

Money can make some people benevolent.
With most it makes them extremely extravagant.
Praise can make a wise man modest, for a fool, it usually makes him arrogant.

❧

That money talks, one cannot deny, I hear it so oft, it says, "'Goodbye."

❧

Prudent thrift you can't truly nurse, when you've reached the bottom of the purse.

❧

My logger friend says, "Money grows on trees;"
Obviously the reason governments collect stumpage fees.

❧

When it comes to finances, don't take any chances.
According to statistics be ruthlessly realistic.

❧

If microbes cling to money as so frequently we are told,
Let's learn how they do it so onto money we can hold.

❧

A succinct Scottish proverb, insightful, not funny,
"No alternatives to thrift in the absence of money,"

❧

Money, daily bread, it's pervasive leaven.
It's a universal passport, but it won't take you to heaven.

❧

It's great to have plenty of money and the things that money can buy.
Check now and then, make certain you haven't lost things you can't buy.

❧

If you have money to burn, there is no need for dispatch.
You'll always find that someone to give you a ready match.

❧

Money is better than poverty in most seasons; be it primarily for financial reasons.

❧

If you expect money to jingle in your pocket,
You must be the owner of a mobile hip socket.
Or one might say, "You must shake a leg."
This terse maxim does wistfully beg.

❧

Some latch onto money, it gives them a thrill.
Paul said, "The love of it is the root of all evil."
I would like to remind you, though it's tax deductible,
You can't take it with you, eventually it's destructible.

❧

Some investments - a painful heartache; at times, the best are the ones you don't make.

MOODS

To truly accomplish, why wait for moods;
Much more importantly, bear in mind the "shoulds."

Today's society seems to be in the mood
For something different, like fat-free junk food.

Beware of your moods, don't let the low fool,
They can be deceptive, you must keep cool.
Folk don't always realize how moods will run;
When moods are down, try them to shun.
Negative feelings come when moods are low,
However, positive thinking is the way to go.
The next time you're low, for whatever the reason,
Just say to yourself, "This isn't the season."
When you're in a good mood, communication is easy,
But you must be wary, lest it become cheesy.
Life isn't as bad as the scene may seem;
You must strive to create a positive dream.

Never give way to melancholy, incline to be consistently jolly.

MORALITY

There can be no high civility, without a deep morality.
-Emerson

You're bound to increase your moral accountability
By increasing your ability, stability and responsibility.

True morality is doing what is right, during day hours and throughout the whole night.

Never allow your fastidious morality to be threatened by your arrogant authority.

Intellectual pride is exceedingly important, but greater is moral principle.
Without the latter distinct attribute, sustaining true progress is impossible.

Most moralists are prone to decide that quickening conscience is a singular guide.

*Our unstable footings we can ill afford.
We must strive to have moral props restored.*

Austere morality we must assume; a truth that's perpetually in full bloom.

MOTIVATION - INCENTIVE

The love of truth, and a sense of responsibility to glorify God, are the most powerful of all incentives to the improvement of the intellect.
-E. G. White

Incentives are external, motivations are internal.

Lofty, upright motivation encourages one's poetic creation.

With lofty motivation we must daily cope; the mystery of motivation is visionary hope.

*If with motivation you seriously keep toying,
Eventually a secured habit will keep you going.*

*The impossible by many is shunned, likewise, by many it is eyed.
Determine to fulfill your dream; the impossible is oft the untried.*

One can't be motivated by dismal mope; the secret of motivation is visionary hope.

*Motivation gets you started, habit keeps you going.
Just keep on pedaling and you mustn't stop rowing.*

D - R - I - V - E
D – Dedication
R – Responsibility
I – Integrity
V – Vision
E – Enthusiasm.

Motivation can fade if you don't give it aid.

*Likelihood may not appear in the wings - it may appear totally improbable.
However, when one is highly motivated, it's easier to accomplish the impossible.*

*There's no abject failure except in no longer trying.
There is no utter defeat unless motivation is dying.*

Lofty motivation must be compelling; militantly overcoming you must be willing.

Harbor an incentive that is credibly preventive.

Incentives are spurs that goad; they motivate to carry the load.

Man with ambition, incentive must integrate,
Lest he regress and slowly disintegrate.

Encouragement, incentive and industry are related;
Freedom and achievement, likewise are affiliated.

THE MOUTH

In order to eradicate incessant yap, we must develop a better "mouth-trap."

Keep a tight-fitting muzzle on the muscles of your mouth.
Curtail the frequent travel of your jaw, north and south.
The chances of you blowing it are directly proportional
To the amount of time spent with horizontal mouth vertical.

Idle gossip, constant chatter, oft difficult to weather;
Narrow mind and a wide mouth usually travel together.

A foul mouth is a mark of a polluted soul.
A source of wisdom should be your set goal.

A loud, nettlesome mouth can be so repugnant.
Don't allow an opinion to sway good judgment.

Don't let your sins tell your mouth what to say.
Continuing in wrongdoing gives evil full sway.

Actions speak louder, let's be unique.
Mouths, give your hands permission to speak.

Reasons for a closed mouth there are but two,
Suggestions that are bound to truly help you,
When vile words of anger you're about to spurt,
And when you're offered delicious dessert.

The jawbone of an ass is as treacherous today
As it was years ago in wise Samson's day.

Big mouths shouldn't say, lest there be tears,
What shouldn't be heard by little perked-up ears.

A LIFESTYLE PORTRAYAL From A TO Z

The entity oft opened in error is mail -
You're wrong, it's the mouth, so oft it does assail.

Before opening your mouth, you must clearly think;
Your cool brain with tongue you must synergistically link.

A fool may possess a scholarly look;
When his mouth is open we know he's not a book.

Some prancing lower jaws should be restricted by laws.

This Philippine proverb let us strive to net,
"Into a closed mouth a fly doesn't get."

Both tongue and mouth should be discreet;
A mouth that's closed, gathers no feet.

The mouth has but a relatively little hole, yet, it can swallow a great big soul.

Take a tip from God's nature, a sober thought, not a quiz,
"Ears aren't meant to close, but a yapping mouth is."

When your mouth says "Yes," and your gut says "No,
Stress in your life is definitely on the go.

MOVIES

When movies were invented, I'm sure 'twas inconceivable
That they'd go from silent, to talkies, then unspeakable.

People who are coughing don't feel very groovy.
They should see their doctor and not go to the movie.

MUSIC

Music is well-said to be the speech of angels.
-Thomas Carlyle

An opera, a form of drama where music is king,
Where a guy gets stabbed, instead of bleeding he sings.

A LIFESTYLE PORTRAYAL From A TO Z

The most difficult instrument, without question, it's no riddle.
Ask a great conductor, he says, "Second fiddle."
To find someone who'll play second fiddle with enthusiasm,
To conductors is a problem, it's not a phantasm.
If second fiddle is missing in any seraphic symphony,
There's something that's missing - it's goose-pimply harmony.

❧

Music is a restorative for the sin sick soul, it revives and heals, helps to make man whole.

❧

MYSTERY

One of life's mysteries keeps making its rounds,
How a piece of plain chocolate causes gain of five pounds.

❧

NEW YEAR

Cartoonists invariably depict the New Year as a newborn wearing a white diaper.
This is because many changes will be made - throughout the whole year they'll occur.

❧

A Happy New Year, I wish you, my dear.
May the best day of this one be the worst next year.

❧

Things To Remember This Blessed New Year

Your presence is a gift to the people of this world.
May your love to mankind be graciously unfurled.
You're a unique personality, just one of a kind,
One of your pattern would be difficult to find.

Within your soul there are so many answers.
To the wisdom of this world strive to be an enhancer.
Kindness and compassion, go a long way.
Don't let the devil discourage or sway.

Do the extraordinary in an extraordinary way,
And always remember to keep tongue at bay.
Count your blessings and not your troubles,
And don't always try to be on the double.

Reach for the top, your goal, your prize,
Your hopes, your dreams, strive to realize.

A LIFESTYLE PORTRAYAL From A TO Z

In choosing your friends, use enlightened discernment,
Consider a friendship as a wise investment.

Nothing wastes more energy than fretting and stewing;
Frankly this isn't what we should be doing.
Take care of your body, God doesn't make junk.
Be cognizant of the fact, there's no spare in your trunk.

Decisions are too important to leave to chance,
Do make it a point to ask God in advance.
Honor you family, your spouse, your begats,
Live a life of serenity, not a life of spats.

Always be courageous, stouthearted and strong.
In the family of God is where you belong.
Take your days just one day at a time.
Remember the Sabbath, the day that's sublime.

Treasure your faith and your trips to the steeple.
Remember the downcast, they too are God's people.
And never forget how special you are,
For you God is preparing a home up there.
-Anonymous

A very nice thing about the month of December
Is letting others know we care and remember.
But why do we wait until the end of the year
To give unto those that we love so dear?

NOISE

*N*oise pollution is a relative thing, comparable to motors and watches.
In an urban setting, it's a plane taking off, in a convent it's a pen that scratches.

NONSENSE

"*I*f plain sense makes good sense, seek no other sense, lest you find nonsense."
-Henry Feyerabend

*T*hey talk about beauty being only skin-deep,
That's deep enough, don't over it lose sleep;
You wouldn't want the pancreas to the surface creep.

They call it "Horse Sense," it's indeed a mind-boggler, this conundrum one cannot hide.
Would you let someone put a saddle on you, and then give that person a ride?

OBEDIENCE - DISOBEDIENCE

Wicked men obey from fear; good men from love.
-Aristotle

Obedience is more than obeisance - it's compliance, submission, allegiance,
Deference, respectfulness, subservience, resignation, servility and acquiescence.

Every great person has learned to obey, whom to obey and never betray.

Disobedience is an offensive evidence of perversity.
Harmony is a pleasing expression of diversity.

When we look up to God, and earnestly behold,
We're in the attitude to do what we're told.

OBESITY

Diabetes and obesity have a synonym– 'Diabesity.'

Some link excess weight to time spent at the table,
Relating so many quaint legends.
For excess avoirdupois, don't blame the minutes,
The cause is the gastronomical seconds.

Two of mankind's most pressing problems,
A concern that should be at the top of our slate,
Is how to prevent populations from starving
And the millions from getting grossly overweight.

Many people become poor, they live beyond means;
Some are overweight, they live beyond seams.

It begins at home – we call it charity.
We can say the same for insoluble obesity.

Those people who know that they've had enough,
I would say are fashioned of the wiser stuff.

A LIFESTYLE PORTRAYAL From A TO Z

*S*eeing a luscious pie, drooling in the oven, fails repeatedly one's appetite to govern.

*I*f excess calories you persistently coddle,
Eventually you won't walk, you'll wiggle and waddle.

*W*hen I have the urge to exercise my knees,
I promptly lie down and the feeling quickly flees.
When I have the desire some victuals to munch,
It's strange how that feeling seems to drive me to lunch.

*Y*ou can trust a fat man, he may be slow, but he'll never stoop to anything low.

*T*hough goopy and slimy, how the oyster man assails,
Without giving thought of removing its entrails.

*T*he exercise superb that's best for overweight - this isn't an impious fable,
It is to exercise wiser discretion at the dining room table.

*M*y wife is perpetually dieting, doing it in her own unique way.
Her plan is to take off tomorrow what she knowingly puts on today.

*W*ith my body and fat, there's a difficult trend,
For as I get older we become great friends.

*T*o take weight off so many are thinking,
But to most of us it's wishful shrinking.

*I*f you overindulge, inevitably you will bulge.
To be fit as a fiddle you must watch your middle.

*S*o frequently people will have a gross pig-out.
They gorge on basic foods, canned, frozen and take-out.

*W*hen a hostess urges seconds, many folk can't deny it.
They find it's as easy as falling off a diet.

*W*hether you shouldn't or whether you ought to,
Determine to know enough when to know not to.

*I*nstead of talking it, do try walking it.

*T*oo much goes to waist as we reach middle age;
You expend less energy, so our intake we must gauge.

A LIFESTYLE PORTRAYAL From A TO Z

*T*he cause of diet failure, just one I wish to mention,
Like trouble and weeds they thrive on inattention.

❧

*B*reakfast like a king, eat lunch like a prince, like a pauper for dinner is hard to convince.

❧

*S*aid a patient to a physician, "I've got twinges in my hinges."
Responded the physician, "Do avoid those big binges,"

❧

*W*hen you're invited to a luscious dinner table,
Observe courtly etiquette, keep a happy mood.
Remember not to go stark, raving mad,
When your eyes feast on delectable food.

❧

*P*utting on weight is a reprehensible state,
It's something that we shouldn't permit.
A result I am told of an appetite bold;
The consequence of exceeding the food limit.

❧

*O*besity for certain is widespread - extremities, torso and the head.

❧

*D*estiny shapes our ends, it's not a puzzling riddle.
It's caloric intake that shapes our burgeoning middle.

❧

I frequently wonder, of all the inventions,
Why don't they make scales that delete pounds for intentions?

❧

*S*aid a doctor to an overweight patient, "I wish to make this perfectly clear.
I'm not going to prescribe a special diet, just leave your uppers and lowers here."

❧

*W*hy wait to feel great – consider losing weight.

❧

A fat man has difficulty his appetite to appease
Because of an oppressive hand-to-mouth disease.

❧

*P*eople who diet go to great lengths
To elude great widths, using limited strengths.

❧

I know that I could shed some weight
If I only ate what was on my big plate,
But my good intentions have a way of fading,
I continue to munch what I should be evading.
No foil-wrapped crumb escapes my theft,
I eat what's right, then I eat what's left.

❧

A LIFESTYLE PORTRAYAL From A TO Z

"What are you doing in the pantry, my dear?"
Queried my wife with words loud and clear.
What could I say, I couldn't tell a lie,
"I'm struggling with temptation, fighting hard," said I.

Mirror, mirror on the nine-foot wall, why don't you ever make me look slim and tall?

Of all the substances I think otiose, it's my hefty 20 pounds of flabby adipose.

One day I said to my aunt Jemima, "You live alone, yet so much you bake!
I truly believe, in some parts of the world, villages could live on your gross intake."

Three square meals in this country abound.
They can be a detriment, they can make one round.

Some folk aren't nutritional achievers - in dieting they're not true believers.

Gluttony is not a secret device, it's very much a visible vice.

Overeating can result in a big fat buttock.
It can also make you thick to your stomach.

Inch by inch, dieting could be a cinch.

Brain cells come and brain cells go, but with adipose it's seldom so;
My excess avoirdupois remains my foe.

You strive for an hour-glass figure, the results aren't always a laugh,
For the sands of time always end in the pear-shaped heavier bottom half.

Too many luscious rolls or delectable buns will put fat in rolls on your plump, round buns.

If with obesity you precariously flirt, you're probably in the habit of taking dessert.

A midnight snacker is a 'Frigidaire' raider; for prudent dieting he's not a crusader.

Losing avoirdupois will take loads off my heart.
'Twill also prevent pant seams coming apart.
I've got to eat less, got to watch what I eat,
This abominable state I've just got to beat,
And putting on weight I must not repeat.
I must lose pounds, and, yes, several inches,
Then when climbing stairs there'll be no need for winches.

If 'heavies' would lose avoirdupois, with life they'd much easier cope.
Another side-benefit, without question – they'd use considerably less soap.

OBSERVATION

Careful reflection in every direction; the boys in blue are waiting for you.

OCCUPATION

Occupation is the necessary basis of all enjoyment.
-Leigh Hunt

Enduring occupation helps prevent temptation.

Occupation pays debts, while despair collects.

One's occupation is life's donation.

OPENNESS

Choose thoughtful openness and harmonious cooperation,
Not arduous conflict and shameful degradation.

OPINION

Popular opinion is the greatest lie in the world.
-Carlyle

A truth, I affirm, the hardest - not your inion,
It's to keep to yourself your candid opinion.
[Inion- the hard, bony protuberance at the base of the skull.]

You're entitled to your candid thinking, though sound credibility it lacks.
Never are you entitled to an idea that is totally based on bare facts.

An opinion, oft prejudice with unrelated fact;
Very frequently transmitted with very little tact.

Man's a strange creature, he's prone to have dominion,
But reluctant to stand alone in his liberal opinion.

*M*any an opinion could have some merit; when fully aware, do give it credit.

A differing opinion should never offend,
Never a motive for separation from a friend.

*R*isk not on the opinion of the man full of booze,
Likewise, on the one who has nothing to lose.

OPPORTUNITY

*P*ass Over Opportunities Repeatedly, and you'll be POOR immediately.

*T*oo many people think of security, instead of acting on promising opportunity.

*T*his is a fact, it isn't any bull – the door of opportunity is "Push" and "Pull."
[Bull, comes from the French word boule, meaning mistake, originally a lie]

*W*ith "Push" and "Pull", don't be clueless - without zealous "Push," "Pull" is useless.

*R*oadblocks don't have to be barriers, they could be opportunity's carriers.

*T*o the door of opportunity most people aren't rushing,
On realizing that it involves considerable vigorous pushing.

*S*eek golden opportunity before long-term security.

I questioned opportunity, "Are you far or near?"
Her succinct reply, "I'm always here."

*F*or opportunities to be multiplied and highly perfected,
They must be seized, lest they die neglected.

*O*pportunity doesn't wait nor does it set bait.

*W*hen opportunity knocks, answer it with poise,
And don't ever complain about the dull noise.

'I would be difficult to hear opportunity knocking,
When your lazy, downy pillow, sonance is blocking.

*W*hen the window of opportunity chances to appear, some deem they've got it made.
In their excitement with no productive thought, they inadvertently pull down the shade.

A LIFESTYLE PORTRAYAL From A TO Z

*O*pportunities are oft missed through thick and thin,
Because we're broadcasting rather than tuning in.

*G*olden opportunity continues to knock, but too many people keep watching the clock.

*O*pportunities are never lost, dear Chris; someone will find the ones you miss.

*B*e ready for ample opportunity, when it comes;
They won't be announcing it with booming drums.

*N*o business opportunity is lost the least bit;
If you should bungle it, a competitor will find it.

*O*pportunity by most isn't promptly recognized,
For it is invariably as hard work disguised.

*I*nstead of seeing difficulties in a matchless opportunity,
Discern the opportunity in a problematic difficulty.

*O*pportunities will grow if them you seize.
Most certainly they'll die on choosing to freeze.

*E*very duty implies responsibility, every opportunity, a singular obligation.

*N*ot only do we have the opportunity to be free,
We can be the best, the best we can be.

*O*pportunities are byproducts of your daily existence.
You'll be amply rewarded if you utilize persistence.

*W*hen opportunity knocks, invite it to come in.
Watch out for temptation, it kicks the door in.

*T*his world would be better with more work and less talking.
Furthermore, if we would let opportunity do the knocking.

*T*hat golden opportunity that you are seeking,
That matchless possibility to earn gainful pelf,
Is not in the environment, not in luck or chance,
It is totally found in one's inner self.

*F*or outstanding opportunities one should never wait.
Latch on to the ordinary and make them great.

Take hold of opportunities - an exhilarating experience.
They do not wait for your greater convenience.

Decide not to wait for so-called ideal chances.
Opportunity may come regardless of circumstances.

Opportunities are missed by most people, limitless possibilities they shirk.
It's because it's dressed in overalls - it looks too much like work.

OPTIMISM

Youth must be optimistic. Optimism is essential to achievement,
and it is also the foundation of courage and true progress.
-Nicholas Murray Butler

An optimist is a person, says Ben, who starts a crossword puzzle with a pen.

An optimist, a calm creature, endorse his meek soul.
He sees the fresh doughnut, his opposition the hole.

Optimism is an intellectual choice; it can make your spirit rejoice.

"Optimism is that faith that leads to achievement."
Omit hope and confidence, you end up with bereavement.

An optimist envisions light where there's none.
The pessimist is inclined to extinguish where there's one.

For an optimistic opportunity, seize hard work.
For that perfect occasion, industry do not shirk.

Don't be a pessimist about probabilities, instead, be an optimist about possibilities.

It'll never hurt you to be ardently optimistic.
You can always weep later, be distinctly realistic.

The optimist is an envisioned driver, his peers, they won't deny it.
He thinks the empty space at the curb won't have a hydrant beside it.

The pessimist thinks "O" is the last letter in zero,
To singular success he has no affinity,
You'll find that the optimist thinks so very much differently,
He negates the "O's" in Golden Opportunity.

ORATORY

Streams of oratory do not always come from mountains of thought.
-Charles Grant

The object of oratory is persuasion; so oft of authenticity there's evasion.

Oratory it would seem is just blowing off steam.

PARENTING

All persons who bear the title of "parent"
have the personal responsibility
to see that their children are growing up fully appreciative
of the rights of God and their fellowmen.
-T. Edgar Hoover

Why would you think of wielding a big stick,
When tactful guidance could be a glowing wick.

Fathers and mothers, be a friend to your child;
You must speak kindly with a voice that is mild.
In time you'll find you'll be loved by a grandchild,
If you should live a life undefiled.

What a child hears from its father and mother, it will eventually emphatically repeat.
The irony of it all, too frequently we find, it invariably spills it out on the startled street.

PARTNERSHIP

Partnership can produce protection, it can also result in affection.

To have Almighty God as your partner, there mustn't be any doubt.
There is no failure more disastrous than success that leaves God out.

PATIENCE

Only those who have the patience to do simple things perfectly
Will acquire the skill to do difficult things easily.
-Johann Schiller

A LIFESTYLE PORTRAYAL From A TO Z

Patience, the ability, one's motor to idle, and his sharp tongue to promptly bridle,
While one's temper to the boiling point nears, as he fully feels like stripping his gears

✥

Patience is a cohort of wisdom, we need it throughout all Christendom.

✥

Gracious patience is love at rest - this type of patience is the best.

✥

Patience isn't an absence of overt action,
It's waiting, it's timing for the right transaction.

✥

Patience is recommended - with courage may we blend it.

✥

Patience, though it can be a minor form of despair,
It somehow, so oft, helps to clear the air.

✥

Do conduct yourself with untiring patience; fortify your soul with unfaltering allegiance.

✥

To keep your arguments in total abeyance,
Be a sympathetic audience, show sheer patience.

✥

A still, clear conscience has of patience a preponderance.

✥

All things come eventually to those who wait;
Take wrinkles for instance, age is the bait.

✥

There are souls who hurt, be patient not curt.

✥

Patience is the ability to hold back snobbish scoff.
It employs a countdown before blasting off.

✥

With patience and time the mulberry becomes silk.
Lord, give me the patience of blessed Job's ilk.

✥

Patience is a quality that you fully admire
In the driver behind you, whose temperament isn't ire.

✥

Be patient with stupidity, likewise with rigidity.

✥

We get a chicken by hatching the egg – not by breaking it, patience it does beg.

✥

The man who is something in the realm of accomplishment,
Will have to be prepared for critical assessment.
The final analysis of his esteemed greatness,
Is how he endures critics without resentment.

✥

A LIFESTYLE PORTRAYAL From A TO Z

There must be patience on our part as saints;
Obeying God's commandments without any complaints.

❧

Be patient, be watchful, and do be careful
With the words you're about to deliver.
Never insult a hungry alligator until you have crossed the river.

❧

Tolerance and self control, unruffled equanimity,
Imperturbability and poise endorse.
One must remember that gentle patience, always works better than force.

❧

Some folks boast of patience, they claim they never lose it.
Still, they'd much prefer to never have to use it.

❧

Patience is power, never let it sour, it won't devour, display it every hour.

❧

Untiring patience takes time; do something in the meantime.

❧

Patience is indeed a most salient virtue,
For certain it is an amazing capacity
To calmly endure the long dissertation
Of someone else's red-hot appendectomy.
To serenely remain just completely silent
As you listen to one's long detailed narration,
Though recently, you've so personally experienced
The very, very same identical operation.

❧

Patience is a virtue, virtue is a grace,
When they're combined they make a honorable face.

❧

Untiring patience involves prudence and silence.

❧

Patience is a trait of character, par excellence,
A characteristic that isn't at all easy to attain;
An attribute consisting of pure sterling quality,
So frequently the result of very deep pain.

❧

O Lord, I pray, give me added patience, for often I grow so weary and faint.
Some day I hope to amply overcome, and to be numbered as God's holy saint.

❧

Patience is a virtue that carries with it wait.
It's an enviable state that bears no hate.

❧

Create practice periods for untiring patience, 'twill make life's attributes rhyme.
You'll be able to fashion a capacity for heavenly patience over time.

❧

A succinct definition of patience, the art of concealing one's impatience.

∾

*P*atience is a basic requirement, it's not an aesthetic elective.
Placid patience allows one to keep a remarkably calm perspective.

∾

PEACE

*G*lory to God on the highest, and on earth peace- goodwill toward men.
-New Testament: Luke 2:14

∾

*P*eace is not made at the council table,
It's in the hearts of men; be willing, you're able.

∾

*P*eace is costly but it's worth the expense,
And you'll agree, it has its recompense.

∾

"*H*ey, do be careful while you're out there,"
This admonition I humbly share.
Much better to have a full cup of tranquility
Than a full barrel of implacable hostility.

∾

*P*eace is divine for the freedom that is mine.

∾

*J*udge your success by the degree of your peace,
And by the amount of precious good you release.

∾

*D*ivine, enduring peace gives us sweet release.

∾

"*G*reat peace have they who love the Lord;"
Disobeying His precepts we can ill afford.

∾

*B*egin in your own home when working for peace.
If you follow this dictum, enmity you'll decrease.

∾

*H*ave peace of mind, worry is a curse;
God is supreme manager of His vast universe.

∾

*O*ccasionally permit yourself to be bored,
From all activity determine to cease.
After some practice you'll experience release;
Boredom will be replaced with a feeling of peace.

∾

*I*f you want inner peace you can't live as you please.

∾

No God, no peace; know God, know peace.

❧

If you do not have peace within, ask Jesus to forgive you your sin.

❧

To have perfect peace, practice awed silence.
The key to most everything is untiring patience.

❧

The prudent and the wise lead peaceful lives.

❧

If you wish to experience peace of mind, aspire to leave conflict behind.

❧

PERFECTION

Nature has perfection, in order to show that she is
the image of God; and defects to show that she is only His image.
-Blaise Pascal

❧

The closest most people can come to perfection
Is when they fill out a job application.

❧

Perfectionism in one's mind is in a state of danger.
In an imperfect world it's a total stranger.
Perfection's not brought on by a singular act,
It's a gift of Christ, a scriptural fact.

❧

PERFORMANCE

An acre of performance is worth the whole world of promise.
-Jeremiah Howell

❧

To be a most credible performer, follow the advice of your mentor,
And you must truly be certain that your ego is not the center.

❧

He who has a tendency to belittle, usually performs very little.

❧

PERSEVERANCE

To keep a lamp burning you have to keep putting oil in it.
-Mother Teresa

❧

A LIFESTYLE PORTRAYAL From A TO Z

Perseverance is persevering through thick and thin.
If you keep believing it, greater chance you'll win.

Perseverance and patience, in its breadth and length,
Accomplishes much more than frustration and strength.

Capability made a poor appearance
Until Diligence married Perseverance.

Perseverance is the father of luck;
Accomplishment is the mother of pluck.

Choose the way of patient persistence, rather than the path of least resistance.

A pertinent word to remember is adherence.
Great deeds are accomplished by persistent perseverance.

Ardent, unabated persistence is hampered by indignant resistance.

It's our humble duty to proceed and persist as if the limits of our abilities don't exist.

The pearl of great price begins with pain, it's not in the proverbial buttock.
It's not in the chest, nor is it in the brain, it originates in the oyster's stomach.

Courage and perseverance do not ever banish.
Your difficulties will disappear and obstacles will vanish.

Great works are accomplished not by strength, it's perseverance,
Steadfastness, persistence, patience and adherence.

Tenacious activity can result in productivity.

Perseverance accomplishes much more than violence.
Hyphenate it with patience, diligence and intelligence.

Persistence and determination are a powerful combination.

Perseverance is not just one big long race,
It's made up of short ones with which to keep pace.

Persistence with purpose address, 'twill eventually result in progress.

PERSONALITY

Being a personality, a Greek or a Hun is not the same as having one.

≈

PERSUASION

Kind persuasion, unassuming persuasion, should be adopted
to influence the conduct of men.
-Abraham Lincoln

≈

To firmly persuade you don't have to be a sleuth.
The wisest, luring venue for persuasion is truth.

≈

To persuade little children one must be a sage,
To convince them that at bedtime they're at retirement age.

≈

If you're to persuade, using ears don't evade.

≈

PESSIMISM

A pessimist is one who makes difficulties of opportunities.
An optimist is one who makes opportunities of his difficulties.
-Reginald B. Mansell

≈

Don't be a pessimist, rewards are for optimists,
Avoid mountains of worry and strife.
No one has ever ruined perfect vision by looking at the bright side of life.

≈

When a pessimist feels good, conjointly he feels sorrow,
For he knows that he'll feel worse on the day called morrow.

≈

Resolve to be realistic, avoid being pessimistic.

≈

Pessimism is mental rheumatism; it's akin to cruel criticism.

≈

Postulate that the best will happen, pessimism one cannot afford.
"All things work together for good to those who love the Lord."

≈

No sense in being pessimistic, you're not being at all realistic.

≈

Today you have things to accomplish, pessimism must be off your list.
Bear in mind, you'll never see a monument erected for a proven pessimist.

≈

*A*ttempt avoiding being a pessimist, don't let things bother your soul.
Obstacles are things you see, when you take your eyes off your goal.

*P*essimists are usually talkative – their blood type is always B-Negative.

PHOTOGRAPHS

*T*he office staff photos had just arrived.
"It does everyone justice," so uttered fellow Percy.
Plump Phyllis replied, "I don't want any justice,
What I'm in great need of is some tender mercy."

PLEASURE

*T*he man is the richest whose pleasures are the cheapest.
-Henry David Thoreau

*P*leasure is more powerful than fear of the shameful.

*B*e mindful of what pleasures you habitually seek.
Sin invites cup of joy to spring a leak.

*C*hoose such pleasure that has qualitative measure.

*T*o get most pleasure out of life, avoid mental worry and strife.

A soul's minor treasure is its room for pleasure.

*T*he prettiest flower in nature's pleasure path,
For certain is not one's scorn and wrath.

*R*estrain your pleasures, restrict your powers,
For a life that's worthwhile, count the swift hours.

PLEDGE

A pledge is a debt that should always be kept.

A LIFESTYLE PORTRAYAL From A TO Z

POETRY

Poetry is indeed the dress of thought.
It can with choice words be so beautifully wrought.

Poetry, simple truth decked in dress-up clothes.
So many folk prefer it to non-rhythmic prose.

POISE

Calm poise is an art when challenging spoof.
Try raising your eyebrows instead of the roof.

Poise is the ability to be so at ease that you do inconspicuously as you jolly well please.

Poise is that quality that ignores other's gawking,
When you walk on stage with a run in your stocking.

Poise ignores noise.

POLITENESS

One of the greatest victories you can gain over a man,
is to beat him at politeness.
-Josh Billings

Two men were on a bus, one had his eyes closed.
Pat questioned his friend, "Are you indisposed?"
Mike feigned to be sleeping, Pat an answer was demanding.
His friend softly whispered, "Hate to see women standing."

To exhibit politeness, there's no room for fuss,
The only thing you may lose is a seat on the bus.

A forte of politeness is timely consideration.
To make it effectual, try implementation.

Politeness comes from within - with it you're more likely to win.

It takes little energy, the body it doesn't tax;
Refined politeness is what warmth is to wax.

POLITICS

Politics is too serious a matter to be left to the politicians.
-Charles De Gaulle

The origin of the word "politics," has singular, conspicuous features.
The cropped word "poli," means many, "tics," blood sucking creatures.

Though voting is a right, it requires insight.

So many of our elected officials, profess they're instruments of change.
Actually they're only wind instruments, yet we elect them, how strange.

A political campaign, to me it appears, is stifled threats, mud-slinging and smears.

Politics has become so expensive, many haven't the sense to quit.
It even takes a massive heap of money to get thoroughly trounced with it.

So oft in voting "Yes," we follow the politician.
There are times that we must lead with a negative petition.

Politicians wish to work for the greatest number;
With at least five figures; the taxpayer they encumber.

Political campaigns are dominated by speakers
Who their own praise love to sing.
Invariably the candidates air each other's linen
While trying to avoid static cling.

A politician is busy, we frequently do discover,
He's running for office or scrambling for cover.

Political campaigns are based on the premise
That you can't sue a fellow for blaming.
It's uniquely the time that money is spent
For digging up dirt and defaming.

Politicians and diapers have one thing in common,
Regularly to be changed, for the same reason.

Why would you put out good money to trace the family tree?
You could go into politics - the opposition would do it for thee.

Politics and morality have drifted far apart.
Just ethics have abandoned things dear to one's heart.

POSE

He's no better than you, disregard his pose.
We all stand naked in our picture-book clothes.

POSSIBILITIES

Some folk have an abundance of opulent possibilities.
Sad to say, they're negated by contingent liabilities.

The impossible mustn't ever be readily denied;
Tragically, it's frequently naively the untried.

To the timid and hesitant much is improbable.
To them it appears, absolutely impossible.

As you travel life's pathway, a word of precaution,
"Impossible," must be used with the greatest of caution.

Whenever probable, make it possible.

POSTERITY

We are too careless of posterity, not considering that as we are,
so the next generation will be.
-William Penn

Remember when planning for posterity,
Tradition and virtue aren't hereditary.

POUTING

If you always pout, your friends will go out.
If you smile, not grin, your friends will come in.

Pout has no clout; when you sulkily pout, you ventilate doubt.

A LIFESTYLE PORTRAYAL From A TO Z

POVERTY

Of all the advantages that come to any young man, I believe
it to be demonstrably true that poverty is the greatest.
-James Freeman Clarke

To those who deem themselves poor, to those who poverty face,
Material poverty in itself is neither virtue nor disgrace.

Poverty of purse is not a curse, poverty of purpose is considerably worse.

The quickest way to be hopelessly broke is to leisurely sit around waiting for a brake.

Poverty in a life of faith within is better than plenty in a life of sin.

Statistics do show amongst those who are poor,
Two out of three families live right next door.

If you're struggling with pinching poverty,
Have a inclination to be overly thrifty.

"*The* richest heritage," said a well known celebrity,
"That a man can be born to is pinching poverty."

POWER

Power is the grim idol that the world adores.
-William Hazlitt

The unbridled power does reign, to fulfill the power for gain.

Power is an idle so many adore; before you seek power, add up the score.

Authority and influence go to the top of the tower.
Ingredients they are for the foundation of power.

Two eagles once flew in the brilliant blue –
Were blowing the breeze as they soared.
When a sleek modern jet on a straight course set,
Shot passed them as onward it roared.

One bird turned his head then quickly he said.
"I wish I could fly like that flier."

The other said, "Good, and maybe you could
If you had two tails both on fire."

The thought comes to me as I share it with thee,-
We all could go faster and higher.
If we know this to be true in whatever we do,
We'd accomplish much more when on fire.
-Adlai Esteb
❧

Most powerful is he who has himself in his own power.
-Seneca
❧

PRAISE

Those who are greedy of praise, prove they are poor in merit.
-Plutarch
❧

Why not invest in endearing praise; your exciting endorphins it will surely raise.
❧

There's a creative element in praise.
The voice of censure seldom raise.
❧

Can praise and worry be comprehensively inclusive?
Can't live in the same house, in agreement they're exclusive.
❧

Do not neglect ways to give others sincere praise.
❧

Modesty is sure bait if for praise you wait.
❧

Acclaim and laudation, not mocking and jeering;
Praise does great wonders for the sense of hearing.
❧

'Twill be to someone's joyous jubilation
If you show high praise and sincere appreciation.
❧

Every new day gives us new reasons
To sing God's praises throughout the seasons.
❧

'Twas Norman Vincent Peale who duly provided
A succinct thought-initiating witticism -
"Most of us would rather be ruined by praise
Than saved by adverse criticism."
❧

A LIFESTYLE PORTRAYAL From A TO Z

Joyfully shout to the Lord all ye land,
Serve and obey Him with whole heart and hand.
Come ye before Him with grateful songs of joy,
He is our God, sacred reverence do employ.
We are His people, the sheep of His pasture,
He is our Creator and total Benefactor.
Enter His gates and His courts with joyous praise -
With songs of endless gratitude your gladsome voices raise.
The Lord is truly good, He is kind to all nations,
His faithfulness goes on to succeeding generations.
  -Psalm 100, (paraphrased)

❧

Praise is a most valuable asset; never to be used to pay a debt.

❧

You will find with some, praise is their talk,
But an axe for wax will not cut rock.

❧

Mealy-mouthed praise endorphins won't raise.

❧

Diamonds and gems are somewhat a rarity;
Like praise, its value lies in its scarcity.

❧

If you should live only for the praise of men,
You'll lack the approval of most of them.

❧

Withhold not giving God reverence and praise;
With soul-piercing voice, a joyous anthem raise.

❧

PRAYER

The spectacle of a nation praying is more awe-inspiring
than the explosion of an atomic bomb.
  -J. Edgar Hoover

❧

We should earnestly pray three times a day;
Prophet Daniel did – ferocious lions stayed away.

❧

God, grant health enough to make work a pleasure,
Wealth enough to support others' need,
Strength to battle and difficulties to overcome,
Sound wisdom to guide and not mislead.
Grant grace enough to confess my sins,
Patience enough to accomplish some good,
Charity enough to help my neighbor,

A LIFESTYLE PORTRAYAL From A TO Z

Will enough to do as I should.
Grant faith enough, things of God to make real,
And love enough, to others hope reveal.
-Johann Wolfgang Von Goethe. (paraphrased)

֍

The only vital power for which man should aspire -
It's Holy Spirit power, available per prayer wire.

֍

Frequent, fervent prayers can lessen daily cares.

֍

With God some have a semblance of communication publicly,
But they're very reluctant to talk to Him privately.

֍

Jesus' top priority was to pray, that should be ours every day.

֍

Prayer is an attribute that Satan cannot rate.
It's an effective weapon that he can never duplicate.

֍

So oft when we pray we're in the 'give-me' mood;
Give me this, give me that; we must pray for sainthood.

֍

Prayer should not be primarily a supplication,
More importantly, more oft, a friendly conversation.

֍

Prayer is the avenue through which men reach
The Deity of heaven, the God they beseech.

֍

To make the most of the day, in your spare moments pray.

֍

"No prayers are to be said," is a government rule.
As long as there are exams there'll be prayers in school.

֍

On our sincere prayers God never does frown.
When prayers go up, blessings will come down.

֍

We must pray that grave danger won't check in too near,
That an angel will be nearer, then why should we fear.

֍

"If you hear a prayer that moves you, by its humble, pleading tone,
Join it, do not let the seeker bow before his God alone.
Why should not a sincere brother share, the strength of two or three in prayer."

֍

Today, Lord, I pray for added discernment.
My mind-frame needs adjusting with visual alignment.

A LIFESTYLE PORTRAYAL From A TO Z

Being totally immersed, completely in self
Is putting myself in solitary confinement.

When I'm tempted to say, "Lord, look what I've done,
All that I've accomplished entirely by myself."
Remind me seeing a turtle on top of a fence post,
I know that that turtle didn't get there by itself.

I knelt to pray but not for long, I had too much to do,
I had to hurry and get to work for bills would soon be due.
I knelt and said a hurried prayer, and jumped up off my knees,
My Christian duty was now done, my soul could rest at ease.
All day long I had no time to spread a word of cheer,
No time to speak of Christ to friends, they'd laugh at me I'd fear.
No time, no time, too much to do, that was my constant cry,
No time to give to souls in need but at last the time to die.
I went before my Savior Lord, I stood with downcast eyes,
For in His hands He held a book, it was the book of life,
While looking at His book he said, "Your name I cannot find,
I fully intended to write it down but never found the time.
-Anonymous

Many have a gregarious propensity of having a conspicuous inclination
To pray for implored forgiveness, rather than to fight temptation.

Mortal man should never despair, knowing that God always answers prayer.

Prayer for a Christian is the spice of life;
Not intended to be a labor-saving device.

Dear Lord, you know how busy I'll be,
If I forget you, please, don't forget me.

When worldly problems call on you, call on God - troubles He'll subdue.

The Publican prayed with accents loud,
Proclaiming he was a cut above the crowd,
But in God's sight to be smug and proud
Is not acceptable, character it does cloud.

"Unceasingly pray – give not the Lord rest;"
His ears are always open to your request.

Weigh what you say before you pray.

A LIFESTYLE PORTRAYAL From A TO Z

Are you despondent, discouraged, depressed? Contact Jesus today.
No matter how far you have run from God, He's only a prayer away.

Before God our prayers of thankfulness must run
As naturally as the sunflower turns to the sun.

In prayer, God hears more than the words you impart.
He listens selectively, he listens to your heart.

Prayers do not change Almighty God.
They change the ones that are made from sod.

It's not the body's posture, some preachers say,
It's the heart's attitude that counts when we pray.

Prayers are not meant to gain selfish booty;
For praise and adoration, and to report for duty.

Lord, what I am, does make a big difference,
Please make my life a positive influence.

Earnest, sincere prayer brings recompense.
Prayer, my friend is practical common sense.

Omnipotent God, my superintendent, – my boss.
I thank Him for Jesus, for recompense of the cross.

We must firstly talk to God about people,
Before we talk to people about God.

He who dashes from God in the morning
Isn't prone to see Him the rest of the day.
It therefore behooves us, one and all,
Firstly, not to forget in the morning to pray.

Why live a life of quiet desperation?
Begin with prayer, you'll improve life's relation.

To expect God to hear midst doom and gloom,
We must turn down the world's volume.

In prayers we oft ask, and then we give up,
When God puts us on hold we mustn't hang up.

A LIFESTYLE PORTRAYAL From A TO Z

Prayer should be offered at dawn and at night.
It's the key to the day and the lock to the night.

*

If your prayer life is right, you'll quickly see the light.

*

Prayer is talking to someone who loves you, Jesus, the loyal friend, eternally true.

*

"The fewer the words the better the prayer." These words from Luther, I humbly share.

*

Don't let bitter feelings cause heartache and despair.
They can be sweetened, mention them in prayer.

*

Your remark about prayer,-"What's the big deal?"
For just a brief moment my thoughts I'll reveal.
As most reverently before the Almighty I kneel,
I thank Him for His blessings, I tell Him how I feel.
My wicked, sinful habits I no longer conceal,
For His total forgiveness I most humbly appeal.
I ask him to guide me, I pray He will heal,
I ask that His will for me He reveal.
To serve Him faithfully, it gives me great zeal.
I tell you, my friend, it's no painful ordeal.
I can honestly say, "To me God is real."

*

Thank you, Lord, for this day and for its bountiful blessings;
Be our guest, we do pray, bless our moments together.
Glory to Thee, may you hear our prayer; guidance do not sever.
Bless our food, bless us all; keep us faithful forever.
 -A prayer at mealtime; can be sung
  to the German tune, "Edelweiss."

*

Talking about problems can be a big chore.
We should pray about them considerably more.

*

If a serious problem needs a decision and you sense it's beyond your control,
Take your problem to your friend, Lord Jesus, trusting Him will calm your soul.

*

Frequent kneeling will keep you in good standing.

*

When you pray for rain, have faith, young 'fella,'
And remember to carry a great big umbrella.

*

Preparation, Enthusiasm and Prayer, mean Progress, Efficiency and Power.
Collectively they spell the word "PEP;" blessings on you God will shower.

*

A LIFESTYLE PORTRAYAL From A TO Z

It is by anger and our flippant airs that we invariably spoil our prayers.

Intercessory prayer is the way to drive wicked angels away.

The word of God has explicitly commissioned
That we keep our homes thoroughly prayer-conditioned.

On Sabbath Christians pray. "Our Father," they speak,
But they act like little orphans the rest of the week.

Take time to pray, several times every day;
Remember that prayer is as important as air.

When you're in trouble and your knees begin to knock,
Just kneel on them friend - with the Lord have a talk.

Whatever your cross, whatever your pain, there'll always be sunshine after the rain.
Perhaps you may stumble, you may even fall; God is always there, He will hear your call.

There will be more power in the pulpit, when there's more prayer in the pew.
The redemptive strength of the sermon will depend a great deal upon you.

Sincere fervent prayer dispels anxious care.

For certain, prayer is not a spectator sport;
To communicate in private I must daily resort.
Prayer we are told is the breath of the soul.
It positively aids us to become spiritually whole.

The devil can trip you, the treacherous tease;
Remember, you can't stumble when you're on your knees.

Don't worry about tomorrow - God is already there.
So why would you nervously fret? Contact Him today through prayer.

There's immeasurable power in prayer, it's just as important as air.

God gave the Israelites their request; what they got was not for their best.
Quail meat filled their bowl – leanness ravaged their soul.

No yesterdays are wasted for those who pray,
For those who give themselves to precious today.

Dear Lord, so far today I've been doing alright,
I haven't at all gossiped, nor a bit have I griped.

A LIFESTYLE PORTRAYAL From A TO Z

I haven't lost my temper, I haven't been grumpy,
Haven't been self-centered, nor have I been jumpy.
But in a few minutes, this one thing must be said,
I'm going to need help for I'm getting out of bed.

❧

We must diligently pray for perseverance and expectancy,
Passionately avoiding devil-prompted reluctancy.

❧

For mental capacity we pray while we're living,
To learn more and more the blessings of giving.

❧

Get down on your knees before the Master.
You'll be up on your feet considerably faster.

❧

In the midst of daily chaos, quality time seems rare.
Do remember A. S. A. P., – ALWAYS SAY A PRAYER.

❧

People want God to answer their prayers,
But refuse to listen to wise counsel He shares.

❧

The demons in power are arrogance and pride.
In your daily living don't let them be your guide.
The demons in money are selfishness and greed;
To avoid them, with God you must sincerely plead.

❧

The Almighty God of creation can handle every situation.

❧

In loving obedience to the commandments of God
There is a sickening, deplorable dearth.
Lord, do hasten the day that the devil
Will no longer inherit this miserable, wicked earth.

❧

Time spent in prayer dispels despair.

❧

We must not forget to pray, we must do so every day!
When we get up and when we go down, when we go out or come in from town.

❧

He who kneels before the infinite one is promised to stand tall before anyone.

❧

I knelt to pray when day was done, I prayed, "O, Lord, bless everyone.
Lift from the saddened heart the pain, and let the sick be well again."
And when I woke up another day, and so carelessly went on my way,
The whole day long I didn't even try to wipe the tear of any eye.
I did not try to share the load of any lonely brother on the road.
I did not even go to see the sick man just next door to me.
Yet, once again when day was done, I prayed, "O, Lord, bless everyone."

A LIFESTYLE PORTRAYAL From A TO Z

But as I prayed, into my ear, there came a voice that whispered clear,
"Pause my child before you pray, whom have you tried to bless today?
God's richest blessings always flow to those who serve Him here below."
And then I hid my face and cried, "Forgive me, Lord, my life has lied.
Please, let me live another day and I will live the way I pray."
-G. H. Clement

❧

May the words of my mouth, Lord, and the thoughts of my mind,
Be always compassionate, considerate and kind.
May they always be coupled with good judgment and sound thought;
Never with falsehood allow them to be fraught.

❧

"The prayer of a righteous man availeth much;" may the Spirit lead that I may be such.

❧

It's totally impossible for the soul to flourish unless with prayer you it daily nourish.

❧

Lord, give me a childlike radiance - likewise, its instinctive obedience.

❧

As you go through the day, do take time to pray?

❧

A great deal of kneeling will keep you in good standing.

❧

Your early morning thoughts could well determine
Your laudable deportment for the rest of the day.
Firstly, make it a habit to consult the Almighty;
I respectfully submit that you earnestly pray.

❧

May the words of my mouth and the meditations of my heart,
Love and compassion perpetually impart.
May my life exalt you – never a blasphemer,
Jesus, my strength, my Savior, my Redeemer.

❧

Lord, I need thee every precious hour.
Give me a full measure of the Holy Spirit's power.

❧

I trust you, Holy Spirit, you're my helper and guide.
All my daily needs you'll abundantly provide.
During times of distress you'll be by my side;
Because of your presence inner peace doth abide.

❧

Fill my dull soul with good works, O God,
With the Holy Spirit do constantly prod.
Not that my good deeds above others may tower,
But to Jesus' glory and the Spirit's power.

❧

A LIFESTYLE PORTRAYAL From A TO Z

*L*ord, though at times it is difficult to cope,
I thank the Holy Spirit for the ark of hope.
I know you are striving with me in my flesh;
I pray, with thy love you will daily refresh.

&

*L*ord, I'm reminded of Joseph your anointed,
How to Pharoah's court this young man you appointed.
I do not aspire to be placed in high places,
Just simply inspire me to put a smile on faces.

&

*L*ord, give me a vision of that perfect love;
Inspire me to contemplate that vicarious summary,
By lifting my head and opening my eyes –
Not only to look at but to see Calvary.

&

*L*ord, with the help of the helper you've provided,
Lead and guide in my plans.
You know that the adversary is ready to attack –
I leave the battle in your hands.

&

*M*y Father, I pray, in this world of chaos, deep darkness, vile tension and strife –
I plead that Thy Spirit may enter in to turn on the light in my life.

&

*J*ust as Thy Spirit hovered o'er the waters,
When the earth was without form and void,
So, hover over me with Your Sweet Spirit –
Show me how sin to avoid.

&

*S*low me down, Lord,- lead me by your Spirit,
Don't let me go into a tail-spin.
Grant me the desire to strengthen my resolve
To be totally victorious over sin

&

We Must Pray Expectantly

*P*eter continued knocking; and when they saw him
they were astonished.
Acts 12: 16

A story is told of a man who obtained
A municipal permit to build a pub in a town.
The members of a church were strongly opposed,
They prayed that God on the project would frown.

A LIFESTYLE PORTRAYAL From A TO Z

A few days preceding the opening of the tavern,
It was struck by lightning, and it burned to the ground.
The church people were surprised, but exceedingly pleased,
Even though little faith in their prayers did abound.

Shortly thereafter, a subpoena was served,
The owner of the tavern was suing them.
He alleged the church prayers were the cause of the fire;
He claimed loss of building and business per diem.

At the conclusion of the hearing the judge wryly said,
"At this point I don't know what my decision will be.
It seems that the pub owner believes in prayer,
But the church people don't, it appears to me."

When old apostle Peter was put into prison,
Christians, earnestly prayed for his reprieve,
But when they were told that he was at the door,
Somehow they couldn't, in fact, didn't believe.

So oft we're comparable to first century Christians,
We have little faith though we pray fervently.
Lord, we do thank you for answering our prayers,
But Lord, do help us, that we pray expectantly.

❧

*L*ord, as this day stretches before me, I do not know what problems I'll face.
Help me to remember to seek your guidance, before my energies I indelibly erase.

❧

*I*n earnest prayer, our weary hands clasp - God opens His to eternally bless.

❧

*K*eep on praying, don't give up; when God puts you on hold, don't hang up.

❧

PREACHERS - PREACHING

*W*hen a person is down in the world, an ounce of help
is better than a pound of preaching.
-Bulwer-Lytton

❧

A preacher is speaking, a minority is awake,
Most are not listening till he makes a mistake.

❧

*S*ome preachers are like gamblers, so oft it's been said,
They lack sense to quit while they're still ahead.

❧

*E*xamine all preaching in the light of God's teaching.

*I*t's easy to see a hordeolum in the man behind the podium.
[Hordeolum - a stye,]

*W*hen Henry Ward Beecher was the padre at Plymouth church,
Father Tom volunteered, "Do not for another search."
The church was overflowing, but when the people heard
That Henry Ward was absent, many left,- about a third.
"All those who have come to worship Padre Beecher
May leave at this time for I am the preacher.
Those who have come to worship their God,
Will remain in their pews, the Spirit doth prod."
The exodus ceased though Father Tom preached.

A clergyman had enjoyed a hearty chicken dinner at the home of a rural parishioner.
While gazing out the window he casually remarked,
"That rooster is a mighty proud strutter."
Quick as a flash, with a thought apropos, to share 'twas a matter of courtesy,
So the hostess replied, "Why, he should be proud,
His son has just entered the ministry."

PRECISENESS

*T*he famous, astute Professor Williams, a leading authority in zoology,
Was leading a prestigious expedition into the upper regions of the Nile.
A student came running, out of breath, "Professor," he cried excitedly,
"Your wife has been swallowed by an alligator, up the river, about a long mile."
Surprise and a look of consternation came over the professor's face,
"Now, surely, Jackson," he casually said, "You mean a mouthy crocodile."

*N*o dice, be precise, concise and cool as ice.

PREJUDICE

*T*he greatest and noblest pleasure is to discover new truths
and is to shake off old prejudices.
-Frederick the Great.

*H*e that's possessed with arrogant prejudice
Will frequently retain in his heart deep malice.

*A*rrogant prejudice is a biased brittle tool.
Too often it's an instrument of a bleating fool.

*P*rejudice is an opinion when judgment is shrinking.
It's merely an idiot's substitute for sound thinking.

*P*rejudice is oft sustained with blunt verbal violence.
'T would be better for all if it were kept in silence.

*P*rejudice that's pious always seems to be in season.
It is a great pity that it lacks sound reason.

*B*lunt prejudice, a time spender, it so negatively impacts.
It lets you form opinions without getting basic facts.

*P*rejudice is virtually being down on, on an entity that one isn't up on.

*P*rejudice instead of truth will dismally fail.
It's weighing the truth with the thumb on the scale.

*O*ft prejudice is bias, preconception, prejudgment.
Frequently it's an opinion that lacks sound judgment.

*I*ntense, pious prejudice is a vagrant opinion.
It usually is propelled by a languishing pinion.

*P*rejudice distorts what it vaguely perceives,
Destroys when it acts, when it talks it deceives.

*Y*ou may call it intolerance, bigotry or muckraking,
Prejudice is a lazy man's substitute for thinking.

*G*od's standard for justice leaves no room for prejudice.

*P*rejudice never aims to please; it always distorts what it sees.

*P*rejudice is a villainous vagrant retort without any viable means of support.

PREPARATION

*P*roper preparation prior to implementation will help to prevent a pitiful presentation.

'*T*is better to look ahead and amply prepare than it is to look back in mute despair.

There's absolutely no substitutive creation for a genuine lack of needful preparation.

PRETENSE

We had better appear what we are, than affect to appear what we're not.
-Francois De La Rochefoucald

Don't ever pretend to be, what you never intend to be.

People will judge you by your visible ascension,
Not your intention or your feeble pretension.

Never make your intentions weak, groundless pretensions.

Some folk accomplish little, they make feeble pretense;
Should the boss nudge a little, they take great offence.

Your faith in God mustn't be a pretense; trusting in Him fully is your sure defense.

One can pretend to be serious - never try being mysterious.
Some humor is scornful pity - never pretend to be witty.

Pretending can make a small child jolly,
However, for an adult it can be flagrant folly.

If you only pretend to be, that invariably you'll never be.

One can't make sense out of nonsense, nor salvage truth out of pretense.

False assumption is specious pretense; dollars go further when accompanied by sense

PRIDE

Pride is a form of selfishness.
-David Lawrence

Pride is an abomination, found in the opinionated.
He who's truly humble cannot be humiliated.

Pride that dines on flattered vanity has no stature in profound Christianity.

A LIFESTYLE PORTRAYAL From A TO Z

A character that's virtuous you cannot hide
If that person shuns pertinacious pride.

*Vanity, arrogance and pride, make some people feel taller;
Conscience, the small, still voice that makes one feel much smaller.

*Pride does not heed and it feels no need.

*Cold, arrogant pride will berate; sound intellect annuls grim fate.

*So many proud folk their minds will air.
It would be more prudent if they were closed for repair.

*Pride frustrates its own desire; it is an ire that can backfire.

*People have enough trouble with their own amorous pride.
They won't swallow yours, in humility confide.

*Occasionally, swallow your pride - it has no calories to hide.

*When you are filled with pride, you push profound wisdom aside.

*Pride is as persistent a beggar as want; your character it will wreck if you let it haunt.

*If you're proud of virtue, it's bound to hurt you.
It's a sin one can't hide, self-exultant, guiltless pride.

*A succinct thought I hesitatingly confide, arrogant pride is destined to deride.
Never allow pride, your sinful being guide.

*The prouder a man, the less he deserves.
When he thinks of self the less he serves.

*Nothing is more infamous nor more fraught with fragility
Than the puffed-up soul that's proud of humility.

*He loves himself, you can tell it at a glance.
With him it has been a lifelong romance.

*Pride is the epitome of sin, with it you can never win.

*'Twas Dante, well read, who years ago said,
"Pride, envy and avarice are the sparks that have set fire in human hearts."

The demon in power is pride, your life, do not let it guide.
The demon in money is greed - avoid these thugs I do plead.

❧

Pride isn't synonymous with wisdom, with it you cannot enter Christendom.

❧

Pride will berate - one's intellect guides fate.

❧

Pride leads to utter destruction, it has no viable function.

❧

Why should we mortals be proud, when matchless humility is allowed.

❧

Pertinacious pride is vanity, it's not a virtue of Christianity.

❧

Never harbor pride within, pride is the mother of sin.

❧

PRINT - PRESS

The press, more than the pulpit, more than even parliament
and the people, is really the guide to the destiny of a country.
-M. E. Nicholls

❧

In debasing print, elect not to grovel, the pen can be dirtier than a barnyard shovel.

❧

Many oral testimonials are but frank flattery.
On the other hand, press releases, oft assault and battery.

❧

If a news reporter a criticism does log, remember, no one ever kicks a dead dog.

❧

Always read carefully a contract, you may think it has made your day.
Remember that big print giveth, while small print taketh away.

❧

No benefit from a lecture if through it you snooze.
Likewise, fine print is not at all good news.

❧

When talking to the press, watch what you address.
Do avoid the absurd, they have the last word.

❧

Freedom of religion and freedom of the press,
Life's highly valued entities democracies should address.

❧

PRIORITY

One must never confuse the will of the majority
With the will of God - He has priority.

❧

PROBLEMS

All the problems of this world could be settled easily
if men were only willing to think.
-Nicholas Murray Butler.

❧

I shall try to be totally explicit, our problem definitely is not the deficit.
Many people earned income choose to avoid; taxes are not paid by the unemployed.

❧

Much of the problems of this our human race
Are due to the lack of the knowledge of business.
The knowledge of what is their private business,
And then there's the entity that's none of their business.

❧

Large cities have so many problems, considerably more by far.
Inductive experience informs us that's where most people are.

❧

You can't get it to work, you surmise imperfections.
Look in the waste basket for explicit instructions.

❧

There's a ubiquitous problem that exists in our land.
So many are wearing a catcher's mitt on each hand.

❧

Problems are always present, for them you needn't hunt.
They all become much smaller when them you decide to confront.

❧

The shortest distance between a problem and a solution
Is the distance between your knees and the floor.
So you have a problem – that distance eliminate;
Talk to the Lord – your heart to him pour.

❧

So oft one's problems are guidelines; not always are they meant to be stop signs.

❧

Dodging problems though small, could eventually be your downfall.

❧

Heads, hearts and hands, and contribution of alms
Could settle world's problems much better than arms.

❧

A LIFESTYLE PORTRAYAL From A TO Z

PROCRASTINATION

"Why always, 'Not yet?' Do flowers in spring say, 'Not yet?'"
-Norman Douglas

He who hesitates invariably procrastinates.

Repeated procrastination inflames confrontation.

Procrastination is delaying that stack of "should."
Why not complete it with a positive "would".

"Do write her today," that silent voice obey.
With gross procrastination don't ever get smitten
For tomorrow's delayed letters seldom get written.

Habitual procrastination is the thief of time; to warn of its vileness I stress in rhyme.

Procrastination in verity is definitely the wrong course.
Delays we must shun, they breed gnawing remorse.

On the journey to the kingdom, procrastination is folly.
One mustn't make plans to take the last trolley.

Timorous hesitation is life's assassin; keep putting off and it won't happen.

Putting off doing never plan; procrastination is opportunities hangman.

An optimist glories in his speculative possibilities.
A procrastinator suffers with hardening of the 'oughteries.'

Addictive procrastination, opportunity's assassination.

PROFANITY

Nothing is greater, nor more fearful sacrilege than to prostitute
the great name of God to the petulancy of an idle tongue.
-Henry Taylor

Calamitous verbal profanity borders on dire insanity.

Shocking profanity smells, what you frequently laugh at tells.

When people lack confidence in the validity of their speech,
To give it emphasis, for profanity they reach.
Why should humanity be burdened with inanity?
It's verbal insanity, this oppressive profanity.

Profanity is the effort of a careless, feeble mind.
It forcibly expresses with vocabulary unrefined.

Shocking profanity is a curse of humanity.

Profanity is the mark of a conversational cripple.
His offensive language causes quite a ripple.

Profanity, blind effort of a vulgar feeble mind.
It's ill-mannered, uncouth, and socially unkind.

Profanity is never nice, some think it's brutal vice.

PROFESSION - PROFESSIONS - VOCATIONS

I hold every man a debtor to his profession.
-Francis Bacon

Whatever profession or career it may be,
Man is put on earth to serve humanity.

Profession without action is putrefaction.

There are people who profess that they always live right.
So many are wearing their halos very tight.

Medicine is a profession that labors with persistence
To eliminate sound reason for its own existence.

Of his ability and knowledge, a physician can be complacent,
But if he's his own doctor, he has a fool for a patient.

"About the magazines in the office," the nurse heard a patient state,
"I certainly hope that the doctor is considerably more up-to-date."

The thing that most people do better than others
Is reading their own writing - some have to persist.

A LIFESTYLE PORTRAYAL From A TO Z

Not so with me - I fail repeatedly -
I eventually have to take it to my pharmacist.

❧

Doctor:
"Your check came back, your money ran out."
Patient:
"Yes, Doctor, it did, but so did my gout."

❧

Said a doctor to his patient, "Good news, Mrs. Johnson."
Her emphatic reply, "Doctor, it's Miss Johnson!"
A turnabout response, "It's bad news, Miss Johnson."
Facts, frequently in the wings, are at times stubborn things.

❧

When you get too much color in the cheeks that you treasure,
You must see your doctor to check your blood pressure.

❧

Ben came to his doctor with two scorched ears.
The doctor remarked, "Bad burns, it appears.
And how did this happen?" the doctor inquired,
"It seems it's been caused by something that's been fired."
"I was pressing my slacks, had the phone on the board,
Suddenly the phone rang, to my ear the iron soared."
"What happened to the other ear, do tell me Ben?"
"Believe it or not, the same fellow called again."

❧

In an optometrist's window - "It's a crystal clear case,
If you can't see what you want you've come to the right place."

❧

I heard this conversation between a dentist and his patient.
"Had high temp last week, I just couldn't sleep,
I shivered and shook, I tried to count sheep."
"Did your teeth chatter while you were under the weather?"
"Well I really don't know, we don't sleep together."

❧

The vocation of everyone should be to serve mankind with dignity.

❧

In these difficult times the optometrist is the guy,
The only person you can see eye-to-eye.

❧

Orthodontia, a profession that keeps teeth trapped.
It keeps children braced and their needy parents strapped.

❧

A dental surgeon is driven to extraction
On seeing a tooth with a deep impaction.

❧

A LIFESTYLE PORTRAYAL From A TO Z

To the dentists, I say, if you can't collect a bill,
Just wait, be patient, a fresh toothache will.

Of all the vocations, 'tis my candid impression,
Podiatrists have a foothold on the health profession.

A chiropractor causes many a patient to moan
As he vigorously works his fingers to the bone.

In caring, whoever the patient, you'll make him feel more at ease,
By caring for him as a person than the features of his disease.

The mark of a doctor is virtually incredible.
What really should be said, "It's totally illegible."

Somewhat annoyed, a psychiatrist said, to his relief receptionist spouse,
"Please, tell the people that we're very busy, never, this place is like a madhouse."

Going to a psychiatrist one needn't be reprimanded,
One just needs to have his head examined.

Philosophers contend, avoid the far right,
Not too far to the left, keep your course in the middle."
Then what do I find in the middle of the road,
Just a narrow yellow line and a dead armadillo.

A neurotic is a person who builds castles in the air.
A psychotic moves in with no fanfare.
A psychiatrist collects rent, so some declare.

Whatever your vocation, forget not vacation.

For what I'm going to say, you can slap my wrist.
Shrink-wrap is an overcoat designed for a psychiatrist.

Fishing is an old art of jigging and casting,
Of spinning while swatting and freezing while fasting.

Cold soft-boiled eggs are beyond repoach.
Our young café chef I will have to recoach.

The weatherman and doctor always sing the same song.
They expect to be paid even when they're both wrong.

A LIFESTYLE PORTRAYAL From A TO Z

*S*aid a nurse to her patient, "You're on a special diet,
And there isn't much point in trying to defy it."
She went on to explain, "For the next day or two,
You can only have things that you can see through."
The patient, astute, thought but a brief moment -
"Okay, then have them send me a freshly baked donut."

∼

"*H*e will see you inside," said a nurse to a patient.
"Oh, no," said the latter, "Hadn't planned an operation."

∼

*A*n undertaker laments, "Things have been slack,
But I'm happy to say we're still in the black."

A middle-aged banker, somewhat a satirist,
"Over the past several months we have lost much interest."

An ardent fruit farmer was ready for quits,
"Because of early frost it's become the pits."

A pediatrician remarked while making his rounds,
"I would say it is growing by leaps and bounds."

I also asked a poet, his reply was terse,
"I am quite thankful, it could be much verse."
-Anonymous

∼

*I*n selecting a vocation, enlist sound scrutiny;
Choice not chance, determine your destiny.

∼

*E*very week she would say, "I'm having my hair done."
So one day I went and looked;
And lo and behold, to my utter amazement,
I witnessed her hair being cooked.

∼

"*Y*ou must put more stamps on your letter, my friend.
It's far too heavy," said the clerk.
"And that will make it much lighter, my dear?"
The customer queried with a smirk.

∼

PROGRESS

*T*hose who work for the world's advancement are the ones who demand the least.
-Henry Doherty

∼

Progress begins with the firm belief that what is necessary is possible.
We must believe that we can be the ones to make that progress demonstrable.

You are a tangible undertaking in progress; copious sweat you must address.

PROMISES

They promise mountains, but perform molehills.
-Charles Hadden Spurgeon

Never let promises go to sleep - all promises are meant to keep.

"It's easier to make a promise," said a father to his son,
"Much easier than it is to make good on one."

Make promises sparingly, then keep them faithfully.

Your word be it written or spoken is a promise that must never be broken.

A promise is a debt you must never forget.

God never made a promise to me and you
That was far too good to be heavenly true.

God's precious promises to humanity unfurled is our business in this wicked world.

A promise of a new home in His word is unfurled.
God's retirement plan is out of this world.

A politician's promises prompt stark dismay.
His pledge of yesterday are the taxes of today.

A promise is an onus.

PROPAGANDA

Propaganda, all too oft to us is brought - it's baloney disguised as food for thought.

PROSPERITY

Prosperity is only an instrument to be used, not a deity to be worshipped.
-Calvin Coolidge

❧

If you should choose to prosper, abandon being a loafer,
Use the past as a springboard, never use it as a sofa.

❧

Here's an English proverb with profound solemnity,
"In times of prosperity, friends will be plenty.
In times of adversity, not one in twenty."

❧

Prosperity provides enough credit it seems
To live far beyond one's individual means.

❧

If you're to design a blueprint for prosperity,
Keep fully in mind, virtue isn't hereditary.

❧

PROVERBS OF SOLOMON
(In Poetic Paraphrase)

The fear (reverence) of the Lord is the beginning of knowledge;
But fools despise wisdom and discipline.
-Proverbs 1:7 (NIV)

❧

In Solomon's proverbs there's a wealth of wisdom;
A merited benefit, it prepares for Christendom.

❧

Proverbs will teach you self-control, and they'll teach you how to make you whole.

❧

Proverbs will teach you to be honest and fair,
And how to avoid evil by avoiding a dare.

❧

A wise man will listen and increase in learning.
A man of understanding of wise counsel is discerning.
-Proverbs 1:5

❧

My child you must listen to your father's preaching,
And do not forget your mother's teaching.
-Proverbs 1:8

❧

My child, if sinners try to lead you astray,
Courageously tell them, "God's showing me the way."
-Proverbs 1:10

❧

A LIFESTYLE PORTRAYAL From A TO Z

*H*ow long will you fools love your simple ways?
How long will you delight at the pernicious to gaze?
Proverbs 1:22

❧

*I*f you listen to me you will live in safety.
You will be at peace without fear of injury.
-Proverbs 1:33

❧

*G*od's victory is in store for those who are shameless.
He's a shield to those whose daily walk is blameless.
-Proverbs 2:7

❧

*G*od guides the course of the meek and the just;
Protecting the faithful to Him is a must.
-Proverbs 2:8

❧

*C*ry out for wisdom, pray for understanding,
Search for it like silver; this I'm demanding.
Proverbs 2:3,4

❧

*H*e guides the course of the meek and the just;
Protecting the way of the saints is a must.
Proverbs 2:8

❧

*D*iscretion will protect you, understanding will guard you.
-Proverbs 2:11

❧

*W*isdom will protect you from the ways of wicked men,
From their perverse words and their iniquitous den.
-Proverbs 2:12

❧

*M*y son, don't forget my teaching, and keep my commands in your heart.
They'll prolong your life for years, and prosperity for you they'll impart.
-Proverbs 3:1,2

❧

*T*rust in the Lord with all your heart
And do not lean on your own understanding.
In all your ways acknowledge Him;
The straight narrow path you'll be comprehending.
-Proverbs 3:5,6

❧

*F*orsake not wisdom, she will protect you;
Love her and she will watch over you.
-Proverbs 4:6

❧

A LIFESTYLE PORTRAYAL From A TO Z

If you listen my son and accept what I say,
Prolonged years of life will not betray.
-Proverbs 4:10

୬

My son, pay attention to all that I say,
Listen closely to the words that I sincerely convey.
Do not let them ever be out of your sight,
Keep them within your heart real tight.
-Proverbs 4:20,21

୬

Go watch the ants you lazy man; watch what they do, enact their plan.
-Proverbs 6:6

୬

A worthless person, a wicked man is the one who designs a sinful plan.
Proverbs 6:12

୬

Six things the good Lord greatly hates, there are seven that He harshly rates:

Haughty eyes, a lying tongue, hands shedding innocent blood,
An evil heart that devises wicked schemes like a flood;
Nimble feet that are quick to rush into ominous evil,
A false witness that initiates with falsehood an upheaval;
And the man that He greatly detests above all others,
Is the one who stirs up dissension among his brothers.
-Proverbs 6:16-19

୬

My son, observe the commands of your father,
And do not ignore the teachings of your mother.
Bind them continually on your mind and your heart,
From their admonition you must never depart.
-Proverbs 6:20,21

୬

I hate pride and bragging, evil ways and lies;
Get wisdom and understanding, I strongly advise.
-Proverbs 8:13

୬

A wise son invariably brings happiness to his father,
But an absurdly foolish one, grief to his mother.
-Proverbs 10:1

୬

Riches obtained by fraud are of no worth.
Right living will delay in your grave a berth.
-Proverbs 10:2

୬

A LIFESTYLE PORTRAYAL From A TO Z

The mouth of the righteous is a fountain of life,
But violence overwhelms the mouth filled with strife.
-Proverbs 10:11

He who heeds discipline reveals life's pathway;
By ignoring strong correction he goes astray.
-Proverbs 10:17

When prim pride comes, then comes disgrace;
With honest humility, just wisdom you'll face.
-Proverbs 11:2

Wealth is worthless in the day of wrath,
But righteousness delivers from eternal death.
-Proverb 11:4

A discretionless woman though beautiful casts doubt,
As a ring of gold in a filthy swine's snout.
-Proverbs 11:22

One man gives freely, yet richer he'll grow;
Another withholds - poverty he'll know.
-Proverbs 11:24

A generous man eventually becomes prosperous.
He who refreshes others himself becomes vigorous.
Proverbs 11:25

The wisdom of the wise wins praise; respect for warped minds has delays.
-Proverbs 12:8

Evil people are trapped by their own wicked talk;
Good people avoid it, in righteousness they walk.
-Proverbs 12:13

Worry, a heavy load, kind words are a goad.
Proverbs 12:25

Spend time with the wise, wisdom you'll realize.
Proverbs 13:20

He who walks uprightly reveres the Lord;
The devious despise the Author of accord.
-Proverbs 14:2

A LIFESTYLE PORTRAYAL From A TO Z

No one can know your sadness, strangers can't share your gladness
Proverbs 14:10

≈

There is a way that seems right to a man,
But death was not considered in his plan.
-Proverbs 14:12

≈

In labor there is profit and prosperity; mere talk leads only to poverty.
-Proverbs 14:23

≈

He who is slow to anger and strife
Has within him great understanding.
He who's quick-tempered, exalts folly and wrath;
In the end he will have a bitter landing.
-Proverbs 14:29

≈

He who oppresses those who are poor
Shows blatant contempt for his Maker.
Being kind to the needy honors Almighty God,
He'll not be shamefully forsaken.
-Proverbs 14:31

≈

An unkind word brings about wrath; a gentle word is a perfumed bath.
-Proverbs 15:1

≈

The tongue of the wise makes knowledge acceptable;
The mouth of fools spouts folly - regrettable.
-Proverbs 15:2

≈

Better a meal of vegetables where there is love,
Than a fattened calf where there's hatred and shove.
-Proverbs 15:17

≈

A hot-tempered man stirs up dissension,
But a patient man calms all apprehension.
-Proverbs 15:18

≈

Better a little with righteousness
Than acquiring much gain with covetousness.
-Proverbs 16:8

≈

Pride goes before destruction, a haughty spirit before a fall.
Honest humility is the answer, in other's eyes you'll stand tall.
-Proverbs 16:18

≈

A LIFESTYLE PORTRAYAL From A TO Z

Better to be lowly in spirit and oppressed
Than in sharing plunder to be obsessed.
-Proverbs 16:19

The mind of the wise makes his speech judicious,
And adds persuasiveness, not at all suspicious.
-Proverbs 16:23

A worker's hunger, lethargy will shirk; his desire to eat, drives him to work.
-Proverbs 16:26

It is better to eat a dry crust in peace
Than to have a feast when anger you release.
-Proverbs 17:1

A hot furnace tests silver and gold; the Lord tests hearts, so I'm told.
-Proverbs 17:3

Whoever insults the poor, definitely insults his Maker.
While enjoying another's troubles, of blessings he'll not be a partaker.
-Proverbs 17:5

A heart that is evil will find no success;
Words that are wicked the Lord cannot bless.
-Proverbs 17:20

An unfriendly person pursues selfish ends.
He defies sound judgment, his spirit seldom bends.
-Proverbs 18:1

The words of idle gossip to some are tasty food.
Don't gobble them up – don't spread them, it's rude.
-Proverbs 18:8

The name of the Lord is a sturdy tall tower;
From it the righteous gain strength and power.
-Proverbs 18:10

The tongue has power to air joy and wrath.
It also has power over life and death.
-Proverbs 18:21

Better is a poor man whose walk is upright.
The man with perverse speech is foolish in God's sight.
-Proverbs 19:1

A LIFESTYLE PORTRAYAL From A TO Z

A man's practical wisdom gives him genial patience.
It is to his glory to overlook an offense.
-Proverbs 19:11

*M*ental laziness casts one into a deep sleep.
He will be hungry, in poverty he'll steep.
-Proverbs 19:15

*B*eing kind to the poor is like lending to the Lord.
He'll abundantly reward you, you needn't at all hoard.
-Proverb 19:17

*L*isten to advice and accept correction.
Heeding the above you'll more wisely function.
-Proverbs 19:20

*H*e who robs his father and disowns his mother,
Disgraces himself, his sister and brother.
-Proverbs 19:26

*A*voiding instruction - to knowledge an obstruction.
-Proverbs 19:27

*W*ine is a mocker, beer makes one loud.
It's not wise to be drunk, it's disrespectful to the crowd.
-Proverbs 20:1

*N*o one can say, "I'm innocent,
I've never done anything wrong."
Your sins will surely find you out;
Can't pretend innocence for long.
-Proverbs 20:9

*M*ost guilty people live dishonest lives;
The honest do right, they're unquestionably wise.
-Proverb 21:8

*T*o the cry of the poor, he who shuts his ear
Shall some day cry but no one will hear.
-Proverbs 21:13

*W*hoever loves pleasure becomes poor.
I read this in Solomon's brochure.
-Proverbs 21:17

A LIFESTYLE PORTRAYAL From A TO Z

A good name is better that riches that mold.
One's honor is better than silver or gold.
 -Proverbs 22:1

*T*he rich and the poor have a common connection.
The Lord is their Maker, He is their protection.
 -Proverbs 22:2

*T*horns and snares are in the path of the perverse.
He who guards his soul will escape that curse.
 -Proverbs 22:5

*T*rain up a child in the way he should go;
When he becomes old his goodness will show.
 -Proverbs 22:6

*T*he sluggard says, "There's a lion outside.
I'm very fearful - I might lose my hide."
 -Proverbs 22:13

*T*he mouth of the adulteress is a very deep pit;
Be careful, be watchful, lest you fall into it.
 -Proverbs 22:14

*F*olly is bound up in the heart of a child.
The rod of discipline will make him mild.
 -Proverbs 22:15

*L*isten very carefully to what the wise say;
Pay attention to their teaching, it will make your day.
 -Proverbs 22:17

*H*ave I not written to you excellent things
Of counsel, of guidance and knowledge,
To help you to know the certainty of truth?
I trust that this fact you'll acknowledge.
 -Proverbs 22:20,21

*D*on't wear yourself out trying to get rich,
And never your thoughts with greed ever hitch.
 -Proverbs 23:4

*W*ealth can vanish in the wink of an eye.
For certain, 'twill disappear when you die.
 -Proverbs 23:5

A LIFESTYLE PORTRAYAL From A TO Z

*D*o not envy sinners, respect the Lord.
To have hope for the future, keep faith on board.
-Proverbs 23:17

*L*earn sacred truth and never reject it;
Get wisdom, understanding, self-control, perfect it.
-Proverbs 23:23

*W*ho has troubles, who has deep pain?
He who drinks wine will always complain.
He'll have big bruises and blood-shot eyes;
Imbibing the stuff is not being wise.
-Proverbs 23:29

*D*on't envy evil people or be friends with the wicked.
Their minds plan violence, their iniquity is unrestricted.
-Proverbs 24:1

*W*ise people have power,
Those with knowledge have strength.
Trusting in the Lord gives life breadth and length.
-Proverbs 24:5

*D*on't envy evil people, don't be jealous of the wicked.
They have nothing to hope for; length of life is restricted.
-Proverbs 24:19,20

*A*gainst your neighbor never testify,
Especially when you know it's an outright lie.
-Proverbs 24:28

*I*f you brag about giving, that's utterly inane.
It's like wind and clouds that have no rain.
-Proverbs 25:14

*T*o your neighbor's house, do not go too often.
To much of you, friendship will soften.
-Proverbs 25:17

*D*on't give false testimony about your neighbor.
It's like a sharp arrow, when falsehood you belabor.
-Proverbs 25:18

Do not give fools a foolish answer.
To their wisdom you'll not be an enhancer.
-Proverbs 26:4

If for others you dig a deep pit, you're bound eventually to fall into it.
-Proverbs 26:27

A lying tongue hates those it crushes.
A flattering mouth utter ruin rushes.
-Proverbs 26:28

Do not brag about the days of tomorrow.
They may bring you nothing but worry and sorrow.
-Proverbs 27:1

Let another choose to praise you, not your own vocal cords.
Let it be a total stranger's, not your own flattering words.
-Proverbs 27:2

A constant dripping on a day of steady rain,
And a contentious woman are considered the same.
-Proverbs 27:15

As still waters reflect your face,
So your mind is a mirror of grace.
-Proverbs 27:19

It is better to be poor, to be blameless and innocent,
Than to be very rich, but in character deficient.
-Proverbs 28:6

Some people get rich by overcharging others.
They overlook the fact that the poor are their brothers.
-Proverbs 28:8

If anyone turns a deaf ear to the law,
His prayers will be detestably 'blah.'
-Proverbs 28:9

At times rich people may think they are wise.
The poor with understanding their wisdom can't disguise.
-Proverbs 28:11

*W*hen good people triumph there is true happiness.
When the wicked get control there is deep sadness.
-Proverbs 28:12

*I*f sins you try hiding you will not succeed;
Confess them, reject them, beg mercy I plead.
-Proverbs 28:13

*H*e who works his land, will have an abundance of food.
The one who chases fantasies lives in famished solitude.
-Proverbs 28:19

*B*y justice a ruler gives a country stability.
One greedy for bribes lacks implicit credibility.
-Proverbs 29:4

*B*loodthirsty men hate a man of integrity.
They hasten to eradicate the upright celebrity.
-Proverbs 29:10

A fool gives full vent to his violent anger.
Self-control to the wise is no fiendish stranger.
-Proverbs 29:11

*D*iscipline your children, teach not to be loud.
They'll give you peace, they'll make you proud.
-Proverbs 29:17

*C*harm can be very deceptive, skin-deep beauty is fleeting.
A woman who reveres Almighty God, for honor is not competing.
-Proverbs 31:30

PRUDENCE

*M*ake haste slowly. -Augustus Caesar

*L*et every man be swift to hear, slow to speak, cautious to steer,

*P*rudence. generates the greatest good; to latch onto this virtue all of us should.

PUBLICITY

If immediate publicity you wish to make,
Become involved in a great big mistake.

PUNCTUALITY

Punctuality is the stern virtue of men of business,
and the graceful grace of princes.
Bulwer-Lytton

A secretary that is good must never be rude.
She must look like a girl, be on time, rain or fog.
She must act like a lady and work like a dog.

Punctuality, so oft distressful, ask me not to initiate it.
The trouble with being on time, there's no one there to appreciate it.

Don't ever keep people waiting, your faults they will be debating.

More important to meet ghastly deadlines than it is to make screaming headlines.

At four-thirty p.m. most workers are punctual.
Their prompt departure is a captivating ritual.

QUALITY

It is the quality of the work that will please God
and not the quantity.
-Mahatma Gandhi

Top quality is important, it's absolutely essential;
Definitely keep in mind, it has great potential.

Quality is not an act, not a habit, it's a bent;
Not always is it inclined to be heaven-sent.

Fine quality should be in a proprietor's recipe.

QUESTIONS

Judge a man by his questions rather than by his answers.
-Voltaire

The debatable question is important 'tis true.
Perhaps, more important than one's I. Q.
I find so frequently, it's the curious that learn.
Eventually they're the ones who will much more earn.

Never hesitate to ask dumb questions, routine monotony it invariably breaks.
They are so much more easier to handle, than the proverbial stupid mistakes.

Some incisive, debatable, probing questions
Don't have concrete answers nor compelling suggestions.

I mustn't only contemplate what this day has brought,
I must stop and question, "This day what have I wrought?"

Allow prime time for appropriate questions;
Answers and opinions could give inner peace.
Another positive benefit would ultimately be acquired,
Your listening skills would dramatically increase.

In all your reckoning, never stop questioning.

QUOTATIONS

Some for renown on scraps of learning dote,
And think they grow immortal as they quote.
-Edward Young

A quotation is something that someone has said,
That seemed to make sense when casually read.

When Adam spoke he was aware it would score,
For he knew that no one had said it before.

An appropriate quotation is so often sought,
That has a profound thought that cannot be bought.

RACISM

*When white and black and brown and every other color
decide they are going to live together as Christians,
then and only then are we going to see the end of these troubles.*
-Barry M. Goldwater

*Today's man is indeed a conundrum, he can break the barrier of sound,
But to break the ubiquitous race barrier, the ability does not seem to abound.
Why not reach over my friend, touch him, let him know you're around.*

*Racism, so extensive, so pervasive it would seem,
That no minority lives in an atmosphere of freedom.*

*Let us not build big walls in our snow-thatched town.
All over our sad world they should be coming down.*

REASON

Reason can in general do more than blind force.
-Gallun

Be attracted to sound reason, it's never out of season.

*If with sound reason you reinforce, you needn't raise your crisp voice.
If with good sense you augment, you're bound to win the argument.*

REASSURANCE

Reassure, buoy up, be a zealous mentor; you'll brighten a room whenever you enter.

RECOGNITION

Recognition for a job well done is high on the list of motivation.
-John M. Wilson

*Shining a spotlight of appropriate recognition
Should be a supervisor's cognitive ambition.*

*At times a recognition communicate in private;
Some humble coworker may not survive it.*

A LIFESTYLE PORTRAYAL From A TO Z

*E*mployees are bettered, knowing they are trusted.

*M*an's ego is markedly boosted, when given direct responsibility,
And he'll accomplish considerably more, when given a shot of credibility.

*N*eglecting attention to all his employees, a supervisor cannot afford.
Personal recognition is extremely important, no one likes to be ignored.

*L*ook for the good things, ignore the faults,
Crown it with compliments rather than assaults.

*I*f you wish your merit to be known, acknowledge what others have wisely sown.

*L*earn how to pay a good compliment; an asset your personality will supplement.

*W*e pay ourselves the highest tribute,
When recognition to humanity we unselfishly contribute.

*R*ecognizing someone's contribution, in essence, is gratitude's solution.

*G*ive recognition to personal ambition, though its fruition creates suspicion.

RECOLLECTION

*I*sn't fortunate how selective our recollections usually are.
-Malcolm S. Forbes

*R*ecollection is the only paradise from which we can't be ostracized.

REFLECTION

*D*iscourses on morality and reflection on human nature
are the best means we can make use of to improve our minds.
-Joseph Addison

*I*ntuitive, glowing moments of peaceful reflection
Kindle the cold heart with love and affection.

*I*n choosing your battles, take time, be reflective.
In winning important ones you'll be far more effective.

Many young folk take time for reflection
In front of a mirror, to note imperfection.

REGRET

For all sad words of tongue or pen,
The saddest are those, "It might have been."
-John Greeleaf Whittier

Regret for things we've done in the past
Can be tempered with the passing of time.
It's regret for the things we've absentmindedly neglected
That are considered a pitiful crime.

Regret is an appalling form of energy; it's comparable to substitution with lethargy.

RELATIONSHIP

Almost all of our sorrows spring from our relations with others.
-Arthur Schopenhauer

To have a relationship with a neat, swell guy, whom for many a week she has eyed,
Is many a maiden's deep longing desire, to determine if he's fit to be tied.

Need to repair a relationship – forgiveness don't ever try to skip.

Guard your relationship against painful erosion;
Especially do avoid sharp verbal explosion.

Relationships need not be bound with tight bands;
Disagree agreeably and still hold hands.

The quality of a relationship you are bound to enhance,
When your jaws are not in a continual prance.

A good relationship is difficult to impart.
It comes not from books, it comes from the heart.

Broken relationships are restored by forgiveness,
Not by argument and impulsive explosiveness.

If for a much stronger relationship you seek,
My friend, why don't you attempt to be meek.

Long term relationships are hard to establish,
At times even harder to permanently banish.
Choose them carefully, select them prayerfully.

A maxim I have learned from experience in the past,
"If you put yourself first, relationships won't last."

A wolf is a Romeo who wants to play ball,
But reluctant to provide a diamond for his doll.

RELIGION

America needs a great revival of religion inspired by faith rather than fear.
-Ralph W. Sockman

It's difficult for many to accept religious creed,
Of some when observing their outrageous, filthy greed.

Atheism is what the devil tries to prod;
"By nighttime an atheist half believes in God."

Religion, like water may be free, except when they pipe it to thee.
In deciding to help pay for the piping - do so without any griping.

God gives us the ingredients for our daily bread.
He expects us to bake it, what more need be said?

Your religion is what you do after the sermon is through.

There isn't any power, not even a smidgen
That regenerates character, none, except religion.

In religious activity we should all take part,
But it isn't a substitute for an obedient, honest heart.

Measure not a man by Sundays - but what he does on Mondays.

Religion should not only be a cloak unfurled,
It should be a protective, shiny armor in this world.

A LIFESTYLE PORTRAYAL From A TO Z

To experience the merit of one's religion, do business with him, be it but a smidgen.
ও
Some turn to religion when the need is dire; only in an emergency, like a spare tire.
ও
Without religious preparation in early childhood, union with God is less likely in manhood,
ও
Forgetfulness of religion, be it race or clan,
Leads to forgetfulness of the duties of man.
ও
All nations in this world need a revival in religion,
Some people have of it but a mere smidgen.
You can't get rid of wickedness and sin,
Just by staying away from atheistic Kremlin.
The pleasures of heaven one can't enjoy or sell,
Just by staying away from inextricable hell.
It must be inspired by faith, not fear;
The end result can be such a joyous tear.
ও
Several farmers passed the day at a feed supply store.
The merits of religion they questioned o'er and o'er.
The eldest said little while he sat chewing a straw;
One of the men asked, "What do you think, Grandpa?
"You may argue," he said, "which road gets you there,
To that storehouse in the sky, to that big bin in the air.
When that final access to the great elevator you gain,
They'll just want to know, how good is your grain."
ও

REPENTANCE

Repentance includes sorrow for sin and a turning away from it.
We shall not renounce sin unless we see its sinfulness.
-E. G. White
ও
If repentance for our sins with our God is to sit,
We must be very sorry, sorry enough to quit.
ও
You cannot repent too soon, for you don't know how soon is too late,
For the hour and day of demise, never can one set a date.
ও
He who has committed a grievous sin, and of sin he has fully repented,
Is totally freed from that sinful transgression; his soul will never be tormented.
ও
"If only," is a common lament; be thankful you can still repent.
ও

REPRIMAND - REPROOF

Forbear reprimanding and censuring.
-E. G. White

❧

Think for a moment before you reprimand.
Talk is very cheap, supply exceeds demand.

❧

If you choose to judge people, judge from where they stand;
Be kind and compassionate, and seldom reprimand.

❧

Don't point a finger or publicly reprimand,
Instead, determine to give a helping hand.

❧

Cut down on the occasions you harshly reprimand;
Example is a language that all can understand.

❧

You won't get an upper hand if you choose to reprimand.

❧

Man should have virtue to fully withstand
An occasional, deserving, rigorous reprimand.

❧

REPUTATION - POPULARITY

'Tis thus that on the choice of friends, our good or evil name depends.
-John Gay

❧

It's not what your parents say, it's what your neighbors convey.

❧

Nobody can raise his own reputation
By lowering others - an unparalleled summation.

❧

You can't build a reputation on what you're going to do,
For you cannot always see what is not in full view.

❧

You can't build a reputation on your future endeavor,
Or for that matter, on the thought that you're clever.

❧

You can't build a reputation on rapt self-admiration.

❧

Your reputation depends on the company you keep,
And on the many lessons that you didn't reap.

❧

Your reputation is what others think you are.
Upright character, the result, of what you bar.

❧

Many would prefer a reputation for generosity.
You'll never get accolades for bloated pomposity.

❧

One's popularity you can never rob; it is a daily do-it-yourself job.

❧

Most people would prefer a rising reputation
That stood for judicious generosity.
Then there are those who would prefer to buy it,
And wear a façade of religiosity.

❧

RESCUING

When a church stops rescuing the lost,
That church hasn't counted the cost.

❧

RESENTMENT

People vote their resentment, not their sincere appreciation.
-William Bennett Munro

❧

Prior to foes dying, let all resentment cease.
Make peace with death, death shall give you peace.

❧

Resentment negates contentment.

❧

Resentment and envy, many jealously hoard.
It's a form of hate than no one can afford.

❧

Resentment, a form of hate - a negativity we mustn't emulate.

❧

Hanging on to impotent resentment, to cordial brotherhood is germane.
It's letting someone you greatly despise live rent-free in your brain.

❧

Resentment, uproot it, if forgiveness is to flower.
For strength to weed it, God gives the power.

❧

May this truly be your singular policy, "Bitter resentment is not for me."

❧

You ignore, you pass by with a turned up snout;
Forget the past, do try reaching out.

RESILIENCY

Man hasn't made anything of super-eminent merit
That is as resilient as the human spirit.

The storms of life have a tendency to bend us,
But the resilience of our spirit is unable to break us.

RESPECT

Respect is what we owe; love is what we give.
-Philip James Bailey

A gentleman is a man who makes it a cinch
For a woman to be a lady - he respects every inch.

The surest way to gain due respect, be compassionate, be kind and avoid neglect.

Many poor folk are willfully neglected, this is disappointingly deeply regrettable.
Do not expect to be respected, if you can't be highly respectable.

Show due respect for all living things, all of God's creatures, not just human beings.

Respect gray hairs, they don't put on airs.

Many folk who command due respect are spurned.
Respect can't be commanded, it must be earned.

Respect can't be purchased, acquired or learned,
It has to be gradually over many moons earned.

Respect for the teacher every child should fulfill.
Likewise, the teacher should respect the pupil.

These provocative, wise words, by my mother,
"Let's safeguard and serve, and respect each other."

RESPONSE - REPLY

"Theirs not to make reply, theirs not to reason why."
From such expect no empires to be built, no inventions made,
no great discoveries brought to light.
-Bruce Barton

❧

If friends don't respond to words deemed influential,
Attract them with a packet marked, "Strictly confidential."

❧

RESPONSIBILITY

Recently excessive emphasis on rights, inadequate on responsibilities.
-Paxton Blair

❧

People who assume high responsibility must equally generate explicit credibility.

❧

Action springs not from thoughtful probabilities.
It comes from readiness for immense responsibilities.

❧

No job can compete with responsibility, in molding and shaping credibility.

❧

The day one accepts personal responsibility,
Is the day that manhood becomes a possibility.

❧

Not bold self, it's our responsibility that we should take totally seriously.

❧

RESTRAINT - SELF-CONTROL

Calmness of mind is one of the most beautiful jewels of wisdom.
It is the result of long and patient effort in self-control.
-James Allen

❧

If you should become irritable, practice mute restraint.
Though displeasure be present, avoid frequent complaint.

❧

Greed and avarice restrain, lest it cause inward pain.

❧

Do not restrict your good deeds to scheduled sense of duty.
Do practice impulsive kindness and serendipitous acts of beauty.

❧

RESURRECTION

Two thousand years ago a lovely flower bloomed brightly in a far off land.
Two thousand years ago its tiny seed was placed within a dead man's hand.
Before the Savior came to this earth that man had lived and loved and died,
And fragrantly in that far-off-time that flower had spread its perfume wide.

Suns rose and set, years came and went - that dead hand kept its treasure well;
Nations were born and turned to dust while life was hidden in that tiny shell.
The shriveled hand is suddenly robbed -the seed has sprouted in the earth,
And lo, its life, long hidden there, into a seedling has now burst forth.

Just such a plant as that which grew from such a seed when buried low,
Just such a flower in Egypt bloomed and died two thousand years ago.
Then will not He who watched that seed and kept its life within its shell,
When those He loves and laid to rest watch o'er their buried dust as well?

And will not He from beneath that sod cause something glorious to arise?
Aye,- though it sleeps through centuries, yet through that buried dust shall rise,
Just such a face as you see now, just such a form as we here bare,
Only much more glorious will arise to meet the Savior in the air.

Then will I lay me down in peace when called to leave this vale of tears,
For in my flesh I shall see God, even though I sleep two thousand years.
-Author Unknown

∽

When I see a funeral procession,
I'm reminded of the devil's insurrection.
When I see a leaf of springtime,
I envision the promised resurrection.

∽

Resurrection of the righteous will result in perfection.

∽

RETALIATION

Retaliation is a confession of pain, on your character it can be a stain,
On your spirit a great big drain; my friend, consider it inane.

∽

"An eye for an eye, and a tooth for a tooth,"
This concept many think is quite ruthless.
How can viability continue to exist when both become eyeless and toothless?

∽

RETIREMENT

Looking forward to retirement, won't be leisure time galore.
You'll end up doing many jobs you will never get paid for.

୰

REVENGE

Revenge is the abject pleasure of an abject mind.
-Juvenal

୰

Revenge, disdain, it's a confession of pain.

୰

He who studies and retains revenge is certainly not prone to make amends.

୰

Revenge puts you even with your subtle enemy;
Forgiveness above him, a luminous epitome.

୰

The man who is consumed with revengeful desire
Doesn't wear the cloak of Christian attire.

୰

May your life portray enthusiastic accord;
Revenge, an infliction you cannot afford.

୰

Revenge is a temptation of those with power.
Avoid it like a plague lest character it sour.

୰

REVERENCE

True reverence for God is inspired by a sense of His infinite greatness.
-E. G. White

୰

The fear of man will bring on tears.
Reverence for God eliminates all fears.

୰

Resolutely persevere, avoid being austere,
With vile words never smear, always of good cheer.
Have courage not fear, from truth never veer,
Eternal, Almighty God, your Creator revere.

୰

REVIVAL

Revival and reformation start not with the preacher,
They start in your heart, the Holy Spirit is the teacher.

≈

RICHES

Riches are soulless, they're of little worth
If they aren't blended with gracious charity.
Riches are for certain not an honor to oneself
If they are not shared with crystal clarity.

≈

Riches are not forbidden unless selfishly hidden.

≈

RIGHTEOUSNESS

Righteousness is more than an attitude, it's an attribute personified in God.
Christ is the believer's sole righteousness, the precious Holy Spirit does prod.

≈

Christ's robe of righteousness, not a raiment for adornment,
It's to fully mantle my pitiful performance.

≈

Frenzied furor avoid, right direction explore,
Loving kindness implore, the vilest of evil abhor.
A frosty snub ignore, unkindness do deplore,
True faith restore, and Christ's righteousness adore.

≈

For those who hunger and thirst for righteousness,
There is a firm promise, "They shall be filled."
To grow in Christ make your desire intense,
You shall be blessed and spiritually thrilled.

≈

RIGIDITY - STUBBORNESS

My neighbor is a conservative, he's a stubborn old gent.
I find his both feet are planted in cement.

≈

Avoid pompous rigidity, instead, favor flexibility.

≈

Be patient with stupidity, query stern rigidity.

≈

RISKS

*H*e who bravely dares must sometime risk a fall.
-Tobias G. Smollett

*S*ome risks are challenges that we are to meet,
Not hasty rationalization and then retreat.

RUDENESS

*I*t seldom pays to be rude, it never pays to be half rude.
-Norman Douglas

*S*ome people are rude and downright crude;
Somehow, it appears, they don't think too good.

*B*ad manners and impudence are rudeness; an inexcusable form of crass crudeness.

A woman at a checkout to the clerk was very rude.
'Twas obvious to the lineup, she was in a bad mood.
To the pert young checker she tossed a flea collar,
"Why, look at this thing, 'tain't worth a measly dollar."
Said a lady in the lineup, who could no longer bear it,
"When you get the collar home, don't forget to wear it."

*A*t a time when evil rudeness is on a dizzy rise,
Let's make an honest effort to bring its demise.
Let's eliminate cruel words, duly shun push and shove,
Let us start an epidemic of sincere forgiving love.

*T*o prevent downright rudeness this one thing I must mention,
Never snap your fingers to attract one's attention.

*D*esignated, precious fruits of the Spirit
Are faithfulness, gentleness and goodness,
Love, meekness, peace, patience, and temperance,
Please note, it excludes vile rudeness.

RUMOR

*T*hat talkative maiden, Rumor.
-George Eliot

A LIFESTYLE PORTRAYAL From A TO Z

*N*ow why would you cherish a false sense of rumor,
When you could bring mirth with a sense of humor?

*B*e cautious with rumor, it's so easy to mutter,
But as difficult to unspread as Skippy's peanut butter.

*I*t is most difficult to quash a rumor
As it is to unring a sounding bell.
However, you can try to help prevent
A person from going to damnation's hell.

*N*othing more painful than malicious humor.
Nothing more universal than ugly false rumor.

*W*ild winds produce storms that sink many a ship;
Rumors produce waves that ruin one's friendship.

*M*alicious, ugly rumor gets thicker as one spreads it.
Do try to avoid it, not just dread it.

*F*alse rumor travels fast, so oft it's uncouth.
It doesn't stay put as long as does truth.

SABBATH

*R*emember the Sabbath day to keep it holy.
-Exodus 20:8

*I*t's strange how on Sabbath desirable attributes abound,
But he's not the same person, when Monday rolls around.

*O*n Sabbath people pray, "Our Father," they speak,
But they act like little orphans the rest of the week.

*C*hrist kept the Sabbath in the village of Nazareth.

SAFETY

*W*hile carrying a cocked rifle, climbing a fence, a bad habit;
Chances are you'll be survived by your wife and the rabbit.

Always choose an auto that's made from steel.
Choose firstly for safety than for appeal.
Be mindful of the nut that holds the steering wheel.

SALVATION

Don't ever rely on your denominational affiliation,
Or your past or present ministry, for your salvation.
-Garrie F. Williams

Our promised salvation - not a human invention.
It's a gift of God, it's His loving intervention.

Salvation isn't something that we personally achieve,
It's a priceless, precious gift that from God we receive.

Believing in Jesus is the foundation of our personal assurance of salvation.

"Only believe," not enough for salvation; you must have faith and with God a relation.

It's not what we do, nor is it our endurance;
The precious word of God is the source of our assurance.

Christ believed is salvation received.

One can obtain tons of religion, of salvation not even a smidgen.

We're not saved by hoping and trying, we are saved by Jesus Christ dying.

Salvation is free, you must receive it; to truly obtain it you must believe it.

If you keep rejecting the "Come" of salvation,
You'll have to accept the "Depart" of damnation.

Salvation is a gift, freely received, not a veiled goal to be personally achieved.

To be almost saved, there is a cost – invariably, it is to be totally lost.

SARCASM

Sarcasm is the language of the devil, for which reason
I have long since as good as renounced it.
-Thomas Caryle

❧

Good humor, proper dress for fashionable society.
Sarcasm and shady witticism, a despicable impropriety.

❧

Be much too kind to say things cruel; avoid making someone appear like a fool.

❧

Sarcasm and cynicism open doors to strife.
The oil of courtesy takes friction out of life.

❧

He who jabs verbally with cutting sarcasm,
And tags it firmly with a laugh that is hearty,
Has undoubtedly the unenviable distinction
Of inevitably being the dull knife of the party.

❧

Your pleasant conversation, do season with wit, as you leisurely partake of your food.
Ugly words of sarcasm, most certainly avoid, never employ words that are rude.

❧

Infamous, silent treatment doesn't breed enthusiasm,
Nor is much accomplished with deep, chilling sarcasm.

❧

In the list of human traits, is irrepressible enthusiasm.
In the dastardly column, abominable sarcasm.

❧

SATIRE

Some girls will scream on seeing a little mouse,
And yet they'll entertain a shrewd wolf in the house.

❧

Scathing satire, a form of envy, at times it could be an attempt at wit.
It may gratify a simple mind, far as truth, there's just none in it.

❧

Never with satire a friend offend; 'tis best to lose a jest than a dear friend.

❧

SATISFACTION

Purpose is primary, motivation, then action,
Sweat and tears follow, the result, satisfaction.

❧

SCIENCE

Science can predict an eclipse of the sun,
Scores and scores of years in advance,
But accurately it cannot predict the weather,
Whether to wear shorts or long pants.

❧

SCRIPTURE - HOLY BIBLE

Every man is in the Bible; your life is mirrored there and so is mine.
-Albert J. Penner

❧

A Bible that is known is worth a dozen you may own.

❧

The Holy Bible is a thought-initiating book.
It gives us examples how our lives should look.

❧

Regardless of sect many Christians expect
The world to reject the book they respect,
The book that they themselves so grossly neglect.

❧

We're to study the Scripture when we meet 'neath the steeple.
We can learn perfect truths through imperfect people.

❧

The Bible has wisdom to convey, and it has instant replay.

❧

The Good Lord has sent us germane messages galore,
In the Bible many letters prevail.
These letters are so relevant to our needs today,
But we just don't read our mail.

❧

The precious word of God, habitually try to heed it.
We should ask its author to be present while we read it.

❧

The Bible should be every man's manual,
For life it has many a sound illustration.
Eventually to mankind in verity it becomes
A beautiful treatise, a captivating illumination.

❧

God's holy word, full of life-saving instruction,
To study it we procrastinate a lot.
God will not open the door to divine wisdom
To the one who keeps his Bible shut.

❧

A LIFESTYLE PORTRAYAL From A TO Z

The Bible may be old but its truths are gold.

❧

If with divine strength you are to be gird,
Partake of the nutrients of God's Holy Word.

❧

There is no book in the world more knowing,
No words more indispensable, nor more disclosing.
Not only should we the Bible be beholding,
We should in verity the Scripture be upholding,
That our lives in conformity with Christ's we be molding.

❧

Dear God, I'm thankful your word is not a secret.
Thank you for your messages the prophets have writ.

❧

You can't perform justice to a meal, munching with only one tooth,
Nor obtain scriptural harmony playing but one string of truth.

❧

The Bible is bread, abundant daily rations.
It's not cake baked for special occasions.

❧

I love God's word, it gives me light,
It tells me what's wrong, it shows me what's right.

❧

Knowing Scripture is vital, to know the God of the Bible.

❧

When we read Scripture, it's an act of worship;
God through His word is personally talking to us.

❧

In a world of painful uncertainty, the Bible provides us certainty.

❧

There isn't a great difficulty that couldn't be solved
If following the teachings of Scripture we resolved.

❧

The Bible is a compass, germane thoughts for reflection.
It points the believer in the right direction.

❧

The signals of Scripture are for our correction,
Direction, protection and our divine perfection.

❧

Bibles that are visibly falling apart, undoubtedly belong to a loving, obeying heart.

❧

Most books of knowledge are for dispensing information.
The Holy Scripture is for our spiritual transformation.

❧

A LIFESTYLE PORTRAYAL From A TO Z

*If your treasured Bible is in first class shape,
The probabilities are, spiritual fitness you escape.*

❧

*Read your Bible more than a bit,
For certain, 'twill help you keep spiritually fit.
There are those who only sample the Bible;
They haven't really acquired a taste for it.*

❧

*The roots of stability, I long ago heard,
Come from being grounded in God's holy word.*

❧

An unread Bible, a fairly accurate sign of a starving believer, of a soul in decline.

❧

Brush up on your Bible every day, it will prevent vital truth decay.

❧

*If your life depended on knowing the Bible,
How long would be your ultimate survival?*

❧

*If you memorize Scripture, your subconscious works;
It takes out of life unwholesome, queer quirks.*

❧

*Man is in need of scriptural insight.
It's available to those who have spiritual eyesight.*

❧

*Scripture is the standard for faith and behavior.
Salvation is by faith, in Christ, our Savior.*

❧

God's Holy Scripture is the profoundest of literature.

❧

*Don't let the attraction of worldly pleasures
Draw you away from scriptural treasures.*

❧

*For John the Isle of Patmos was an isolation chamber.
For us he wrote much to study and remember.*

❧

*The scripture records a female financier -
You will probably remark, "Ah, get off it."
Pharoah's lovely daughter went to the bank of the Nile
And drew out an amazing prophet.*

❧

*Getting to Paradise, won't that be great!
In the meantime, turn right and then go straight.*

❧

SECRECY - SECRET

To keep your secret is wisdom, but to expect others to keep it is folly.
-Samuel Johnson

Keeping a secret, very few plan, therefore assume that no one can.

If you should wish another to keep your very own deep secret,
Firstly learn that you must be the only one to keep it.

Inviolate, profound, strict secrecy, is part and parcel of true decency.

When evil secrecy and mystery begin, roguery and rascality are sure to win.

You can take care of a secret's span, much better care than another can.

Very few will repeat what they hear and no more.
Most everyone prefers to embellish secret's store.

You've passed the true test of respectable maturity
With a will that is gracious and strong,
When keeping a secret gives you more satisfaction
Than passing that secret along.

Nothing so burdensome as a deep dark secret.
Eventually comes a time when you heedlessly release it.

If you wish to keep a secret, you must never carelessly spill it.

So you want to have a secret concealed;
Even to a best friend don't have it revealed.

Share not information personal or financial,
Unless you should feel it's absolutely essential.

SECURITY

Happiness has many roots, but none more important than security.
-E. R. Stettinius, Jr.

It's not the cage bars that make inmates abide,
It's the narrow spaces that keep the prisoners inside.

Primarily in growth, reform and change,
Absolute security you're more likely to arrange.

Age is a high price to pay for maturity;
Yet folk for old age will aim for security.

To gain security one must grasp opportunity.

Our security depends on our listening and remembering,
On obedience to God's word, and to Jesus surrendering.

SELF-ESTEEM - SELF-IMAGE - SELF-RESPECT

To have respect for ourselves, guides our morals.
    -Lawrence Sterne

You may think that I'm nothing, just a worthless punk.
I know that I'm something, God doesn't make junk.

Self-esteem must entertain a degree of responsibility,
Trustworthiness, a clear conscience, and utmost accountability.
It engenders due care, gallant charge and capability,
Solemn duty, obligation, commitment and answerability.

When self-esteem is low, negatives begin to flow;
Contradictions begin to grow sour, they have very little power.

Self-respect is confidence in our right to be happy.
Not being lackadaisical, it's being downright snappy.

Command self-respect - you'll never regret.

Positive self-esteem is a basic human need.
Confidence in achievement should be our creed.

With high self-esteem folk tend to be more ambitious.
They're far from being suspicious, nor notoriously vicious.
They do not act officious, nor are they injudicious,
They avoid being malicious, and they're never pernicious.

Self-image sets the boundaries of individual accomplishment.
    -Maxwell Maltz

SELFISHNESS - UNSELFISHNESS

To feel much for others and little for ourselves,
to restrain our selfishness and exercise our benevolent affections,
constitute the perfection of human nature.
-Adam Smith

The Sea of Galilee and the Dead Sea are one.
They come from the same source, their streamlets have fun.
They flow cool and clear from the heights of Hermon,
And from the highlands of the cedars of Lebanon.
The bright Sea of Galilee fashions beauty of it,
For the Sea of Galilee has a living outlet.
It gathers in its riches with a goal to give
To the vast Jordan Plain that others might live.
The Dead Sea, I pray - bow your head and weep!
You have no outlet, your aim is to keep.
An allegory
By Henry Emerson Fosdick
(paraphrased)

Unselfishness, ennobles, and it satisfies; both recipient and donor it gratifies.

SELF-PITY

We pity in others only those evils which we ourselves have experienced.
-Jean Jacques Rousseau

Self-pity do not share, it will get you nowhere.

Get out of your own way, avoid self-pity.
Accept the inevitable and don't feel guilty.

Contemptuous self-pity isn't at all that witty, nor is it ever pretty.

SERENITY

A humble spirit is a treasure,- it's prone to accept pain and pleasure.
With an even, serene calm mind, it is always unmoved by either.

SERVICE

"Service," emphatically is not "Serve Us."

&

Service is the rent that we pay for living.
Gratitude, what we get when we're involved in giving.

&

Some choose to operate on the cafeteria plan,
Self-service only, never give though they can.

&

If business is to prosper, this one thing you must note,
It's the customer alone who casts the winning vote.

&

Business is like tennis, not meant for amusing.
If you don't serve well, you will end up losing.

&

How can I confer better service today?
"Top Service" should be my motto each day.

&

To govern today takes nerve; you don't have to govern if you serve.

&

Service, what life's all about, you'll agree.
We must be involved in our community.

&

From a helping vocation incline not to swerve.
Your destiny will be happiness if you aim to serve.

&

Serving humanity is the path to success.
If you follow this pathway, God will surely bless.

&

You attract your lover with love and appeal.
Labor for your brother with the same fervent zeal.

&

Am I for certain my brothers' keeper?
Listen to the answer from the Divine Doorkeeper.

&

SEX APPEAL

The sexes were made for each other,
and only in the wise and loving union of the two
is the fullness of health and duty and happiness to be expected.
-William Hall

&

Today much is said about sex-appeal; to you my friend, what does it reveal?
More importantly, have you pondered – what does it conceal?

SILENCE

Silence is true wisdom's best reply.
-G. K. Chesterton

Hushed silence is practiced by those who mourn.
For many it's an expression of vile hatred and scorn.

Profound, mute silence is a singular preference,
Especially when one retains his primitive ignorance.

Silence is an argument that is difficult to refute.
Furthermore, it is something that we cannot dispute.
It's an attribute that we should frequently salute.

Silence is part and parcel of conversation, be it between one's sisters or brothers.
It is that part of any conversation that cannot be misquoted by others.

So frequently silence should be your first choice.
There are those times that it has the clearest voice.

It's natural for the elderly pensive quietness to tout.
They have so much more to be quiet about.

Be aware when involved in prolonged communication.
Silence is the safety valve for sedate conversation.

Methinks some folk are a senseless riot.
They'd prefer to be wrong rather than be quiet.

There's a thing about silence, it's so admirably discreet;
Another pensive thought, you can it repeat.

Awed silence is the ultimate, a weapon of power;
Above other virtues it so oft does tower.

So frequently a fool when silent is wise.
When he closes his lips he tells no lies.

There is an advantage to silence, I'd say, few entities can beat it.
Why, if you haven't said anything, you won't be asked to repeat it.

A LIFESTYLE PORTRAYAL From A TO Z

If silence for a wise man is a timely good rule,
How much more important must it be for a fool.

Silence profound, doesn't always mean consent,
Sometimes the ear hasn't been philosophically bent.

Awed silence, an entity that cannot be quoted.
It's seldom for silence that one is demoted.

"*And* how do you wish to be trimmed?" A barber asked Hortense.
The client meekly replied, "Please - in total awed silence."

Why be argumentative to the point of a riot?
You will have to agree, it's best to keep quiet.

I regret so often that silence I have broken,
But rarely have I regretted for not having spoken.

Do not attempt any parlance unless you can improve the silence.

Many people remain silent, they don't say a word.
They choose to be silent in order to be heard.

The way to save face with no "If" "And" or "But,"
Is to keep the lower half of your face tightly shut.

With silence you can win, so don't put your foot in.

Silence isn't always golden, this thought remember, young fellow.
Sometimes it appears to me that's it's definitely just plain yellow.

At times you must hyphenate compliance
With the much looked-forward-to silence.

The gift of speech by some is embellished.
On the other hand, by many, silence is relished.

A well-timed silence is more eloquent than words.
In the vernacular of the scientist, it increases one's hertz.

It is best at times not to say a single word.
Consider being silent in order to be heard.

Silence, so frequently should be your clear choice.
There are times that silence has the loudest voice.

Learn from the fish, he would not get caught,
If instinctively he'd learn to keep his mouth shut.

Silence is effectual, it does not leak; obtain vital facts before you speak.

Silent, silvery, singular silence – usually seeks solitary, secret compliance.

Silence is wisdom's response, it can be used more than once.

Always duly ponder what you intend to say.
It is considerably more expedient that way.
Don't always express what you surmise or think.
Silence with thought you must always link.

Remember, while involved in sedate conversation,
"Silence" is a safety valve for all communication.

Take time to be silent, you'll be less defiant,
You'll be more reliant and you'll end up compliant.

Silence can be valuable, don't ever try to break it,
Unless you are positive that you can improve it.

It is better to be silent and be considered a fool
Than to speak out and have dark doubt overrule.

SIN - SINFULNESS

He that falls into sin is a man; that grieves at it is a saint;
that boasteth of it is a devil.
-Thomas Fuller

Man's greatest sin is inhumanity to one another.
To overcome this transgression delay not my brother.

It's so uplifting to the soul, doing what isn't called sin.
Try to do something good rather than doing someone in.

Mortal sin can't exist in the presence of God's might,
No more than stark darkness in the presence of light.

Sin is not judged by the way we see it,
It's judged by the way that God reveals it.

A LIFESTYLE PORTRAYAL From A TO Z

"To be moderate in sin," the preacher saith,
"Is no more possible than moderation in death."

❧

Minor sins add considerably to one's wretched troubles,
Subtracts from one's energies, and difficulties it doubles.

❧

Man calls sin a helpless infirmity – the Almighty sees it as hideous iniquity.

❧

What could be worse then being under sin's curse?

❧

Sin, great or small - Jesus forgives all.

❧

Heinous sin displays an inviting entrance; to enter therein, don't give it a chance.

❧

Some run from sin, be they male or femme;
Others crawl away, hoping it will catch them.

❧

A tiny little sin like a pebble in a shoe,
Tires the human soul, 'twill tire you too.

❧

To avoid sin's painful tragedy, be aware of the devil's strategy.

❧

The letters S-I-N, to some spell a riddle.
To me it's quite clear, "I" is in the middle.

❧

Sin is an offense that the devil tries to prod;
An offense to humanity and Almighty God.

❧

Every act of sin that by man is employed
Is done by an act that he can avoid.

❧

We can never say that we are sinless.
We deceive ourselves and the truth is not in us.

❧

Regardless from where the cause may stem,
We're not punished for sins, we're punished by them.

❧

The exit of evil will never, never hurt you.
It promptly allows the entrance of virtue.

❧

Much nobler for evil to suffer than it is vile evil to offer.

❧

Righteousness by faith doesn't give license to sin,
Nor allow mortal man amendments to spin.

❧

A LIFESTYLE PORTRAYAL From A TO Z

Sin is a disease, I'm sure; Christ is the only sure cure.

You don't become guilty by fate; somewhere you've opened the gate.

Sin cannot flourish if godliness we nourish.

Sins that are obvious in others, we must never assail or belabor.
We must acknowledge our own, not those of our perfidious neighbor.

Vile sins focus on short term desires,
Resulting in baleful, devastating fires.

If you admit your sin, to the devil don't give in,
Abruptly choose to quit, you then are bound to win.

The most deadly sins do not leap up at us,
They just have a tendency to creep up on us.

Sin cannot flourish if godliness we nourish.

It has many branches, that tree called sin.
It has but one root; it's man's within.

We tend to keep on carelessly sinning,
But God is willing to be forgiving.

To get rid of evil, do give it the boot.
Don't strike at the branches, get rid of the root.

Evil is wrought by lack of good thought.

To repay evil with good is what every man should.

A bite of sin, so oft in haste, will leave a bitter after-taste.

The fruit of the devil determine not to cart.
Staying out of his orchard is a sensible start.

If for eternity you hope to be a winner,
You must avoid being a wretched sinner.

It's strange how minor our own sins seem,
But others' appear to be on high beam.

*W*ith God's forgiveness there can't be complaint.
He can change a sinner into a heavenly saint.

*I*n this earthly battle between good and evil,
Contemplate, "What is our worldview?"
To place Jesus Christ in the center of the picture
Is a mission we must all pursue.

SINCERITY

*S*incerity is impossible unless it pervades the whole being;
and the pretense of it saps the very foundation of character.
-James Russell Lowell

*T*here is no replacement for sparkling clarity,
Nor is there a substitute for impeccable sincerity.

*W*hy not make of yourself a sincere, honest man.
You'll be certain to make one less rascal in the land.

A sanguine blush, can't be counterfeited.
Insincerity in one's life should daily be omitted.

SINGING

*S*o often we learn our songs when it is too late to sing.
-Emily Carr

*T*he happy wish to sing, they don't wait for long;
You'll find that invariably they'll come up with a song.

*I*t's not an idle question, please lend me your ear-
In the seventh inning stretch, why should we sing, and cheer,
'Take me out to the ball game,' when we're already here?

*T*his morning, let us take a few moments,
I think it would be well worth our while
To compare what we frequently sing
While portraying our Christian Lifestyle.

"O, IF WE COULD HAVE A THOUSAND TONGUES,"
To sing our blessed Redeemer's praise,

A LIFESTYLE PORTRAYAL From A TO Z

But we utilize not the tongues we have,
We habitually neglect His banner to raise.

"THERE SHALL ALWAYS BE SHOWERS OF BLESSINGS,"
A lovely promise He is honestly maintaining.
Why then from the church should we choose to stay
Away, just because it's miserable - it's raining?

"I LOVE TO TELL THE BLESSED STORY,"
This song we gladly, so frequently sing,
But to share it with our next door neighbor,
The doorbell we're reluctant,- we're afraid to ring.

" O BLESSED BE THE TIE THAT BINDS,"
We seem to sincerely and solemnly sing,
But then, along comes an offense to sever;
Our fellowship's heart, it takes full wing.

This is the scriptural, loving injunction,
You must duly "CAST THY BURDEN ON HIM."
Why should we agonize, fret and worry,
Nurturing a lifestyle that's unutterably grim?

"O DAY OF REST, O DAY OF GLADNESS,
O day of joy and blessed light."
We make weary trips on the Lord's Day,
Heavy traffic we nervously fight.

How oft we sing, "THROW OUT THE LIFE-LINE,"
And truly for souls we should prayerfully pine,
But then our souls we choose to gratify
By casting from our dinghy the pearly fishing line.

"THERE IS SUNSHINE IN MY SOUL TODAY,"
However, to worry and pessimism we cling.
Our countenance doesn't bear the caption out,
Our voices with happiness fail to ring.

"HAVE THINE OWN WAY, LORD," we pray and sing,
But then we keep doing our very own thing.
"Search me and try me, dear Lord, today,"
Oh, how we refuse to follow and obey.

We sing the promise, "I WOULD BE LIKE JESUS,"
In country, home and in a huge throng,

A LIFESTYLE PORTRAYAL From A TO Z

But then, our actions, they fail to show it,
With people we just don't seem to get along.

"NEARER, STILL NEARER TO THEE," my Lord,
Draw me my Savior, I earnestly pray,
But then so oft I'm not anywhere near Him,
Repeatedly from Him I choose to stray.

"ALL THE WAY MY SAVIOR LEADS ME,"
We sing early morn and on going to bed,
But so frequently we take a wide detour,
We go where angels fear to tread.

"TAKE THE WORLD BUT GIVE ME JESUS."
In most of our joys we fail His name.
Invariably and consistently, we forget our Savior.
We find that our lifestyle, the world doth proclaim.

"WHAT A FRIEND WE HAVE IN JESUS,
All our sins and grief to bear,"
But so frequently we refuse to confide,
Reluctant our cares with Him to share.

"BE SILENT, BE SILENT," a tacit injunction,
This sweet song does so fully admonish,
But while we're in church, our chatter in the foyer,
Our minister and congregation it does astonish.

With enthusiasm we sing, "AWAKE MY SOUL,"
As we gently press with vigor on,
But as soon as the minister begins to speak,
There comes that abhorrent, the biggest long yawn.

"ONWARD CHRISTIAN SOLDIERS," we sing o'er and o'er,
We sing this song in a militant way,
But then invariably we wait to be drafted;
Let us no longer choose to delay.

"WE'RE MARCHING TO ZION," so oft we sing,
But we fail to march to Sabbath School and church,
Thus leaving the Sabbath School Superintendent
And our dear Pastor in the lurch.

We sing "O JESUS I HAVE PROMISED
To serve thee faithfully to the end,"

But those devout promises we keep on breaking,
Those blithe promises we deliberately bend.

"PRECIOUS, JESUS SAVIOR, - PILOT ME!"
The trusty binoculars we carry on the shelf,
Then somehow, we have a change of heart,
"Master, I'd rather do it by myself."

"GIVE ME THE BIBLE," we love to sing,
But on its hard cover grimy dust we allow.
Habitually God's word we do not study,
Beginning with prayer we fail to bow.

❧

When we pleadingly sing, "Lord, do fill me now,"
We should earnestly request, "Empty evil, somehow."

❧

A person who never sings is like a wagon without springs.
You can prance if you can walk, you can sing if you can talk.

❧

SKEPTICISM

It's strange that skeptic rhymes with septic.
Some think it inconsequential, methinks it's providential.

❧

SLANDER

To murder character is as truly a crime as to murder the body.
The tongue of the slanderer is brother to the dagger of the assassin.
-Tryon Edwards

❧

Spiteful slanderers slaughter reputation; their final reward is hell's damnation.

❧

The devil is an expert in subtle malicious slander.
Let not slippery tongue in his territory meander.

❧

Some minds meander – tongues turn to slander.

❧

Our tongues were not given to rip others apart,
They were given to build, to give folk a good start.

❧

SLOTHFULNESS

Slothfulness can cater to success an immunity.
If you should kill time, you'll bury opportunity.

SMILE - SMILING

There's a smile of Love and there's a smile of Deceit,
And there's a smile of Smiles when two smiles meet.
-William Blake

A sincere, broad smile doesn't vex or rile, it does not mislead nor does it beguile.

A smile can change many a man's fate.
It's a curve that has a tendency to make things go straight.

A smile can erase an accusing poker face.

Seek out the man with a smiling face; the shadows of life he will help to erase.

Why fret, fume and fuss, gripe pout and stew?
A smile duly adds to your face value.

Smiling is infectious, you catch it like the flu,
When someone smiled at me, I started smiling too.
I came around a corner and someone saw my grin,
When he smiled I realized that I passed it on to him.
I thought about that smile, then recognized its worth;
A smile like mine could travel 'round the earth.
When you feel a smile beginning, don't leave it undetected,
Let's start an epidemic and get the world infected.
-Anonymous

A lovely, cheery smile – one's attention it hooks.
It's a low-cost way of improving one's looks.

Can you readily smile when things go wrong,
Or do you have someone in mind to blame it on?

A cheerful, smiling leader who adds a little fun
Wins more cooperation than a grim or gloomy one.

A smile is never out of style, it always should be your clear choice.
Smile when you pick up the phone, the caller will see it in your voice.

A LIFESTYLE PORTRAYAL From A TO Z

A smile is an antidote for distress, daylight to those who are bleary.
A smile is sunshine to the sad, it's rest to those who are weary.

A smile is intimate exchange, how true,
Worth more than its endearing face value.

A big gracious smile is on the face of my brother;
It unblushingly introduces one charmed ear to the other.

A great big smile is always in style.
For a grouch, spoil the day, give him a smile.

*Y*ou can make yourself happier simply by smiling,
Putting your anxieties and your worries to full flight.
A lovely happy smile initiates brain changes
That occur during moments of spontaneous delight.

*W*hat sunshine is to flowers, smiles are to hours.

*S*ome people will smile, though unhappy, I'm told;
They're just showing off a bright inlay of gold.

*W*e should never rile - much better a smile.

A smile is most certainly a magical thing,
You can treasure it, keep it or pass it along.
A smile can erase an aching heart,
A smile can put in your heart a sweet song.
A smile is a ray of dazzling sunshine.
A smile is a beautiful expression of love.
A smile, a gift that comes back to you
With bountiful blessings from a Power from above.
-Anonymous

A smile that lights up a face, coldness of heart will erase.

SMOKING

*M*uch smoking kills live men and cures dead swine.
-George D. Prentice

"*S*ir," said a lady to a smoker, "Smoking makes me sick as a pup."
Replied the man sarcastically, "Why don't you try to give it up?"

"Smoking," or "Non-smoking," where will it be?
Where will you be sitting in eternity?"

Incessantly smoking is so oft provoking.

Do resolve today that you'll no more smoke,
And that you'll never repeat a dirty joke.

One must determine to earnestly stop smoking
Before emphysema begins to start choking.

In the consumption of cigarettes, there is a conundrum,
An expression that's dull-witted, some might call it dumb.
We call him a smoker, when his lips he does pucker –
It's the cigarette that smokes - he is the sucker.

SNOBBISHNESS

There are five types of men who fail in life;
the machine, the miser, the hermit, the snob and the brute.
-Walter Wilber Gruber

A pointed nose in the air can cause another's despair.

The penalty of success, this the prosperous will eschew,
Is to be bored by people who used to snub you.

SOCIALISM

All socialism involves slavery. That which fundamentally distinguishes
the slave is that he labors under coercion to satisfy another's desires.
-Herbert Spencer

There are two places where socialism fills the bill,
One is the beehive, the other the anthill.

SOLITUDE

For the self-development of men and women it is absolutely
necessary that they should be "alone with themselves"
at least one hour each day – to get the blessings of solitude.
-William J. H. Boetcker

❧

Solitude with sobriety, oft the best society.

❧

Occasional solitude to the soul, is inclined to make man whole.

❧

Think me not unkind and rude that I walk alone in grove and glen;
I eagerly go to the God of the wood to fetch His word to meditative men.
-Emmerson

❧

SORROW

If sorrow would not talk it would die.
-Serbian-Croation

❧

The sorrows in life are hyphenated with tears.
The worst of sorrows are its harrowing fears.

❧

Cease your sorrow, put your trust in tomorrow.

❧

There are two thieves that bring on sorrow,
Regret for yesterday, and fear of tomorrow.

❧

Do not of yesterday sorrow – make memory for tomorrow.

❧

SPECIAL - SPECIALNESS

It is natural for every man to wish for distinction
and the praise of those who can confer honor by their praise.
-Sydney Smith

❧

'Special' is a word that is used to remind us
Of something precious, something one of a kind.
'Special' are personae who act from the heart,
Doing for others set them clearly apart.

❧

A LIFESTYLE PORTRAYAL From A TO Z

'Special' is the soul that speaks love with a smile,
Happy at all times is her (his) charming lifestyle.
"Special' is that someone who is dearly adored,
One's faith in humanity is so fully restored.
'Special' is that person who is faithful, true blue.
"Special' is that expression that bests describes you.

S - signifies Sincerity -
This quality so genuine she portrays sincerely.

P - stands for Poise -
A salient trademark she displays very clearly.

E - denotes Elegance -
This graceful distinction she does truly possess.

C - utters Charm -
A treasured refinement, no more, no less.

I - speaks Idealism -
A pure, golden virtue that she holds very high.

A - announces Attractiveness -
A winsome, flawless mark that catches many an eye.

L - proclaims Loveliness -
A precious inner grace that inspires admiration.

L - too is for Love -
On occasions exclaiming, "What a beautiful creation!"

SPEECH

You must speak clearly, if you speak at all;
Carve every word before you let it fall.
-Oliver Wendell Holmes

I'm reminded today of the law of the wheel.
It's a message to speakers how the audience may feel.
I trust that my words may please and not ire,
The longer your speech the less you'll inspire,
For the longer the 'spoke' the greater the tire.

A LIFESTYLE PORTRAYAL From A TO Z

After all is said and done, do shut up and then sit down.

ప

They always talk who seldom truly think, they usually have the least to say.
Talk less, listen more, you'll learn the true score,
And you'll find it will make your day.

ప

It's wise to choose what you're about to say, before you choose to tactfully convey.

ప

Respond, don't react and don't be a baiter;
Be careful not to utter, then regret later.

ప

Some people will say, "Please, let me tell you."
I try not to accommodate, but talk they do.

ప

In your daily speech use words that grab; never, yes, never use words that stab.

ప

One doesn't always have to have the last word.
At times be silent in order to be heard.

ప

Do not ever answer an angry word in kind.
If you follow this dictum it'll blow their mind.

ప

To be a good talker avoid being a squawker;
Aptly learn to listen, don't ever be a knocker.

ప

What's in that deep well of your very own heart
Will invariably come up in the bucket of your speech.
Be cognizant of this adage if others you're to reach;
Both the young and the old this truism we must teach.

ప

Some well-meaning folk when with people they're among,
Miss invaluable opportunity to hold their sharp tongue.

ప

For certain it isn't the ship in the water, it's the water in the ship that sinks it.
It isn't so much what's on your mind, it's what you might say that could shrink it.

ప

Verbally express not what a good man should be.
Be that humble man with gentle benignity.

ప

If you should do wrong, who takes the blame?
If your words cause embarrassment, do you bear the shame?

ప

It is better to refrain from words when you part
Than to utter vacant words that don't come from the heart.

ప

A LIFESTYLE PORTRAYAL From A TO Z

*Y*ou'll miss a good chance your image to enhance;
When you yap like a pup, have you thought of shutting up?

*M*any of us into verbal quagmire sink.
We usually speak twice before we think.

*M*an's brain is so wonderful, noon, night and early morn,
It doesn't stop functioning from the day he is born.
A response I request, a sound answer I beseech,
Why does it cease functioning on getting up to make a speech?

*A*n appropriate speech, a solemn responsibility;
Make certain it contains implicit credibility.

*I*n our writings and in our speech, there are many glaring signs,
One should make an honest effort to read between the lines.

"*I*'m delighted to speak to this audience today,
In your new auditorium, so grand and so full.
I presume you're aware that "auditorium" is derived
From "Audio" to hear, and "Taurus" the bull."

*C*ourage is what it takes to speak while standing up.
Wisdom is what it takes to sit down and shut up.

*T*alk is cheap, including reprimand, it's daily supply far exceeds demand.

*H*ave something to say, no sarcastic mocking;
Make it profound and then stop talking.

*K*ind words one must never neglect.
Sharp words can dull one's respect.

*D*o speak kindly, it won't hurt your tongue,
And you'll be elevated by those you're among.

*T*he difference between wretchedness or a blessing,
Is frequently found in your manner of speaking.

*R*ather than putting others in their place,
Try putting yourself in that same space.

*B*e mindful what you say, make it profound;
A man who slings mud inevitably loses ground.

A LIFESTYLE PORTRAYAL From A TO Z

*T*ake a long pause before moving your jaws.

A good speech is gracious, full of thought and strength,
But the best part of a speech is it's depth, not it's length.

*O*rators so oft with caustic words have stung.
It doesn't always pay to have a golden tongue.

*M*any disturb silence by venting vengeance,
Speaking utter nonsense; give your speech substance.

*I*t takes a wise person to know what to say.
For this divine wisdom continually pray.

A vessel is known by its sound,
Whether it be square or round.
Men likewise are proved by their speeches,
Whether they come from wise creatures.

*H*e is a wise person who eliminates all squawk.
He perceives the big difference between free speech and cheap talk.

*B*e careful what you say when your words you do mike.
If you say what you think the response you won't like.

*B*e watchful what you say, lest your speech betray.

*O*ur speech should add light - vengeful ire won't do it.
It should reduce heat and then you should cool it.

A missing ingredient isn't always the seasoning.
In most of our talking it's usually the shortening.

*B*e careful what you say, avoid boorish bluffing,
Think twice before speaking and then say nothing.

*T*here should never be a ready welcome mat
For an envious thought or a gossipy chat.

*S*ay pleasant things, proclaim them to the ceiling,
It will help to create a warm, fuzzy feeling.

*Y*ou'll suffer acute indiscretion if you speak before reflection.

A LIFESTYLE PORTRAYAL From A TO Z

*D*on't let your sins tell your mouth what to say;
Continuing in wrongdoing gives evil full sway.

*M*ost experts advise, "Begin with a joke."
My advice, don't ever at others fun poke.

*S*peak little and well if yourself you're to sell.

*B*lunt, starched words of monosyllabic brevity
Do not promote friendship, compassion or levity.

*D*on't blow your trumpet about years spent in college,
Lest you darken counsel with words lacking knowledge.

A human learns to talk, about year two; it takes fifty or more to learn when not to.

*E*veryone is guaranteed the right of free speech,
Providing the loyal listeners don't have to hear screech.

*D*on't attempt to convey, when you've nothing to say.

I've noticed many audiences by dry speech are beset,
Oft caused by speeches that are usually all wet.

*M*any men's speeches are like broiled lobster,
You have to be cautious of the heat,
And you will have to pick through much of it
To find so-called edible meat.

*M*ares don't have colts if they haven't been bred,
Likewise, don't explain what you haven't said.

*B*e cautious, be careful, lest your clever retort
Have no visible means of viable support.

*S*ay what you mean, mean what you say,
But don't make it mean, it's best that way.

*B*e certain your speech is better than silence,
You won't have to utter passionate defiance.

*I*n delivering a speech, vary pace and pitch,
And eventually don't forget a conclusion to hitch.

A LIFESTYLE PORTRAYAL From A TO Z

*A*bout your announcement, I have this report,
If idiots could take off this area would be an airport.

*R*iding an old horse that is steady and sure,
Gets you much farther than a young one that balks.
A minute of clear thought is better by far
Than an equivalent amount of loose, loud squawk.

*Y*our incensed loud voice is usually much crisper.
Your answer should be soft - people listen to a whisper.

*H*e that speaks much is frequently mistaken;
Though invariably loud, he's completely forsaken.

*O*f "Someday" so many repeatedly speak.
Remember, my friend, it's not a day of the week.

*S*peech has power to persuade, to convert, compel and give aid.

*T*ake heed, lest your speech portray cruel belligerence,
Intolerance, indifference, and sarcastic inference.
Particularly do avoid articulating ignorance,
Arrogance, malevolence, and blasphemous irreverence.

*K*eep fully in mind this entity - you must never attempt to give up,
And another thing to remember, when you must totally shut up.

*C*ontrol the tone and the volume of your voice;
Propelling loud yell should not be your choice.

*S*mooth talk can be threatening, some question its worth,
One wonders if the sleek will inherit the earth.

*S*peech both conceals and succinctly reveals.

*K*eeping some words as a prized possession
Will prevent one's spirit from going into a recession.

A mama whale said to her baby, while over it she lovingly swooned,
"It's when you are visibly spouting, chances are you'll get harpooned."

*S*tand up to be seen, speak up to be heard,
Know when to sit down, always honest in word.

Let your eloquent speech be filled with grace,
Seasoned with kindness, allowing others space.

❧

Be much to kind to say things cruel; avoid making someone look like a fool.

❧

The man who is modest in his every day speech,
And excels in his actions, his goal he will reach.

❧

So much thoughtless speech on this earth does abound;
The vessel that is empty makes the greatest sound.

❧

The true, just value of a good dissertation is not only in remembering what was said,
It is in retaining what you candidly think – the result of what to your brain was fed.

❧

Speak no evil of man, instead, all the good you can.

❧

Some salesmen speak much while attempting to sell,
But have an inherent problem, they do not speak well.

❧

When asked to give a speech, prolong not your brief chat.
When asked to say a few words, try to keep them at that.

❧

There are many folk who love to talk,
Their tongues, incessantly travel like a piston.
So oft, surprisingly, you will discover, they're the ones who hate to listen.

❧

"I am deeply concerned about ischemic necroses,
So let us stand up and relieve what hurts the 'mostess.'"

❧

"I believe your standing has somewhat relieved it.
Thank you, my friends, you may now be seated."

❧

SPIRITUALITY

The basic need of the world is spirituality.
 -Douglas MacArthur

❧

The less spirituality that there is in a church, a path we should be shunning,
The more festivities, drama and entertainment it takes to keep it running.

❧

You're responsible for the depth of your spiritual understanding;
God's Spirit will assist you if you work at comprehending.

❧

A LIFESTYLE PORTRAYAL From A TO Z

Some are deemed spiritual by faithful church attendance,
An exercise that could be mere ritual.
It's the study of God's word, His grace and abiding love
That inclines a soul to be spiritual.

~

There are no byways to spiritual maturity,
Nor are there shortcuts to eternal security.

~

Flowers that bend toward the warm sun,
Do so on cloudy days - for Christians a lesson.

~

To gain spiritual strength acknowledge your weakness,
In profound humbleness and genuine meekness.

~

Spiritually bankrupt and filled with agony,
The man who serves God only for money.

~

We must be spiritual, we must be right-minded,
To prepare for heaven we should,
But we must not become so heavenly-minded
That we are no earthly good.

~

Life oft is a series of collisions with the future.
In days to come, spirituality I must nurture.

~

To keep yourself spirituality fit, use the Great Physician's kit.

~

The crisis of most nations is their pitiful morality.
They must rid themselves totally of rascality and brutality.
They must aim to discourage sensuality and artificiality,
Think less of materiality, and eliminate criminality.
To prevent finality in their staggering totality,
They must give full freedom to instinctive spirituality.

~

Keep spiritually fit, faith never banish.
Keep your eyes on Jesus and your fears will vanish.

~

A person who is almost persuaded, by the devil is not evaded.

~

Criticism and fault-finding are not spiritual gifts.
They aren't the attributes that will give us a lift.

~

A sagacious maxim with no 'ifs' or 'buts,'
God wants spiritual fruit not religious nuts.

~

A LIFESTYLE PORTRAYAL From A TO Z

SPIRITUALITY'S LIFESTYLE RATION IN AN ABECEDERIAN SCRIPTURAL FASHION

Anxiety
Fret not about anything, pray about everything;
If you follow this dictum, calm peace God will bring.
-Philippians 4:6,7

Believe
"Do not be afraid, only believe.
She will be made well," Christ doesn't deceive.
-Luke 8:50

Conscience
To live in good conscience I must include obeisance.
-Acts 23:1

Duty
Obedience to duty is in God's plan.
Keeping His commandments is the duty of man.
-Ecclesiastes 12:13

Exercise
Apostle Paul advised, godliness we must exercise.
-First Timothy 4:7

Fearlessness
Fear thou not, don't be afraid, I am your God, I'll give you aid.
-Isaiah 41:10

Greed
He who is guilty of gainful greed, his life's journey, death will impede.
-Proverbs 1:19

Humility
Before high honor comes honest humility.
The latter will give you peace and tranquility.
-Proverbs 15:33

Integrity
"Let wholesome integrity and uprightness preserve me."
To this profound precept I bend my knee.
-Psalm 25:21

A LIFESTYLE PORTRAYAL From A TO Z

Joy
A joyful, merry heart doeth good like a medicine.
To employ this entity we shouldn't be reticent.
-Proverbs 17:22

❧

Knowledge
The fear of the Lord is the beginning of knowledge.
Fools despise wisdom, they deplore attending college.
-Proverbs 1:7

❧

Love
Love doesn't act rudely, doesn't seek its own,
Not easily provoked, its heart is not of stone.
-First Corinthians 13:5

❧

Meekness
Of gentle meekness there's considerable dearth;
Blessed are the meek, they'll inherit the new earth.
-Matthew 5:5

❧

Name
A good name is fulfillment, better than precious ointment.
-Ecclesiastes 7:1

❧

Omnipotence
Omnipotent God! Man is from sod.
-Revelation 19:6

❧

Prosperity
"He who covers his sins will never prosper;" to ask for forgiveness do not defer.
-Proverbs 28:13

❧

Quitting
To live a spiritual life, one must not quit; most importantly, quench not the Spirit.
-First Thessalonians 5:19

❧

Remember
Remember the Sabbath to keep it holy; an old commandment for the rich and lowly.
-Exodus 20:8

❧

Security
Not only is Jesus our surety, He is our eternal security.
-Hebrews 7:22

❧

Thought
As a man thinketh in his heart, so is he.
Temperate in all things he should try to be.
-Proverbs 23:7

Understanding
In all your ways acknowledge Him, and lean not to your own understanding.
This admonition, the young and the old, should be fully comprehending,
-Proverbs 3:5

Vanity
How long will man love vanity? It borders on incipient insanity.
-Psalm 4:2

Worry
Worry and fretfulness your soul can't afford;
Things work for good to those who love the Lord.
-Romans 8:28

eXample
Christ, our supreme example, this should be more than ample.
-First Peter 2:21

Youth
Remember your Creator in the days of your youth;
Avoid using speech that's offensively uncouth.
-Ecclesiastes 12:1

Zeal
For meritorious good deeds, avoid timid shirks.
Attempt to be zealous for good, wholesome works.
-Titus 2:14

In the desperate battle for one's survival,
Have you considered a spiritual revival?

All that happens in world history rests on something spiritual.
If the spiritual is strong it creates world history
-Albert Schweitzer

SPORTS

The least one can say about pole-vaulter Kirk,
Wholeheartedly he throws himself into his work.

A LIFESTYLE PORTRAYAL From A TO Z

On golf courses the Professional won't allow any beagles;
Surprisingly he encourages to shoot birdies and eagles.

Athletics is America's most favorite exercise;
We sit down and watch and incessantly criticize.

SQUABBLING

When squabbling with a fool may patience be your guide;
Make certain that you aren't similarly occupied.

STATISTICS

Statistics on death don't lie, ten out ten people die.

While reading statistics, a lady pondered the logistics.
She said to a man, "I don't tell lies -
Every time I breathe – a human being dies."
Obviously in haste, he said, "Try toothpaste."

STATURE

No man can add one cubit to his stature.
-E. G. White

The true measure of a man is how he handles power,
And how he comes across to those who are much lower.

Quite oft on this stepstool stood a big man,
His greatness defied physical stature.
Compassion and kindness to the young and his peers,
He made it a point to nurture.
His faithfulness to God and love for his neighbor
Have been absent from signs of dizzy lurch.
He's been exceedingly steadfast to duties assigned;
Overflowing has been his love for the church.

A man never adds to his stature, by treading on others' toes,
Nor does he increase prestige by telling more than he knows.

STEALTH

There is little doubt, our people practice stealth;
Our country is abundant with unreported wealth.

STRESS

Man should not try to avoid stress any more
than he would shun food, love or exercise.
-Dr. Hans Selye

In attempting to reduce stress, ways to happiness address.

You have to have stress if you wish to get ahead.
If you don't have stress in time you'll be dead.

To those who say, "I've been working real hard,"
Their behavior we emulate, stress we disregard.

The ever-present stress on our life demands
That we take hold of it with both feet and hands.

A brook loses song if it had no rocks.
It's best we be graduates of the "School of Hard Knocks."

Be patient, be diligent, avoid being a fool;
Cope with life's pressures without losing your cool.

STUDENT - STUDY

To students I say. midnight oil, do burn.
Investment in knowledge gives the best return.

SUCCESS

The secret to success is constancy to purpose.
-Benjamin Disraeli

If you exercise and sweat, success will be met.

A LIFESTYLE PORTRAYAL From A TO Z

The most difficult thing about triumphant success,
Lasting achievement you must persistently address.

～

The foundation for ultimate success - confidence and prayer do not shirk.
Actively engage yourself daily with purpose and might while you work.

～

An escalator to success? No, you must climb, using the stairway one step at a time.

～

In the race for success in your life, make certain you marry a good wife.

～

Plan your work then work your plan; an axiom that is followed by the successful man.

～

Said the boss to apprentice Stu, "You can't spell success without U."

～

For success, go straight if you expect survival; every crooked turn delays one's arrival.

～

Awareness you must fully address, insight is the key to success.

～

You must go forward if success you're to nurture.
You can't walk backward into the unknown future.

～

A successful salesperson with obtrusion is bolder.
He finds instant cure for the common cold shoulder.

～

Hard work applied diligently and intelligently is something one must fully address.
One's thinking in an organized manner is bound to lead to success.

～

The reason so few ever reach to the top is that so many choose to sit still.
No successful method has ever been devised for anyone sitting to slide up hill.

～

To be successful, let me give you a clue, ideas won't work unless you do too.

～

Success and great fame many aim to address.
Do not confuse fame with well-merited success.

～

The chances of success in any undertaking
Is measured by the belief in self you are making.

～

For business to be successful, priorities do arrange;
The only constant factor is never-ending change.

～

There's no set code of conduct to help most anxious beginners.
Coupled with mediocre talent, inner drive can make them winners.

～

A LIFESTYLE PORTRAYAL From A TO Z

To be successful in business, true facts in any clime,
Three things are always paramount, knowledge, persistence and time.

If the mountain of success you're to successfully scale,
You must in your thesaurus avoid the word "Fail'"

May this singular concept in your memory forever last,
'No one can be successful in the fleeting past.'

Success I have found requires responsibility;
A very close second, prompt availability.

For success in business, this thought is crucial,
You must strive to avoid, 'business as usual.'

To be a success you must be daring, you must be different, you must be caring.

If you think you're successful and give credit to your skill,
It's best to take inventory, you may be sliding downhill.

A person to be successful must have capacity for thinking,
And from positive action he mustn't be shrinking.

Not man's appearance or the manner of his dress,
It's his unselfish service that spells true success.

Though inertly you may fall, trying repeatedly is all.

Failure won't stand in the way of success, providing the "why?" you painstakingly address.

Be it high rank and wealth aplenty, in the absence of fulfillment, success is empty.

If supreme endeavor you fully address, sweat plus sacrifice will turn into success.

A man can succeed, a philosophical truism,
At anything for which he has unlimited enthusiasm.

A totally enterprising, successful man makes more money than his darling wife can.
A successful woman is one who can through diligent search find such a man.

If success is to be a viable movement, commit yourself daily to self-improvement.

Success in itself can be shallow or hollow; aim for service, success will follow.

A LIFESTYLE PORTRAYAL From A TO Z

If you dauntlessly dare to fail, if industry you energetically assail,
Eventually success will prevail.

❧

If you're to succeed, weigh all admonishment.
When you do succeed, hide your astonishment.

❧

You'll attain success much faster if you give of your best to your master.

❧

For a successful toehold in how you deal, I justly caution, don't act like a heel.

❧

To achieve success in all that you do, think things through, then follow through.

❧

The penalty of success, this the prosperous should eschew,
Is to be bored by people who used to snub you.

❧

"We must believe in pure luck," the man at the podium did mike,
"How else can we fully explain the success of those we don't like."

❧

Analyze the present - plan the future, review the past - success you'll nurture.

❧

Those who are destined to become successful,
Make the hours live by making them useful.

❧

If you should ever feel that you cannot succeed
In doing the job well, don't others impede.
If you feel that the task does not give you a thrill,
Step aside, pass it on to someone else to fulfill.

❧

An enduring passion for any objective is bound to ensure success;
For your ardent desire will point the way to that which you wish to address.

❧

For you to become truly successful, your ambition you must seek to arouse.
Be aware, you'll only travel as far as your intellectual horizon allows.

❧

Enthusiasm and persistence you must fully address.
They're singular attributes that lead to success.

❧

To attain success, a prudent goal declare, don't ever despair, of shysters beware,
Weigh prudently a dare, you must always play fair, honesty never spare, do learn to care,
Keep in mind share, dilemmas mustn't scare, and passionately do not omit daily prayer.

❧

How can one say, "Life isn't a success,"
When getting food on the table is no longer duress.

❧

*S*ingular success isn't measured by the dollar,
Neither does brilliance make a true scholar.

*Y*ou have to begin if your desire is to win.
Enduring success comes from daring to begin.

*I*f success is to become a viable rendition, take proper aim and have right ammunition.

*Y*ou've reached the pinnacle of success and authenticity,
When you're no longer seeking wanton wealth and publicity.

*I*n attaining success, avoid violence and indolence;
Determination, the main chapter in the book of excellence.

*S*uccess in one's life exacts a worthy goal; to aim, strive and gain is up to your soul.

*S*uccess is invariably due to one's will; suave equanimity is one's peace being still.

SUPERFICIALITY

*D*eep down some folk are relatively superficial.
This candid oxymoron may appear prejudicial.
In some, I reckon it could be interstitial.
Nonetheless, I'll agree, it is not official;
Perhaps a prudent judge his input would initial.

SYMPATHY

*W*e are living at a time when creeds and ideologies clash,
but the gospel of human sympathy is universal and eternal.
-Samuel Hopkins Adams

*P*latitudinous pity has no monetary value,
Compassion alone doesn't seem to ring true.
Fulfilling specific need we must keep in full view.
Our pattern of sympathy we must fully review.

TACT

*T*act is one of the first mental virtues, the absence of which is often fatal.
-William Simms

A LIFESTYLE PORTRAYAL From A TO Z

Tact is a knack of making a point
Without putting someone's nose out of joint.

❧

Subtle tact is when your mouth gets the cue
Just before someone shuts it for you.

❧

At times tact has with it a needful bit of spoof,
Like raising your dark eyebrows instead of the roof.

❧

Tact is convincing that you are thinking
That they know more, and that you them adore.

❧

Genuine tact, the unsaid part that one tries to keep close to his heart.

❧

Rare tact teaches you when to be silent.
Wisdom indoctrinates when to be compliant.

❧

A lack of tact is the ability, to step on another person's toes;
To put a foot in one's mouth and say considerably more than one knows.

❧

Discriminating tact is uniquely sublime.
It's the knack of being quiet at the right time.

❧

In graceful communication one must have tact.
No way of dodging it, this is a known fact.
"Don't know how we're going to be without you, Miss Frye,
But beginning on Monday we're going to try."

❧

Lincoln defined tact as the ability, to see others as they see themselves.
What a marvelous trait to possess, this singular characteristic never shelve.

❧

Administrative talent is no match for tact; we see its failure in an aggressive act.

❧

Talent can be power with inordinate skill; talent knows how, tact, when to be still.

❧

Discriminating tact is uniquely sublime, it's the knack of being silent at the right time.

❧

TALENTS

Talent is only a starting point in business – you've got to be working that talent.
-Irving Berlin

❧

Talents with persistent practice are unfurled.
Character is created in the tempests of this world.

❧

*Share your talents while alive, to the grave you them cannot take.
The one who buries his talents is making a grave mistake.*

*With ordinary talent and extraordinary adherence,
Most things are attainable with indomitable perseverance.*

Talent is power, tact is skill, love is caring, giving is will.

Talent inspires fulfillment of duties, it also creates its own opportunities.

TARDINESS

Better three hours too soon, than one minute too late.
-Shakespeare

*Some folks are perpetually on time being late.
It's indeed a conundrum how lateness they calculate.*

*Being late to so many is a captivating ritual,
And so, for leisure time they aim to be punctual.*

*A lackadaisical cannibal, unquestionably much older,
Was penalized for tardiness, he got the cold shoulder.*

TEACHERS - TEACHING

*The best teacher is the one who kindles an inner fire,
arouses moral enthusiasm and inspires the student with a vision.*
-Walter R. Rutherford

*Said an astute teacher to an indolent student – the latter, his studies he neglected,
"The afternoon invariably intuitively well knows what the morning never suspected."*

There are scores of teachers - how many are educators?

*In the throes of teaching some almost come to blows.
It's impossible to teach one when he thinks he more knows.*

*The professor remarked about indolent Clem,
"He has great gifts - too lazy to unwrap them."*

Though obstacles obstruct they can also instruct.

One of the great gifts that parents can bestow
Is teaching a child when to say, "No."

We teach far more by what we are, what we do and what we bar.

A teacher's habitual astuteness, captures a student's attention.
She is prone to quickly dispel a child's groundless apprehension.

A first grade pupil slouched back in his chair –
He appeared somewhat peaked - was in no one's hair.
His shirt was unbuttoned, his pants were down,
His tummy was exposed – he wasn't acting a clown.
His teacher inquired, "What's wrong, Robbie?
He meekly replied, "I have a sore tummy."
"Pull your pants up – do it real soon."
"But the principal told me to stick it out till noon."

Our teachers today are a strong mainstay, not fully appreciated until a rainy day.

"You're to sit still while I try to instill," this sound precept teachers aim to fulfill.

Teachers try helpfully to open the door,
But it's up to the students to diligently store.

A teacher with serenity and gentle benignity can effect eternity.

A noble teaching art that's blest, is knowing how to positively suggest.

An announcement came out, a retired teacher to honor;
The bulletin in itself caused quite a ripple -
"You're invited to come to honor this person,
She has class no more, nor has she any principal."

TELEVISION

Television has transformed an idealistic subject
From an irresistible force into an immovable object.

The boob-tube couch potatoes, part and parcel of the human race,
Leisurely select their options while gradually broadening their base.

Media, Television and Radio, one would say, with words are replete.
Not always are they candid communication, more oft they're a one-way street.

A LIFESTYLE PORTRAYAL From A TO Z

A TV commercial is a time that depresses,
And I might add, there are times it refleshes.

Television opens doors, of them, many scores.
You'll find that they're mostly refrigerator doors.

Television has added new dimensions to pain;
Obesity, a sore bottom, and uncomfortable eyestrain.

Turn off periodically the TV and computer;
Exercise your mind, it could be your tutor.

In the production of videos, I would certainly much rather
They be strictly designed to the capacity of my bladder.

There'd be fewer problems with children, if they did more rowing and hoeing,
And if they had to chop wood to keep the television going.

TEMPER

A tart temper never mellows with age; and a sharp tongue
is the only edged tool that grows keener with constant use.
-Washington Irving

A temper that's ungoverned governs the whole man.
So temper your temper, control it, you can.

When a person's temper gets the best of him,
It succinctly reveals the worst in him.

Uncontrollable temper, undeniably it's the worst.
To control it in others with temper some burst.
Before you control others, control your own first.

To lose your temper, if so you choose,
You'll find invariably that you will lose.

When you lose your temper you lose your head;
When you lose your head,- what more need be said?

Of men it can be said, "They're comparable to steel,
When they lose their temper they lose their appeal."

Temper is a quality that at a critical moment, brings out the best in iron and steel,
But on the contrary, it's the worst in people, a petty childish trait it so oft does reveal.

~

Temper is the entity that gets us into trouble.
Pride is what keeps us from being contritely humble.

~

A reckless temper, like a raging fire; it's very destructive when controlled by ire.

~

A boiling hot temper and a tongue that's loose
Are frequently responsible for cooking one's goose.

~

Permit not yourself to exhibit hot temper;
Of a cool temperament be an admirable exemplar.

~

If temper you're inclined to lose, destiny is bound to refuse.

~

TEMPERANCE - INTEMPERANCE

"Classic temperance is a bridle of gold." Use it, my friend, your life to mold.

~

The man who skillfully masters himself
Has singular priorities that are far above pelf.

~

The toughest test of one's self-control
Is to listen to someone define it in whole,
Describing the same ailment you have in your own soul.

~

Some are comparable to a steamboat, when they've had too much grog.
You'll find that they toot the loudest, when they're in a dense fog.

~

It's been said that some people drink like a fish - I think the concept is bunk.
Just dial your mind to memory's recall, have you ever seen a fish drunk?

~

TEMPTATION

Whoever yields himself to temptation debases himself
with a debasement from which he can never rise.
-Horace Mann

~

Temptation rarely comes in appointed busy hours.
It is in leisure times that temptation powers.

~

Temptation is for certain to ring your doorbell,
You might even think that he's a real winner.
True, you've no control of him coming to your door,
But don't ever ask him to stay for dinner.

Temptation usually comes, it's been frequently spoken,
Through a door that's been left deliberately wide open.

When temptation knocks make use of the locks.

Half the sacred art of Christian living is shunning temptation and loving and giving.

No virtue is so strong that it is beyond temptation.
Take heed, ask for strength to overcome this tribulation.

One's drinking causes the loss of inhibitions.
It results in socially embarrassing exhibitions.

Sound advice to temptation - SCRAM! Forbidden fruit makes bad jam.

Into temptation we'll fall, if we don't flee from its call.

When fleeing temptation's duress, don't leave a forwarding address.

TENSENESS

A youngster, somewhat nervous, graphic words imparted,
"Feel in a hurry all over, but I just can't get started."

TESTIMONIALS

Many testimonials are but frank flattery.
Conversely, press releases oft assault and battery.

THANKS - THANKSGIVING

The personal blessings we enjoy, deserve the thanksgiving of a whole life.
-Jeremy Taylor

Teaching a child to be thankful, a virtue a parent must prod,
Lest, when he becomes a man he doesn't take time to thank God.

"Thank You," two words that are very essential.
"I'm Sorry," two words with tremendous potential.
❧

Try to remember to start each day thinking of someone to thank.
That shouldn't be difficult for at top, your heavenly Father must rank.
❧

A customer chided a clerk, "With a thank-you, you're not replete."
The clerk's witty repartee, "It's printed on your receipt."
❧

Your thank-you notes should always be prompt,
Even though with chores you're continually swamped.
❧

When you get to the top of the stair, thank those who helped you get there.
❧

A thankful heart is a parent of all virtues.
It's a trait that we all should elect to choose.
❧

Thankfulness in prayer can lift a load of care.
❧

Be thankful for a job, be it mixed with disdain;
Complain not of the clouds when you've prayed for rain.
❧

We don't need more to be thankful for, we just need to be thankful considerably more.
❧

If you believe that life is worth living, you'll be involved in gracious thanksgiving.
❧

Be thankful for every heartbeat and breath.
In life there is nothing as certain as death.
❧

When you've thanked the Lord for every blessing sent,
You'll have little time to murmur or lament.
❧

THOUGHT

They are never alone that are accompanied with noble thoughts.
-Sir Philip Sidney
❧

Our thoughts, our words, our actions, or be they imaginings of the heart,
Stop for a moment, take inventory – what portrait do your thoughts impart?
❧

There is a succinct thought that we've frequently heard,
"One thing you can give and still keep is your word."
❧

A LIFESTYLE PORTRAYAL From A TO Z

You may think great thoughts, but expression you've curtailed,
If you don't get them across, without question you've failed.

Boundless happiness for what God has wrought
Depends in large measure on the quality of our thought.

If thoughts could be read some faces would go red.

Politicians using eloquence to transfer leading thought;
By many this sole attribute is so eagerly sought.

Research is to see what others have sought,
And to think of something no one else has thought.

No one thinks happiness when he is benched,
Nor can one give when fists are tightly clenched.

Thinking can makes us good or bad, happy or sad, calm or mad.

Some folk are hasty in thought - about them I have some illusions.
Why not provide a safety net for those who jump to conclusions.

I note that many a train of thought has too many directions and motives;
Could it be that one's confused brain has too many moving locomotives?

There is this one thing we must never ignore,
Most things have been thought of or said years before.

The glow of a warm thought can never be bought.

If someone should casually request, "Follow my train of thought,"
Make certain that they're on track before a ticket is bought.

I questioned my wife about the cookbooks she bought.
Her candid reply, "They give food for thought."

With positive thoughts you'll do more than survive,
You'll definitely thrive and project you're alive.

If you think like doing an impulsive foolish thing,
Think for a moment, what joy will it bring.

If habitually you allow machines to do your thinking,
Before long you'll find your brain will be shrinking.

A LIFESTYLE PORTRAYAL From A TO Z

If you learn to think big, success you will dig.

~

When eating fresh fruit think not of the fee,
Think of the person who planted the tree.

~

Is the glass half empty or is it half full? Tell me, what response do you read?
Methinks an engineer's response would be, "Twice as much glass as you need,"

~

Is the glass half empty or is it half full? A question that occasions some thinking.
I've come to the conclusion, it totally depends on whether you're pouring or drinking.
I'm pouring - 'half full', - 'half empty', I'm drinking,
Don't you agree that this is sound thinking?

~

It's not what you know in inexhaustible amounts,
It's what you think of in time that counts.

~

A thought expressed may cause you to blink;
A provocative question may cause you to think.

~

Watch your thoughts, they can become words;
Adorn them with beauty, imitate songbirds.

~

Some people get lost in thought, unfamiliar territory they've sought.

~

Thinking a long time can be wrong-doing for thinking too long can be one's undoing.

~

The thought of being alive can be a joyful high-five.

~

A rose is attracted to the eye even though its stem is thorny.
There could be an element of truth in ideas that are thought to be corny.

~

Our lives would run smoother, they would be less cursed,
If we only permitted second thoughts to come first.

~

A multiplicity of words so often is wrought;
So frequently it indicates utter poverty of thought.

~

Though there can be prophetic power in thought,
Deep, revered wisdom cannot be bought.

~

Habitually dive into the sea of thought;
You'll come up with pearls that can't be bought.

~

Evil thought of a brother on retiring do not link,
Nor should you go to bed with dirty dishes in the sink.

~

A LIFESTYLE PORTRAYAL From A TO Z

The farther back in your thoughts you can be,
The farther forward you are likely to see.

❧

Cultivate fertility of thought - an attribute that should be sought.

❧

A public opinion poll, has to be bought, be it nation-wide - not a substitute for thought.

❧

If you pause to think you'll have cause to thank.

❧

Innovation requires deep thought, to some it's totally disdainful.
To folk that are somewhat complacent, I find that thought is painful..

❧

Though great thinkers perish their thoughts we do cherish.

❧

If you rest your firm chin in your hands while you think,
It will keep your mouth shut, your thoughts you'll better link.

❧

What you daily think determines what you do,
And of your character it provides a good clue.

❧

Thoughts that are private should be kept at bay.
They can be silent – they're best that way.

❧

Thoughts that are pleasant are softly spoken;
One's trusted secrets should never be broken.

❧

Don't try to impress people with the deepness of your thought.
Using vagueness of language, victory can't be wrought.

❧

While in deep thought, you're disturbed by a child;
Do you see it's innocence or do you go wild?

❧

Why entertain thoughts - depressing or distressing?
Multiply your joy by counting your blessings.

❧

Think big thoughts, enjoy small pleasures;
These attributes in life can be true treasures.

❧

Take occasion to be caught in this wide world of thought;
Could be a rare moment pensive thought has wrought.

❧

What people think of you, don't agonize; how seldom they do would be a surprise.

❧

Every thought-through thought is a germinating seed;
Grievous, impending failure it is bound to impede.

❧

A LIFESTYLE PORTRAYAL From A TO Z

If you want to get your clever thoughts across,
It's quite imperative that you don't get cross.

Getting lost in thought, not at all a rarity, the cause is usually unfamiliar territory.

Putting great thoughts into intelligent action could oft result in a positive impaction.

In hell's damnation you could be sinking if you leave God out of your daily thinking.

He that will not command clear thought, should be counseled - for certain he ought.

We know what we are and what we should bar,
But what we could be our thoughts run afar.

Be the author of a salient precious thought; be the instrument that others have sought.

He purchased a new gadget, unassembled of course,
After rereading the instructions, he had but one recourse.
He sought help from his handyman who was in the backyard –
A humble old gent, not at all a blowhard.
He picked up the pieces – began assembling the device –
Amazingly from the instructions he sought no advice.
The contrivance in a short time had its full function.
"That's amazing," said the boss, "with no help from instructions?"
"It's a fact," said the handyman, with a sly, gleeful wink,
"When a fellow can't read he's got to know how to think."

For thought-through thoughts there's a tremendous dearth;
Before spewing off, let's think things through first.

Only five percent of all the people in our society take time to think.
Fifteen out of a hundred think they think, eighty-five percent do anything but think.

To read and to think, both we should do; readers of plentiful, thinkers are few.

Reserve a place in your thoughts for fantasy;
Imagination rehearsed could result in ecstasy.

Stretch your thoughts to the max - an entity that governments can't tax.

THREE "B'S."

"Remember the three "B's," said a mother to her Shirley,
"B" careful, "B" good, and "B" home early."

THREE "R'S"

Remember the three "R's" – for self, Respect -
Regard for others - Responsibility ne'er regret.

TIME - TIMES - DAYS - YEARS

The inaudible and noiseless foot of Time.
-William Shakespeare

I've been given but a tiny precious minute, there are merely sixty seconds in it.
I can assure you, I didn't seek it, nor was I given the chance to choose it.
It's been forced, I couldn't refuse it, been strictly told, I must wisely use it.
Been warned I'll suffer if I should lose it - an account I must give if I should abuse it.
Merely sixty seconds – eternity could be in it!

When someone tells you, "It won't be but a minute,"
He's probably very truthful, most times he's definite.

Time is a singular benefactor, it's an acid test of one's character.

You'll much higher climb if you're the master of your time.

Some long for tomorrow, they humbly for it pray.
They forget that tomorrow is just another busy day.

A sure way to get to appointments on time, initiate early leave, do it every time.

The hours you put in could greatly amount.
It's what you put into the hours that count.

One can never rush future's rhyme, it usually comes one day at a time

Time is an entity that can't be retrieved - it is that something that must be believed.
One can regain lost friends or money, when time is lost, so is opportunity.

Wasting the gift of time, by some it's deemed a crime.

A LIFESTYLE PORTRAYAL From A TO Z

My time, my life is God's gift to me; what I do with my days is up to me.

∽

Each new day comes with its own special gift.
Untie the bow, your countenance it will lift.

∽

Have you noticed that folk who have time to waste,
Invariably want to spend it with someone in haste?

∽

What good is a precious hour or two
To the person who doesn't valuable time pursue?

∽

"I've been allotted three minutes to speak," said a man with a voice somewhat meek.
"But I don't know just where to begin," said he, with a wry, sheepish grin.
A drawl from the rear, loudly heard, "Ah, why don't you begin with the third."

∽

Precious, lost time is never found again; a fact oft quoted and writ with pen.

∽

Today, just as much can be done as tomorrow; do not put it off, time you can't borrow.

∽

The prism of precious time, o'er the years, months and days,
Can alter one's perception in strange, magnetic ways.

∽

Killing auspicious time murders opportunities.
Avoid any involvement in trivial importunities.

∽

Be mindful of minutes, lost time is never found;
Always be diligent, keep your nose to the ground.

∽

You won't be wasting your "YESTERDAYS,"
If inclined to utilize your precious "TODAYS."

∽

Ben Franklin's message continues to be sound, "Precious, lost time is never again found."

∽

Our greatest possession is fleeting precious time.
Cherish the golden hours if your aim is to climb.

∽

Why would anyone precious time waste? Good, honest work has a special taste.

∽

It's been said, "Time heals ills, caused by sickness or sword."
It's been proven by sitting it out in the emergency ward?

∽

The length of a minute solely depends upon, which side of the bathroom door you're on.

∽

It's precious time that you're 'hasting,' when talking about time you're wasting.

∽

A LIFESTYLE PORTRAYAL From A TO Z

*T*urning the tap off saves water every time,
But you can't stop the clock in order to save time.

*O*ur days are identical suitcases, you'll note they're all the same size;
Some folk can pack more in them; they're the diligent and the wise.

*M*uch can be accomplished with loose shreds of time;
Minutes are valuable, they initiate climb.

*B*e thou a sophisticate or an uncultured peasant,
Be cognizant that there is no time like the present.

*Y*esterday is gone, it's floated down the river;
A space of precious time that we can't recover.

*T*he people who complain, "There isn't enough time,"
Are the ones who usually abuse life's rhyme.

*T*ime spent getting even, it can be truthfully said,
Is time that is lost for one forging ahead.

*V*aluable time is something we all possess; our success depends on how time we address.

*U*nlike space, time has direction; allow time's arrow to lead to perfection.

O'er the years of time, I finally saw the light.
It's difficult to argue with someone who is right.

*F*leeting time, not recyclable, for no longer is it mine;
Exceedingly precious - now it's fated, totally wasted time.

*B*e on the watch to perceive the prime
Of life as it occurs, whatever the time.

*T*ime is a mender, it examines the offender.

*T*ime lost can be regarded as a bitter curse;
Like a run in a stocking, it can only get worse.

*T*hat times are better - a shattering illusion,
For today's dreadful calamities are in utmost profusion.

*A*s requested by his father, said her little boy Abel
To his mother in curlers at her dressing room table,

A LIFESTYLE PORTRAYAL From A TO Z

"Daddy wants to know just how very soon
Does his beautiful butterfly emerge from her cocoon."

❧

*L*ife is too short to be small or to belittle; time is too precious just to lazily whittle.

❧

*T*hough time is precious you cannot rank it, you can try to save it but you cannot bank it.

❧

*D*ays, daily mount - make the days count.

❧

*T*hat today is here, you don't have to be clever.
On the other hand, truthfully, tomorrow – never.

❧

*W*hen as a child, I laughed and wept - time crept.
When as a youth, I dreamed and talked - time walked.
When I became a full-grown man - time ran.
When older I became, I daily grew - time flew.
Soon I shall find in travelling on - time's gone.
-Anonymous

❧

*A*s I lay on my pillow, reminiscing of the past,
Oh, how time flies - I'm totally aghast.
Stop, go backwards, swift time in your flight,
Make me a little lad just for tonight.

❧

*A*ppointed time is of solitary essence, it does a great deal to gratuitously bestow.
Mounting precious years, they zealously teach us what the fleeting days will never know.

❧

*P*recious days break, though they never fall.
The nights always fall but never do they break

❧

*T*ime is a gift, use it to be wise, read, meditate, therein wisdom lies.

❧

*R*emember, in the budgeting of time, if more hours you should seek,
One seventh of your life is spent each day of the seven day week.

❧

*T*ime is the most valuable entity I can spend; in the use of time what aches can I mend?

❧

*A*re you catching up with your yesterday,
Programmed doing things your usual way?
Will you find on the morrow at the same precise hour
That you'll be ready for the next precious day?

❧

*T*ime can't be expanded, accumulated or imparted,
Nor can it be mortgaged, hastened or retarded.

❧

A LIFESTYLE PORTRAYAL From A TO Z

A kindly reminder, the future don't resent, the future is purchased by the daily present.

*D*o be careful how you approach precious time;
Watching the clock will never initiate climb.

*S*pend not too much time on cushy recliners, lest you get a tendency to major in minors.

*C*ount not the hours you daily put in, it is what you put into hours to win.

*Y*our employee's time is valuable too, so, don't keep him waiting, he's part of the crew.

*D*o all in your power to improve the hour.

*I*f you elect to give honest value to time, the ladder of prosperity you'll inevitably climb.

*B*e careful, be watchful, while consuming the hour.
The past can't be changed, the future's in your power.

*Y*esterdays were days of the future, amazingly they didn't long last.
I'm deeply disappointed for I expected so much from them in the past.

*T*ime is very valuable, at times very solemn, it can be meditatively sublime.
One can stop the hands of a clock, but no one can stop precious time.

*O*ur days are not a static thing, seize today and see what it brings.

*E*ach precious day comes bearing a gift; untie the bow, your soul it will lift.

*T*ime will pass - will the whole class?

*B*efore you take time an old rag to chew, remember other's time is valuable too.

*T*ime is very valuable, for idleness do not vote,
The man pulling oars hasn't time to rock the boat.

*O*ne thing you can learn while watching the clock, hands move time - never do they balk.

*T*o find precious time, you must make it; to get rid of a habit, you must break it.

*T*he clock of life is wound only once, no one has unlimited power
To tell when the hands of the timepiece will stop, at a late or an early hour.
Now is the only time that you own - live, love and toil with a will.
Place no faith in the days of tomorrow, for the clock may then be still.
-Anon.

A LIFESTYLE PORTRAYAL From A TO Z

All clocks in China's vast country conform; a one time zone is considered the norm.

At income tax time our governments receive;
They remind us that it's better to give than to deceive.

It's a paradox, indeed, when a man retires, for a retirement gift a Rolex he acquires.
I think the event doesn't make good sense for time is no longer of urgent importance.

What the year brings will greatly depend on what to the day you graciously lend.

Too much money and happy time can adversely affect life's rhyme.

Time deals gently with those who give it plenty.

All yesterdays become human history, tomorrows you'll agree are a mystery.
Today is a gift, truly pleasant, that's why it's called the present.

Precious days are given for worthy employment,
Happy hours are allocated for your enjoyment.
All time comes from God, be careful lest in haste
Those God-given moments you carelessly waste.

Using the time and date digital clock, a timepiece that we mustn't ever knock;
Nineteen eighty nine was the year that sequential numbers on the face did appear.
It happens only once in a whole century, it won't happen again for me to see.
It was on June seven, I wish to state, for those who put month, first in the date.
For those who place month after the day, the sixth of July was the precise day.
It was a very minute moment in time: 0 1 2 3 4 5 6 7 8 9.
(01:23:45, 6,7, 89)

I may never see tomorrow, there's no written guarantee,
And things that happened yesterday belong to history.
I can't predict the future, I cannot change the past,
I've just the present moment, must treat it as my last.
My time I must use wisely for it will soon pass away
And be lost to me forever as part of yesterday.
I must be compassionate, help the fallen to their feet,
Be a friend unto the friendless, make an empty life complete.
Things unkind I do today, may in the future ne'er be undone,
Friendships I failed to win, may never more be won.
I may not have a chance on bended knee to pray,
And thank God with humble heart for giving me this day.
-Anonymous

A LIFESTYLE PORTRAYAL From A TO Z

There's a time to be born and a time to die,
There's a time to laugh and a time to cry.
There's a time to be silent and a time to speak,
There's a time to be proud and a time to be meek.
There's a time to debate and a time to be quiet,
There's a time to indulge and a time to diet.
There's a time to mourn and a time to dance,
There's a time for caution and a time for chance.
There's a time to tear and a time to mend,
There's a time to resist and a time to bend.
There's a time to plant and a time to uproot,
There's a time to stay put and a time to scoot.
There's a time for everything and everything in its time,
There's a time for beauty and all that's sublime.
There's a time to work and a time to play,
There's a time to say "Yes'" and a time to say, "Nay."
There's a time to wreck and a time to rebuild,
There's time to gloss over and a time to gild.
There's a time to subtract and a time to add,
There's a time to be sad and a time to be glad.
There's a time to sell and a time to buy,
There's a time to oppose and a time to comply.
There's a time to give away and a time to keep,
There's a time to stay awake and a time to sleep.
There's a time to search and a time to give up,
There's a time to fast and a time to sup.
There's time to hate and a time to love,
Above all, take time for your God above.

❧

Forgive, forget – grievances don't conceal,
There is no remembrance that time cannot heal.

❧

In the sands of time one cannot conceal
The footprints of a soul or the marks of a heel.

❧

Years teach us much that the days cannot touch.

❧

The clock in the work place will never be stolen;
It's watchfully by many employees beholden.

❧

When your day is done, initiate retrospection,
Lest you learn too late, "Time has no resurrection."

❧

A LIFESTYLE PORTRAYAL From A TO Z

While shunning the devil with indomitable persistence,
Waste not precious time solely for existence;
Use it serendipitously for much needed assistance.

✌

I get those brief moments that are free from worry;
Those respites of panic, flurry, hurry and scurry.

✌

A delightful Joyous Christmas and Happy New Year.
May the happiest of this one be the worst next year.

✌

God bless your year, your coming in or going out,
Your daily repose, your travelling about;
The rough, the smooth, the bright the drear –
Again I say, God bless your year.

✌

If you would that your days be joyous and sublime,
Remember to live just one day at a time.
If you would that your days be compassionate and kind,
Remember, you must always keep others in mind.
If you would that your days exhibit thankfulness,
To your many joyous blessings, thankfulness address.
If you would that your days be of service to mankind,
You must keep the down-hearted and the needy in mind.
If you would that your days include singular living,
Use a portion of your time for some needful giving.

✌

Time begets experience to the latter add adherence.

✌

Vice, virtue and time do not stand still; vice we should kill, virtue instill.

✌

Spend not allotted time that gives cause to repent;
Bear in mind, precious time is daily heaven-sent.

✌

God-given days used wisely can amaze.

✌

Wasting the gift of time, insults the Giver Sublime.

✌

"Nothing is worth more than this day," so said, Johann Wolfgang Von Goethe.

✌

In weather forecasting, I watch the weathercock.
In telling the hour my stomach is the clock.

✌

The bee is such a energetic, busy soul – he has no time for birth control;
So that is why in times like these we have so many sons of bees.

✌

"If you keep one eye on tomorrow - the other on yesterday,"
I'm told by an ancient philosopher, "You're bound to be cockeyed today."

It's been said o'er the years that time changes things.
You are the agency that subtle change brings.

When times are bad, keep your perspective.
It's well, now and then, to be reflective.

In times like these, be they plight or ease,
It's best to recall there've been times like these.

The year, 10 02 2001, the astute will observe is a palindromic date.
Likewise, 05 31 1350, - someone elected to use his pate.

"Redeem misspent time that's past, live this day as if it were thy last."
-Bishop Thomas Ken

TIPPING

When a tip is left under a dinner plate, the waiter can expect that it won't be great.

For courteous, efficient service, tipping, you should.
Tip on all occasions, 'twill make you feel good.

Had a meal in a café with a gifted, friendly bard,
I elected to pay with my trusty credit-card.
When I looked for my pen to sign the charge slip,
Said the waiter, "Use mine, it has a larger tip."

TITHES - OFFERINGS

"A man must not rob his God, yes, you are stealing from me."
You say, "Just how could this be?" "In tithes and gifts, don't you see.
This day you are cursed with a curse; you're robbers, what could be worse?
You must bring in the whole tithe when you've finished working with the scythe.
Test me," says the Lord of hosts, "Set back the sturdy granary posts.
The windows of heaven will be open; all records for blessings shall be broken."
-Malachi 3:8-10 (paraphrased)

Let us be faithful in our tithes and our gifts, let us purpose to give God's cause a big lift.

"*B*ring in all the tithes," so says the sacred scroll.
Take God off your charity list, put Him on your payroll.

*T*wo mites were all the poor widow could give;
Two tiny bronze coins that others might live.

*T*he gospel of Christ is the water of life, we all know this offer is free,
But it costs for the plumbing and all of the pipes to bring that gospel to thee.

TOASTING

*W*hen a man is being toasted by more than a few,
You can bet that he's deliberately being buttered up too.

*H*ere's to the woman who came after man,
And has been after him since time first began.

*T*o the man who has earned true respect, not money;
To the man whose home is a place of harmony.

*M*ay your mind always be stretched out in friendship,
And ne'er the occasion be extended in want.
May happiness prevail throughout your day,
Come nighttime ne'er sleeplessness bewitchingly haunt.

*M*ay God be with you in the journey you travel.
May the tiny silver threads of intellect ne'er unravel.
May occasions be few to use the gavel.

*B*e poor in misfortune, but rich in blessings,
Slow to make enemies but quick to make friends.
Whether rich or poor, be you quick or slow,
Have nothing but happiness until your day ends.

*M*ay you have warm hands on a bitter cold evening,
A bright full moon on a dreary cold night;
A great big umbrella if it should pour,
And a road downhill all the way to your door.

*H*ats off, not to him who rashly dares,
Invariably to him who nobly bears;
Consistently to the heart that's compassionate and cares,
And to that someone who continually shares.

May you have happiness to make you sweet, trials to make you diligent and strong,
Sorrow enough to keep you human, fond hope to spur in your heart a song.

TOLERANCE

He knows not how to wink at human frailty or pardon weakness that he never felt.
-Joseph Addison

A measure of courage you portray, when few eye-to-eye with you see.
The cup of tolerance you exhibit, when with a minority you agree.

Be tolerant with your child, when he makes a mistake.
Just how many times have you won the sweepstake?

Bigotry creates enemies, tolerance makes friends;
To impatience and indignation, forgiveness makes amends.

Letting other people find happiness their way,
Instead of your way, is tolerance in full sway.

Tolerance is as great an emblem of freedom, as is sincere love for our fellow man.
We must make allowances for man's infirmities;
Our gracious concessions are part of God's plan.

THE TONGUE

The clean tongue, the clear head, and the bright eye
are birthrights of each day.
-William Osler

Eyes need glasses, ears need trumpets,
Knees need replacement when a man becomes stout;
So oft I have wondered, 'tis indeed a conundrum,
The tongue works the hardest but it never wears out.

The tongue, the truth it so frequently does bend,
And so many hearts it unmercifully does rend.
We can be thankful that it's attached at one end.

He who has burned his tongue has acquired an informative scoop.
You will find in years to come he will always blow his hot soup.

A LIFESTYLE PORTRAYAL From A TO Z

*T*eeth so frequently bite a master's tongue,
And so they should if the tongue has stung.

*B*e careful lest you mutter words considered cheap,
That's when you'll wish that your tongue were asleep.

*M*any a sharp missile a man's tongue will fling;
At times it can be a very painful thing.

*K*indness does not hurt the tongue; with compassion no one gets stung.

*O*h, so little weight the human tongue, regardless of how one moulds it,
Yet I observe from where I sit, so few are able to hold it.

A tongue is ready ruthless evil to impart, when it's aware of an angry heart.

*T*hough your shiny teeth may be totally false,
Don't let your tongue bitter falsehood waltz.

*Y*ou must prudently confine your tongue, lest by it others get ruthlessly stung.

*R*elatively speaking, the tongue is small, yet it can kill a man six feet tall.

*B*eware of the tongue, be mindful of the tip, it's normally wet, it has a tendency to slip.

*S*ome people have ears that seem to balk, but few with tongues that can talk - talk not.

*N*ever use the tongue to defame or slaughter,
And keep mouth closed when you're in deep water.

*S*o oft the first screw that works loose in one's face
Is the one that firmly holds the wagging tongue in its place.

*I*t may be said, or even arbitrarily sung,
Whatever is in the heart will get to the tongue.

*T*he tongue of the wise makes discourse acceptable,
But the mouth of fools spouts folly, regrettable!

*H*ave you ever reflected after much scoff and mirth,
That a sharp, piercing tongue is a poor tool to work with?

A clear mind, a keen eye - keeping tongue at bay;
This is the inheritance that is ours each day.

A LIFESTYLE PORTRAYAL From A TO Z

A tongue, like an axe, though sharp won't float,
But it has a tendency to cut its own throat.

Though your teeth may be false, may your tongue be true.
Do pray that the latter may be becoming to you.

So amazing the loose tongue, it lives in a small space,
Yet it oft gets its owner into a very tight place.

So oft the human tongue is out of its domain.
It shows no evidence it's connected to the brain.

No echoes return to derisively mock the silent tongue," says Uncle Jock.

Just imagine if your right foot should slip,
Luckily you'll recover your balance;
But if your tongue should choose to meander,
To retrieve your words, not a chance.

Some tongues are so fiery, like instruments of percussion.
They produce more heat than light in a discussion.

It is much better to bite your tongue than it is to shout at the top of your lung.

The tongue can be a blessing or it can be a curse.
There is no question as to which could be worse.

A clean, honest tongue, a clear head and bright eye,
Will help one's life from going awry.

"*The* boneless tongue, so small and weak can crush and kill," so saith the Greek.
"The tongue destroys a much greater horde," the Turk asserts, "than does the sword."
A Persian proverb so wisely saith, "A lengthy tongue, an early death."
It sometimes takes this form instead, "Don't let your tongue cut off your head."
"The tongue can speak a word whose speed," the Chinese say, "outstrips the steed."
While Arab sages this message impart, "The tongue's sole storehouse, is a man's heart."
The sacred writer crowns the whole, "He who keeps his tongue doth keep his soul."
-Anonymous

If anyone deems to be fervently religious, but does not effort to bridle his tongue,
He deceives his own heart, his religion is worthless;
How can he sing the victor's song?

A LIFESTYLE PORTRAYAL From A TO Z

TOURISM

A tourist is one who travels very far to be photographed by the family car.

TRANQUILITY

Great tranquility of heart is his, who cares not for praise or blame.
-Thomas Kempis

The hour is not wasted that engenders tranquility;
Uplifting heart and soul, it postpones senility.

TRANSACTIONS

In transactions of trade it is not to be supposed that,
as in gaming, what one party gains the other must
necessarily lose. The gain to each must be equal.
-Franklin

The times that someone cooks up "A real steal,"
The deluded party usually gets a raw deal.

TRAVEL - TRANSPORTATION

It's better to be last in a traffic obsession than first in a dismal funeral procession.

While travelling beautiful interstate "Five,"
With breaking the speed limit I was carelessly toying,
Then I remembered:
RadaR, a palindrome, same forward and backwards;
The cops usually get you coming or going.

The best of our autos at times have quirks;
Needless to say, some in them have jerks.

When in heavy traffic, you so frequently travel,
Never allow composure or nerves to unravel.

Be careful when you travel, with tires don't throw gravel.

A LIFESTYLE PORTRAYAL From A TO Z

*B*efore you embark on your journey,
Before climbing the tall tower via ladder,
For the first you must fill you gas tank,
For both you should empty your bladder.

*E*ngineers, we want autos that will stop smoking,
Likewise, build vehicles that'll discontinue drinking.

*I*t's strange how a hound dog traverses from birth;
He travels with his nose down vacuuming mother earth.

*T*ravel agents say, "Please, do not stay."
Their business motto is: "Please, go away!"

A suggestion to auto makers: "Make lights that won't blind us,
And please do make brakes that will stop cars behind us."

*T*o avoid blood flowing from shattered glass,
Pull over, don't race - let the idiots pass.

TREES

I think that I shall never see a poem lovely as a tree,
A tree whose hungry mouth is pressed against the earth's sweet flowing breast,
A tree that looks at God all day and lifts her leafy arms to pray.
A tree that may in summer wear a nest of robins in her hair;
Upon whose bosom's snow has lain, who intimately lives with rain.
Poems are made by fools like me but only God can make a tree.
-Joyce Kilmer

*M*en who fall trees have to be tough,
They work very hard with much huff and puff.
Some have a manner that is somewhat gruff,
To add to their image they chew vile snuff.
They burn kals galore, eat mounds of foodstuff
After hours of hard work, 'till they've had enough.
From the wood they cut comes a fibrous fluff
To manufacture newsprint for printing much guff.
I question the wisdom of printing the stuff.

*T*he festive, joyous Yuletide tree points us to the cross of Calvary.

TRIALS

Trials are invariably the raw materials out of which God weaves His blessed miracles.

God permits trials not us to impair,
They're meant to improve us and for heaven prepare.

Repeated trials test trust; for Christians they are a must.

God's chastening isn't cruel, it's His corrective tool.

When faced with a trial, do you sanction denial?

TRUST - TRUSTWORTHINESS

No virtue is more universally accepted
as a test of character than trustworthiness.
-Harry Emerson Fosdick

For one to be trusted, not aside shoved, is a greater compliment than it is to be loved.

Tell a gentleman, there are a billion stars, you'll find that he will believe you.
Tell him that a bench has been freshly painted - he'll touch it to see if it's true.

To consider oneself public property is a must,
When a man who is elected assumes a public trust.

One cannot trust a person in anything who doesn't have a conscience in everything.

Very few joys can equal the presence of one in whom sacred trust is the essence.

A trustworthy friend, a heartache can mend.

Trust God's authority, not man's majority.

Trusting God in good measure, transfers trials into treasure.

We all must have duties to proudly perform, posts of service are a definitive must.
There are a few stations of distinguished honor;
They are responsible positions of trust.

Trusting during trial, in darkness and in light, is walking in faith and not by sight.
It's relying on God with total confidence, it's resting in His love, trusting His providence.

Don't always trust a charming face, lest you be fooled by allure and grace.

❧

Trust and obey, that is God's way.

❧

Would anyone think of believing in God without fully trusting in Him?
Is it possible to trust Him for the big things in life,
Like forgiveness and endless eternity,
And then not trust Him for the little things we need,
Like kernels of dried hominy?

❧

There is a great virtue that is never rejected,
Tried trustworthiness is universally accepted.

❧

Trustworthiness should always be perfected; no virtue is more universally accepted.

❧

The face of a bee is so sweet and kind, but I tell you, my friend, don't trust its behind.

❧

TRUTH - LOGIC

Tell the truth and shame the devil.
-Francios Rablais

❧

There's a fundamental truth that brings on ire,
A fisherman calling another, a blatant, outright liar.

❧

A priest who had spent a futile day fishing,
Scurried to a fish market, hoping and wishing.
Three fat fish remained, "Yes, yes, I'll take them,
But first toss 'em to me, before you wrap them.
You see, I'll be truthful when I say I caught them."

❧

In all your debates may truth be your aim.
In endeavoring to make gain do not expose shame.

❧

A maxim from Ghandi for those who trust, "Truth never damages a cause that is just."

❧

Truth needs no crutches, no dubious alibi, if it limps or hobbles it's an outright lie.

❧

There's a solemn truth that no one can deny, a half truth in verity is always a whole lie.

❧

Remember, you must always tell the whole truth,
You'll have a clear conscience on going to bed,
And you won't ever have to remember, what in the past you haven't said.

❧

A LIFESTYLE PORTRAYAL From A TO Z

"It will never hurt you to stretch the truth," some of your friends may casually surmise,
But it is certain to painfully sting you, whenever it snaps back to its original size.

❧

If austere truth is to constantly prevail, unerring logic do not assail.

❧

Truth that is crushed to earth will rise; it is never dependent on deliberate lies.

❧

Plain truth is not only stranger than fiction, it is a lot cleaner than is stained diction.

❧

'Tis better to know pure truth and beware, than believe a vicious lie and not at all care.

❧

Truth that's profound is sacred, there are times it may be lacking.
Speculative comment is free, oft with very little backing.

❧

When triumphant logic is readily unfurled, it becomes a nice contrast for the real world.

❧

God's sacred truth is the best protection against the wily devil's insurrection.

❧

Some say that error needs truth to exist; the Spirit says, "Truth will always persist."

❧

Sacred truth is stronger than error - God's sweet peace more quieting than terror.

❧

The truth of a matter is not how one sees it,
Nor is it determined by how you may believe it.

❧

For truth the devil won't rush, in fact it makes him blush.

❧

Pure truth is never for or against, it's discernibly free, joyously unfenced.

❧

Plain truth is never sarcastic or uncouth; whenever you speak, may it clearly be truth.

❧

Truth always exists, consensus consented, it's falsehood only that is always invented.

❧

It is easier to see error than to recognize truth,
So realized Goethe in the days of his youth.
For error is on the surface, and it may be overcome,
But truth is down deep, to find it's toilsome.

❧

Avoiding the search for truth is a journey we cannot afford.
Facts don't cease to exist because they're totally ignored.

❧

In stretching the truth or launching a wisecrack, one must be careful lest it snap back.

❧

Non-violence and truth are allegedly indispensable;
Uncompromising deceit is totally reprehensible.

❧

A LIFESTYLE PORTRAYAL From A TO Z

An axiom to be remembered by all, cultivate it during the days of your youth.
"To detect and to avoid earthly error, expose it to the light of God's truth."

~

For truth we must ceaselessly toil, allow it to fall on fertile soil.

~

Be careful what you say, help prevent truth decay.

~

It is much more blessed to give than receive, likewise, to tell truth than it is to deceive.

~

Deception is oft dressed in the garb of truth.
Be cautious lest your residence becomes a steel booth.

~

Truth divine makes sound sense, it shouldn't ever be a pretense.
May it not only solemnly shake us, but also may it gracefully shape us.

~

Truth does not lie and it doesn't assail, it has a distinct character, it is never pale.
To give one direction it will never fail; truth is penetrating, you can't it curtail.
Truth is powerful, never is it frail; truth is everlasting and it never grows stale.
It's something you can't purchase, for it's not for sale,
In fact, it's free,- see the Scripture for details.

~

Sacred truth is free - no payment of a fee,

~

Having truth decay – chances you'll be liable.
There is a remedy – brush up on the Bible.

~

Do tell the truth, be always on the level.
In being truthful you're ignoring the devil.

~

We are to be channels of God's divine truth,
Not mere repositories, like a sound-proof booth.

~

The arrow of truth can't be equated with money.
Before you shoot it immerse tip in honey.

~

May the love of pure truth draw you to read
The words of Holy Writ; this axiom we must heed.

~

If to the chief magistrate you speak sacred truth,
You'll have a better chance of avoiding the steel booth.

~

When in doubt, determine to tell the whole truth.
Keep in mind this precept from the days of your youth.

~

The best mind-altering medicament is truth.
We should never allow our speech to be uncouth.

So oft we believe in matters least known.
Sacred truth we're inclined to arbitrarily postpone.

UNGODLINESS

Ungodliness is not only wickedness that's rife,
It's simply ignoring, leaving God out of one's life.

UNITY - UNANIMITY

Where there is unity, there is always victory.
-Publilius Syrus

Unity to be strong must stand the demand
Of an extremely severe strain without breaking a strand.

Unity to be real must have a high rating;
The test, a severe strain without signs of breaking.

Absolute, peaceful, unanimity, some say,
Is found only in a neighboring cemetery;
Unassuming, unadorned, unclouded unassailable -
Unaccustomed, unadulterated, unblemished unanimity.

Unity amongst believers is truly found, when union with Christ does fully abound.

What trait is there in me that prevents church unity?

Nature in her infinite wisdom knows there's strength in unity.
Why not that selfsame wisdom in man's magnificent diversity?

VACATION

For your next leisurely vacation, why must you your money squander?
Just climb into a comfortable hammock and let your lazy mind wander.

A spot for vacations is a place that they charge
Enough money to make up for the months you're at large.

A LIFESTYLE PORTRAYAL From A TO Z

Ill-nourished, ill-housed, ill-clad, the plight of a third of our nation.
Do not be alarmed or sympathetic, they're happy, they call it vacation.

Vacation - travel time – you hope 'twill be sunny;
You take too much clothes and half as much money.

Vacation is over when your money is spent,
And you have no idea where it all went.

A pause – time out - a trip would be best;
A vacation would be ideal if the wallet took a rest.

VAGUENESS

It's strange how the vague we see eventually,
But the unmistakably obvious it takes a full century.

VANITY

The surest cure for vanity is loneliness.
 -Thomas Wolfe

Vanity we must totally eschew; it isn't a viable virtue.

Diplomas and degrees gauge mental vitality.
Don't let them ever be a mirror of vanity.

Make vanity a matter of pure self-denial.
When your ego is fed you're definitely on trial.

Most prudent people lose their selfish vanity,
When suddenly regaining their forsaken sanity.

Whether you're a left or be you a right brain,
You must always strive not to be absurdly vain.

VERBOSITY

Many folk exhibit their tiresome verbosity,
Animosity, impetuosity and bloated pomposity.

It would be much better to show preciosity,
Angelic compassion and unparalleled generosity.

VICTORY

The greatest victory is the victory over self.

You can truly become a magnanimous philanthropist
By gradually overcoming selfish greed over pelf.
However, no conquest is truly as important
As is totally overcoming singular victory over self.

VIOLENCE

Degeneracy follows every autocratic system of violence,
for violence inevitably attracts moral inferiors.
-Albert Einstein

Those who talk violence don't improve the silence.

If football and hockey didn't have morbid violence,
They could give society examples of excellence.

VIRTUE

Virtue consists, not in abstaining from vice, but in not desiring it.
-George Bernard Shaw

No virtue is ever so strong, that it is beyond one's temptation.
Take heed, ask for strength and power to overcome that tempting tribulation.

All good virtues demand self-denial.
It behooves each one of us to put them on trial.

Virtue doesn't need great skill; it is a distinct act of the will.

Sexual harassment is known to most men, as not at all a problem for virtuous women.

So many sound virtues, I know they all count,
But courage is the ladder on which virtues mount.

The best proof of virtue, not knowingly choosing it,
Possessing great power but never abusing it.

It's exceedingly much easier to fight, for one's immutable principles,
But difficulty is encountered to live up to - of virtue we're not disciples.

Virtue is righteousness non-defiled; the greatest of all is self-denial.

Vanity is sheltered in the heart of man; so many for it consistently plan.

Virtue, a moral excellence we should deeply admire;
A triumphant defense to one's inward desire.

There is a great virtue that is never rejected.
Tried trustworthiness is universally accepted.

Get rid of your vices, replace them with virtues.

Victorious virtue smothers wild fires; a triumphant resistance to one's heart's desires.

Frankness is not always a Christian virtue, it can injure a soul, it can hurt you too.

Virtue and a muscle are alike, with exercise daily them psyche.

Advice, that is evil we initially repel, eventually tolerate and then embrace.
My friend, why don't you replace it with virtue? Why not all evil with virtue efface?

Years ago there was a virtue called charity - today it is reckoned as a viable industry.

Virtue, the right arm, never will it harm, nor cause alarm, its goodness will disarm.

VISION - DREAMS - DREAMERS

The vision of things to be done may come a long time
before the way of doing them becomes clear,
but woe to him who distrusts the vision.
-Jenkin Lloyd Jones

To have clear insight, have a stimulator;
To have inspired vision is so much greater.

If you can dream it, you can achieve it.

A LIFESTYLE PORTRAYAL From A TO Z

Vision communicates a sense of the possible.
It is seeing what others don't think is probable.

Don't let thorny thistles clutter your schemes;
Cultivate and irrigate your flowery dreams.

Beware of speculative and perfidious schemes.
Keep facts in mind when you have those dreams.

He who is narrow of vision has difficulty making a decision.

To become an adult is but a single page; a vision for accomplishment for age is a gauge.

Vision and dedication are a powerful combination.

Creating a better future begins with a vision, and with the ability to visualize revision.

Our myopic, blunted vision needs careful revision.

The voyage of discovery is not travelling new skies.
It involves a broader vision, it's having keen eyes.

Soon after the completion of Disney World, a lady said,
"It's sad that Walt Disney didn't see this vast spread."
An astute director countered, "He did see it, my dear,
He had singular vision and that's why it's here."

Some don't see the light, I underscore and repeat,
Until they begin feeling the proverbial heat.

Though there may be designs, objectives and schemes,
Broad visions triumphantly override small dreams.

Some dream of all they can get, others, of all they must do.
The Master is prone to ask, "Which one of the two are you?"

If you're unable to conceive a vision for the future,
Don't rely on the past your future to nurture.

Admirable virtue is always in season, under the direction of inspired reason.

Beauty catches your vision; virtue wins the decision.

Some build formidable castles, that to heirs they plan to bequeath,
Then realize that they can't even afford the real estate sitting underneath.

A LIFESTYLE PORTRAYAL From A TO Z

The human spirit cannot be paralyzed, if you are breathing, dreams can be realized.

If you want your dreams to come true, don't just sit around and stew.

Reach high for the stars hidden in your soul; dreaming deep dreams precedes the goal.
-Pamela Star

VITAL FORCE

The natural vital force that dwells within us
Is a God-given gift that remedies and heals us.

You may feel that your spirit is spent, you haven't anymore vital stuff.
My friend, you have awesome prayer – that can be more than enough.

VOICE

An incensed voice is usually a lot crisper.
Your answer should be soft, people listen to a whisper.

VOLUNTEERS

Volunteering creates character. it gives a nation such spirit
of confidence, comradeship and compassion.
-Brian O'Connell

The Deacon's Dilemma

The church board had been seeking for some volunteers.
The church hadn't been painted for many, many years.
The paint had been selected, 'twas in fact supplied,
Now they were most anxious to have it applied.
The head deacon consented to do the big job,
But no one suspected that some paint he might rob.
You see, the gifted paint was so densely thick,
He had up his sleeve a sinful heinous trick.
In his mind he spun a slick pernicious yarn -
He thinned the precious paint, painted church and his barn.
That night, heavy clouds, the thunder it roared,
Then came heavy rain, oh, how it poured.

A LIFESTYLE PORTRAYAL From A TO Z

On the morn, the deacon through the shades peaked -
To his utter dismay the barn was all streaked.
He dashed to the church, it was streaked likewise;
His heavy heart and soul were in total demise.
He dropped to his knees, God's heaven to implore,
Suddenly, a celestial voice,
"REPAINT – THIN NO MORE."

*Volunteers so oft perform with equanimity.
Someday they'll discover a golden opportunity.*

People who act as volunteers, outlive those who don't by years.

When I think of volunteers, I think of caring,
Compassionate loving, giving and sharing,
Consideration, understanding, service and courtesy,
Brotherhood, sisterhood, patience and mercy;
Tolerance, affection, amiability, hospitality,
Kindness, meekness, warmth and cordiality;
Tenderness, soft-heartedness, thoughtfulness, largesse,
All beautiful attributes, one must confess.

VOTING

The future of this republic is in the hands of the American voter.
-Dwight D. Eisenhower

"It's the customer alone who casts the vote."
To all prime establishments this axiom please note.

Voters at the polling booth approval will shower
On those who are caring, than on those who seek power.

VULGARITY

The greatness of a speech isn't measured by its length;
Vulgarity is a weak man's expression of strength.

A LIFESTYLE PORTRAYAL From A TO Z

WATER

*W*ater is a liquid, it's a solid, it's vapor, solve its deep mystery I sincerely beg.
How does boiling water soften a hard carrot, and at the same time it hardens an egg?

*"M*ary, please give me the formula for water."
"Yes Sir, it's H I J K L M N O."
"And how in the world did you come up with that answer?"
"Well, yesterday you said, it was H to O."

WEALTH - POSSESSIONS - RICHES

*H*e that will not permit his wealth to do any good while he is living,
prevents it from doing any good to himself when he is dead.
-Colton

*P*ersonal wealth can be a double blessing,
When the needs of others it's routinely addressing.

*T*here isn't much point in being a rich man in a lovely memorial park;
You won't be able to do business there for you'll be totally in the dark.

*P*ermit your wealth to do good while you're living,
Accomplish that good, simply by giving.
You will not experience that pleasure when you're dead.
All said and done, what more need be said?

*S*ome folk amass riches, they expect it to last,
But their enormous wealth can't buy the past.

*A*llow not great wealth and riches to be a lure.
"Not he who has little - who wants more who's poor."

*W*ith most rich people one's inclined to concede,
The parade of their riches they do not impede.

*W*ealth is definitely a link with man's capacity to think.

*N*ot he who is rich has much, it's he who gives is such.

*R*iches are soulless, they're of little worth,
If they're not blended with gracious charity.
Riches, for certain are only honor to oneself if they are not shared with crystal clarity.

A LIFESTYLE PORTRAYAL From A TO Z

Riches do not exist in the possession of treasure,
It's in it's dispersion in the fullest of measure.

❧

Wealth is the product of man's thinking capacity.
Beneficence is the outgrowth of his heart's immensity.

❧

If enormous wealth your goal is to chase, honesty could be a very lonely place.

❧

For glittering gold so many are pining, while doing so they miss the silver lining.

❧

It's not wealth you possess it's what you profess.

❧

One's best companions – innocence and health,
And his best wishes, ignorance of wealth.
-Oliver Goldsmith

❧

WEATHER

Sunshine is delicious, rain is refreshing, wind braces up,
snow is exhilarating; there is no such thing as bad weather,
only different kinds of good weather.
-John Ruskin

❧

This evening these words with regret I commiserate,
'Tomorrow stormy clouds the sun will obliterate.'

❧

In weather forecasting only One has been accurate,
I say this in humble summation.
"Noah, prepare to build a huge boat –
There's a 100 percent chance of precipitation."

❧

WEEPING

Don't cry my dear, you mustn't seek pity.
Moreover, my love, your crying isn't pretty.

❧

They are messengers of love, there's a sacredness in tears;
They're a mark of power, not of weakness or fears.

❧

WELFARE

There are those who joyfully order their own lives,
so that they may serve the welfare of mankind.
-William Graham Sumner

If generations keep growing on welfare, how will our future generations fare?

The problem with welfare that very few are mouthing,
The costs are too great to get something for nothing.

WHOLENESS

To make man whole is to broaden one's soul.
If I'm physically active, my character becomes attractive.
I'll be mentally more alert, avoiding verbiage that is curt.
I'll be totally aware, showing clearly that I care.
Becoming socially attentive, will guide ideals preventive,
And volitionally autonomous, quite frequently anonymous.
Helping one of the least my spirituality will increase.
My soul will surely thrive, becoming spiritually alive.

WICKEDNESS

To see and listen to the wicked is already the beginning of wickedness.
-Confucius

Wickedness in verity is deep pain, vile deviltry has no worthwhile gain,
One's sin a character 'twill stain; iniquity will not forever reign.

WILL - WILLINGNESS

Man is made great or little by his own will.
-Johann Schiller.

A willing will, I would say, it's a fact, is what you need to clean up your act.

To will, gives release, what God wills gives peace.

Holiness is not rapture, it's not great skill,
It is in its entirety the surrender of the will.

A LIFESTYLE PORTRAYAL From A TO Z

The education of self-determined will is the object of our complicated existence.
It can only be truly accomplished with devotion and prayerful persistence.

A uniqueness for will power, believe it or not,
Is the ability to eat just one salted peanut.

With stout mind and good will one can't stand still.

Where there's a will there's a won't;
Where there's consent there's a don't.

A man persuaded against his will is oft of the former opinion still.

The difference between diligence and obstinacy -
One comes from a strong will, the other negativity.

Your will must be greater than your skill.

To keep on pedaling should be part of your will
To turn that sprocket to get up the next hill.

If we cannot do what we will actively,
We must will to do what we can effectively.

WINNERS

Winners never quit to overcome sin; quitters never win, they lack Christ within.

WISDOM

Wisdom is to the mind what health is to the body.
-La Rochefoucauld

Sound wisdom and good humor, more uplifting than rumor.

Wisdom to blossom must be rightly reared; it's in the head, not in one's beard.

If you have sound wisdom and vigorous vitality,
Whatever you believe in will become a reality.

Knowledge is knowing a fact, wisdom is knowing how to act.

A LIFESTYLE PORTRAYAL From A TO Z

Men of wisdom think, they digest things most,
Seldom do they criticize, neither do they boast.

Where wisdom is lacking books give little backing.

Pain makes one think, thought makes one wise,
Wisdom, life endurable, slow to advise.

What Roosevelt said about wisdom is sublime,
"Nine-tenths of wisdom is being wise on time."

Wise is the person who knows what to say,
And gracious when to others he gives the right of way.

Wise is the person who truly knows, when some things he's not to disclose.

The mastery of a person who's wise, cannot be kept in disguise.

Honest wisdom is an ally of truth; do encourage it in the days of your youth.

When does a man start cutting wisdom teeth? Let me give you a tangible clue.
It's when a man searching for wealth bites off much more than he can chew.

Wisdom is an entity we must address; learned more from failure than from success.

If you realize you aren't as wise today, as you thought you were - you're wiser, I'd say.

Those who get wisdom do themselves a favor.
Those who love learning will improve their behavior.

The art of being wise is not an open book, it's the art of knowing what to overlook.

Wisdom is knowing when to mind your speech; speaking your mind will seldom reach.

A wealthy old gent was about to commission
An astute, renowned architect to draw plans for a mansion.
"Money is no object - have but one disclosure,
All walls must possess a southern exposure."
The architect pondered, but for a brief moment,
His comment profound, revealed sound judgment.
"If I'm to comply fully with your eccentric soul,
Firstly purchase a lot spot on the North Pole."

Hindsight is wisdom for ever - you must admit that it's clever,

A LIFESTYLE PORTRAYAL From A TO Z

To enhance your wisdom keep your thinking cap on.
A cap on your thinking you must never don.

≈

Always hire people that are wiser than you.
This will clearly show that you are wise too.

≈

A man is wise to seek wisdom, the rule.
When he thinks he's found it, he becomes a fool.

≈

WISHING

A wishbone doesn't give a good score; backbone accomplishes considerably more.

≈

You must never grow a wishbone, Moe, where a sturdy backbone ought to grow.

≈

To have a great body, to improve muscle tone,
Spend not too much time developing a wishbone.

≈

Mr. Ovid used his wise head when he so astutely said,
"To wish, is of little account; to succeed you must desire.
Desire must shorten your sleep," and you must nobly aspire.

≈

One's idle wishing is a mental hitch, 'twill never make a poor man rich.

≈

WIT

If you have wit, (don't it skirt), use it to please and not to hurt.
-Lord Chesterfield

≈

Subtle wit is indispensable, tomfoolery, reprehensible.

≈

One day I visited a nonagenarian, with me she made a great hit.
When our conversation encountered a hole she'd darn it with her sharp wit.

≈

Season conversation with wit while you partake of your food.
Avoid ugly words of sarcasm; never use words that are rude.

≈

Laugh at yourself now and then, season your day with wit;
Pleasurable, effervescent humor; one can't live without it.

≈

Sharp wit is the seasoning of every conversation.
Choose to learn something, that's my summation.

≈

A LIFESTYLE PORTRAYAL From A TO Z

"Brevity is the soul of wit," - years ago, Shakespeare writ.

ઐ

WITNESS

The true test of civilization is not the census nor the size of the crops, no,-
but the kind of man the country turns out.
-Emerson

ઐ

Your witness is verily your own benefactor.
Indeed, it is only as strong as your character.

ઐ

To be a singular, reputable witness is as important as physical fitness.

ઐ

A witnesser's memory is frequently defective.
So oft a judge finds that it's downright selective.

ઐ

WORDS SPOKEN OR WRITTEN

Young boys flying kites haul in them big birds,
But you can't do that when you're flying words.
"Be careful with fire,"- good advice we all know,
"Be careful with words," ten times doubly so.
Words unexpressed so frequently drop dead,
But even God can't kill them, after they've been said.
-Wilf Carleton

ઐ

Wise words that were spoken by an august old sage,
"Never pacify a man at the height of his rage."

ઐ

One doesn't always have to have the last word,
At times choose silence in order to be heard.

ઐ

One's words are like leaves, for a fall they are bound;
Amongst them fruit of nonsense are so frequently found.

ઐ

Do keep your words, short, gentle and sweet, lest some day you them may have to eat.

ઐ

Words break no bones nor tear joints apart,
But they're well known to break an aching heart.

ઐ

Do note what you say or unkindly convey, a friend they may asunder part.
"Yes, sticks and stones can break our bones, but words can break an aching heart."

ઐ

A LIFESTYLE PORTRAYAL From A TO Z

Your words, well chosen, bitter discord never breed.
Be kind and compassionate - do help those in need.

What word when you add two letters make it shorter?
This question stumps many,- "Short" becomes "shorter."

It's the words your guests say, driving out your driveway.

If with words you are hurt, swift revenge do not seek;
Even a botched haircut is forgotten in a week.

If what you want to say, you speculatively question -
Eating your words could give you indigestion.

Guard your naked thoughts, they may not rhyme,
They may worm into words at any old time.

A wise man's words may express deep thought.
A foolish one's dribble is so oft for naught.

A thousand and one words. regardless how clever,
Will not leave so deep, so lasting an impression
As a solitary, meritorious, delightful deed.
Truly, this is my sincere confession.

For customary proceedings, take notes on the spot.
Words best remembered are when they are hot.

It is much wiser to have an open mind than of an open mouth to be a possessor.
You'll truly avoid much misery and strife and of cruel words you won't be a transgressor.

Right words can be effective, with but a simple clause.
"The prudent," Mark Twain reminds us, "is the rightly-timed pause."

Using cutting words doesn't have my vote; having a sharp tongue can cut one's throat.

If inappropriate words are allowed to escape,
One cannot lasso them to bring back to the gate.

There is a succinct thought that isn't new – 'Why use two words when one will do?"

Those who write words in the name of fiction,
Don't always make use of the cleanest of diction.
Some of what's written, without doubt is hazy;
Some of it I conclude is downright crazy.

A LIFESTYLE PORTRAYAL From A TO Z

The words from your mouth you impart, speak volumes about your stout heart.

❧

Ponder over words you're about to impart;
Your irrevocable words are windows to the heart.

❧

Spoken words are cheap, they are so abundant;
Regretfully I conclude, so oft they're redundant.

❧

Words are thoughts made distinctly audible,
The natural overflow of the mind's wellspring.
Before you determine those thoughts to release,
Select from the genus that does not sting.

❧

Do watch your hasty words, your tongue do tether;
Not so narrow of mind that your ears rub together.

❧

Your word, be it written or spoken, is a promise that mustn't be broken.

❧

Many people hurt, more from blunt words,
Much more than they do from pointy sharp swords.

❧

Thoughtless, cutting words from your mouth should never slip.
With them one should never nip, clip or whip.
Kind words will always a stranger's heart grip.
Be honest in your dealings, don't ever try to gyp,
And I succinctly add, the truth never skip.
If you utter falsehoods, eventually they'll trip.
With phony flattery words your speech should never drip.
Into cesspool of gossip don't let your tongue dip.
With your jealous words one's honor you can't strip.
For kindness and service, remember the tip.
Expressing your gratitude you should never skip.
May the law of kindness be ever on your lip.

❧

Watch your words, don't let them defile; advice to young and old, don't grow senile.

❧

Remember to take time to taste your glib words
Before letting them past your pearly white teeth.
Words can be sharp and pointed like a sword;
Best that they be guarded like a sword in its sheath.

❧

Your words always plan, they make or mar man.

❧

Words are thoughts made audible, endeavor to make them plausible.

❧

A LIFESTYLE PORTRAYAL From A TO Z

*W*ords are comparable to grenades, do not at others sling scoff;
Unkindly, irrevocable, cutting words, have a marked tendency to go off.

*Y*ou don't have to shout if you use the right words.
Words that make sense are always clearly heard.

*C*hoose lovely, sweet words, live happily and rejoice.
To accomplish your selection you must love your choice.

*H*arry Truman, years ago, these action words twirled,
"It is the "C" students who usually run the world."

*C*old words freeze people, hot words burn them,
Bitter words cause anger, they all condemn.
Kind words will calm and comfort the soul,
Producing a beautiful image, making man whole.

A multiplicity of words so often is wrought;
So frequently it indicates poverty of thought.

*T*he word American ends with "I can."

*O*ne's words may show us his knowledge and his wit;
Actions are the ones that tell us he lives it.

*I*f you're favorably inclined to get a bright idea across,
Wrap it with kind words, never act like a boss.

*W*ords, 'Why' and 'How' you can never abuse; they just cannot be too frequently used.

*W*ords can calm or they can cause a storm, like fire, words can either burn or warm.

*I*f you wouldn't write it, sign it and send it - don't ever say it.

"*I*n conclusion," words to many a convenience;
A short phrase that wakes up a majority of the audience.

*A*n empty sack cannot stand up, erroneous words won't add up.

A good speech is judged by its content not its length.
Great works are the result of intellect not strength.

*W*ords are but leaves, deeds are the sheaves.

'*Z*ymurgy' is a word that is very seldom heard; in most dictionaries it is the last word.

A LIFESTYLE PORTRAYAL From A TO Z

*B*lunt, starched words of monosyllabic brevity,
Don't promote friendships or compassionate social levity.

*I*t was Voltaire who succinctly expressed,
"Words are used to hide thought."
Do couple them with good sound judgment;
With falsehood they should never be fraught.

*W*ords carelessly flung, be it workplace or foyer,
Do render frequently a rich, happy lawyer.

*T*hat it be not stained or bent, one takes good charge of his sword.
More so, one should give good care to honest thought and word.

*T*he shortest pair of words are "Yes" and "No.'
With the one you spend, with the latter you save dough.

*"G*entlemen prefer blondes," words expressed by men.
Many men don't heed, "Ladies prefer gentlemen."

*"N*o," a small word - seldom label it rude.
It's one of many words that can't be misunderstood,

*T*o have the last word without a alibi, a concise parting word - just say, "Goodbye."

*I*f your words encourage, empower and enlighten,
You are bound a person's countenance to brighten.

*T*ender words can be brief and easy to say;
Their echoes are endless, they continue to convey.

*W*ood that's decaying cannot be carved; bare words can't feed those who are starved.

*M*r. Walter Heller tells of an experience he had,
While speaking to some bankers in a mid-western town.
A man, way at the rear, so rudely interrupted,
"Ah, you're so stupid,"- causing Heller to frown.

A short time later the man shouted again,
"You're stupid," he repeated, much louder, no rhyme.
Noting a slight slur in his voice, Heller thought,
For him I'll be ready when he yells the next time.
A few moments later the man was heard from again,
"You're stupid," he said for the very third time.

Heller's quick response, "And you're beastly drunk,
You're causing a disturbance, your actions are a crime."

The detractor responded, he was no cupid,
"Tomorrow I'll be sober, but you'll still be stupid."

An insulting retort only makes matters worse.
So often it's best that our lips we purse.
Instead of lashing out, let us turn a deaf ear;
This was David's policy, his psalm makes it clear.

"I'm like a mute who doesn't open his mouth."
-Psalm 38:13

൙

*W*ords that are sotto voce, have a unique persuasive way.
[soe-toe-voe-chay –spoken softly.]

൙

*S*ome words that are flung, some might deem them clever,
But the wound a word opens could fester forever.

൙

*T*en words in a sentence with two letters in each,
A profound, impressive lesson they are bound to teach.
"If it is to be, it is up to me."

൙

*I*deas in the mind are the transcript of the world; words, a replication of ideas unfurled.

൙

*W*ords profound on a ranch or college, could be a unique transcript of fuller knowledge.

൙

*W*hen there's an abundance of words, one's transgression is unavoidable.
He who restrains his fat lips won't be considered deplorable.

൙

*G*od's Irrevocable Word, should always be heard –
Not little-known 'zymurgy,' God's is the last word.

൙

WORK

*G*ood work is a great character builder, the sweetener of life.
—Grenville Kreiser

൙

*T*he largest reward for a person's toil is what you become, not the size of your spoil.

൙

*F*or work well done there's not always a reward,
But to do it another way one can ill afford.

൙

A LIFESTYLE PORTRAYAL From A TO Z

No work is complete, though the goal be in sight.
No question is settled until it's made right.

You go to work daily, you get good pay, so do not let yesterday use part of today.

If your desire is not to work, this one thing you must aptly learn,
A big pile of money you must firstly earn.

Urgently of hotel workers we need a new supply; those inn-experienced need only apply.

Ask God's blessing on your daily work; He promises to bless if work you don't shirk.

You can't sit in front of a fireplace and say,
"Blackie, give me heat in exchange for wood."
Likewise to your employer you cannot suggest,
"Give me pay now, then I'll work real good."

About hard work – if your hope is 'not-to-have-to,'
Work to make enough so no more you'll have to.

Working is overcoming resistance over a specified distance,
During a spelled-out space of time, regardless of inclement clime.

Hard work that's applied diligently and intelligently is an entity we must fully address.
Thinking, formulated in an organized manner is bound to lead to success.

Work that endures with accord, is work that is worthy of reward.

Avoiding daily chores one cannot afford; work in verity has a hidden reward.

Attempting a project, try not to shirk; what isn't tried will never work.

Reading the Forbes list, I choose not to shirk.
If my name isn't there I decide to go to work.

Hard work is the key to success, to work so many do bock.
One finds that they would much rather attempt to pick the lock.

Patient, honest labor, be it heavy or light, is never undignified, if it's done right.

Work can be pleasure as much as leisure.

Our neighbors toil diligently, come rain, hail or fog.
I see them out daily, they work like a dog.

A LIFESTYLE PORTRAYAL From A TO Z

They raise fresh produce, they even grow fennel;
Their aim is to live in a much better kennel.

❧

Why cease your toil, it doesn't make sense;
It's never accompanied by cessation of expense.

❧

Applying elbow grease, life's journey will ease.

❧

Forego wasteful leisure and shortcuts to success.
Wholesome working hours one must fully address.

❧

Honor you won't foil if your honest in toil.
Work always treasure, it's the parent of pleasure.

❧

Work that's hyphenated with a sense of duty
Gives joy to one's life and special beauty.

❧

Neglect not to don your breeches, luck alone won't bring you riches.

❧

If you work very hard, long hours every day,
And be not too concerned about your hourly pay,
Eventually you will be the corporation boss,
Spending long, busy hours on the profit and loss.

❧

Have you ever wondered why so many work shirk?
Unemployment takes the worry out of being late for work.

❧

Work will make you what you ought to be; a benefit to mankind - a sacred duty.

❧

Work never shirk, put dignity into work.

❧

Work, so oft difficult, you mustn't ever shirk, that is the reason why it's called work.

❧

A prospective employer, an employee engages, but it is the product that pays the wages.

❧

In days gone by, to get work was tough, you just couldn't choose and pick.
Today it's much easier, with salary come benefits, those who have a job, call in sick.

❧

In labor or in business, 'good enough' seldom is.

❧

So many people wait for good luck, for work they have an immunity.
They're unaware that luck is when preparedness meets opportunity.

❧

To an ounce of luck add a pound of pluck.

❧

A LIFESTYLE PORTRAYAL From A TO Z

On deciding to do labor, don't go at it half-hearted,
Enthusiastically proceed to get the task started.

God knows that labor for man is the best; he gives birds food but not in their nest.

A man must work if his goal is to eat; a greyhound finds food with his agile, fast feet.

The effects of sustained work, I would say, is unbeatable,
Gives a sense of accomplishment, endorphins are repeatable.

Every job accomplished is a portrait of your presence.
Signature your work with distinction and excellence.

I rent, I borrow, I owe - so off to work I must go.

Don't just put in a day, add something that will stay.

So what if you work up some old fashioned sweat.
You first have to give before you can get.
-Grace Easley

WORRY - ANXIETY - APPREHENSION

The mind that is anxious about the future is miserable.
-Seneca

Our greatest prostration and weariness, comes from worry and dreariness.

When worry walks in, strength runs out, but strength returns when we let go doubt.

If you worry continually, if fretting you nurture,
Tell me, my friend, will it change the future?

Worry can be likened to sitting in a rocking chair.
It'll certainly keep you busy but won't get you anywhere.

The bridges we're to cross oft give us the shivers,
But so very frequently they're over absent rivers.

Do not concentrate on the blues of the past;
Rosy thoughts of the future are the ones that'll last.

If you should worry about missing the boat, don't get into needless panic.
You might consider how lucky you are - remember, my friend, the Titanic.

A LIFESTYLE PORTRAYAL From A TO Z

If you should get wrinkled with worry and care,
Have your faith lifted - it'll cure grim despair.

Constant mental worry is interest paid on trouble.
Its impotence is comparable to a pricked soap bubble.

To worry about tomorrow is to live with sorrow.

Worry one should shirk, it's more exhausting than work.

Worry encourages mental strife; friendships are the flowers of life.

Incessant worry and distress are not one's life requirement.
Celestial spiritual strength, should be man's sacred environment.

Worry has the propensity to make energy stall.
It's as useless as having a handle on a snowball.

Ulcers can be painful, they result in high bills;
A malady one gets climbing mountains over molehills.

Apprehension is fretting in a hurry; don't burden yourself with worry.

Worry and fretfulness are satanic; trusting in God's power prevents panic.

Less energy to worry and more to your goal -
You'll have greater incentive to be gentler to your soul.

Don't worry, don't fret, be joyful, be circumspect - this to yourself you owe.
If you cannot find the precious pot of gold, make an effort to enjoy the rainbow.

Clammy apprehension - need I mention,
Must duly generate your prompt attention.

To those who worry this one thing you should know,
God is infinitely stronger than the fiercest foe.

Why worry, fuss and fret, constantly stewing; why not switch over to blessed well-doing.

The perfect cure for worry is trust; to trust in God, the Almighty is a must.

Worry is an abominable, a sordid creation, it's a misuse of one's despicable imagination.

I must have peace, worry is a curse, God is top manager of His universe.

A LIFESTYLE PORTRAYAL From A TO Z

*B*lessed is that zeal-filled person who is much too busy to worry;
To sleepy to worry at night, he goes to bed in a hurry.

*W*orry does not free tomorrow of its sorrow,
Neither does it strengthen today or the morrow.

*T*o carry your cares to your sack, is to sleep with a pack on your back.

*W*hat torments of pain so many have endured
From evils perceived, but have never occurred.

*M*en do break down from hard work and tribulation,
However, much more so, from worry and dissipation.

*S*ome people are troubled by things in the Bible that they don't seem to understand.
Then there are those who are likewise concerned by the things they do comprehend.

*W*orrying and stewing is fretting without doing.

*W*orry subdue lest it control you.

*W*orry doesn't improve the future, it only ruins the present.

*F*aith is a cure for worry and fear - it quickly suppresses many a tear.

*T*oday is the first day of the rest of my life; today I shall set aside all worry and strife.

*S*o you've been offended – why worry and fret?
The best way to get even is to forget.

*W*ith worrisome mental worry go slow,
It never produces a bright glow,
It gives small things a big shadow.

*Y*ou may be in haste, but don't be in a hurry,
Lest it result in despair and worry.

*W*orry is Satan's sardonic, wicked curse,
Showered upon his restricted universe.

*D*on't worry, don't fret about past misdeeds.
A good garden invariably will have some rank weeds.

*M*ental worry causes fret, to your soul it's a threat,
It's as useless as blet, and 'twill never pay a debt.

A LIFESTYLE PORTRAYAL From A TO Z

Worry is the most miserable of all sensitivities,
And the most unproductive of all human activities.

Anxiety successfully never bridged any chasm,
It frequently results in a mental spasm.

WORSHIP

The worship most acceptable to God, comes from a thankful, cheerful heart.
-Plutarch

Never misconstrue sacred worship, as a binding, boring arrangement.
Hallowed worship duly involves our decisive, active engagement.

YAWNING

When you see someone in your audience yawning,
Don't let it for a moment your composure shake.
Nor of vile anger allow there to be spawning,
Be thankful for the fact, some are still awake.

Just a polite warning, don't talk while yawning.

When someone yawns, and his tonsils are glistening,
It's an airy way of saying, "I'm not listening."

YEARNING

Much mental distress is caused by our yearnings.
The latter gets far ahead of our meager earnings.

If you are yearning to succeed, this maxim you must fully heed,
'Identify the skills you'll need, then assertively, methodically proceed.'

Some pensively yearn for the 'Good old days' –
Really, would you want to wear those stiff metal stays?

He who to seek answers is yearning,
Maintains a keen hankering for learning.

YOUTH

*W*e think our fathers fools, so wise we grow;
Our wiser sons, no doubt, will think us so.
-Alexander Pope

*A*n axiom for you, an idiomatic, witty phrase,
"Hang on to enthusiasm, forget your birthdays."

*I*t's perfectly true, you're only young once,
But it's hardly good reason for being a stupid dunce.

A teenager's years are usually comprised of
Agony, confusion, tribulations and puppy love.

*S*o many of our youth will avoid the norm.
Their wish is so oft with their chums to conform.
They will so invariably follow their peers;
Sad to say, the result, they get bum steers.

*W*hen you're young and pretty, know what you stand for,
More importantly you should know what you won't fall for.

*Y*outh would be an ideal state if it came a lot more late.

*Y*outh is primarily experimental, and it is ruthlessly judgmental.

*W*hile staying youthful attempt to be useful.

*A*t times you may wonder about your wayward occiput.
Remember, today's oak was yesterday's nut.

*W*e vote for youth in old age, every time.
It's a pity it comes but once in a lifetime.

*T*here would be miracles if youth would more know,
And if old age would continue to flow.

A switch in time could help to prevent crime.

*L*et no one look down on your abounding youthfulness.
Let your speech and purity be examples of truthfulness.

A LIFESTYLE PORTRAYAL From A TO Z

ZEAL

Zeal without knowledge is like a fire without a grate.
-Julius Bate

❧

Zeal is like fire - needs both watching and feeding.
Hyphenate to the above, common sense and much reading.

❧

Zeal and initiative are intelligent; poverty can't overtake the diligent.

❧

A successful salesman, to be for real, must have appeal, coupled with zeal.

❧

Zeal without knowledge is a runaway horse.
This sagacious maxim our minds should endorse.

❧

The man or woman of a zealous trend,
A magnetic influence is destined to vend.

❧

Though fellow employees may scornfully scoff,
Your incredible zeal is bound to pay off.

❧

Zeal without knowledge is blight, comparable to a lamp without a light.

❧

Blind zeal assails - intense zeal prevails.

❧

With untiring zeal, knowledge is obtained;
The greater the enthusiasm the more is retained.

❧

Zeal is a great vehicle, but to be a survivor,
It must be driven by a shrewd, skillful driver.

❧

He appears to have zeal, he acts so jolly,
But zeal without knowledge is the sister of folly.

❧

Zeal is love that's on fire - never let your love retire.

❧

For achievement, capability is not always the keel.
To ardor and vigor we must devotedly appeal.
Much success is due less to ability than to zeal.

❧

What you aim to accomplish and zealously pursue,
Must be carried through by indomitable you.

❧

Zeal is oft blind, frequently unregulated,
When on the rights of others it's curiously contemplated.

❧

A LIFESTYLE PORTRAYAL From A TO Z

Obedience is the epitome of duty; zest is the secret of all beauty.

A seal of approval is definitely for real to those exhibiting true, lofty zeal.

Zeal, if it's real, has worthy appeal.

Blind zest can be a pest.

An ancient proverb, this mentally realize, "Untiring zeal is only for the wise."

Blind zeal can harm and can also alarm.

Indomitable zeal, never seasoned with jest;
Zest comes first, then action, then rest.

Zest is one's radiant beauty; it's life's magnificent booty.

Though you may jolly, zeal alone is folly, you could miss the trolley.

A LIFESTYLE PORTRAYAL From A TO Z

ADDENDA

MAN'S BIZARRE BEHAVIOR AND STRANGE ANATOMY

*A*natomy is the science of a phantasmal structure,
Of an amazing, statuesque, vibrant human body,
And its relationship to its innumerable parts
That are based on meticulous, intricate dissection.
However, I'm amazed, I'm in a total quandary,
When it approaches its phantom nomenclature.
I am totally confused, I'm completely befuddled,
Its ambiguous terminology hasn't reached perfection.

How far can a man journey on a litre of gas,
At what mileage does he need his valves ground?
Do his knees knock because he's burned a bearing?
How does he throw his heavy weight around?

For forty five years,- a practicing physician –
Still man is a fascination, a puzzlement to me.
Much mystery surrounds him unanswered to this date;
I have questions about his strange anatomy.

With the ball of his foot, what game does he play,
And why the hook in his big prominent nose?
So oft I do wonder what function it does serve,
Does he ever use it to hang up his clothes?

From the bangs in his forehead I never hear a sound,
I frequently do wonder how he can doze.
By the way, who scribbles the lines on his face?
They oft remind me of the feet of hopping crows.

The anvil with the hammer, why does he pound?
Obviously, I observe, it's so he can hear,
But why the tip of his humerus would he strike?
Wouldn't think it's funny, it's atypical, it's queer.

What lovely tall flowers besides the Iris does he grow?
What valuable treasures does he store in his chest?
What traffic through the arch of his foot does there flow?
Which one of his organs does he deem to be the best?

A LIFESTYLE PORTRAYAL From A TO Z

I wonder, is he sharp 'cause his head comes to a point?
Tell me, what victuals does he cook in his pot?
Which joint do you see him leisurely smoke?
The answers to these questions to date I have not.

Have you ever seen his knuckles knuckle down,
And how with his neck does he flirtatiously neck?
Seriously, how serious an accident must he sustain
Before he can be reckoned a total mangled wreck?

And why would he ever put his foot in his mouth?
Would he really place a wrench is his back?
Have you ever seen him stick his neck out,
And how does he actually blow his stack?

Where can a man buy a cap for his knee,
Or the treasured key to the lock of his hair?
Can his eyes be called a creditable academy
Because there are visible pupils there?

In the crown of his head, what gems can be found,
And who ever crosses the bridge of his nose?
Can he use in shingling the roof of his house
The many short nails from his fingers and toes?

Should the crook in his elbow be sent to jail,
If not, what should we be inclined to do?
How does he sharpen his shoulder blades?
I wouldn't know, tell me, would you?

Can he sit in the shade of the palms of his hands?
Have you ever seen him beat the drums of his ears?
Can the calves in his legs eat the corn in his toes?
Why not grow edible corn in his ears?

Why is his derriere so oft called a bum,
And his big yellow liver be proclaimed a liver?
With what part of his body does he throw a curve?
Tell me, what sign does he take to deliver?

How fit must a man be to be fit to be tied?
What reason would he give for cooling his heels,
And why would he ever choose to chew a rag?
Could there be a nutrient missing in his meals?

A LIFESTYLE PORTRAYAL From A TO Z

Why doesn't the heavy-weight lose his weight
Where the lean, skinny guy can readily find it?
A twofold benefit would obviously eventuate -
I for one, certainly wouldn't mind it.

I have peeked into many a thick skull through the years -
No wheels on any dimension have I ever found.
So oft I do wonder just where they're concealed,
And just how fast they are moving around.

How do noses run, and how do feet smell?
Why would some people keep themselves in a shell?
How do heated arguments cause atmospheres that are chilly?
These baffling conundrums, I'd say are a dilly.

Where is the horn that he persistently keeps tooting,
While his friends dodge to stay out of his way?
He has senses, touch, taste, sight smelling and hearing -
But where is his common sense - has it faded away?

How clear and broad a vision do his eye-teeth have?
Do they enjoy window shopping in the mall stores?
From furniture how can they tell basic man apart,
When his big chest slips into his drawers?

So there you can see what a conundrum man can be;
A navel detachment I have never seen.
Does his nose run until his breath is spent?
To be sure, man's lifestyle isn't always serene.

A LIFESTYLE PORTRAYED RATION IN A POSITIVE ABECEDARIAN FASHION

Slow to ATTACK - quick to DEFEND;
This truly is being a sincere, loving friend.

Slow to BELITTLE - quick to ELEVATE;
The meek and the lowly we must emulate.

Slow to CONDEMN - quick to JUSTIFY;
Jealousy we must strive to keep out of our eye.

Slow to DEMAND - quick to GIVE;
Watch your words, put them through a sieve.

A LIFESTYLE PORTRAYAL From A TO Z

Slow to EXPOSE - quick to SHIELD;
To evil temptation we must never yield.

Slow to FIGHT - quick to PEACE;
Our tensions of hate we must quickly release.

Slow to GRIPE - quick to THANK;
With pure gratitude fill your tank.

Slow to HATE - quick to LOVE
Our fellow man, the wish from above.

Slow to IRRITATE - quick to SOOTHE;
Out of contentions rut we must move.

Slow to JUDGE - quick to FORGIVE;
This, our direction on how to live.

Slow to KEEP - quick to RELEASE
Despicable grudges, thus ensuring sweet peace.

Slow to LAMENT - quick to REJOICE;
This sound admonition should be our clear choice.

Slow to MALICE - quick to GOODWILL;
This will ensure that our peace will be still.

Slow to NEGLECT - quick to CARING,
With help to the needy we mustn't be sparing.

Slow to OUTRAGE - quick to FORBEARANCE;
This attribute in life must be a high preference.

Slow to PRIDE - quick to be HUMBLE;
One's arrogance comes before the tumble.

Slow to QUESTON - quick to AGREE;
Making decisions with maturity.

Slow to RIDICULE - quick to EULOGIZE;
This beautiful trait we must fully prize.

Slow to SARCASM - quick to WORDS NICE;
Disregarding this precept puts friends on ice.

A LIFESTYLE PORTRAYAL From A TO Z

Slow to THREATEN - quick to REASSURE;
This counsel heeded builds character demure.

Slow to USURP - quick to SURRENDER;
Our feelings to others should be warm and tender.

Slow to VILENESS - quick to GOOD DEEDS;
We must give of our time to supply others' needs.

Slow to WORRY - quick to TRUST;
Instruction from the Scripture, follow it we must.

Slow to eXPEL - quick to RETAIN;
The advice of our elders our lives should proclaim.

Slow to harsh YELL - quick to SWEET CALM;
Doesn't make sense to cause much alarm.

Slow to ZIG-ZAG - quick to GO STRAIGHT;
Our lives the Divine Pattern we must emulate.

❧

A FREE PARAPHRASE OF FIRST CORININTHIANS THIRTEEN

Though I'm able to speak to Almighty God, to presidents, ambassadors and kings,
But if I speak not with genuine love, with kind words and a sweet tone that rings,
I am but an old, noisy washing machine, a mixmaster that goes rippity rapp,
Or an ancient, whirling garbage disposal that rattles a stray bottle cap.

I may be able to tune an old car so that it runs and purrs like a kitten.
I may be able to fix an old oil furnace, so that the house is warm as a mitten.
I may bravely jettison myself into traffic to remove a child off a car hood,
But if it's not done with reassuring love, it does me absolutely no good.

Yes, I may be extremely eloquent, before great crowds and huge throngs,
And I may even fathom my computer, and know where every chip belongs.
Love is clearly being very, very patient, not thinking or uttering a harsh word,
While patiently waiting for my darling spouse, as she primps and preens like a bird.

Though I may give away my new typewriter, a new dress, or the new microwave
To someone who is considerably less fortunate, and get pats on my back that I gave.
I may have faith that all of my baking will always turn out to perfection,
But if I do not retain abiding true love, I can expect but total rejection.

A LIFESTYLE PORTRAYAL From A TO Z

True love is verily being duly kind, crawling out of bed in bare feet
To get your loved one an extra blanket that her body may retain more heat.
Love, is in no way being the slightest bit jealous, it's being eager about her success;
Must think of it as my own good fortune – no room or time for redress.

Love is being not the least bit ill-mannered, like pointing out a minute fault
In front of family, my friends or neighbors – true love has no room for assault.
Love is for certain not being at all selfish, repeatedly having my own way,
Not pushing, not shoving, not selfishly grabbing to get the best bargain of the day.

It's not being egotistical, self-seeking, self-centered, self-interested self-indulgent, self-concerned,
Not greedy, not possessive, nor self-regarding, uncharitable closefisted, unconcerned.
In truth, true love is not being irritable, 'cause he left his socks on the floor!
Not resentful of many past offences, like forgetting to bring groceries from the store.

Veritable love is not being angry, - "Remember, I told you so,"
When there is loss in a monetary business and relationship loses its glow.
Steadfast love, truly rejoices, when a prudent business decision is made.
This verily strengthens the entire family, now overdue bills can be paid.

Undaunted love, literally bears all things, for instance, when the children were ill,
Like many a sleepless, miserable, restless night – like the marbles they'd repeatedly spill.
Like the lonely times of long separation, when duties would take hubby away,
Or the frequent times of too much togetherness, when jobless for many a day.

Unswerving love, believes all things- believes he'll come to the Lord;
Believing that in the not too distant future his health will be fully restored.
True love does justly endure all things because a commitment was made,
To love, to hold and to dearly cherish – may the memory of that day never fade.

Patient love doesn't get easily provoked, when my dinner is not on time,
Nor does it at all exasperate – unswerving love is sublime.
Genuine love, never, never ends, it comes from above and beyond;
God's love is wide and deep as the ocean – our love can be likened to a pond.

When I was but an immature youth, my dreams would drift off very far,
Marriage was a most beautiful wedding, a new home and a spanking new car.
It was an energetic, handsome young couple, storybook, romance-filled. carefree,
Indeed, it was living blissful young lives – raising a lovely family.

But then, after several years of marriage – contentions, financial problems galore,
Illness, harsh words, outbursts of anger – innumerable adjustments to be sure;
God came with the gift of His infinite love, he provided so much it would seem,
And so, two totally different weary lives he blended into a loving team.

A LIFESTYLE PORTRAYAL From A TO Z

Since I became a grown mature man, I put away many selfish ties,
Like man can never say, "I'm truly sorry," the notion that a man never cries.
My earthly view of life is so hazy, like gazing into a grimy, tarnished mirror,
But with God's help as I grow older the long narrow path is much clearer.

So now abides faith, hope and true love, the magnificent, incomparable three.
Strong faith and belief that all of our loved ones will dwell with us eternally.
Invincible hope, is verily that day, a beautiful, peaceful new world,
Free from agonizing strife and divorce – a complete, perfect era unfurled.

But deeper than faith and bright buoyant hope
Is the virtue, God-given to man -
LONG-SUFFERING LOVE, a most precious ingredient;
It conforms to God's Holy plan.

ON CHOOSING A NEW MINISTER

A tall task the church faced –'twas in choosing a new minister.
The chairman of the board acted in a manner somewhat sinister.
Yes, applicant after applicant was rejected by the committee;
The whole process was painful – another name came to the kitty.
The moderator read a letter, purporting to be true,
This one from another applicant, he was number twenty-two.
"Dear ladies and gentlemen; I hear your pulpit is vacant.
I'm truly interested in this worthy engagement.

I would like to apply for this honored position,
I trust my application won't meet much opposition.
I have qualifications, good, bad, some indifferent,
Trust my curriculum vitae will be more than sufficient.
I've achieved as a preacher – great success as a writer,
Some say that I've been a most efficient organizer.
I've been a good leader most places that I've been,
I've worked hard and long to help stamp out sin.

My age, I'm over fifty – I try to be thrifty;
Lengths of stay have been short – some say I've been shifty.
Some places my work has caused discord and riot;
I'm exceedingly frugal – can exist of meager diet.
Must admit I've been in jail some three or four times,
Not caused by wrong-doing or some serious crimes.
My health is not perfect, but I accomplish a great deal.
I can assure you dear folk, my achievements are for real.

The churches I've preached in have been very small;
With some of the leaders I didn't get along at all.
I'm not very tall, perhaps somewhat overweight,
My memory is not good, this others will substantiate.
My vision is poor – a secretary is imperative;
I must truly admit, I'm somewhat argumentative.
So there you can see, I'm really tried and true,
'Tis my hope you can use me – shall do my best for you."

The board chairman paused to note the reaction,
"Well what do you think, shall we call him into action?"
He eyed them keenly, he didn't further stall,
He then informed them, "It's signed, Apostle Paul."

THE CONCERT VIOLINIST

A young concert violinist was playing the main continent;
Music critics exhausted their stores of top compliment.
An editor wrote a column in a journal 'twas the latest,
"Of all the violinists, he is the world's greatest."

His first concert in England was marred by adverse column,
Written by a caustic critic, causing the artist to be solemn.
"It is safe to assume that most people will come
To hear the Stradivarius – purchased with a large sum."

Hundreds were in attendance at a performance in Britain.
The audience sat spellbound – with his artistry they were smitten.
At the conclusion of his first number rafters rattled with applause;
"Ah for certain," said a critic, "The Stradivarius was the cause."

The artist humbly bowed, acknowledging their enthusiasm,
But he could not forget the critic's sharp sarcasm.
Then suddenly all were stunned – just how could this be!
As abruptly the instrument was smashed upon his knee,

The audience was horrified – there must be an explanation;
He proceeded to relate with a short crisp narration.

"I've finished my first number on this lovely violin,
Purchased from a pawn shop, frequented by sin.
The instrument I've been using has been truly vicarious;
I shall continue the concert using my Stradivarius."

A LIFESTYLE PORTRAYAL From A TO Z

The critic was so wrong, 'twas uniquely not the instrument,
'Twas the master with the bow that resulted in accomplishment.
Methinks there's a dogma in this story I discern,
From this touching, vivid episode there's a lesson we can learn.

We perhaps cannot be the best instrument in the land,
Our real value is found in the blessed Master's hand.
There's so much that we of ourselves cannot do.
We must never underestimate what through us God can do.

❧

POETIC RUMINATIONS ON THE SUCCINCT SUFFIX "TUDE"
(Condition or state of being)

Your thoughts, your actions, your feelings and behaviour
Reflect you sensible mental ATTITUDE.
Your natural or acquired abilities or bent
Are reflected in your outstanding intellectual APTITUDE.
Your singular attitude, your versatile aptitude
Could rank breathtaking, unbelievable ALTITUDE.
Blessed are the merciful for they shall obtain mercy –
A limitless, infinite, blessed BEATITUDE.
To have full trust, dependence and security,
Is having self-assurance, total CERTITUDE.
The sanctified Sabbath, do keep it holy –
A precious, so gracious, venerated CONSUETUDE.
Make straight your way, correct false notions –
Irreproachable, infallible, rigid CORRECTITUDE.
Keeping your body in the state of DESUETUDE,
Results in subtle, onrushing DECREPITUDE.
Unerring precision and absolute accuracy,
Puts you in the realm of precise EXACTITUDE.
Your patient strength of mind in the face of adversity –
Unshakeable, matchless, enduring FORTITUDE.
Sincere thankfulness on receiving a favour,
Express with humble, heartfelt GRATITUDE.
Avoid incompetent words and actions –
Futile, fruitless, foolish INEPTITUDE.
Avert state of weariness, mimicking fatigue –
So dreary, despairing, languorous LASSITUDE.
Have freedom from narrow mental limitations –
Beloved, boundless utmost LATITUDE.
The beauty of the stars, the vastness of the universe,
Declare God's infinite, majestic MAGNITUDE.
Adopt refinement and polished behaviour –

A LIFESTYLE PORTRAYAL From A TO Z

Unassuming, intelligent, stately MANSUETUDE.
Commonplace verbiage and obvious truisms.
Are considered as sugared, worthless PLATITUDE.
Eschew not the state of blessed abundance –
Share of your peculiar, overflowing PLENITUDE.
Endorse fully the habit of being on time –
An envious characteristic, unfailing PROMPTITUDE.
Embrace the evidence of mysterious charm –
So beautiful, so rare, inexplicable PULCHRITUDE.
Trusting the almighty, believing in His word,
Result in peaceful, comforting QUIETUDE.
Be wise in judgment, upright in principle –
Conscientious, guileless, virtuous RECTITUDE.
Relish the state of marital solemnity –
Scared, profound, angelic SANCTIUDE.
Reverence to God and obedience to His precepts,
Proclaim your loving, implicit SERVITUDE.
Deep concern and irrepressible anxiety,
Signal affectionate, tender SOLICITUDE.
It's truly inclined to make man whole –
To the virtuous soul is hallowed SOLITUDE.
Shun perversion, degradation and impurity –
Inherent, sinful, putrid TURPITUDE.
So many things have the appearance of truth –
Carefully scrutinize VERISIMILITUDE.
Take changes in their stride, your fortune, varied seasons –
It could be sweet, sublime, sudden VICISSITUDE.

Tell me, my friend, what's your state of being?
What's your response, – which way are you leaning?

"TUDE" DEFINITIONS

ATTITUDE – state of mind, behaviour or conduct.
APTITUDE – natural or acquired ability or bent.
ALTITUDE – a high place or rank.
BEATITUDE – supreme blessedness or felicity.
CERTITUDE – complete confidence.
CONSUETUDE – custom, habitual practice.
CORRECTITUDE – correctness.
DECREPITUDE – a decrepit or enfeebled condition.
DESUETUDE – a condition of disuse.
EXACTITUDE – in an exact manner.
FORTITUDE – strength of mind in the face of adversity.

A LIFESTYLE PORTRAYAL From A TO Z

GRATITUDE – thankfulness, appreciation.
INEPTITUDE – the state or quality of being inept.
LASSITUDE – a state of weariness or fatigue.
LATITUDE – tolerance or liberality.
MAGNITUDE – greatness or importance.
MANSUETUDE – mildness, gentleness (archaic).
PLATITUDE – a dull or commonplace statement.
PLENTITUDE – plentiful, complete or abounding.
PROMPTITUDE – quality or habit of being prompt.
PULCHRITUDE – beauty, grace, physical charm.
QUIETUDE – a state or condition of tranquility.
RECTITUDE – uprightness in principle and conduct.
SANCTITUDE – a state of sacredness and solemnity.
SERVITUDE – the condition or duties of a servant.
SOLICITUDE – the state of being solicitous, having concern.
SOLITUDE – the sate of being solitary.
TURPITUDE – inherent baseness, vileness.
VERISIMILITUDE – appearance of truth, likelihood.
VICISSITUDE – changes or variations as of fortune.

TWO WOLVES

One evening an elderly, sinewy bronze Cherokee,
While standing pensively 'neath a tall church steeple,
Told his young grandson about a mental battle,
That continually goes on, inside of most people.
"The conflict erupts, Spring, Summer and Fall,
It's between two wolves, that's inside of us all."

"One wolf in impetuous, his name is Iniquitous!
He's envy, hot anger, dull sorrow and jealousy,
Fond greed, regret, brash arrogance and self-pity;
Resentment, inflated ego, dread guilt, and pomposity,
He's falsehood, false pride, and so full of animosity."

"The other wolf is congruous, his name is Virtuous!
He's genuine happiness, ardent love and serenity,
Loving kindness, benevolence, crystal truth and empathy,
Stellar faith, compassion, and matchless courtesy;
His name is renowned for his amazing generosity."

The young grandson then thought, but for a brief minute,
Then asked his grandpa, "Which wolf eventually wins it?"

The old Cherokee replied, "My answer, do heed –
The wolf that wins the battle is the one that you feed."

WHO IS THIS CHRIST WHOSE BIRTH AND LIFE WE CELEBRATE AND HONOR?

To God the Father, He's the beloved Son.
To an accomplished artist, He's altogether lovely.
To an eminent architect, He's the solid Cornerstone.
To an empowered ambassador, He's the Prince of Peace.
To the searching astronomer, He's the bright, Morning Star.
To the village baker, He's the Bread of Life.
To a prominent builder, He's the Sure Foundation.
To the local botanist, He's the Rose of Sharon.
To the knowledgeable biologist, He's the Giver of Life.
To the town carpenter He's the Master Craftsman.
To a young child, He's the Babe born in Bethlehem.
To a discerning doctor He's the Great Physician.
To an intellectual educator, He's the Master teacher.
To the florid florist, He's the Lily of the Valley.
To a sinewy farmer He's the Lord of the Harvest.
To a hard-working geologist He's the Rock of Ages.
To an investigative genealogist He's the Son of David.
To a happy horticulturist He is the True Vine.
To a creative inventor He's the Creator of all.
To a judicious jury, He's a staunch, True Witness.
To an inspired journalist, He's Tidings of Great Joy.
To the pricey jeweler, He's the Pearl of Great Price.
To a lawful king, He's the King of Kings.
To an honorable kinsman, He's the Elder Brother.
To a gray-haired lawyer, He is the Law-giver.
To a skilful metallurgist, He is Pure Gold.
To a magnanimous monarch, He's the Mighty Ruler.
To the well-known naturalist, His creation is awesome.
To an ophthalmologist, He's the Light of the World.
To a distinguished ornithologist, He's the Eagle hovering over its young.
To the lone prisoner, He's the miraculous Deliverer.
To the zealous preacher, He's the Word of God.
To the eloquent philosopher, He's the Wisdom of God.
To the generous philanthropist, He's the Unspeakable Gift.
To the prudent psychologist He's the Wonderful Counselor.
To the quartermaster, He's the Supplier of all of life's needs.
To the fleet-footed runner, He rewards the imperishable wreath.
To the capable scribe, He's Alpha and Omega.

A LIFESTYLE PORTRAYAL From A TO Z

To the faithful servant, He is the Good Master.
To the seasoned seaman, He's the Master Pilot.
To a lowly sheep rancher, He is the good Shepherd.
To the symbolic sculptor, He's the Living Stone.
To the stately statesman, He's the Desire of all Nations.
To the wayworn traveler, He is the Sure Way.
To the scholarly theologian, He's the Author and Finisher of Our Faith.
To the life underwriter, He is Life Eternal.
To the devoted vicar, He is the High Priest.
To the well-driller, He's the Water of Life.
To the wary xenophobe, He is a True Friend.
To the skilful yachtsman, He's Chart and Compass.
To a zealous zoologist, He's the Lover of Creatures, great and small.
To the repentant sinner, He's the Lamb of God that taketh away sins.
To a devout Christian, He is the Son of the Living God,
Our Redeemer, Our Savior, coming in the clouds of glory.

WHAT IS HE TO YOU?

ISBN 155212620-X